## RADICAL
## TRADITIONS

### THEOLOGY IN A POSTCRITICAL KEY

#### SERIES EDITORS

*Stanley M. Hauerwas, Duke University,*
*and Peter Ochs, University of Virginia*

RADICAL TRADITIONS cuts new lines of inquiry across a confused array of debates concerning the place of theology in modernity and, more generally, the status and role of scriptural faith in contemporary life. Charged with a rejuvenated confidence, spawned in part by the rediscovery of reason as inescapably tradition constituted, a new generation of theologians and religious scholars is returning to scriptural traditions with the hope of retrieving resources long ignored, depreciated, and in many cases ideologically suppressed by modern habits of thought. RADICAL TRADITIONS assembles a promising matrix of strategies, disciplines, and lines of thought that invites Jewish, Christian, and Islamic theologians back to the word, recovering and articulating modes of scriptural reasoning as that which always underlies modernist reasoning and therefore has the capacity — and authority — to correct it.

Far from despairing over modernity's failings, postcritical theologies rediscover resources for renewal and self-correction within the disciplines of academic study themselves. Postcritical theologies open up the possibility of participating once again in the living relationship that binds together God, text, and community of interpretation. RADICAL TRADITIONS thus advocates a "return to the text," which means a commitment to displaying the richness and wisdom of traditions that are at once text based, hermeneutical, and oriented to communal practice.

Books in this series offer the opportunity to speak openly with practitioners of other faiths or even with those who profess no (or limited) faith, both academics and nonacademics, about the ways religious traditions address pivotal issues of the day. Unfettered by foundationalist preoccupations, these books represent a call for new paradigms of reason — a thinking and rationality that are more responsive than originative. By embracing a postcritical posture, they are able to speak unapologetically out of scriptural traditions manifest in the practices of believing communities (Jewish, Christian, and others); articulate those practices through disciplines of philosophic, textual, and cultural criticism; and engage intellectual, social, and political practices that for too long have been insulated from theological evaluation. RADICAL TRADITIONS is radical not only in its confidence in non-apologetic theological speech but also in how the practice of such speech challenges the current social and political arrangements of modernity.

## RADICAL TRADITIONS

# Praise Seeking Understanding

*Reading the Psalms with Augustine*

Jason Byassee

WILLIAM B. EERDMANS PUBLISHING COMPANY
GRAND RAPIDS, MICHIGAN / CAMBRIDGE, U.K.

Published 2007 by
Wm. B. Eerdmans Publishing Co.
2140 Oak Industrial Drive N.E., Grand Rapids, Michigan 49505 /
P.O. Box 163, Cambridge CB3 9PU U.K.

Printed in the United States of America

12  11  10  09  08  07     7  6  5  4  3  2  1


Library of Congress Cataloging-in-Publication Data

Byassee, Jason.
    Praise seeking understanding: reading the psalms with augustine / Jason Byassee.
        p.        cm.        — (Radical traditions)
    Includes bibliographical references and index.
    ISBN  978-0-8028-4012-7 (pbk.: alk. paper)
    1. Augustine, Saint, Bishop of Hippo.   2. Bible. O.T. — Criticism, interpretation, etc.
    3. Jesus Christ — Person and offices —Biblical teaching.   I. Title.

    BR65.A9B93   2007
    221.6'409 — dc22

                                                    2007027526

www.eerdmans.com

*For Jaylynn*

# Contents

# Foreword

"Allegorical" exegesis of Augustine's sort ". . . is sufficiently expansive to include modern historical critical insights as well as figurative, christologically based Augustinian ones. It is usually not the case, however, that overly historicist versions of interpretation can allow for the continued existence of hermeneutics such as Augustine's" (Byassee, 93). Of the many illuminating dicta in Jason Byassee's fine book, this one must be a great comfort for theologians of a certain sort. Perhaps I may be permitted two paragraphs about one such.

As a beginning theologian, I accepted that the Bible was to be the "norm" of theological inquiry. But that the Bible was itself interesting, and could be a participant in reflection, dawned on me only after a time. And it was works of historical-critical scholarship, more specifically of form criticism — Gunkel, Mowinckel, Jeremias, and the like — that opened my eyes. Those weird stories in Judges — not very apparently apt to settle the systematic-theological debates in which I was invested — had actually been told and retold in life-situations where they made a spiritual difference! Those parables were not just illustrations of moral or homiletical truisms! I am, therefore, unwilling to join those who now eschew historical-critical labors.

On the other hand, years of seminary teaching taught me how little or even negative was the payoff from the critical methods in which we drilled students. On Sunday mornings Blanche Jenson and I would sometimes visit congregations served by recent graduates. Again and again the preacher would first dutifully retail the historical information about the text, and then preach the same sermon — often excellent, we had some good students — he or she would have given without ever having heard of such matters. Moreover, it became ever plainer: the text authoritative in the church's life has to be the church's canonical Scripture, and not a "more original" text constructed by a scholar; nor can the history Scripture tells be replaced in the church's memory and imagination by scholarly guessing about what "really" happened. Therefore I currently participate in the revolt against historical-critical hegemony in exegesis, and have even turned my own hand to the writing of commentaries. Indeed, Byassee does me the startling honor of putting me on a very short list of notable allegorical exegetes.

It will be apparent that those — and they are in fact many — who, like me, straddle this uncomfortable fence, some threatening to fall off on one side and some on the other, should be grateful for help in maintaining their balance, or even perhaps in remodeling the fence while sitting on it. They should therefore read Byassee on Augustine. For if indeed such habits of reading as Augustine's can make place for modern critical moves — while the reciprocal is by proclamation of the moderns themselves not possible — we have the way to go.

Seekers should not be diverted by Byassee's first chapter, which mostly reports on pioneers of the revolt against historical-critical hegemony; the book derives from a dissertation and occasionally shows it. And the chapter has its own use: if you want to know what, e.g., Steinmetz said in a famous essay, Byassee will tell you.

But Byassee finds his role when he turns to his book's great case in point, Augustine's *Enarrationes in Psalmos*. With elegance, subtlety, and love, he shows us how Augustine's exegesis really works. And he is just as good when he continues a short way on his own, to describe the hermeneutics he thinks the church, following but not enslaved to Augustine, might with blessing adopt.

I will not spoil things for readers by reporting much of that in advance. About Byassee's actual matter I will append only a few scattered and personal remarks, with a query embedded in each.

The church's classic exegesis is often denounced as uncontrollable: with enough ingenuity the allegorical exegete — it is alleged — can make any text say anything. After reading a bit of patristic and medieval exegesis in recent years, I cannot altogether repress sympathy with this critique. But at least for Augustine and at least for Augustine's commentaries on the Psalter, Byassee persuades me that a very clear control is operative: an interpretation is right if, in a way peculiar to the given text, it draws the reader on in the love of God, patterned and enabled by Christ. This criterion works, of course, only if one believes that God does indeed mold us to life in Christ and thereby move us into God. Which is what Augustine did believe. Query: Where do we now find preachers and teachers who believe this, and so are in position to do what Augustine did? One fears the real problem is a problem of faith.

Thus the control of our biblical interpretations should — if we follow Augustine-according-to-Byassee — be exerted by our Christology. The ancient church, however, knew other Christologies than Augustine's, and I confess to some doubts about his — except for his wonderful and powerful notion of the *totus Christus*. Query: Would a different Christology have resulted in different interpretations? I hope not, since I greatly admire Augustine's interpretations as Byassee displays and analyses them. But if different Christologies do not fund different interpretations, how does Christology control?

Augustine's exegetical enterprise, as Byassee presents it, is itself preaching and teaching, done in the very face of a congregation. Exegesis is now practiced as a subject in seminaries and divinity schools, where it is supposed to be preparation for preaching and teaching. Query: Does the modern church's institutional structure have a location where Byassee's book — or Augustine's *Enarrationes in Psalmos* — might appropriately be read? One again has that fear mentioned above.

Byassee's penultimate chapter has a section "A Surprising *Sensus Litteralis*" that contains some of the book's most profitable pages. The line between "literal" reading and "figural" or "allegorical" turns out to run differently for Augustine than it does for us — if indeed there is any one such line for Augustine. For Augustine can find christological and ecclesiological gist in the Psalms by attention to the mere words on the page, without need for what one might usually call allegory. I like that. In trying currently to elucidate Ezekiel, I find it is regularly what happens. But then I have a query about Augustine's general project: Does not affirming that it is "literally" Christ who, with his body the church, prays the Psalms — and speaks generally in the Old Testament — require a little more revision of inherited metaphysics than Augustine undertakes? The Augustinian move Byassee reports, that Christ dispatched some members of his body to pray the Psalter, is neat. But how did time work when Christ did that?

Any who have gotten this far will have noticed: the author of this preface is delighted to have the job. Read the book.

*Robert W. Jenson*

# Acknowledgments

I am grateful to Stanley Hauerwas at Duke and Peter Ochs at Virginia for accepting this book in their Radical Traditions series, and especially to Peter for the extra bit of editing he did (and rewriting he made me do!) to make it a better book. I'm grateful also to Jon Pott at Eerdmans, as well as my copyeditor there, Jennifer Hoffman. David Heim is a dream of a boss for whom to work and a model of Christian charity at *The Christian Century*. It helps that he's also a world-class journalist with an eye keen enough to spot what's important before others do.

It is a thrilling and humbling thing to have a collection of world-class scholars pore over your work and offer both praise and constructive criticism, as those who participated in my studies at Duke University did. I am especially grateful to my doctoral director, Reinhard Hütter, and also to Stanley Hauerwas, Ellen Davis, and Warren Smith for their careful and generous attention to this book. When a friend finished reading the first draft of what would become this book, he said, "It reads like a work of journalism." I'm not sure he meant that as a compliment! I think he meant that it was clearer than many other academic works. I had no idea at the time that he was speaking prophetically: that I would become an actual journalist, despite having made no plans for such a career.

Many others at Duke fueled and shaped my love for theology over the years, especially Geoffrey Wainwright, Richard Hays, David Steinmetz, Willie Jennings, Stephen Chapman, Amy Laura Hall, Greg Jones, and Karen Westerfield Tucker. Lewis Ayres, David Hart, Kathy Grieb, and Robert Wilken taught me much during the short periods in which I was privileged to study with them. My friends in Hütter's doctoral circle made this work better and its writing more joyous — thanks to Jeff McCurry, Holly Taylor Coolman,

Beth Felker Jones, and Edgardo Colon-Emeríc. Friends and fellow graduate students Kavin Rowe and Chris Franks provided great conversation, encouragement, and ideas. Will Willimon has shaped the way I think in so many ways I'm not aware of them all, but I am at least thankful for them.

I am deeply grateful to the people of Shady Grove United Methodist Church for their encouragement and support of me while I was writing this book and serving as their pastor from 2002 to 2004. They often appear obliquely in its pages. I'm grateful also to administrators and students at the schools where I have taught since then: Garrett-Evangelical Theological Seminary, North Park Theological Seminary, Wheaton College, and Northern Seminary. Friends at A Foundation for Theological Education (AFTE) encouraged and helped me greatly.

I am most of all grateful to my wife, Jaylynn Warren Byassee, who was my pastor and preacher during the first part of the writing of this work, full-time mother to Jack, Sam, and Will during the last, and pastor of Winfield Community United Methodist Church sometime in the middle. The work is dedicated to her, my dearest friend.

# Introduction

This book was born out of the experience of leading a congregation. As a preacher I spent a great deal of fruitless time seeking biblical commentaries to help me read scripture well for the sake of the church. I have found modern commentary helpful for certain things — in clarifying historical events or linguistic problems with greater confidence than ancient commentators could, for example. Yet I found ancient commentators more helpful in doing the most important thing that Christian preaching and teaching must do: drawing the church to Christ. So while modern commentary was better equipped to translate a psalm's inscription and say when and why it may have been added to the canon, Augustine could tell me that the "sons of Korah" are etymologically the "sons of the bald," or that *calvus* in Latin is a word linked to Calvary. The sons of Korah mentioned in many psalm inscriptions then are the sons of Christ's passion who teach us to hear these words in a christological key and be shaped accordingly. Now, Augustine's ability to translate is legendarily limited, and he himself laments it. His hermeneutics and his actual exegetical leaps often call for mockery among modern students of biblical hermeneutics. And yet, for all that, his exegesis itself is lovely, and it is more precisely aimed at the church's goal of reshaping persons in the image of Christ than ours tends to be. Even when he is "wrong," there is often a certain beauty to his readings. His readings then are like those of an exegete who "is deceived in an interpretation which builds up charity . . . he is deceived in the same way as a man who leaves a road by mistake but passes through a field to the same place toward which the road itself leads."[1]

---

1. Augustine, *On Christian Doctrine* I.28.40. English trans. D. W. Robertson (Upper Saddle River, NJ: Prentice Hall, 1958), 31. Augustine follows these famous words by going on to say that

Now, let me hasten to say that I have not thrown away my modern commentaries! I actually reach first for *Interpretation* or *New Interpreters* when preparing to preach, and second for patristic commentators — and often the contemporary material serves where the ancient does not. Close attention to language, and then to narrative themes, is crucial for getting at the literal sense of the text. The rampant anti-Judaism so prevalent in ancient writers is thankfully absent from most contemporary ones. Above all else historical-critical interpreters pay close attention to the words on the page, written in languages most of us cannot read, and draw out meaning the rest of us can then put to good use. The most important contribution of historical criticism has been to make the Bible strange again. Allegory can domesticate scripture so that its readings become a sort of "new literal" sense and no longer need to be argued for or demonstrated with theological rigor.[2] And Augustine, to be frank, can bore for long stretches. So perhaps ancient and modern reading traditions can learn from each other here.

This book is an effort to offer Augustine as a new, or at least recovered, resource for the church's biblical interpreters. I offer Augustine's *Enarrationes in psalmos* as a model for Christian hermeneutics and exegesis now. I do this in conjunction with a patristic and Augustinian renaissance already underway. In this new flowering we have not only Catholic publishing efforts that have been ongoing since before Augustine's death, not only Anglican and magisterial Reformation academic efforts with their centuries of maturity, but also Baptist, Anabaptist and otherwise evangelical Protestant reappropriations of his work. This is all to the good — new readers make for interesting new readings. It is also noteworthy that those branches of the tree of the Reformation that have often defined themselves in opposition to Augustinian positions are now turning to him as a resource in efforts to redescribe church, scripture, and more daringly, God.[3]

This work is another offering in the young tradition of evangelical re-

---

such an exegete is "to be corrected and shown that it is more useful not to leave the road, lest the habit of deviating force him to take a crossroad or a perverse way."

2. One could argue, however, that this task has long since been completed, and it is more theologically robust exegesis that is no longer familiar in the church or academy.

3. See the work of Gerald Schlabach, *For the Joy Set Before Us: Augustine and Self-Denying Love* (South Bend, IN: Notre Dame, 2000); and Barry Harvey, *Another City: An Ecclesiological Primer for a Post-Christian World* (Harrisburg, PA: Trinity, 1999). Signs of evangelical interest in patristic exegesis more broadly include Christopher Hall's two books, *Learning Theology with the Church Fathers* (Downers Grove, IL: InterVarsity, 2002) and *Reading Scripture with the Church Fathers* (Downers Grove, IL: InterVarsity, 1998), and the InterVarsity Press publishing endeavor called the Ancient Christian Commentary on Scripture series, edited by Thomas Oden.

readings of Augustine. My own Methodist tradition has produced great historians, but has not necessarily defined itself as an Augustinian church to the degree Catholic, continental Reformation, and Anglican bodies have, especially diverging with the late Augustine over issues of grace and free will. This is also not a technical work of historical scholarship. It is rather a theological work, properly speaking. I read Augustine's *Enarrationes in psalmos* as a guide to rethinking the church's scriptural hermeneutics in our new location. I read him here because I am convinced that the fathers generally and Augustine specifically have been almost entirely excluded from modern conversations about exegesis and from its actual conduct in seminaries and churches. While the fathers have their exegetical faults, they also have much to teach us. Most importantly, their *telos* in exegesis is often right, precisely where ours is frequently wrong. They see exegesis as one of the tasks the church undertakes as part of its pilgrimage to the heavenly city, to use Augustinian language. Certainly the patristic tradition makes mistakes in its steps toward this goal, often severe ones. Yet its attempt to progress toward a specifically Christian goal, to conduct exegesis with this *telos* in mind, is a great improvement on exegesis done with no such eschatological orientation. Augustine does exegesis as though Jesus *is* head of the body of the church, and we who are doing the exegesis *are* members of the body united under this head. Christians should be hard-pressed to disagree.

My book is part of a growing field known as "theological exegesis," many of whose primary practitioners are discussed below. I write with scholars who for generations now have mounted a quiet but steady drumbeat in opposition to overly hasty dismissals of patristic exegesis and for creative reappropriations of the fathers' readings of scripture. I detail many of these theologians in Chapter 1 where I treat them together as what I call the "Return to Allegory School." In their work these largely Protestant theologians[4] draw on previous

---

4. Of the six theologians I treat in Chapter 1, one is a Methodist (David Steinmetz), one Orthodox (Andrew Louth), two are Anglicans (Stephen Fowl and Lewis Ayres), and two Roman Catholics (Robert Wilken and Nicholas Lash). I maintain that these are "largely Protestant" figures not just because Louth and Wilken are converts from Anglican and Lutheran–Missouri Synod upbringings, respectively, but also because even the non-Protestants teach mostly Protestant students at traditionally Protestant institutions — Wilken is at Virginia (a state school, but so naturally more Protestant than Catholic), Louth at Durham, and Lash is retired from Cambridge (Fowl is the exception, working at Catholic Loyola in Baltimore; Ayres is at Emory and Steinmetz at Duke). In other words, most of these were brought up in and taught in Protestant institutions, even with their current Catholic leanings. If anything, they seem to have a broadly Anglican center of gravity, reflecting the Anglican Church's *via media* between traditional Protestant insistence on the primacy of the Word and Catholic emphases on sacramental practice and the Magisterium's authority in arbitrating doctrinal disputes.

generations of *Nouvelle Theologie* pioneers such as Henri de Lubac and Hans Urs von Balthasar who did so much to help us read the fathers well again after many of our churches had forgotten how. Many of these also draw on the work of Karl Barth, who though not an apologist for patristic allegory as such, did himself read the Old Testament in extraordinarily rich ways that resemble Origen and Augustine more than he may have realized. The work of post-liberal theologians in the United States after the inspiration of Hans Frei and George Lindbeck at Yale has given rise to a generation of younger theologians devoted to specifically theological exegesis.[5] "Radical Orthodox" theologians in England following the work of a previous generation of Thomist scholars[6] draw from both *Nouvelle Theologie* and Barthian wells[7] and contribute to the presumption that these sorts of readings are newly acceptable. My description of the "Return to Allegory School" attempts to show the key reasons each figure privileges ancient Christian multivalent readings over exclusively modern ones. I use them to build a cumulative case based on increasingly strong dogmatic arguments for why we should again read scripture like Augustine.

In my second chapter I turn to christology, the heart of Augustine's psalms commentary. Here I argue that anyone who purports to share Augustine's christology ought also share his approach to biblical exegesis. For Augustine, christology is not merely a fact to which to assent, repeating in rote fashion the church's doctrinal formulae. Rather, christology names a dramatic action of God by which we are joined in Christ as members to a body. As those joined to this head, we notice that when Jesus speaks in the New Testament it is often to cite psalms. He does so at particularly crucial times in his ministry, such as in his passion. The cry of dereliction of Jesus from the cross becomes a starting place for Augustine. Jesus has made the *kenotic* motions of what we call the lament psalms his own, for the very abasement and destitution described repeatedly in the Psalter find their climax in Christ's abase-

5. For example, Rusty Reno (*In the Ruins of the Church: Sustaining Faith in an Age of Diminished Christianity* [Grand Rapids: Brazos, 2002]) and Ephraim Radner (*Hope among the Fragments: The Broken Church and Its Engagement of Scripture* [Grand Rapids: Brazos, 2004]) both offer compelling arguments for reappropriation of ancient church practices of biblical interpretation.

6. Such as Herbert McCabe, Nicholas Lash, Fergus Kerr, and Brian Davies.

7. Notwithstanding the frequent disavowals of interest in Barth from John Milbank, Catherine Pickstock, David Hart and others in this fledgling tradition. Here Rowan Williams, David Ford, and Graham Ward show better the importance of Barth to Britain's younger theologians. Interestingly, these figures are split on whether we ought to read like the fathers. Williams in moments of hermeneutical reflection seems to think not, Ford tentatively to think so, and Ward unreservedly to approve (perhaps too quickly). More on each of these below.

ment and destitution. Yet, as Jesus' use of the Psalter elsewhere demonstrates, the darkness of desolation is not the last word. Jesus also prays psalms of exultation and joy, for his taking on of human sin is only to break its power over those joined to him, to have them share with him in the divine life. As Christians notice Christ's use of the Psalter in these ways we become adept at seeing christological motifs throughout that book of Israel's prayer, not only in lament and exultation, but also in narrative, in cursing, in enthronement psalms, pilgrimage chants, even in absurdities and contradictions. Jesus, for Christians, is at the heart of scripture. Just so the fulfillment of the covenant is for us surprisingly apparent also throughout the breadth and depth of the biblical record of that covenant to those of us looking back at scripture *ex post facto.* We for whom the gradual working out of our salvation is partly through the chanting of psalms will see the means and end of their salvation — Christ — illuminatingly present in every word we pray.

This claim naturally raises questions. If we are simply to find Christ on the page of the Psalter, why read the Psalter at all? Why not simply read, say, Colossians, where Christ is patently present instead of only mysteriously or allegorically so? Chapter 3 seeks to answer this question with a glance at Augustine's aesthetics. The answer is that it is beautiful to find Christ present where we had not expected to find him. A perplexing biblical passage that initially offends somehow invites deeper contemplation. As we come to see Christ in the place that initially perplexed us, we find a surprising congruity between his story and the words on the page. This new vision brings illumination and delight. Reading the Psalter for Augustine is not simply the gleaning of information, the record of something past. It is the actual working out of salvation now through seeing Christ anew in the words and the liturgy that we "perform" in worship. Now, this description naturally raises a host of further questions. What if someone does not find it beautiful to see Christ where not previously anticipated? This cannot be easily answered. Arguments over beauty are so messy we in modernity usually pass them by. Yet this is a mistake on Augustinian grounds. The church is a place where claims about physical beauty are often made and indeed argued about. Using Augustine's account of the spiritual senses in his Psalms commentary I describe the process by which we come to see, hear, touch, taste, and smell as Christians. Augustine is not unaware that perceiving Christ here in the Psalter (or anywhere) is difficult, and so his preaching is dedicated to converting and training his hearers into being skilled discerners of Christ.

In Chapter 4 I turn to a common and important objection to my claim that the church should again read like Augustine. What of Augustine's awful missteps, such as his frequent denunciations of the Jews? Unfortunately, practiced readers of the church fathers either become accustomed to stock denunciations of Israel in those pages, or else they stop reading. These occur so frequently one must either become numb to them or do something else with one's time. Yet precisely this numbness is what led to the worst of Christian violence against Jews, above all in the last century. It seems then grossly immoral to claim Augustine as an exemplar when our worst moments have been shaped by readings like these. In reply to this important charge I first look at Augustine's own theology of Israel. This, for all its faults, gives the most prominent place to Israel as Israel of any western patristic figure. Then I turn an important Augustinian theme against Augustine. His standard reading of the cursing psalms is to object to their literal sense, for Christians cannot pray with retribution even against their enemies due to Jesus' explicit command. Therefore such psalms must be read as invocations to transform our enemies into friends. Reading this Augustinian theme back against Augustine allows us to see a way past Augustine's and the church's blind spots and dead ends in thinking about Israel. A proper Christian response to sin is not to ignore it or pretend it has not previously existed, it is rather to *confess* it, to use a crucial Augustinian category. The presence of this harmful tradition in Augustine and this potentially salutary Augustinian counter-tradition actually enhance my argument that we should read him as we conduct our exegesis. For we can confront our worst exegetical and moral failings as well as the best resources of hope for redemption within our own tradition as we seek genuine friendship with Jews.

In Chapter 5 I gather up these fragments and offer an Augustinian theology of scripture from the *Enarrationes.* The reading of scripture is, for Augustine, an activity of "praise seeking understanding." Christians are those who, as part of the working out of our baptisms, gather frequently around the scriptures to hear preaching and celebrate the mysteries. As part of this liturgical existence the preacher exegetes the psalms only after we have chanted them, often antiphonally, normally with a Trinitarian doxology appended. The Psalms are always already set in a liturgical context for us. So the proper way to understand psalm exegesis is to note that we are people who habitually praise with the psalms. How now shall we understand the words with which we have just praised God? I suggest here that, *mutatis mutandis,* this model of "praise seeking understanding" ought also apply whenever Christians read any portion of the scriptures. Further, in conjunction with the christology presented in Chapter 2, I argue that Augustine's approach to the literal sense of a biblical text is *not* a non-literal approach. That is, we can see in him what we may call a form of "christological literalism." The question this chapter struggles to answer is, surprisingly, can we have an Augustinian allegory at all? If the words of scripture are understood in a christological manner without allegory, what is left for allegory to do?

Finally, in a conclusion I return to the contemporary theological and ecclesial scene. I survey recent theological exponents of exegesis who make dogmatic arguments for why Christians should canonize historical criticism as essential to its life. I dissent from these claims, and respond that the best analogy for understanding scripture in the Christian life is not to compare it to the Trinity or to christology, but to the sacraments. Augustine often describes the words of scripture as *sacramenta,* as barely concealing mysteries that must be shown forth in worship, broken and poured out and distributed in celebration, and reflected upon in preaching. Then I address the question of what to do now with historical criticism. I suggest we place it in its proper place in a cross-generational "midrashic" conversation. Historical critics can, like any other age in the church's readers, offer better readings than previous interpreters. The church in any given time and place must determine which of the readings offered through the history of exegesis is most appropriate for its own situation — or if it should come up with a new one. For allegorical interpreters there can be more than one acceptable reading, even if these clash with one another. What I want to avoid is an approach that handicaps the midrashic exegetical workshop in advance by claiming historical critics have the best access to what a text "originally meant." Christian readers ought not cross a line from confidence to presumptive arrogance that cuts off exegetical debate. I maintain instead that modern approaches to scripture have just as much an opportunity to offer exegesis as ancient ones. The fundamental form of this exegesis would then be the medieval gloss, which presents exegetes roughly in chronological order and selects those that stay in the margins of texts and those that fall out based on how they help readers and communities at prayer. I close by arguing that the Christian life itself is allegorical: a series of attempts to live out in new circumstances that which we read on the page of scripture. I then suggest that the ways churches and seminaries train their ministers ought to be reshaped accordingly.

If this book offers anything new it is the theological claim that we church members ought to go and do what some of our theologians have been saying we should as we read scripture. Academic conversations about why we should return to allegory are intellectually rich but insufficient. If indeed ancient Christian forms of exegesis have things to recommend them then we should go and read scripture like the fathers did. Otherwise we risk being stuck in the sort of methodological prolegomena that so often haunts theology — we clear our throats unendingly and say nothing. If there is any color in these pages it is in the actual exegesis Augustine undertakes. I probably have too many examples of his actual readings of the psalms here. Augustine is so captivating I cannot help but pile on citations of him, to the point of overwhelming the text with examples from Augustine himself. I would like for readers to be similarly taken with the beauty of Augustine's exegesis. Once enough of us read scripture like Augustine, both in the church and in the academy, then we can look back and ascertain whether doing so makes for more faithful exegesis. I offer this work as an experiment of sorts, hoping to encourage Augustinian readers so that the shape of our life sometime in the future may show whether this sort of exegesis is truly to be commended. My hope is that church members and academicians may return to reading theological commentaries as avidly as we modern people now devour popular entertainment, for Augustine's commentary can indeed be thrilling for those whose taste is properly schooled. Even more, I hope more of us will lead lives shaped in Augustinian ways after the image of Christ. Such lives would be the best "readings" of scripture.

# 1  The "Return to Allegory" Movement

There remains a general discomfort with ancient Christian allegory in today's theological academy. We do not normally teach ministerial students to read scripture allegorically, so it is unlikely that they will teach those skills to catechumens preparing to join churches. We train them to attend to the literal sense of a text and its implied and actual historical background so as to set their exegesis on as solid a foundation as possible. Classical Christian figural readings of the Old Testament are often left behind as either fanciful or dated. Systematic theologians usually keep to the New Testament when speaking of expressly Christian doctrines. Homileticians and practical theologians discourage readings that depart from a text's *sensus literalis*. There are good historical reasons for this discomfort and its correlative reading strategies.

Yet one crucial area of ecclesial teaching and practice in which allegory is not ruled out of court is in liturgical studies and practice. It would be difficult to do away with allegory here without fundamentally redoing the calendar of the Christian year so that we do not read Isaiah in advent, or the lament psalms in Holy Week. Yet this is no mere aesthetic holdover from an unenlightened era. The Christian year is structured in accordance with the incarnation itself; its rhythms set to immerse Christian people in the feasts and fasts that mark God's saving presence with us, first in Israel, then in Christ and now in the church. Think for a moment about a baptism at the Easter vigil. The church traditionally reads and celebrates Miriam's song of victory with its celebration of God's work in casting the horses and chariots of the Egyptians into the sea (Exodus 15:1-18). Those enemies do not stay safely in the past, however, but leap up into the present life of those who sing this song anew. Our own sin, fear, and violence are now drowned in the waters of baptism, granting freedom to Israel once more. Christian liturgy is itself an alle-

9

gorical act, a reading of Israel's scripture in "another sense," one that would be misunderstood or lost if it were not for baptism and the church's continual liturgical celebrations. Even more importantly, baptism, that ecclesial act that initiates Christian salvation itself (1 Peter 3:21), *inscribes* a certain set of reading practices from the very moment of Christian initiation.[1] Christians are born amidst allegory. This is precisely the sort of "reading" — normally eschewed in the modern theological academy — on which Easter, baptism, indeed the whole of the Christian mystery, is founded.

Because of our liturgy and our canon, then, Christians cannot but practice allegorical exegesis. Since modern biblical interpretation frowns on these sorts of exegetical approaches, what we have in modernity is unrestrained allegory. That is, the very thing of which modern interpreters accuse the fathers is what they leave to today's churches. Allegory, like any form of reading, must be fought over, argued about, disciplined by various complex sorts of "controls." Allegory is not always done well, nor is it always harmless. For example it can be employed to exclude or even mock the literal sense of scripture instead of reading it more deeply on the way to more mystery-laden interpretation (more about all this to come). But since allegory is ruled out of court in seminaries, pastors and Christian thinkers are left without the resources to practice allegory well. And since Christianity is an inherently allegorical faith, we are left with no tools for doing that which we always already do other than our own personal resources, or lack thereof. I would like to see the church reclaim its ancient practice of figurative biblical exegesis so as to teach its pastors and members well how to use it and how not. Only then can we even begin to argue over whether such readings as the three offered above are *good* readings, on specifically Christian grounds.

1. Critics of allegory recognize this as well. After an essay in which he dismisses christological exegesis of New Testament hymnic passages, Robert Morgan writes that "only a historicist and positivist Scrooge will fail to enjoy the myth [of a preexistent Logos becoming incarnate] at Christmas," in "Jesus Christ, the Wisdom of God (2)," in *Reading Texts, Seeking Wisdom: Scripture and Theology*, ed. David Ford and Graham Stanton (Grand Rapids: Eerdmans, 2003), 36. Morgan follows in the tradition of Maurice Wiles in arguing that the New Testament celebrates being drawn into Jesus' saving mission, but does not encourage anything like later metaphysical descriptions of Jesus' eternal preexistence or *kenosis*. Yet his mention of Dickens's character Scrooge suggests a willingness to set aside objections and enjoy Christmas mirth, like a parent who indulges childish belief in Santa Claus. If Morgan really believes that later doctrinal and liturgical description of Christ is false to the biblical witness, Scrooge's posture of refusing to celebrate should not be benignly shrugged off, but emulated.

## The Proposal in Detail

Think with me, for a moment, of the problems inherent in this ostensibly simple claim: "we should read the Psalter like St. Augustine."

Each of the words of the phrase is open to debate. Who is the "we"? For this book the "we" is the Christian church, gathered to worship the risen Christ as Lord in the power of the Holy Spirit. Others will, I hope, be able to learn from our reflections here. But I presume to make a claim primarily on the faith and practice only of orthodox Christians.[2] Others may wish to write for a more general audience, or no audience in particular. But as Jon Levenson has argued, such an effort is often tantamount to asking committed Jews or Christians to be something other than what they are.[3] In fact, the best dialogue takes place when partners committed to their own traditions in some depth come together to discuss both similarities and differences.[4] That is, the way to genuine diversity and tolerance, and to good disagreement, is to have each party deepen its own religious roots rather than pull them up.

What of the "should"? Its cohortative mood is not accidental. As Stephen Fowl and David Dawson[5] have recently shown, any particular approach to

2. By this I mean, roughly, those who confess the Nicene creed.

3. Jon D. Levenson, *The Hebrew Bible, the Old Testament, and Historical Criticism* (Louisville: Westminster/John Knox, 1993): "For Spinoza, the excommunicated Jew who never became a Christian, the idea of inspiration was simply another shackle constricting the exegete. No longer need exegesis take place within the believing community. . . . Jews and Christians can participate equally in the Spinozan agenda only because its naturalistic presuppositions negate the theological foundations of *both* Judaism and Christianity" (5).

4. I take this to be the secret behind the success of the Society for Scriptural Reasoning — an ecumenical dialogue that depends on adherents from each of the three Abrahamic faiths reading their own texts loyally and others' respectfully.

5. Both Fowl and Dawson are essential to this project and will be discussed further below. For now, we can say that Fowl's project is largely an attempt to reintegrate Christian biblical interpretation with key Christian beliefs and practices. His *Engaging Scripture* (Oxford: Blackwell, 1998) demonstrates the importance of the presupposition of Christian community and its key practices to faithful exegesis.

Dawson shows even more clearly the political nature of exegesis in his older work, *Allegorical Readers and Cultural Revision in Ancient Alexandria* (Berkeley: University of California Press, 1992). He correctly (if unromantically) describes interpretive conflict as a result of "efforts by readers to secure for themselves and their communities social and cultural identity, authority, and power" (2). Even seemingly straightforward evocations of a text's "plain sense" are necessarily reflective of a community's political interests. "This is true even, or perhaps especially, when ancient allegorists themselves choose to speak of their readings as the recovery of meaning rather than as the exercise of power" (5).

I could easily have included a section in this chapter on Dawson, or on any number of other important figures who write about patristic exegesis and its contemporary reappropriation:

reading presumes a politics, a claim to authority by some peoples over others, such as pastors over parishioners or bishops over broader stretches of the church. Naturally we shall hope that politics to be peaceful, though we should not pretend authority is not being exercised. Specifically Christian "authority" is exercised in reflection of a shepherd who lay down his life for the sheep (John 10:11). For all the good reasons we have to be skittish about church claims for authority, the way forward is better authority (for example, that tempered by better biblical exegesis!) rather than none.

It is far from obvious what "read" means. Fowl has taken a rather minimalist approach to this word in his important work. "Readings" cannot ever be spoken of without reference to shared commitments of the community doing the reading. It is never obvious what "reading" means in advance of political, social, intellectual, and other shared agreements and practices in a particular community. That said, of course communities can and should argue over whether they are making better or worse sense of the words on the page. So we are already in the midst of interpretive dispute. And this is a good thing! What else is the history of Christian doctrine besides a multi-generational exegetical workshop, as Christians continue to engage scripture in an effort to follow their Lord?[6] I, for example, wish to hold that Christians who make orthodox confessions of their faith ought to read more like Augustine — to include multiple levels of readings and not limit themselves to one.[7] I have substantive suggestions to make for how practices of reading ought to

---

Gary Anderson, Frances Young, Brian Daley, Rusty Reno, Ephraim Radner, and many others. The group of those I treat is not meant to be comprehensive.

6. One image that originally attracted me to this sort of project was what I took to be a quite Jewish approach to biblical interpretation: "rabbi so and so said of rabbi so and so's interpretation of scripture that. . . ." That seemed to me precisely the way Christians ought to see their scripture — to look at it only through the lenses of previous fathers' and mothers' readings. Said more strongly, the move away from the gloss tradition in the church is the abandonment of a particularly Jewish *form* of biblical exegesis (even if the *content* of much of the medieval gloss tradition must be adjudged reprehensible with regard to its take on Judaism).

7. Fowl and Francis Watson are united in their avoidance of explicit criticism of historical criticism. Fowl cites approvingly Watson's response to a critical review: "'So far as I can remember my book contains no disparagement at all of 'the historical-critical method,' largely because I do not believe that such an entity exists in the singular form that is normally envisaged. What does exist is a shifting set of convictions, never clearly defined and constantly under negotiation" (Fowl, *Engaging Scripture*, 22, citing "A Response to Professor Rowland" in *Scottish Journal of Theology* 45 [1995]: 518). My sense is that Fowl's and Watson's critics are right to suspect in their work a fundamental criticism of historical criticism, even as they draw upon it in constructive ways. Though we cannot give a "Platonic" definition of it, nor a creedal demarcation of what counts and what doesn't, there is enough of a "family resemblance" to its tasks that we can speak of it "existing" long enough to complain about it.

look in an Augustinian light. But I am not claiming some a-historical "meaning" present "in" Christian texts can be unearthed which will show I am right. I am rather suggesting that those who self-identify as Christians ought to come, by virtue of their beliefs, to engage in the sorts of reading practices to which Augustine devoted his life.

It is far from obvious what "the Psalter" is. Manuscript production is itself a political act. Certain persons decide to make texts available for purposes designed to serve communities' specific ends. For Augustine the Psalter was a set of 150 psalms translated rather poorly from the Septuagint into a variety of local Latin translations in the place to which he was called by God to do ministry. These texts were always read in an ecclesial context. Even if Christians were reading them in solitude, this act of reading was part of a greater effort of growth toward knowledge and love of God in communion with fellow Christians. Versions of the book would have been copied by hand, probably with a complex set of practices liturgical and technical, by previous generations of similarly minded Christians with an eye to ecclesial use. It normally would be read out loud, if alone in a practice that would issue in medieval *lectio divina;* if in a group it would be read "with interpretation," that is, with preaching as part of a greater liturgical practice. For us moderns, the "Psalter" is something we can buy in any bookstore, or be handed by any Gideon, that then decorates our book shelves or the inside of drawers in hotel rooms. That is, its very physical existence is not necessarily an ecclesial truth with liturgical ends. Modern printing has made books cheap, in both senses of that word, and divorced them from the weighty ends communities once had to have to go to the effort and expense of reproducing them. Even modern critical editions produced by highly learned scholars inscribe a certain set of political claims — among them, that anyone with the appropriate technical skills can and should have at this book, that the marginal *glossa ordinaria* that ancient communities tended to assume necessary for scripture are in fact a hindrance to good reading. It is not obvious that my NRSV translation of the Psalter ought be preferred to Augustine's motley collection of ancient Latin and Punic translations — a wide range of issues would have to be hashed out by a community to say it is so. Modern translations surely have better reconstructions of historically reliable manuscripts in their favor; ancient ones that are more like those used by the writers of the New Testament and Augustine. A simple question can show how hotly debatable manuscripts and translations are: should Isaiah 7:14 be translated "a young girl," after Hebrew "originals," or "a virgin" after Greek ones? Who precisely shall be with child? Not only is every translation also an interpretation, but so is every attempt to sort through ancient manuscripts and every contemporary effort to produce new ones.

What is the force of "like"? If we were simply to repeat what Augustine said with the most wooden precision, we would in fact *still* be "changing" him, for the same words and interpretive moves made now have different significance and resonance than they would have then.[8] Faithfulness to a predecessor is always still a rhetorical performance of some sort, which must be judged better or worse by communities in light of their ends. This "like" is made all the more difficult by the fact that we have in our hands tools Augustine would have deeply coveted, such as the improved manuscripts, translations, and background technical knowledge he occasionally longs for in the *Enarrationes in psalmos*. Yet for us those interpretive "advantages" are imbedded in a host of problematic assumptions and practices that accompany the historical-critical method that Christians rarely even notice now. Precisely what the force of this "like" is will be a major subject of this work.

The word "saint" is hardly plain in meaning. It is a descriptor used by the church to say that a particular life evinces holiness sufficient to merit imitation by latter Christians. It can be used in a stronger and specifically soteriological sense by Roman Catholics to say that a certain person has no purgative work to do before the beatific vision. When the Reformers worked to clarify the word "saint" they argued it should be used as Paul did — to refer to all Christians (e.g., Romans 1:7; 2 Corinthians 1:1; Philippians 1:1). So if Protestants are still to speak of St. Augustine or St. Paul they ought also call themselves and all their fellow church members "saints." When this book argues that biblical exegesis ought to be done so as to produce saints, it is using the word in some sense in between traditional Catholic and Protestant usage. It assumes both that certain figures can be distinguished as exemplary for the sake of the whole church's emulation, and also that the whole church is called to be no less holy. It is also making a theological and political claim: that it is most desirable to be a certain sort of person, trained out of vice and into virtue, given the right sort of love for the right things, spiraling into ever more intimate union with God and therefore also with others.

Augustine. Why is Augustine our subject here? For one, Augustine's *Enarrationes* covers the whole breadth of the Psalter more thoroughly than

---

8. Nicholas Lash shows that even the most ardent conservative cannot resist all change: "If, in thirteenth-century Italy, you wandered around in a coarse brown gown, with a cord round your middle, your social location was clear: your dress said that you were one of the poor. If, in twentieth-century Cambridge, you wander around in a coarse brown gown, with a cord round your middle, your social location is curious: your dress now says, not that you are one of the poor, but that you are some kind of oddity in the business of 'religion.' Your dress now declares, not your solidarity with the poor, but your amiable eccentricity" ("What Authority Has Our Past?" in *Theology on the Way to Emmaeus* [London: Society for Christian Mission, 1986], 54).

any other extant patristic commentary. Moreover, the text has become available in a good English translation. It is time for theologians to make good use of the treasure now available in the form of New City Press's printing efforts. There is also now good historical work available on the *Enarrationes*, but not the avalanche that meets anyone who tries to read most of Augustine's great works. The choice of Augustine is also an argument. He is, by common agreement, the most significant theological voice in the Christian west. Yet the *Enarrationes* are not often read in the church or the academy. It is no accident we have had no good English translation until now. This is because modern theology has relegated biblical interpretation to the tools and tasks defined by historical criticism. Historical criticism was, from its origin, a certain sort of rebellion against the church's established and dogmatically informed biblical exegesis, a stripping away of tradition in order scientifically to appraise an author's intention in its original historical context (normally ignoring or even disdaining later ecclesial contexts in which the words read differently).[9] Augustine's own works could then be studied quite successfully on historical-critical grounds: his best original manuscripts imaginatively reassembled, his context appraised, his own communicative intent surmised, and so on. Yet what Augustine himself *does* when he reads scripture usually cannot in any way be emulated by modern biblical exegetes if these wish to pass muster either in church or academy. This is all the more true when Augustine reads the Old Testament. For while we may be willing to grant a certain theologically robust reading of the New Testament, which no one doubts to have been written by Christians for Christians, how can we possibly allow a specifically Christian and allegorical reading of the Psalter, which no one can imagine possibly to have been written by Christians or for Christians?

The best recent patristic scholarship has argued persuasively that patristic theologians were concerned with nothing other than the interpretation of scripture. The enormous fights that led to, say, Nicea, were above all

---

9. In his recent book *Reading the Bible with the Damned* (Louisville: Westminster/John Knox, 2005), Bob Eckblad reads the Bible with convicts, exiles, and others on the margins. His work with people in such social location yields this consideration of historical critical exegesis: "In contrast to 'scientific exegesis,' which claims to be objective and unbiased theologically, the socially engaged biblical scholar must both encourage people to directly question and challenge assumptions about God that most oppress them and invite them to consider a liberating alternative way of reading" (73-74). Prisoners' readings indeed illuminate, say, Genesis's description of Jacob's various ethically questionable wiles. As Eckblad reads with prisoners, so this book reads with Augustine as a contrast and complement to the dominant historical-critical paradigm.

exegetical fights.[10] The results which a council like Nicea codified were, above all, exegetical results. For example, the *homoousion* represents a solution to an exegetical debate about conflicting biblical accounts of Jesus' relationship to God, and also a sort of interpretive plumb line for future exegetical work. To ignore or impugn patristic exegesis is then to undercut the foundation and intelligibility of the *homoousion,* and so to render problematic the confession of that term in a liturgical setting. In other words, if Christians wish to adhere to conciliar dogmatic decisions, as most do, they must recognize that they also implicitly agree to patristic exegetical assumptions and conclusions, at least to some degree. You cannot have patristic dogma without patristic exegesis; you cannot have the creed without allegory.

If I can show this to be true of Augustine, the cornerstone upon which theology in the west is founded, then I can show by implication that the theological heritage treasured in common by Protestants and Catholics alike rests upon a "foundation" of allegory. Perhaps by some attention to this underread portion of Augustine some new ecumenical avenues may surprise us. Yet I suspect that both Catholics and Protestants will be very nervous about this entire project. Catholics have recently worked very hard simply to avail themselves of historical criticism, and have quickly gone from Vatican I's rejection of it to a post-Vatican II setting in which Catholics have been busy producing some of the academy's best practitioners of modern biblical scholarship. There are memories of martyrs and confessors to this great effort. On the Protestant side there would be a similar fear of retrogression, of return to a pre-critical era in which fear kept history at bay in order to protect dogma. Were not Enlightenment-based techniques of scriptural study an in-breaking of a new dawn over against an age of darkness in both the church and the academy — again, one that required heroic sacrifice to bring about? Both will have well-founded worries about the loss of the extraordinary *rapprochement* recently possible with Jewish exegetes through critical examination of the historical moorings of the New Testament's anti-Semitism. Both will worry about the loss of an ability to pry loose "fundamentalist" students from rigid and narrow conceptions of the historicity of the Bible. The modern biblical academy as a whole has developed its own "saints" — those mentioned with *gravitas* by former students, anecdotes of whose life and study are repeated for joy and emulation. All have given a great deal to be part of an academy that demands rigorous scholarship, extraordinary expertise and the renunciation of other possible (more lucrative) professions for their pursuit.

---

10. See here above all Lewis Ayres's *Nicaea and Its Legacy: An Approach to Fourth-Century Trinitarian Theology* (Oxford: Oxford University Press, 2005).

Notice that the forms of these worries, which I hope will be widely recognizable through their presentation here, are specifically *Christian* forms, recast in secular guise. The turn from pre-critical flights of fancy to rigorous and clear-eyed modern exegetical technique is often spoken of as a sort of conversion. Indeed, many accounts of patristic exegesis until recently treated it as a history of more or less failed efforts on the inevitable way to modern historical consciousness, with all participants evaluated for how closely they resemble modern critical techniques.[11] The concern to safeguard dialogue between Jews and Christians, and the strong moral claim that the latter will inevitably do violence to the former without the pacifying influence of historical criticism, is another *simulacrum* of Christian reasoning: one that casts historical criticism in messianic guise as the only thing that can save us from violence. It also overstates its case. Classical Christian exegetes can and have been friends to Jews; not a few historical critics have been their bitter

11. This is why "Antiochene" exegesis and theology has traditionally been praised at the expense of "Alexandrian," for its supposed closer approximation to modern theological agendas. Recent historical scholarship from Dawson, Elizabeth Clark, John J. O'Keefe, Andrew Louth, Frances Young, and many others has now questioned any sharp division between Alexandrian and Antiochene hermeneutics and criticized the comparison between Antiochene exegesis and modern historical criticism. This newer scholarship claims that Antiochenees like Theodore of Mopsuestia, Diodore of Tarsus, and to an extent Theodoret of Cyrus should be seen as adhering closely to the reading strictures of ancient rhetorical schools and reacting against the versions of "Origenism" that were ruled heretical in their day. See here Frances Young's *Biblical Exegesis and the Formation of Christian Culture* (Cambridge: Cambridge University Press, 1997); and Elizabeth Clark's *Reading Renunciation: Asceticism and Scripture in Early Christianity* (Princeton: Princeton University Press, 1999). O'Keefe goes further and criticizes Antiochene readers for an unwillingness to read Old Testament texts in light of Christ. The distinction to be made between the two schools is not that one practiced allegory and the other did not — Antiochene exegetes occasionally criticize Alexandrian ones for being overly literalistic! It is rather an unwillingness to let a specifically Christian dogmatic claim — Christ as the fulfillment of God's promises to Israel — challenge an *a priori* philosophical commitment to the reading techniques of the rhetorical schools. See O'Keefe, "A Letter That Killeth": Toward a Reassessment of Antiochene Exegesis, or Diodore, Theodore, and Theodoret on the Psalms," *Journal of Early Christian Studies* 8, no. 1 (2000): 83-104. O'Keefe makes a similar criticism of recent historiographical praise of Antiochene christology. Its adherents in the ancient church were few and it was rightly condemned for its unwillingness to give up philosophical commitments to divine impassibility that had to be retooled in light of the incarnation, as Cyril of Alexandria saw clearly but Nestorius could not. O'Keefe, "Impassible Suffering?" *Theological Studies* 58 (1997): 39-60. Exemplars of the older historiography include Beryl Smalley's *The Study of the Bible in the Middle Ages* (Oxford: Clarendon, 1941) and, closer to our topic, Gerald Bonner's article "Augustine as Biblical Scholar," in *The Cambridge History of the Bible*, vol. 1: *From the Beginnings to Jerome,* ed. P. R. Ackroyd and C. F. Evans (Cambridge: Cambridge University Press, 1970), 541-63.

enemies. As Fowl argues, Jews and others will have nothing to fear from Christians not when these are sufficiently policed by modern interpretive strictures, but when Christians obey their Lord and foreswear violence.[12] The concern to be able to separate young fundamentalists from their blindly historicist assumptions and free them from spiritual and political rigidity is another quasi-evangelical effort, a desire to bring about intellectual and spiritual flourishing of a certain sort.[13] It is admirable in a way, but should be recognized as a call for a sort of religionless conversion, an altar call without altars. The historical critical guild is itself a sort of shadow church, with saints, canonized texts, hallowed processes of training novices, calls for ascetic renunciation and deferred reward, with its own glosses filling the texts of manuscripts, its own orthodoxy, its own heretics, its own desired political and spiritual ends. Much of this is admirable to a degree, and has much to teach Christians and others. But it is not by itself an objection to the sort of project I call for here.

That is nothing less than the restoration of classical Christian allegory. By "restoration" I do not mean simply the publishing of books like this one, but rather the restoration of the institutions that once provided the skills necessary to discern the mystery of Christ on every page of scripture. As things stand there is no place one may go to learn to be a doctor of the sacred page. One can earn degrees in a variety of fields such as Bible or church history or dogmatics, but as I said above these are strategically cordoned off from one another to prevent the sort of biblical exploration executed by Augustine. One could go to the monastery, but the monks trained there are no less sub-

12. See his "Vigilant Communities and Virtuous Readers," in *Engaging Scripture,* 62-96, where he argues that the answer to previous Christian misreading is not more historical criticism but better practice of penance and vigilance over future readings.

Jewish and Christian dialogue about scripture is a mostly modern phenomenon for which we have reason to be grateful. Yet Ephraim Radner has recently argued that monolithic social orders were often surprisingly hospitable to outsiders, while those that champion enlightened liberty could be extraordinarily hostile to actual difference. He writes that toleration in medieval Europe is often overlooked by those holding to an "Enlightenment caricature" of history that ignores Christendom's surprisingly frequent tolerance, in contrast to the "cruel impatience" of later revolutionary Enlightenment social orders. He cites a revisionist scholarship on this matter that includes *Beyond the Persecuting Society: Religious Toleration Before the Enlightenment,* ed. J. C. Laursen and C. J. Nederman (Philadelphia: Pennsylvania University Press, 1998). See Radner's *Hope among the Fragments: The Broken Church and Its Engagement of Scripture* (Grand Rapids: Brazos, 2004), 27.

13. Fowl ironically uses the historical critical guild, with its extraordinary concentration of the best intellectual habits of extremely capable scholars, as a model (under the venerable rubric of "plundering the Egyptians") for the church to restore specifically theological exegesis in *Engaging Scripture,* 187-90.

ject to the forces here described than anyone else.[14] One can go to the church, but the church is no less "in the ruins" with regard to scripture than with every other aspect of its life.[15] Further, where there are calls for allegory, one indeed has to worry about a sort of reactionary spirit — either outright *fear* of modern inquiry, or a conservatism unwilling to question its own assumptions or fairly to evaluate the claims of others: theology as an effort to be right rather than to be faithful. And so, to restate my project without all the polemic: I offer Augustine as an experimental case, to evaluate whether he shows an ability in his Psalms commentary to absorb the strengths of modern exegesis, and to correct his own weaknesses without fundamentally reorienting his exegetical foundations. In short, I seek to provide Augustine as a model for a genuinely post-critical form of biblical interpretation.

I offer this work as part of an impressively broad array of scholars who make up what I call the "Return to Allegory" movement. Broad, in that they include Old Testament scholars, New Testament interpreters, church historians, theologians, and practical theologians.[16] These scholars also come from places that traverse the spectrum of theological traditions. We are not surprised to find Orthodox, Catholic, and Anglo-Catholics here, but may be to find more mainline Protestants, such as Methodists, and evangelicals. Perhaps again this cohesion across disciplinary and denominational lines suggests an original unity whose division only barely masks a more basic reality, an original peace of a genuine *catholica*. I do not mean by calling this a "movement" to suggest that they are all of one mind, nor that they are neces-

14. At Mepkin Abbey in South Carolina, a place where much of this work was originally conceived, I discovered that the monastery's annual visiting lecture in scripture was to be given by none other than Bart Ehrman — a distinguished critic of New Testament and early Christian literature, to be sure, but also precisely that: *a critic*. There is no escaping the world. See Ehrman's *The Orthodox Corruption of Scripture: The Effect of the Early Christological Controversies on the Text of the New Testament* (Oxford: Oxford University Press, 1993).

15. The phrase is Radner's, from *The End of the Church: A Pneumatology of Division in the Christian West* (Grand Rapids: Eerdmans, 1998), notably picked up by R. R. Reno in his *In the Ruins of the Church: Sustaining Faith in an Age of Diminished Christianity* (Grand Rapids: Brazos, 2002). I am concerned about the possible distortion suggested by the phrase, for when has the church *not* been in ruins? As long as it does not imply a pristine Edenic state and instead turns our attention to this particular set of ruins and the implied possibilities for "building" we now face, it can do metaphorical work.

16. Liturgists do seem to be the only people for whom allegory is not foreign. As Robert Wilken often argues, the church's liturgy inscribes allegorical practice into the very fabric of Christianity. Liturgists perhaps best can see this above peers of other disciplines. On the link between ancient Christian exegesis and liturgy see, for example, his chapter "An Awesome and Unbloody Sacrifice," in *The Spirit of Early Christian Thought* (New Haven: Yale University Press, 2003).

sarily in collaboration with one another, though a disproportionate number come from Yale School and English institutions and are indeed colleagues and friends to one another. What gives them sufficient similarity to call this a movement is the cohesion of their arguments: namely, that allegorical reading of Christian scripture is a viable theological endeavor that, in some way, should be restored to church practice. My discussion of each in turn will hopefully help locate my own argument that the church and its academies would do well to imitate Augustine's exegesis in his *Enarrationes*.

### "Reading the Bible like any other book . . ."

"To interpret a text is to ascertain the original author's intended meaning." Students of modern hermeneutics do not have to work very hard anymore to show this description to be inadequate. Yet it is still very much alive in theoretical discussions of biblical interpretation. This is so for a number of complex reasons. One, the modern insistence that a biblical text be investigated scientifically, without input from the interpreter or from previous noncritical interpretation, seems to have yielded such spectacular results in our understanding of the Bible's historical origins. Since Benjamin Jowett first said we must "interpret the Scripture like any other book,"[17] modern critical scholarship has advanced to the point of being able to produce a scholar like E. P. Sanders, whose groundbreaking work on the deeply Jewish nature of the New Testament has benefited the church, the synagogue, and the academy immeasurably. That benefit has also been deeply theological, as it has helped the church to rethink its doctrine on such key matters as Christ and the church to reflect more faithfully on our Jewish roots and to do so in ways that encourage *rapprochement* between Jews and Christians.[18] A second reason for

---

17. *Critics of the Bible 1724-1873* (Cambridge: Cambridge University Press, 1989), 143.

18. To give just a few examples, Michael Wyschogrod's extraordinary essays in *Abraham's Promise: Judaism and Jewish-Christian Relations*, ed. Kendall Soulen (Grand Rapids: Eerdmans, 2004); and *Christianity in Jewish Terms*, ed. Tikva Frymer-Kensky et al. (Boulder: Westview, 2000). See there the extraordinary document from Frymer-Kensky, David Novak, Peter Ochs, and Michael Signer, *Dabru Emet*, and the response to it from Christian theologians Wolfhart Pannenburg, David Hart, David Burrell, and Barry Cytron in *Pro Ecclesia* 11 (2002): 5-19, and further reflections upon it in Robert Jenson and Carl Braaten, eds., *Jews and Christians: People of God* (Grand Rapids: Eerdmans, 2003). See also the collection of older essays by John Howard Yoder, recently released by Michael Cartwright and Peter Ochs, eds., *The Jewish-Christian Schism Revisited* (Grand Rapids: Eerdmans, 2003). This list could be expanded a great deal. It is not obvious to me that these sorts of constructive and respectful theological endeavors done by Jews and Christians in cooperation with one another would have been possible without modern

the durability of the stock description of interpretation as an attempt to divine an original author's meaning is that it seems to have the implicit backing of theological authority. Protestants have placed enormous emphasis on such doctrines of scripture as *sola scriptura* and such theological categories as revelation, which together drive interpreters toward such a formulation as the above. Most importantly, it contains a degree of truth! Many acts of reading indeed place a great deal of store by the discovery of an author's "communicative intent," whether we are speaking of such mundane "texts" as a note from a spouse, an article in *Time,* or the interpretation of an essay. The description has a sort of "common sensical" ring to it — which is partly what makes it so problematic in its application to biblical interpretation.

The fact that theoretical conversation about biblical interpretation is still so fascinated with talk of "gaps," "ditches," and various sorts of "bridges" over these quite physical metaphors suggests an absence that must be addressed: that of the church.[19] What if the "vehicle" meant to bear a community across the otherwise unbridgeable chasm between a text's origin and our reading today is *there* but simply being ignored? In truth we have no direct access to the other side of the chasm, to the point of origin in which a text was first penned, handed on, redacted, and so on. Modern scholarship has served us well by demonstrating this reality to us. What we have is a complex historical process by which a diverse array of people across time and space has "handed on" teaching, one to another, until it reaches us (1 Corinthians 15:1 and 3). This handing on process cannot but have affected the form and content of that which they have handed on — and this fact should only worry those who would wish to have at that point of origin directly. For those with anything like a theological account of "tradition," of the process of handing on church teaching as part and parcel of the Spirit's work of shaping a people in the image of Christ, this quite mundane and human process of handing on and shaping teaching over time will not first be a cause of worry, but of celebration. For where there would be a "gap," an

---

biblical scholarship's impetus to Christians to reevaluate their own scriptural and traditional claims about Judaism.

19. Stanley Hauerwas's *Unleashing the Scriptures: Freeing the Bible from Captivity to America* (Nashville: Abingdon, 1993) redirects a hermeneutical debate that has long been almost exclusively focused on political disputes in America, and how to make America more "just" or more "religious," to one centered on the church. The "gap" to which we must attend in reading the scriptures well is not between us and an ancient book, creed, or messiah, but between us and the holiness to which we are called, without which we cannot read scripture well. The saints are the true exegetes of scripture. Along these lines see also Kenneth Surin's "'The Weight of Weakness': Intratextuality and Discipleship," in *The Turnings of Darkness and Light: Essays in Philosophy and Systematic Theology* (Cambridge: Cambridge University Press, 1989).

"unbridgeable chasm" between us and, say, Jesus, is precisely where the church stands, handing on teaching from one generation to another, giving us access to the God who has gifted us with scripture.

## David Steinmetz: The Superiority of the Pre-Critical

A crucial essay by the Methodist historian of the Reformation, David Steinmetz, broke ground in criticizing historical-critical scriptural inquiry a quarter of a century ago.[20] Steinmetz opened "The Superiority of Pre-Critical Exegesis" with an attack on Jowett's work. For all the benefits historical critical study has brought us, the theory upon which it rests is "demonstrably false." The reasons are primarily ecclesial. As Steinmetz writes, with unforgettable piquancy,

> How was a French priest in 1150 to understand Psalm 137, which bemoans captivity in Babylon, makes rude remarks about Edomites, expresses an ineradicable longing for a glimpse of Jerusalem, and pronounces a blessing on anyone who avenges the destruction of the temple by dashing Babylonian children against a rock? The priest lives in Concale, not Babylon, has no personal quarrel with Edomites, cherishes no ambitions to visit Jerusalem (though he might fancy a holiday in Paris), and is expressly forbidden by Jesus to avenge himself on his enemies. Unless Psalm 137 has more than one possible meaning, it cannot be used as a prayer by the church and must be rejected as a lament belonging exclusively to the piety of ancient Israel. (29-30)[21]

Steinmetz's essay forthrightly and clearly lays out the primary tenets of classical Christian allegorical exegesis. Different genres in scripture call for different sorts of interpretation. The difference in time, place, and above all, morality, of the church from ancient Israel call for some sort of non-literal reading. Ancient Christian readers share with us moderns a desire for discerning the intent of scripture's author. Yet for them, scripture's primary author is always God! (31). And when Christians speak of scripture, there is a wide "field" of

---

20. In *Theology Today* 37, no. 1 (1980): 27-38; reprinted in Fowl, ed., *The Theological Interpretation of Scripture: Classic and Contemporary Readings* (Oxford: Blackwell, 1997). Page references to this article in *Theology Today* will be given parenthetically in the text.

21. Francis Watson makes just such a rejection of Psalm 137 on New Testament grounds while arguing for the interrelationship between Old Testament and New Testament in his *Text and Truth* (Grand Rapids: Eerdmans, 1997), 119-22.

possible meanings any one of which can be viable in the church's effort to exposit its scripture. Further, any good historian knows that a great figure's work always escapes the confines of its origin. In Steinmetz's own field of Reformation studies "there was not one Luther in the sixteenth century, but a battalion of Luthers" (36). For all these reasons "the notion that a text means only what its author intends it to mean is historically naïve" (37). Origen could not have made the case for allegorical reading any more concisely.

Steinmetz's enthusiasm here for pre-modern exegesis is no signal that he has whole-heartedly embraced a post-modern enthusiasm for interpretation disconnected from authorial intention. There is a battalion of Luthers loose in scholarship of the sixteenth century, but some of these are better Luthers than others! Steinmetz worries that modern literary criticism has "become a jolly game of ripping out an author's shirt-tail and setting fire to it" (37). He worries about interpretation that so dismisses a text's literal and historic sense that exegesis is relegated merely to the issue of "the problem of the regeneration of its interpreters" (32). Medieval biblical exegesis steers a middle way between extremes, since it is capable of careful "application and avoids the Scylla of extreme subjectivism, on the one hand, and the Charybdis of historical positivism, on the other" (38). Steinmetz's response to Jowett is that if indeed we should read the Bible "like any other book," *no* great historical work is read well in the way Jowett describes. Further, speaking more ecclesially now, the church's historical practice of allegory is theologically defensible and should be emulated. Medieval commentators read Jesus' parable of the workers in the vineyard as a comforting word to grieving parents that their small children, though they worked but an hour, will still receive the full reward of eternal life. Steinmetz argues that such a reading, though deeply pastoral, ought nonetheless be permitted on textual grounds. The refusal or inability to see this will restrict the historical-critical method "to the guild and the academy, where the question of truth can be endlessly deferred" (38).

The success of Steinmetz's essay is in the clarity and wit of its polemical broadside rather than in any programmatic description of how exegesis ought to look now. Many questions are left unanswered. What then do we do with historical criticism? It seems useful for biblical interpretation no less than for such important Reformation scholarship as Steinmetz's own, but precisely how? While a host of lovely examples of allegory could be rolled out and displayed as Steinmetz does here, an equal number of abominable examples could be trotted out in response — on what grounds do we determine which is which? Perhaps more poignantly, precisely how do we tell when a reading slips outside the acceptable field of biblical meaning and has become part of the jolly game of setting the author's shirt afire? Steinmetz gives a negative example of Jacques Lefèvre d'Etaples' argument that true interpretation is, above all, about the spiritual regeneration of the interpreter, with no reference to a text's historical origin. Over against it Steinmetz celebrates the medieval church's capability for "sober and disciplined" exegesis (32, 38). Yet is it not also true that good exegesis is fundamentally bound up precisely with the regeneration of the interpreter, as Origen first demonstrated?[22] And how do we tell when "sobriety" and proper fields of meaning have been left behind?[23] More pointedly we might ask what precisely represents "intoxicated" exegesis? It cannot simply be identified on the basis of a presumed authorial intention, since Steinmetz has shown that fallacy does not even work in Luther scholarship, let alone on a text whose first author is God, whose "intentions" humans can never claim to know with transparency. Steinmetz's own example of the various possible meanings of the parable of the workers would suggest the answers to such questions must, for Christians, be deeply ecclesial. Steinmetz's essay suggests a deeply Protestant confidence in the ability of the Word to speak anew to the church for its ongoing edification without need for the blessing of the academy's exegetical guild. But how would we take stock of ecclesially shaped exegesis that, on the surface, looks so contrary to a text's historical origins as Augustine's commentary on the Psalms? Would the *Enarrationes* fall within the field of ecclesially shaped yet "sober" exegesis? Or would Augustine be adjudged to have set the Psalmist's shirt on fire?

## Nicholas Lash: Performing the Scriptures

The Roman Catholic theologian Lash coined a metaphor that has now become widely celebrated and utilized in the literature on theological exegesis: that of "performing the scriptures."[24] A simple observation opens up profound depths in Lash's hands: different sorts of texts call for different *actions* on the part of their readers. Some texts will be merely decorative and will call

22. Dawson makes this argument to great effect in his *Christian Figural Reading and the Fashioning of Identity* (Berkeley: University of California Press, 2002).

23. This description of "sober" exegesis as a contrast to allegory reminds me of two passages: first, John 2, in which Jesus allows an already-drunk wedding party to continue now with even better wine, and second, David Bentley Hart's beautiful retelling of the entire gospel through the image of wine, which, in Christian scripture, "is first and foremost a divine blessing and image of God's bounty," in his *The Beauty of the Infinite: The Aesthetics of Christian Truth* (Grand Rapids: Eerdmans, 2003), 108.

24. Lash, "Performing the Scriptures," in his *Theology on the Way to Emmaus*, 46. Page references to this essay will be given parenthetically in the text.

for framing and hanging on the wall; others for reading aloud in a pub; still others for creative application to a particular case at hand; others to the repair of a mechanical device. These brief descriptions of what one does with a work of calligraphy, of poetry, of law, and of a television repair manual quickly show that we cannot speak of "reading in general" and then apply our insights to the Bible in particular. *Any* text will call for certain forms of reading and corresponding actions in life among people. Further, Lash argues, drawing on Raymond Williams, that there *is* no play or symphony in the sense that there *is* a great painting. The latter is at least a somewhat stable object that one can go and look at. A play or symphony, in contrast, only *exists* as performed. The words on the page are then merely notations meant to direct actors or musicians "according to particular conventions." On this analogy, what sort of reading does the Christian Bible call forth, and what correlative form of life?

The answer is: a life of fidelity to the man Jesus, who is the central meaning of history for Christians, expressed in sacramental practice. Lash describes the eucharist as the high point of Christian "performance" of scripture, on analogy to a group of actors' performance of a play. As in theatrical work a performance of scripture can be correct to the letters of the "script," but be adjudged lifeless, conventional, and so unsuccessful. Or, in contrast, the performance even of an old favorite can lead its viewers to a new level of self-awareness, and to the discovery of fresh and unanticipated meaning in a beloved text. There is clearly an extraordinary amount of freedom in how a particular production of *King Lear* might be performed in fidelity to the original that also opens new and unexpected layers of meaning. Yet a good audience will be able to tell the difference between creative reappropriation and the telling of a different story, or telling the same one badly. On analogy to that, Christians' central "performance" of their scripture will be in the liturgy of the eucharist: "that interpretive performance in which all our life consists — all our suffering and care, compassion, celebration, struggle and obedience — is dramatically distilled, focused, concentrated, rendered explicit" (46). This central performance trains Christians to live out further performance of the Christian ministry in all aspects of life, since, as Lash has argued elsewhere, Christianity contravenes the bounds set for "religion" by modernity, and affects all the most interesting aspects of life in politics, art, history, and everything else in creation.[25]

---

25. In his "Ministry of the Word," *New Blackfriars* 6 (1987): 472-83. Lash's own words, as ever, are more memorable: "To *think* as a Christian is to try to understand the stellar spaces, the arrangements of micro-organisms and DNA molecules, the history of Tibet, the operation of

The analogy has its obvious limits.[26] Unlike the actors who perform on a literal stage, Christians never take off the costumes, since the performance of scripture is the entirety of Christian life and practice, and ends "only at death" (46). Yet the analogy can do a great deal of work for us. For example, it gives a crucial place to the academic guild of historical criticism! Every theatrical production is dependent on the hard historical work. Any interpretation of *Lear* will depend on previous work by highly trained scholars in text criticism, the history of Elizabethan drama, literary criticism, philosophy, and so on (41). Yet no one would confuse this necessary but insufficient work with a performance of the play itself. Some texts, such as scripts for plays or the Christian Bible, only yield their deepest meaning in their continual performance by living, breathing people. Therefore the "*poles* of Christian interpretation are not, in the last analysis, written texts . . . but patterns of human action" (42). Lash notes that a fellow scholar has hit precisely on a properly dramatic notion of biblical performance when he brackets the form of the question "what could Paul have meant in his theology of martyrdom?" in order to offer the life of Maximilian Kolbe as a faithful performer of that por-

---

economic markets, toothache, King Lear, the CIA, and grandma's cooking — or, as Aquinas put it, 'all things' — in relation to that uttering, utterance and enactment of God which they express and represent. To *act* as a Christian is to work with, to alter or, if need be, to endure all things in conformity with that understanding" (476).

26. It also has an important new critic. Samuel Wells has argued that the image is entirely too static, at least for thinking about Christian ethics. By extension it seems to him inadequate also for the theology and preaching of the church. Wells charges that the metaphor (1) inappropriately suggests that the "script" of the Bible "provides a comprehensive version of life," (2) suggests that the Bible "encompasses the whole of the church's narrative" leaving no room for the work of post-biblical saints, (3) implies "the recreation of a golden era," as though things were less confusing and difficult in the biblical church, and (4) can "militate against genuine engagement with the world" by suggesting "no significant theological place for the present tense" (Wells, *Improvisation* [Grand Rapids: Brazos, 2004], 62-63). Wells suggests instead the analogy of improvisational theater as a more appropriate one for thinking about the Christian moral life.

These are important checks against misplaced enthusiasm for Lash's metaphor, which indeed may be insufficient for thinking about "ethics." Yet Wells may be charging Lash with claiming more for the image than Lash himself does. The strength of the metaphor seems to me to be that it carves out a limited, if important, place for historical scholarship (on analogy to those who work on the manuscripts of Shakespearian plays) — one that is vital to, but woefully incomplete without, the acting out of the work on stage. Second, it points to the importance of theology's being lived out in the "present tense," with its suggestion of the eucharist as the climax of ecclesial "performance." Third, and most important for our purposes, there is a case in which the scriptures simply are a script: in the chanting of the Psalter! In this case we simply do read the words on the page before us, and the preacher then shows us the christological significance of that which we have read. It is a minor, but important, point to dissent from Wells's dissent from Lash.

tion of scripture.[27] An innumerable host of other saints could also be potentially offered as good performers (not least, hopefully, ourselves).

Lash has an inimitable knack for spotting the philosophical flaws present in standard, almost assumed accounts of theological argumentation. For example, he takes on a much praised (and now much criticized) description of New Testament scholar Krister Stendahl's that distinguishes between what a biblical text once "meant" and what it now "means." He argues that the distinction is dangerously positivistic. What act of historic description (what it meant) is not always already an interpretation? This can be asked without necessarily suggesting any radical relativism. Lash's own corrective is to argue that a good interpreter of an ancient text must also be a good reader of *our own* time and place. The relationship then between history and theology, between critical examination of the past and the present, must be dialectical in order to elude positivist myopia. Further, as all of our "Return to Allegory" thinkers will argue, it is not at all clear what the word "means" means. What was the original "meaning" of *King Lear?* Or, to use another of Lash's examples, of a speech by a politician determined to set up detention centers to administer "'short, sharp shocks'" to juvenile offenders? (78). The examples say enough: whatever "means" means, it is always already bound up with interpretation by a community in light of its ends.[28] For example, some would have celebrated such punishment of juveniles! Finally Lash attacks what he takes to be an implicit metaphor for biblical interpretation: a relay-race model, in which the Bible scholar gets the "baton" of meaning first, and when finished hands it off to the theologian for contemporary exposition. The problem, for theologians like Lash, is that the baton never seems to reach them. Biblical scholars, no less than other academic professionals, will never finish arguing over what a passage "means" so as to be able to hand over their results to theologians. Nor should the latter expect them to. Rather, both should carry out their respective tasks with the goal of rendering more faithful performances of scripture by the church: biblical scholars and historians through their important, but limited, role of critically examining manuscripts, languages, historical background, and so on (never in isolation from

27. In Lash, "What Might Martyrdom Mean," in his *Theology on the Way to Emmaeus,* 90, citing W. F. Flemington's "On the Interpretation of Colossians 1.24," in *Suffering and Martyrdom in the New Testament* (Cambridge: Cambridge University Press, 1981), 183-98.

28. I often think our culture's general derision of former president Bill Clinton's sleight of hand under oath, "it depends on what your definition of the word 'is' is," suggests our inability to take the kind of care necessary for theological language to flourish (no defense of Clinton implied!). Clearly the Reformers' debates over *est* in Jesus' announcement "this is my body" suggest that one's definition of the word "is" matters a great deal and can result in ferocious debate.

critical self-examination nor reading of the current times), and theologians with a task not dissimilar from that of pastors — directing the church in its performance of scripture.

Lash's most important contribution will prove to be his keen eye for metaphors and analogies. He coins new ones with ease and good humor; he dissects bad ones with appropriate élan. His performance analogy sheds light on some key questions, but leaves as many more in the dark. How are Christians to perform texts besides the obvious ones, like the institution narratives we follow in celebrating the eucharist or the praise of God in a psalm? For example, how shall Christians perform the conquest of Canaan? Or the *Haustafeln* in the deutero-Pauline epistles? How shall we perform those texts that are morally repugnant? Or simply theologically useless? There is room in Lash's proposal for bringing all such scriptures into relationship with the Christ at the heart of scripture, yet he himself does not demonstrate how this should be done. He does, however, leave us with what may be an appropriately "underdetermined"[29] description of the church that would allow us to develop further the resources necessary to go and answer such questions on our own. He borrows from the Aquinas scholar M. D. Chenu a description of a theologian as a "philologist," that is, as he says elsewhere, "one who watches one's language in the presence of God."[30] He continues:

> We are required, in politics and in private life, in work and play, in commerce and scholarship, to practice and foster that philology, that word-caring, that meticulous and conscientious concern for the quality of conversation and the truthfulness of memory, which is the first casualty of sin. The church, accordingly, is or should be a school of philology, an academy of word-care.[31]

My goal here is to extend this description of the church as an academy of word-care into the still-open question of how to take particularly Christian care of all the words in the Psalter.

---

29. I borrow the description from Fowl in "Stories of Interpretation," in his *Engaging Scripture*, 32-61. He contrasts the description with a "determinate" theory of meaning, in which we extract meaning from text like we do jam from jars, and an "anti-determinate" post-modern one, in which meaning must always and in principle be resisted. Christians, Fowl rightly argues, can offer theoretical descriptions of what we do in exegesis, yet we should not feel bound to say in advance or abstractly how those will look in the church in specific times and places.

30. In his *Believing Three Ways in One God: A Reading of the Apostles' Creed* (London: SCM, 1992).

31. Lash, "Ministry of the Word," 477.

*Stephen Fowl: Reading in Light of Community-Specific Ends*

Stephen Fowl shares the conclusions of these previous thinkers: that Christians must read scripture in light of their ends and conjunction with the apostolic rule of faith. Further, he argues with them that modern academic disciplinary boundaries make this vocation difficult. Yet he pushes our previous subjects' arguments farther in at least two important directions. One, he continues and deepens Lash's tradition of undoing standard apologetics for the way things are in the biblical and theological guilds. He notes that historical critics will often argue that Jews and Christians have a stake in attending to historical criticism: if God has worked *in history* in the calling of Israel and the ministry of Jesus, then Christians and Jews are theologically licensed, or perhaps even mandated, to explore the historicity of those events with all the tools at our disposal. The problem with this argument for Fowl is that it implies an extremely narrow vision of what counts for "history." Those who espouse it are usually interested in the speculative activity of the reconstruction of histories "behind" texts, rather than in the biblical text's final form. Or, they are interested in the history of the interpretation of those texts in the church or synagogue, rather than the history of what Christians claim the triune God has done in the incarnation. Further, for Fowl, to speak colloquially in terms that are not his, the argument often takes the form of a "bait and switch." When Ernst Käsemann argued a generation ago that Christians who failed to attend to historical criticism are practicing Docetists, what he really did was make a clever, if misleading, category mistake. No amount of historical criticism can answer the question of whether Mary is *theotokos,* and whether Jesus has one or two natures and persons and how these relate to each other — the questions actually debated at Ephesus and Chalcedon. Historical criticism is not designed to ask or answer that sort of dogmatic question, useful as it may be for other tasks. Further, though Docetism would indeed be harmful to Christian interests, the way to avoid it is to practice more explicitly *Chalcedonian* exegesis, not to do better historical criticism.[32]

Fowl does not stop there. He has even less tolerance than our previous thinkers for the idea that texts "have meanings." In response to the common claim that historical criticism is necessary to oppose ideologically problematic biblical texts, Fowl avers that "texts don't have ideologies; people do." He

---

32. This paragraph is drawn from *Engaging Scripture,* 182-86. The key resource here is A. K. M. Adam's crucial article, "Docetism, Käsemann, and Christology: Why Historical Criticism Can't Protect Christological Orthodoxy," *Scottish Journal of Theology* 49 (1996): 391-410. Page references to *Engaging Scripture* will be given parenthetically in the text in this section.

demonstrates his point by showing the dramatically different ways the story of the calling of Abraham has been read by Jews and Christians throughout history, before asking which reading has shown the "ideology" present in the text. Is Abraham Philo's soul in search of wisdom, Paul's exemplar for freedom from the law in Galatians, or Justin Martyr's justification for the supersession of Christian faith over Jewish unbelief? Meaning is always under negotiation in specific communities, it is not a static and easily identifiable "thing." Further, the claim is another category mistake. The right way to avoid harmful misreadings of texts is not to impose a problematic theory of "meaning," but to be sure that a community's practices of repentance and reconciliation are in good working order. In short, for Fowl, talk of "meaning" is only unproblematic until a legitimate dispute arises in an interpretive community. Then such disputes are never solved by appeals to a text's "meaning." Such exegetical disagreement must be addressed by slow, patient, and above all *charitable* debate about words and lives, for which theories of "meaning" are no substitute.

Fowl also has a response for the common Reformation-based description that historical criticism is designed to ascertain a text's "plain sense," which by common Christian logic is meant to discipline and normalize all other senses.[33] He points to quite important recent scholarship by post-liberal theologians who respond that the "literal sense" is that established through ongoing exegetical debate in communities that take the Bible as their scripture.[34] That is, it is not obvious what a text's literal sense is, and this can never be determined independent of actual bodies of Christians offering readings. Fowl grants here that the literal sense may be described as that intended by the biblical text's author. Yet he returns to Steinmetz's point that for the pa-

---

33. Fowl's running engagement in his footnotes here is with Brevard Childs, yet the attempt to offer historical criticism as a descriptor of the *sensus literalis* or of the *sensus plenior* is quite common in theoretical descriptions of exegesis.

34. These are Hans Frei, George Lindbeck, Kathryn Tanner, and, above all, Eugene Rogers. See especially Frei's "The 'Literal Reading' of Biblical Narrative in the Christian Tradition: Does it Stretch or Will it Break?" in *The Bible and the Narrative Tradition*, ed. F. McConnell (Oxford: Oxford University Press, 1986); Lindbeck's "The Story Shaped Church: Critical Exegesis and Theological Interpretation," in Fowl, ed., *Theological Interpretation of Scripture;* Tanner's "Theology and the Plain Sense," in *Scriptural Authority and Narrative Interpretation*, ed. G. Green (Philadelphia: Fortress, 1987); and Rogers, "How the Virtues of the Interpreter Presuppose and Perfect Hermeneutics," *Journal of Religion* 76, no. 1 (1996): 64-81. He does not here mention Bruce Marshall, who has made similar arguments about the literal sense; see Marshall, "Aquinas as Post-Liberal Theologian," *The Thomist* 53, no. 3 (1989): 353-406; and "Absorbing the World: Christianity and the Universe of Truths," in *Theology and Dialogue: Essays in Conversation with George Lindbeck* (Notre Dame: University of Notre Dame Press, 1990).

tristic and medieval church, the first author of a biblical text is God. Therefore there can be an abundance of literal *senses* in any passage of scripture, since God may have any number of things to say to the church through this particular configuration of words. The literal sense of a biblical text is that roughly agreed to by a scriptural community as it seeks to determine God's Word to it in its own time and space in a way that its members can agree amongst themselves is faithful to the "way the words go" on the page.[35]

Fowl's book is intended to demolish the description of exegesis with which I opened this section: "To interpret a text is to ascertain the original author's intended meaning." Naturally then his proposals accord ill with those who have any stake remaining in that description of the exegetical task. Biblical scholars and historians whose very *life* it is to determine an author's intended meaning cannot be enthusiastic about this demolition. Neither can theologians who have a stake in identifying textual meaning as part of any broader theological agenda, whether conservative or liberal. Fowl's work tends to draw faint praise, and then fairly panicky rejoinders. Yet notice how much superior Fowl's proposal on exegesis is to what it replaces. If there is a single authorial intention buried in a text, which the exegete must unearth, then the entire history of biblical interpretation in the church must be regarded as a series of failed excavation attempts before today's climactic discovery (36). While such a view might be good for an exegete's ego or tenure prospects, it simply cannot be true on ecclesial grounds. If the Spirit is indeed leading the church into all truth, as Jesus promised, then the church cannot have been without biblical truth all these years — such a view is simply theologically impermissible. Further, Fowl argues that such a view places Christians in an extremely awkward position with respect to their Old Testament. To give just one example, the authors of the Old Testament clearly intend that their faithful readers would be circumcised (129). Christians must do *something* with those words on the page other than just ignore them, and allegory offers resources for reading them, as Christians have long seen. A theoretical description of exegesis that in principle excludes most of the history of the church's wrestling with scripture, and

35. These points all come from Fowl, *Engaging Scripture*, 37-40. Rogers seems to have introduced this paraphrase of the Thomistic description of the literal sense as "the way the words go" into current conversation in "Virtues of the Interpreter," cited in note 34 above. The description helpfully avoids any impression that interpretation's goal is what may have been in the human author's head. It also shows that the literal sense does not choke off exegetical freedom, but rather offers a surprisingly wide variety of exegetical possibilities, as long as "the way the words go" can bear the exegetical weight exerted when these interpretations are laid on top of it. It could be that "the way the words run" cracks under such pressure, so that the proposed interpretation must be discarded.

that precludes Christians from reading the Old Testament as Old Testament (that is, as a witness to Christ),[36] ought at least to raise concerns.[37]

If we have foresworn theoretical descriptions of "meaning" and "authorial intent," how then should we speak of what we are doing when reading Paul, or Thomas Aquinas, or Stephen Fowl? Fowl suggests that instead of the problematic description of "meaning," we speak of an author's "communicative intent" (58). This linguistic shift allows us to wield the best exegetical tools available to get at what, say, Paul is doing in Galatians, or Thomas in the *Summa*. Yet it does not pretend thereby to have exhausted the exacting process by which a community determines the sense of a passage for its life before God. Further, the description seems to leave more space for what the church has traditionally called "allegory," and what Fowl, following David Dawson's work, calls "counter-conventional" interpretation. For a heavy-handed theory of "meaning" would seem to relegate other readings to a netherland of "un-meaning" or, to speak more plainly, of nonsense. To speak of the author(s) of Genesis' "communicative intention" leaves space for historical critical observation, for communal discernment of literal sense, and also for the possibility that St. Paul might offer a counter-conventional interpretation in Galatians that, far from violating the "way the words run," may in fact illumine it in ways that are helpful for the community's life. Fowl concludes with a stunning observation on the preconditions for reading scripture well that dovetails nicely with Lash's observations that we must understand our current time to read scripture well. He points to the odd description in Ephesians 4:28 that Christians must not steal, and notes that people must live in sufficiently close communal quarters, as opposed to, say, gated suburbs, for stealing even to be a threat to the community's life. The way we live now inevitably affects the readings of scripture we produce, and any effort to avoid or elide this impact will simply make for bad theories of reading and bad readings. This marvelous observation and example is at once exegetical and ecclesial, based on the best tools available for reading Paul and a keen eye for observation of our own life and ecclesial setting.

Fowl's best gift to us is his offering of new theoretical tools with which to

---

36. The claim that Christians cannot read the Old Testament as a witness to Christ is often made in an effort to prevent Christians from a supersessionist posture with regard to Israel. Yet it can unwittingly lead to the ancient Christian heresy that is most potentially dangerous toward Israel — Marcionitism — which claims that the God attested to in the New Testament is different than that in the Old, with all the disparaging claims about Israel's scriptures and God that such heretics (and, if they're not careful, Christians) tend to make.

37. I have added a level of polemic not present in Fowl's own quite gentle argumentation, yet I think it not untrue to the spirit of his work here.

speak of exegesis. His only limitation, if it is that, is an unwillingness to extend himself theoretically in a way that may prove indefensible. For example, he will be loathe to offer too general a description of how a community ought to identify good or bad literal or counter-conventional readings: such decisions must be made "on the ground," as it were, by particular churches on *ad hoc* bases. This theoretical minimalism works to keep his argumentation from exposing any open flanks that may be attacked. Yet it leaves us with unanswered questions. We are a church that indeed needs reflection on how to read well, and help discerning good literal and allegorical readings from bad. Fowl offers this by way of his own exegetical displays with a clear encouragement to "go and do likewise." So how precisely do we do likewise? If we wish to use Paul as a model for how to read the Psalms, is Augustine's way of doing that an exemplary one? We are inclined to say that Fowl would say "yes." This book then may be seen as a Fowl-informed display of Christian reading of the psalms that Fowl himself does not give. The only other problem, if it is that, with Fowl's work, is that in theoretical moments he argues with Augustine, Aquinas, and modern defenders of their ancient hermeneutics. Yet in most of his exegetical moments, his footnotes are filled with E. P. Sanders, Richard Hays, N. T. Wright, and other present-day exegetes. This is no surprise: Fowl is a modern exegete and New Testament scholar! And his interlocutors here are nothing short of world-class. Yet the question remains: is there a disconnect, by which the ancients are right about *how* to do exegesis, but when we turn to *actual* exegesis we don't read like these same ancients? Fowl reads more widely and uses sources from more fields than almost anyone else writing in this area. This rich collection of *ad hoc* drawing from such a variety of sources is partly what makes his work such rewarding reading. Yet the disjunction between ancient theory and modern practice remains. An explanation for it may be that his exegetical displays are then more a product of his own training in New Testament studies than any theoretical predisposition for modern exegesis over ancient. If so, then again this book seeks to pick up where Fowl has left off.[38]

*Andrew Louth: The Fallacy of Imitative Form*

The final figure we will examine in this half of the chapter has devoted most of his scholarly career to patristics, yet made a foray into theology once that

---

38. One exception to my criticism of Fowl's omission here is his lovely Augustinian reading of baptism in the Gospels on *Engaging Scripture*, 91-95. This may be more a theoretical than exegetical moment, too, however.

has yet to have the hearing it deserves in the academy. Andrew Louth's *Discerning the Mystery* does deconstructive work as it attacks the academy's use of historical criticism, then constructive work as it offers a dogmatic *apologia* for Christian allegory. We will look at his deconstructive work here and at his constructive suggestions in the next section.

Louth situates the church's confidence in historical criticism within the promise made by the Enlightenment to deliver reliable, objective truth about the world, unclouded by tradition and prejudice. In modernity it is the hard sciences that have delivered on this promise in spectacular ways. Yet it is a mistake, Louth maintains, simply to apply the tools, attitudes, and methods of modern science to the humanities. He uses George Steiner's description of this misplaced confidence as an example of the "fallacy of imitative form."[39] The liberal arts broadly, and literature more specifically, are simply different than the natural sciences. Louth uses the Enlightenment critic Giambattista Vico to describe the natural world, which humans have not made themselves, as that which must remain *other* than us for the scientific method to be an appropriate way of studying it. In contrast, we *have* made our literature. In this arena we are not mere spectators, but are *actors* (19).[40] We create our literature, and then remain never unaffected by that which we have created. Louth uses Hans-Georg Gadamer to show that the creation of any literature is also the creation of a *tradition*, a thing quite literally handed on *(traditum)*. Any literary work, once put to paper, is to some degree set loose from the contingency of its creation, made ready for new relationships to future readers and then writers (31). The best way to describe the "meaning" of any great work of literature, say a poem, is not necessarily to ask what the poet thought she was saying while writing. When the poem is put to paper something genuinely *new* has happened, and the author is not necessarily the best authority to say what that is. In fact, the most interesting new things that happen with a poem may not even be accountable with words, but may be best approached by silence (103).[41]

The Enlightenment's goal of presuppositionless understanding, as well as it may have served the hard sciences, is a fundamentally false theory of interpretation of literary texts. We can never escape the tradition that has taught

39. Louth, *Discerning the Mystery: An Essay on the Nature of Theology* (Oxford: Clarendon, 1983), 10. Page references will be given parenthetically in the text.

40. Louth occasionally notes that modernity's description of the natural world and the scientific method as the best way to study it is not without its critiques — for example it seems to fit physics better than it does biology since practitioners of the latter are increasingly aware of the way they are also agents and not mere spectators of the world.

41. Louth draws here on T. S. Eliot above all.

us to think, that has handed us certain works of literature that have in turn shaped the world around them. The false attempt to do so yields bad readings and bad theories of reading. A truer vision of interpretation would be to attempt to understand the traditions in which we are set in order to bring these into dialogue with whatever new literature that we read. Louth finds this metaphor of a "conversation" quite agreeable. In a genuine conversation the other is not simply an object to me, to be poked and prodded, without revealing anything of myself (as, say, the Freudian analyst relates to the patient [40]). Nor in a genuine conversation are differences between parties smoothed over or ignored. Rather, each is available to the other, open to the other, genuinely willing to do the hard work of listening, responding, being changed (41). As in any good conversation, listeners will have to be open to metaphor, to the mysterious veiling and unveiling of truth, in a way that our literarily tone-deaf academic guilds and churches often fail to be (19).

We have been describing, in quite broad strokes, the work of several important theological and historical scholars as they push toward a way past the strictures that centuries of historical critical inquiry have left with us. Steinmetz, Lash, Fowl, and Louth offer arguments that reductivist versions of historical criticism — the enterprise of interpreting a text is to ascertain the original author's intended meaning — are bad ways to read texts in general. If we must read the Bible "like any other book," then like any other book we must first ascertain the way this particular book seeks to be read. And the Christian Bible seeks to be read *biblically!* That is, with references to smashing babies in Psalm 137 situated within the same covers as Jesus' Sermon on the Mount, copied and passed down to parish priests in France (Steinmetz). Situated with the life and death of the man Jesus at the center, read by and for the sake of a people who seek to live its performance (Lash). As presenting problems that question-begging theories of meaning cannot solve, but that a more specifically Christian way of reading in light of our community's end of greater love of the triune God *can* (Fowl). And as a text that shows in particularly high relief the mistaken nature of the application of (ironically) uncriticized critical methods that produce poor readings (Louth). In short, much of the modern talk of gaps, authors, and texts is mistaken. For where modern theorists identify a gap is precisely where the *church* is meant to be, joyfully reading its scripture (no ordinary "text") as a witness to God, its first and last author. "To read the Bible as any other book," if read aright, can be an apt description of how to read the Bible.

Yet these hermeneutical suggestions remain underdeveloped *theologically*. That is, how does the taking of the Bible as a specifically *Christian* text shape our exegesis in ways that are different than the reading of any other book? The authors we have presented above have their own reasons for not offering robustly *theological* accounts of the Bible or exegesis. Steinmetz is merely wishing to make a point that the way Christians have historically read ought to count as *good* readings. Lash and Fowl work to show that models now long passed down in modern biblical interpretation do not hold on biblical or philosophical grounds. Louth, in the part of his book we have seen so far, shows that scientific methods applied wholesale and uncritically to the Bible produce bad readings. Yet what should we say of exegesis if we take scripture as a specifically *theological* category? If we seek to offer specifically christological readings of the Bible? If the goal of exegesis is to produce saints? In this next section, as we continue our look at Andrew Louth's work and also examine the work of Robert Wilken and Lewis Ayres, we will see specifically theological descriptions of exegesis come to the fore.

## "Reading the Bible . . . in order to see how the Bible is unlike any other book"

How precisely *does* Christian doctrine shape Christians' exegesis of scripture? From the works we have just examined we are left with a strong impression that there is some effect, but precisely what? Steinmetz defends ecclesial and homiletical medieval readings of scripture as good ones. Lash's vignettes leave us a sense of the importance of the mystery of Christ at the center of exegesis and of the eucharist in performing the scriptures. Fowl insists Christians (and others) must read scripture in light of their communal ends. Louth reaches back to early critics of the Enlightenment such as Vico, and more recent ones such as Gadamer, to deconstruct any specifically Christian faith in "scientific" exegesis. Well and good. What do we do now?

### Louth: Discerning the Mystery

Louth was not yet Orthodox when he wrote *Discerning the Mystery,* but was a representative of that part of the Anglican tradition that draws deeply from the eastern fathers. When he writes that "the tradition of the Church *is* the Spirit," Protestant readers will wonder whether we are left with any tools to discern good tradition from bad, failed attempts to "discern the mystery" from faithful ones (88). Nevertheless, Louth gives eloquent voice to the way that specific dogmatic claims should influence exegesis. Christianity, he writes, is not first a tradition of beliefs, a set of tenets to be held, but rather a matter "of fact, or reality. The heart of the Christian mystery is the fact of God made man, God with us in Christ; words, even his words, are secondary to the reality of what he accomplished" (74). Christians are not first to believe certain things, but to *be* certain things: namely, ones to whom the gospel has been handed down (1 John 1:1-3). This continuous handing on of the gospel from generation to generation, from those who actually handled the Word-made-flesh to us who now handle the Word as sacrament, is itself a reflection of the inner-trinitarian divine sendings: of the Son into the world by the Father, of the Spirit upon the church by both. These Trinitarian sendings *ad extra* in turn reflect even more mysterious divine processions within the Trinitarian life: of the Son and the Spirit by the Father (83). Louth uses Irenaeus's work against the Gnostics to insist that what are handed down in the Church are not ideas, hermeneutics, models for exegesis, but a certain sort of life, a fellowship instituted by such material means as the flesh of Jesus, the water and bread and wine of the sacraments, the basic material existence of each of us in the fellowship of the church. This core doctrinal heart to exegesis must be understood, or better lived, for allegory to make sense. Louth quotes Newman to this effect: "'never do we seem so illogical to others, as when we are arguing under the continual influence of impressions to which they are insensible'" (147).

Scripture for Christians is only important as it unfolds to us the mystery of Christ. Christianity is not, properly speaking, a religion "of the book," it is rather a religion of the Word, sent by God to us, passed down from others to us, who continually look for him anew in worship at the table and font and before the pulpit.[42] The question then to ask of any way of reading, whether allegory or historical criticism or some other, is "whether this way focuses our attention on the text of Scripture in such a way that we are more able to hear what it has to say to us, more alert, more sensitive, to the voice of God in the Scriptures" (106). Any form of reading cultivates a specific shaping of the imagination, a certain "habit of attention" that helps readers to catch some things, and necessarily also leaves them likely to miss others.[43] Historical crit-

---

42. Louth uses Henri de Lubac here, and St. Ignatius's famous claim: "for me the archives are Jesus Christ, and the inviolable archives his cross and death and his resurrection and faith in Him" (102). He could also use Luther's marvelous homiletic image of the scriptures as the swaddling clothes of Christ: mere rags by themselves, made unspeakably precious by the One they hold. The Luther analogy from the Table Talk can be found in *Day by Day We Magnify Thee: Daily Meditations from Luther's Writings Arranged According to the Year of the Church*, comp. and trans. Margarete Steiner and Percy Scott (Philadelphia: Muhlenberg, 1950), 108.

43. I borrow this terminology from Lewis Ayres, who borrows it from Simone Weil.

icism has sought to make readers attentive to the original historical context in which a text was written. It has been so successful it is difficult for most of us to read scripture with any other set of commitments! Yet Christians must recognize that this method is only occasionally helpful in the achievement of our primary exegetical goal of the discernment of Christ in scripture. This latter, more specifically Christological goal, involves a different sort of "listening" to the text, a listening "across a historical gulf that is not empty, but filled with the tradition that brings this piece of writing to me, and brings me not only that piece of writing but preconceptions and prejudices that enable me to pick up the resonances of the images and arguments used in whatever it is I am seeking to understand" (107). Allegory seeks to make readers attentive to the image of Christ refracted through the almost unendingly various images throughout the Christian scriptures. It is not accidental that the way of allegory is finally a way of prayer. This is crucial, because otherwise allegory starts to seem like a trick for reading, a clever hermeneutic, and not a form of devotion to Christ through attention to the sacred page.[44] Louth compares it to the mass in a French cathedral built in the Middle Ages:

> The action of the mass takes place; we see the gestures and the movements, we hear the chanting and the singing. The meaning of what we are participating in we absorb in what is potentially almost an infinity of ways. Images contained in the words may draw our attention to something in the cathedral — a statue, an arch, a picture in the glass. Things seen, things heard, may recall other things seen and heard, in the same place, on another occasion. We may be struck with analogies between what we can hear and what we can see. Some of this — not likely very much of this on any one occasion: that would mean we were distracted — kindles our devotion, and focuses our heart on the *mysterium Christi* being done before us. A potentially infinite variety of shape and form and association, all drawn from the mystery of the Eucharist, all drawing us back to the mystery of the Eucharist. That is for me some sort of an image of the way Scripture finds, or is found to possess, an infinity of richness in the bosom of the Church's tradition. (109)

Louth shows that the common description of allegory as a way of solving textual problems — for example, of Christians finding acceptable readings to now problematic Old Testament texts — is not a satisfactory description. It

---

44. As it feels to me in the hands of several prominent secular literary critics who have championed allegory such as Harold Bloom and Paul de Man, and to theologians who have celebrated their work, such as Graham Ward. See his "Allegoria: Reading as a Spiritual Exercise" in *Modern Theology* 15, no. 3 (July 1999): 271-95.

would be better to say that allegory is meant to *preserve* the central difficulty with which scripture presents us, to "prevent us, the church, from dissolving the mystery that lies at the heart of the faith" (71). Heresies were often simplifying movements, seeking to ease the tension with which scripture presents its readers between, say, the unity and the three persons of God by choosing one over the other. Louth's vision of orthodoxy is that it is willing to let mystery remain mystery, rather than attempting to dissolve it into a puzzle that can be "solved" and done away with.[45] Allegory is a matter then not of erasing textual difficulty but of shifting to and preserving a certain sort of difficulty: that of seeing Christ, who may be difficult to see, in a place where we believe he must be present. Once we are clear that it is the mystery *of Christ* we seek to behold on the page, and not the puzzles of textual or historical difficulty or whatever, we can see that a specifically Christian goal of exegesis is to "hold before us that mystery, or better, to hold us before the mystery, so that we are questioned by it, and not allowed to ignore it, or miss it" (114).

Allegory does not "prove" anything, nor is it meant to. The rule that nothing can be argued allegorically from scripture that is not also present literally is as old as Origen. What it seeks to do is to hold us readers "still" before Jesus,[46] to disallow the clever reading strategies by which we would avoid Christ in the pages of scripture. Nor is this quite heavily christological hermeneutic a license for avoiding the particular words and story of the Old Testament. The Old Testament "builds up a context, a matrix, in which the mystery of Christ can be incarnated" (120). Now that Christ has filled this womb, and so this world, with grace, and allowed persons to participate by grace in that divinity which he eternally is, we are given eyes to see his gracious presence not least on every page of scripture, but also throughout the created order. Allegory is no movement away from the particular events of salvation history into a realm of timeless truth. It is rather a movement *into* history: a dogged refusal to allow exegetes to evade the christological significance with which all history is infused after the incarnation. The result, for Louth, is a symphony, as the various and quite distinct notes of the full sweep of scripture are joined into the concert of a "harmonious composition" (113).[47]

Finally, we can find in Louth a response to the common question: are there any controls to allegory? I myself find this an odd question. No one thinks it a good question to ask of any other topic in dogmatics: "what are the

---

45. The key distinction between a "mystery" and a "puzzle" comes from Paul Claudel.

46. I take this description from Rowan Williams in his *Christ on Trial: How the Gospel Unsettles Our Judgement* (London: Fount, 2000).

47. Quoting R. L. P. Milburn.

controls on christology? Or eschatology?" The "controls," if we are to use the term, are the same as for any other topic in systematics: faithful attentiveness to scripture, to the tradition, to contemporary pastoral situations and so forth. Yet the question is still so commonly asked it must be answered. What keeps allegory from wild, uncontrollable misreadings, and keeps it rooted in history and the real world? He quotes the tractarian John Keble that "'Christ set before us in the Creed of the Church will give a fixedness and reality to our symbolical interpretations'" (122). *Christ* is the guarantor against allegorical flights of fancy, the "control" that fixes our readings on the ground. Readings that show forth the church's faith in Christ, and that forge lives of hearers in cruciform ways, are those that invite our trust. Any other answer pretends to the sort of scientific objectivity that Louth has worked so hard to disassemble. Louth's description of how to think of whether readings are acceptable or not is quite similar to Steinmetz's of a "field of meaning," though here with a more specifically christological form: "the idea of a *magnetic field* is an attractive one: one could develop the analogy by thinking of the mystery of Christ as the magnetic pole and the field of force as the *regula fidei*, the rule of faith, in the context of which the Scriptures are to be interpreted and which is itself derived from the Scriptures" (121).

*Lewis Ayres: Reading in a Trinitarian Light*

Lewis Ayres takes the theological observation about the *regula fidei* deeper by strengthening it historically. He points out that the consensus among patristic scholars is that the developing *regula* in the earliest church was key to determining which books became part of the newly developing Christian canon. The *regula* preceded the canon historically, and was a key to determining it. The *regula* itself was nothing other than a complex reading of scripture, especially of those portions of it that most clearly showed the continuity of God's activity from the covenant with Israel to the death and resurrection of Jesus (Ayres offers John 1 and Philippians 2:5-11 as examples). As the church debated the inclusion of New Testament books, it asked whether these could be shown to be in concert with the emerging *regula* and its more clear expositions of the full Christian story in places like John and Paul. These clearer texts were celebrated for their ability to tell coherently the whole sweep of the story from creation to the gathering of the church. To be able to do this required extraordinarily adept retellings of Israel's story through figurative readings of her scripture (see John 5:39-47; Galatians 4:21-31; Acts 8:32-35). The question debated as the church looked to texts that were less clear in their ability to tell the full sweep of the story was whether they could be shown to be in coherence with these faithful retellings: Hebrews was seen as a success apparently, and Shepherd of Hermas was not. Ayres's conclusion is at once historical and theological: the *regula* was, no less than the New Testament, about early Christian exegesis of the Old Testament.[48]

Ayres is skeptical of the now-common theological move of analogizing between the two natures of Christ and two supposed natures of scripture.[49] He speaks rather of the medieval four-fold method of exegesis as an appropriately multivalent manner of paying attention to Christ in scripture. He uses Aquinas to argue that Christians' vocation is to attempt to "grasp the nature of Christ's showing of the Father (and of the consubstantial Trinity) at the heart of multi-form attention to the scriptures" (44). Modern readers of scripture of course have tools that were not available to our forebears; as they had tools now lost to us. Each of these will bring strengths and weaknesses that must be negotiated as they are caught up into the larger *telos* of multi-form attention to Christ on the pages of scripture. It is important for Ayres that all *four* senses, including the "literal," do indeed witness *to Christ* in different ways. To develop Ayres's point in an Origenian direction, we might say that the difference between the various senses of scripture is not that some are christological or allegorical and one is not. They have to do not with styles

---

48. This all comes from Ayres's important long article, "On the Practice and Teaching of Christian Doctrine," *Gregorianum* 80, no. 1 (1999): 33-84. Page references hereafter will be given parenthetically in the text.

In more colloquial, conversational moments, Ayres will say that there is only one "testament": Israel's, with an appendix, called the "New Testament," that tells us how to read the Old. Robert Jenson has given this suggestion a dogmatic hearing in "A Second Thought about Inspiration," *Pro Ecclesia* 13, no. 4 (2004): 393-98: "The Old Testament is — so to speak — the *Scripture* in the church's Scripture. Scripture in the proper sense is text which precisely *as* text, as a sequence of signs inscribed on a surface, is by divine ordination a constant orienting presence in the life of a community. The Old Testament is such Scripture, but the New Testament is not; the New Testament's textuality is instead a *substitute* for something other than text, for a *viva vox*, the voice of the living Apostles. Thus it is the Old Testament which — again so to speak — anchors the Bible as a sheer object of necessary reference in the church's worship and proclamation and catechesis" (394). Luke Timothy Johnson makes a similar proposal in his *The Writings of the New Testament: An Interpretation* (Philadelphia: Fortress, 1986): "the NT writings [can] be regarded as crystallizations of reflection on Torah in light of the experience of Jesus the Lord" (548).

49. See his article with Fowl attacking the Pontifical Biblical Commission's work. Another example of the argument Ayres attacks, to be discussed in the Conclusion, is Telford Work's *Living and Active: Scripture in the Economy of Salvation* (Grand Rapids: Eerdmans, 2002). For Ayres, historical criticism should be spoken of as one of many possible approaches to the letter of scripture as Christians turn to it for continual elucidation of the Godhead of the Son.

of reading at all, but rather with the maturity of the readers. Those who have advanced to some degree will have more profound and difficult ways of discerning Christ in the words that correspond to their greater maturity; those who have not should remain with the literal sense's witness to Christ. These senses then correspond not to hermeneutical differences but to spiritual ones. Perhaps, contra Steinmetz, allegory *is* a matter of the regeneration of the reader.[50]

We have already seen, with Louth and Ayres, the centrality of christology for exegesis. How now shall we fill out this christological vision in an explicitly Trinitarian direction? Ayres turns to Hans Urs von Balthasar and John Milbank for direction in precisely this task. He borrows Balthasar's concept of "transposition." When John's Gospel speaks of Jesus' "hour," and when Paul's talks of Christ's "death and resurrection," these are not mere historical descriptions of Jesus, but rather figurative re-presentations of Jesus offered to frame the way their readers live. What scripture offers is "archetypes," or "persistent patterns of figuration"[51] that shape how its readers see the action of God in the world for the sake of the transformation of their own lives (55-64). "Transposition" is not merely a hermeneutical term. It is rather filled out in Trinitarian particularity. The *way* believers see the form of Christ transposed onto their lives is by the Spirit's drawing them into the Church's mission that *just is* the sending of Christ into the world anew. Ayres offers Balthasar's work on St. Therese of Lisieux and on St. Elizabeth of the Trinity as tangible examples of the "space" opened up in the divine life for his creatures by way of their participation in the Father's sending of the Son and the Spirit.

Ayres borrows from John Milbank the concept of an "aesthetic-hermeneutic" model of the Trinity, in which the triune life is envisaged as the Father's speaking a Word to the full, without reserve, to the point of "exhaustion" we might say, until the Spirit reflects this Word back to the Father, whose delight in his Word causes him to speak again.[52] This response of the Spirit is "eschatologically identical" with the gathering of human beings on the path of deification. The Spirit's response to the *Logos* of the *Arche* that is

---

50. Even this suggestion is not meant to leave behind previous or less mature levels of reading, as though one who is mature enough can be done with the literal and draw nourishment only from tropology. The most mature spiritual masters know these "progressions" include frequent returns to the beginning. Those most practiced in holiness are also the best readers of the literal level of scripture.

51. Ayres credits Fowl with this formulation.

52. Milbank, "The Second Difference," in his *The Word Made Strange* (Oxford: Blackwell, 1997).

the Son is nothing less than the unending variety of roles and missions within the life of the church. Human beings, in an analogous process (at infinite remove) to the inner-divine "process" of interpersonal procession, only discover who we are by an exchange in which we give ourselves over to others, lose control over ourselves, and then learn anew from the other who we are, to speak again. A particularly *Christian* identity is shaped through attention to the history of the saints, who become a "treasury of interpretations of Scripture" as the Spirit shows Christians the form of Christ amidst the pluriformity of lives and works that would otherwise lack coherence. This process of discovery by participation in mission within the life of church is identical with the Father's own reinvigoration to speak anew by the Spirit's reflection of his life back to him in the form of the Son (64-71).[53]

Ayres is more attentive than Milbank to the *fallen* character of human thinking, and its need of divine repair. Scripture offers a sort of divine therapy for damaged human minds to re-teach us the christological ordering of all things: their creation in Christ (John 1:3) and their destiny to be bound up under Christ their head (see Colossians 1:15-23 and Ephesians 1:3-14). It does this by offering "persistent patterns of figuration," archetypes for how to live and see things, progressively deeper and more complicated ones as the process of repair continues in the life of the church. This entire process is inaugurated by the Spirit's work of drawing persons into the Christoform life of the church: the making of persons into members of a body with a head who is Christ. What it means to be Christian at all is to be drawn into Christ's death and resurrection by the Holy Spirit in the church. What it means to *think* as a Christian is to struggle to describe all creation as it truly is and is bound to be, "in Christ." What the history of doctrine does in this process is to offer an almost unending reservoir for seeing anew these persistent patterns of figuration in the text of scripture. Therefore the first task of a *historical* reading of scripture should be to look at the myriad ways Christians have seen Christ in scripture, as part of their being drawn by the Spirit toward the fullness in Christ that is the destiny of the entire created order. It is difficult to imagine a more theologically robust description of the task of exegesis than this.

53. I myself have difficulty seeing how Milbank's model avoids the problem of making humanity *necessary* for the very triunity of the divine life: that is, as necessary to make God God. The way out of this problem is to admit more frankly than Milbank seems able that we speak of God only analogously, and so cannot even describe the way in which our speech fails, but trust by the Spirit's grace that it corresponds to the reality that God is enough to renew our minds, souls, and bodies in the divine image. That is, to realize that even the best human minds are not God's, and that they think only by participation in a divine reality they cannot understand. A healthy dose of traditional theological apophaticism would greatly help Milbank's project generally.

The only problem I would point to in Ayres's work is that it offers very little in the way of actual biblical exegesis. This is odd for someone who has so poignantly described the importance of exegesis in the ancient church in his historical work, and has here pointed to the importance of exegesis as the very manner in which Christians are drawn into the divine life in response to contemporary theological questions. To address this lacuna, we turn to the work of Robert Wilken.

### Robert Wilken: Attending to Words Christologically

Wilken helps us to see the importance of particular *words* in ancient Christian allegory. It is often charged that allegory is concerned only with the abstract at the expense of the particular.[54] That may be with non-Christian allegory, but Wilken demonstrates it is patently *not* the case in the ancient church. The historian in Wilken is impressed with the "omnipresence" of scripture in earliest church's liturgies, rituals, practices, writings, and in their world more generally.[55] Scripture is so often on the earliest Christians' lips for two reasons. One, the gospel was birthed into a world that loved words. No reader of Augustine's *Confessions* will be able to forget the love of words shown not only in the life of this precocious young rhetor, but also in the broader culture into which he was born. Words were the heart of ancient education, in which students memorized great portions of poetry and literature. They were also the staple of classical politics, as combating orators tried to sway people to their cause, of ancient economics, since one could not go far in that world without the ability to persuade, and of entertainment, as even personal letters became sources of literary largesse (69).[56] As some of these educated persons in antiquity became Christians, this love for words carried over and became a hallmark of patristic thought. The Bible, Wilken says, "created a distinctive universe of meaning" in Christian thought, and gave to patristic

---

54. David Dawson tries to defend ancient Christian allegory as practiced by Origen from such clear-eyed modern critics as Daniel Boyarin, Erich Auerbach, and Hans Frei in *Christian Figural Reading*. His most impressive move is to show that these critics misunderstand allegory because they think of it as a hermeneutic, rather than a reflection on the consistent action of God in history.

55. *The Spirit of Early Christian Thought: Seeking the Face of God* (New Haven: Yale University Press, 2003), xvii. Page references to this book will be given parenthetically in the text.

56. Wilken explores the literary culture of antiquity more generally in his chapter on rhetoric in *John Chrysostom and the Jews: Rhetoric and Reality in the Late Fourth Century* (Berkeley: University of California Press, 1983).

thinkers a "vocabulary" that reshaped all their language. Even now Christians cannot hear the word "hyssop," a strangely biblical word, without thinking of David's penance in Psalm 51. They cannot think of the odd word "cleave," without hearing the Psalmist's description that it is "good for me to cleave to God" (Psalm 73:28), or the description in Genesis of Adam and Eve who "cleave" together as one flesh (Genesis 2:24). This description, in turn, is colored by St. Paul's insistence that "cleaving" to God is only possible by the Spirit's pouring out of the divine love into our hearts (Romans 5:5). The words echo through the canon and our prayer. To use another favorite Wilken example, Christians cannot think of the particular texture of the words "living water" without thinking of John 7:38 and Jesus' promise there. That description in turn shapes how they hear the Canticle's description of "living water" in Song of Songs 5. As each of these three examples of scriptural resonance show, the particular texture of the biblical world of meaning is not left behind, far from it. It is rather entered into more deeply as Christians find words they love throughout the scriptures, and thereby are given new eyes to see the world around them as shot through with divine meaning. There is always a particularly *verbal* link that makes allegory possible. When this is lost, specifically biblical allegory is lost as well.[57]

Over against the stock portraits of allegory's critics, Wilken argues for importance of history in allegorical exegesis. Christians hold that something "prodigiously" new has happened in Jesus.[58] The "latter days" spoken of in Isaiah have come. With the messiah's arrival the promises recorded about his coming may read quite differently. Scripture must now be interpreted "in light of this new fact. Paradoxically, the spiritual sense was the historical sense, for if there had been no Christ, no Incarnation, no death and Resurrection, there would be no spiritual sense."[59] A "spiritual" reading of the Old Testament is itself a historical reading of it, if we hold it to be historically true that Jesus is the messiah. If the Old Testament is to be read as Old Testament — namely, that which points forward from itself to the one who is its fulfillment, and not as a historicist's haphazard collection of religious documents from the ancient near east[60] — it will "take on different hues, certain images

---

57. Ward nicely describes the literal sense of scripture as actually the "letteral" sense: one that keeps the letters but may say something quite different (Ward, "Allegoria," 289). That may also work as a description of allegory.

58. The word "prodigiously" is de Lubac's.

59. "*In Dominico Eloquio:* Learning the Lord's Style of Language" in *Communio* 24 (Winter 1997): 865.

60. Wilken is well aware that there are other ways to take these texts rooted in a community's faith identity: especially in the Jews' life and its particular shaping by scripture. It is not

spring to life, persons and events [are] privileged, and everything [is] woven together in a tapestry imprinted with the face of Christ." The Bible is, Wilken quotes St. Augustine, "the face of God for now."[61]

With Augustine, Wilken often distinguishes between a text's *signum* and its *res,* the word itself and the reality to which it refers. This distinction points out the strange newness of a particularly Christian reading. For most readers, ancient and modern, one examines a word *(signum)* in order to learn what its meaning *(res)* is. We can see this in the contemporary churches' practice of continuing to multiply translations of the Bible. We are less interested in the particular words and more in their basic gist, which we often avidly update with ever more contemporary paraphrases. This would never have worked in the ancient church, and not just because books were more expensive to produce, but because the particular words of a received text were so vital. The *signa* were never unimportant. Further, in Christians' case, the *res* to which the Bible's *signa* point is already known: Christ! In a stark reversal of the common ancient and modern approach to interpreting texts, the task of biblical exegesis for Christians is to see how these particular *signa* refer to this *res.* The result is allegory, as words not obviously meant to refer to Christ are shown to do so through readings that turn out to be gloriously beautiful. Wilken, as an apologist for this sort of reading, for all his insistence on its christological particularity, does find contemporary parallels to ancient allegory. Reviews of works of art only become interesting when we have seen the work itself, after which we can engage with the review. Guidebooks to places we visit are only helpful once we are present and can engage with the place itself. How much more, given Christians' view of what has happened in history in Jesus, should we expect that *signa* will be intelligible only in light of an *a priori* understanding of the *res* to which they refer?

Wilken also points to the importance of Christian liturgy in allegory. Paul does something extraordinary with Psalm 19 when he applies it to the work of Christian missionaries preaching to Gentiles in Romans 10:18. This itself, Wilken insists with Origen, is meant to be an example for Christian exegetes, not a mere *brutum factum* for Christians to honor as scripture but then not emulate. Then, something equally important happens when Psalm 19 is assigned by breviaries and Catholic books of hours for reading on Christian saint days. The liturgy itself inscribes allegorical reading practice

---

against Israel's scriptural life that Wilken polemicizes but against those who would limit exegesis to historicist reconstruction. See, for example, Jon Levenson's description of the coherence lent to scripture by the faith life and resulting reading practices of Israel in his *Sinai and Zion: An Entry Into the Jewish Bible* (San Francisco: Harper, 1987).

61. The last two quotes are from *Spirit,* 76.

into the very habit of daily Christian prayer. The lectionary and breviary are themselves allegorical. To use an example beyond Wilken, when Psalm 29 is assigned for reading on Baptism of the Lord Sunday, how can those listening not hear Jesus' baptism described anew in the psalmist's celebration of the "voice of the Lord" that is "upon the waters"? Further, though Wilken does not say this, the new description in the Psalms must necessarily add "something" to that which we already know to be true about Jesus' baptism. It gives us a new set of words for describing that which we know happened: more *signa* with which to describe, and adore, the *res*. Allegory, for Wilken, is about the privileging of scriptural language.[62] Allegory works like poetry in that it gives new, evocative words with which to speak of whatever we like. Yet poetic language that is not scriptural or liturgical will likely lack the staying power of specifically *biblical* poetry — it will fail to stick in most church people's memories, let alone their hearts. Further, the aesthetic surprise of allegory aids its hold on the memory of hearers. To use biblical language for an event that does not seem, at first, to refer to that event, will stick in the craw of Christian readers who love that language and love that referent. Then, when the liturgy inscribes this "spiritual" reading into Christian thought and practice, it *becomes* a sort of new literal meaning, a spiritual-literal meaning of a biblical text, if you like. Christians cannot now hear of "manna" without thinking of the eucharist; cannot now hear of the Exodus from Egypt and through the sea without thinking of baptism. And why should they want to? We can see here the confluence of ancient culture's love of words, with a specifically Christian view of the significance of the history of Jesus, with the observation that liturgy creates a new people whose delight is steered toward God specifically by allegorical exegesis. We should note too that the liturgy functions as a sort of "control" on allegory for Wilken. Those readings of scripture that are remembered and revered in breviaries, lectionaries, and liturgies more broadly may be trusted as good ones. Those that are silently dropped or openly repudiated probably ought not. Wilken leaves us with a glorious description of exegesis from Cyril of Alexandria. The character of scripture can be described as

> the mystery of Christ signified to us through a myriad of different kinds of things. Someone might liken it to a glittering and magnificent city, having not one image of a king, but many, and publicly displayed in every corner of the city. . . . Its aim, however, is not to provide us an account of the lives of the saints of old. Far from that. Rather it seeks to give us knowledge of the

62. "In Defense of Allegory" in *Modern Theology* 14, no. 2 (April 1998): 206.

mystery [of Christ] through those things by which the word about him might become clear and true.[63]

Benjamin Jowett's formulation of exegesis — that we should read the Bible like any other book, so as to discover how it is unlike any other book — has been vilified, altered, and defended *ad nauseam*. I find myself surprised to be using it here. This is partly because it is so malleable that I may use it to ends quite different from those intended by Jowett. Yet I can defend my reading of the phrase according to its particular words — Jowett's intention, whatever that may have been, is less important! In no case do we read a book like any other book. We always read a book according to the particular strictures it brings to bear on its readers. Jowett seems to say that no method should be ruled out of court as "heretical" in advance of particular readings: we should certainly agree. So to read the Bible "like any other book" we read it according to what it is — a collection of books that bear witness to Israel's God so as to shape that God's ongoing redemptive work in creation.

## Allegory as the Gentile Way to Israel's Scripture

The members of what I have termed the "Return to Allegory School" have shown the problems with thinking that "to interpret a text is to ascertain the original author's intended meaning." They have borrowed from important recent gains in hermeneutics to argue that this is a poor description of how interpretation works in general. More importantly they have marshaled impressive theological descriptions for why this fails to suffice for Christians reading their scripture. Christians deal not with a generic "text," but with Christian scripture, which takes its meaning primarily from the Christ to whom it bears witness. Further, the talk of "gaps" in this description are clear evidence for the lack of a *church*, the body that has always already "bridged" any gap that would have been present between readers and writers. Perhaps most importantly the first author of scripture is God, whose purposes, by definition, cannot be divined non-theologically. Theology is itself a matter of discerning what God is saying to the church through scripture. Scripture itself is only one component, one agent, in Christian liturgy — which is the primary place where God speaks with people, and people speak back to God. The true home for Christian exegesis is in the liturgy, as God's presence is mediated through bread, wine, water, word, as people are changed and empow-

---

63. From *"In Dominico Eloquio,"* 863-64.

ered for mission in the world. We might describe a specifically Christian hermeneutic as not more nor less than a commentary on the liturgy. If an exegete were to keep squarely in mind that the text on which she is working is primarily a liturgical text, it would properly situate all the various tasks of interpretation. To return to a previous example, study of a text about the baptism of Jesus should be situated in preparation for preaching and presiding on Baptism of the Lord Sunday, in which we renew baptismal vows and "remember who we are." Perhaps we could simply say exegesis ought primarily be conducted with present-tense verbs! Allegorical exegesis is not primarily about negotiating gaps between us and a long-dead author, it is rather God's action on people, God's formation of a church.[64] And that specific people is continuing on in constant pilgrimage toward the heavenly city. If there is a "gap" to negotiate, it is that between where the church now is, and where it is called to proceed in pilgrimage.[65]

Allegory also performs an important function in reminding Christians they have no unmediated access to Israel's scripture. Contrary to the impression created by modern printing techniques, the Bible is not a book meant to be equally accessible to all-comers. In fact, Israel's scripture is not a book meant for gentiles in any obvious sense at all. Christians' behavior toward Jews over the last two thousand years is reason enough to ask why we ought to have access to their scripture in the first place. Any Christian access to these scriptures is based on a strictly *exegetical* argument, begun by Paul and often forgotten, but worthy to be continued in our day. How can you claim that Christians *are* Israel, and so have access to Israel's privileged status before God, including her scriptures (Galatians 6:16)? Paul's argument in this respect is crucial: God's intention from the beginning of the calling of Israel was to bless "all nations" through his act of election. Israel's prophets anticipated a time in which these nations would stream to Zion at the coming of the messiah and the restoration of Israel, and just so of all things. Christians believe that this restoration has begun in Jesus' death and resurrection, and that we are the gentiles streaming to Zion through life in the church. It is clear that many Jews would have great reason for rejecting this exegetical claim![66]

---

64. This is the central theological argument of Dawson's *Christian Figural Identity*. His charge against Boyarin, Auerbach, and Frei is that their failure to see exegesis as a matter of God's agency on readers now is what keeps them from appreciating its merits.

65. As R. R. Reno argues in *In the Ruins of the Church*, our primary difficulty with the biblical text is not a matter of historical or theoretical "distance," but spiritual dissonance. God in scripture makes moral demands on us to which we would rather not submit.

66. The argument between Dawson and Daniel Boyarin is key in this sense. Boyarin sees Paul as the originator of a body-denying hermeneutic, one that is amplified in Origen, and finds

Christians have reason to worry here as well: it seems we hang from Israel's scriptures by a mere thread. Yet it must hold — we have no other access to Israel's Bible. This is a quite "literal" argument — that the nations prophesied to stream to Zion, in accordance with God's will in establishing Israel's covenant to begin with, are *us*. It would be a key victory for a specifically Christian allegorical approach to the Old Testament for the church to realize it must argue exegetically for our ability to interpret Israel's Bible at all. Because we will see then that our existence must conform with the overall story of scripture in a quite literal way, as allegory always must conform with doctrine according to the literal telling of the biblical story in the *regula fidei*. Then we would see that there are enormous swaths of scripture to be interpreted anew: what now do we make of commands to be circumcised? To avenge ourselves on our enemies? To follow the ceremonial law written in Leviticus and Numbers? The list goes on indefinitely.[67] We must make a specifically Christian sense of scripture that is self-aware enough to recognize that our relationship to these books is tenuous, and needs continually to be exegetically reestablished. Allegory then shows Christians that they bear a certain "weight of weakness" in approaching the Old Testament.[68] Our very *existence* is allegorical. It is supremely fitting to our nature as those grafted, "against our nature" into an olive tree to which we do not intrinsically belong (Romans 11:17-24). As we only belong to Israel tenuously, "against our nature," it is appropriate to read Israel's texts tenuously, "against the letter." As gentiles worshipping Israel's God we do have literal access to much of Israel's scripture, especially key portions in Genesis and the prophets, and perhaps wisdom literature. Yet our access to most of the rest of Israel's scripture — most of the whole — is by necessity allegorical, tenuous, premised on reading it according to some "other sense" that Jews will not likely recognize or count as legitimate. We have a lot of exegetical explaining to do. This requires us to make sense of the whole story of God's action from creation to our inclusion and on to the eschaton, to

---

its true fruit in the attempt to exterminate Jews. Dawson, while not denying the similarity of Paul and Origen, nor the heinous outcome of much Christian thinking, sees a disconnect between these two. Anti-Jewish thought and practice is a Christian aberration, not the real thing. Further, Paul's is not a denial of embodiment, but a new sort of embodiment, one that rests on the Jewish flesh of Jesus, and the bodies of Christians transformed in quite material ways through the reading of scripture. These sorts of debates are crucial for Christians to make sense of allegory, of our relationship to Israel "according to the flesh," and the tenuous connection between the two.

67. Of course, Jews have to make their own exegetical sense of these passages in light of new life situations in which they find themselves, as the rabbis always have. They simply have less work to do to show that they may read this book in this way — it is *theirs* after all.

68. The description is Kenneth Surin's.

make sense of the words on the page, and to do so in ways that honestly reflect our identity with respect to this story and these texts. Allegory, I contend, reminds Christians of who they are with regard to Israel.

In this way we can make sense of the knee-jerk reaction many moderns have to ancient allegory. When we see Augustine interpret the mistake in the Psalm inscription as to which king it was before whom David feigned madness as a clue that we ought to read christologically, we are inclined to protest: there is *no* justification for such a reading in the text! That sense of outrage is appropriate: Christians' claim to be able to read this text *at all* is a scandal of sorts, one that must be justified exegetically in arguments like Paul's in Romans 9–11. We are not Israel according to the flesh, the promises are not intended for us, this is not even our book. Unless Jesus is indeed messiah, and baptismal participation in his death and resurrection indeed grafts us into his covenantal promises to Israel, then we should close Israel's scripture. Allegory should remind Christians this is not, intrinsically, our book, so our approach to it must be tenuous, exegetically grounded, premised both on a contested reading of "the letter" and on many readings according to some "other sense" than anything obviously present on most of its pages.

Now of course allegory has often not functioned in this way. It has often become reified, with Christian access to Israel's scripture merely presumed and neither argued for nor exegetically demonstrated, as part of the long and awful history of Christian anti-Judaism. We shall see more examples of this than anyone should care to in Chapter 4 when we examine Augustine's approach to the Jews in the *Enarrationes*. It may be that we are now, at our current place in history, appropriately situated to see the way allegory ought to work. It ought to be aware of its own burden of bearing a certain weight of weakness with regard to the text, just as Christians' relationship to this book generally hangs from a thin thread. It can realize again that it *proves* nothing, and is not meant to — it is rather meant to illustrate anew that which Christians know from other more literal and patent places in scripture. The only point of this new illustration in an allegory is to surprise, to demonstrate the beauty of the work of God in the world in a way that brings unexpected delight, and so to increase love of God and neighbor (see Chapter 3 for more on this). Allegory is always meant to sit lightly, to be the source of a certain exegetical mirth, or holy play. Like the work of the rabbis in midrash it is meant to bring delight, and like the best jokes it is meant to reorient the way we see. Allegory is then finally a way of prayer.

My own greatest frustration with historical criticism may be that it is another example of modernity's tendency to flatten all biblical meaning into one sense — that intended by the author. This sort of reading is thin gruel to offer to those who wish to grow spiritually. It may be no accident that allegory has largely flourished in the monastery, where monks and nuns are charged with reading scripture slowly, meditatively, for the entirety of their lives. They are searching there for the very depths of holy teaching, "chewing" the biblical text slowly in an effort to have each verse crack and reveal its particular spice.[69] To know that the Psalms are Israel's hymnal, that their literal sense confounds the Donatists' claims to be a holier church, is sufficient for an Augustinian beginning, remedial understanding of the text. Yet a deeper reading requires something more, something only attainable by attending to every word and phrase, every metrical hint and every untranslatable particle, for each of these has a new depth of meaning about Christ to share with readers who will patiently work for it. None of these deeper layers of meaning will *prove* anything to someone who doesn't already hold Christian teaching to be true; it will only serve to delight those who are already sufficiently mature to read in that sense, and not others. It may also, not inappropriately, repel those who do not hold to the truth of scripture's literal story. Allegory is not meant for beginners. Ancient Jews and Christians alike did not hand the Song of Songs to any remedial reader. Such a one had to trudge through the brick-by-brick wisdom of the Proverbs, then the apophatic grimness of Ecclesiastes, in order finally to scale the heights of the Canticle. To read that book too early can cause confusion at best, outright harm at worst. In contrast, modernity has no ability to speak about such deeper levels of meaning, visible only by hard work and patient teaching. And precisely this is indispensable for growth in Christian maturity for ancient readers. No wonder we live in an age of spiritual adolescents. And no wonder that Augustine, in contrast to us, praised the scriptures: "how amazing is the profundity of your words! We are confronted with a superficial meaning that offers easy access to the unlettered; yet how amazing their profundity, O my God, how amazingly deep they are! To look into that depth makes me shudder, but it is the shudder of awe, the trembling of love."[70] This sort of ecstatic, passionate love, with its obvious conjugal echoes, is clearly not for the uninitiated, but for those who boast the familiar sexual relationship of old lovers, for those long since married to the Word and accustomed to adoring every detail of the other's body.

A final introductory note about allegory is this: it is not easy. Its difficulty

---

69. Contemporary theorists often now turn to *lectio divina* as a medieval resource for going forward in post-critical exegesis — see Ellen Davis's work in such places as her commentary on the Song of Songs in *Proverbs, Ecclesiastes and the Song of Songs* (Louisville: Westminster/John Knox, 2000), and the work of Michael Casey in such places as *Sacred Reading: The Ancient Art of Lectio Divina* (Liguori, MO: Triumph, 1996).

70. *Confessions* XII.14.17, trans. Maria Boulding (New York: Vintage, 1998), 282.

derives from its intentionally counterintuitive approach to reading. It cannot be dreamed up by a scholar in a carrel, nor understood by someone outside of the reading practices that make it intelligible. It has to be taught, over the course of years, by one expert to another, as part of the growth in grace intrinsic to Christian living. Rowan Williams has pointed out that the sheer difficulty of reading the Bible well drives those who desire to read it into the tutelage of teachers and fellow students. Any community of this sort will experience conflict and difficulty, for the very stealing Fowl describes will be possible in it! Only through such a grueling process of communal life, and learning to read, will someone be able to produce such allegorical readings as Augustine does, or be able to appraise them well.

This difficulty is why I can offer this book as a sort of experiment. It is not obvious to me that it is now possible to read the way Augustine does. Where are the communities to which one may go to learn to do this? Where are the skills with which to do it well, or appraise it well? My hope is that such places will grow up organically from among us who wish to reinstill these sorts of reading habits in the church, or that we will discover places where such readings are still going on. Until we have communities of readers like Augustine's, we will not be able to tell if it is possible to read this way again after modernity. The viability of allegory is finally an ecclesiological issue. More on this in the final chapter.

## 2 Christology and Exegesis

As we argue for the restoration of Christian figural reading, it is tempting simply to take the moral high ground by pointing to the Bible's description of the exegetical practice of Jesus himself.[1] While contemporary exegetes may wish, for whatever reason, to say that "the stone the builders rejected" of Psalm 118 or "the Lord said to my Lord" of Psalm 110 ought not be read with reference to Christ, Jesus' own exegetical practice demonstrates otherwise and so closes the case for Christian exegetes. Augustine himself is given to this sort of argumentation: "Would anyone have the temerity to assert that he ought not to have expounded [scripture] in the way he did? How much less should anyone presume to gainsay the plain truth when the Lord expounded a parable he had himself proposed?"[2] Not only did Jesus read scripture with refer-

---

1. Most modern exegetes would discourage any high degree of confidence about what we can know of Jesus' own exegesis or self-understanding. N. T. Wright has launched a major effort to reverse this trend with his section, "The Aims and Beliefs of Jesus," in *Jesus and the Victory of God*, vol. 2 of *Christian Origins and the Question of God* (Minneapolis: Fortress, 1996), 477-653. Unfortunately Wright's zeal to make strong conclusions about Jesus' self-awareness drives him to a strange dismissiveness about post-biblical Christian doctrine: "forget the pseudo-orthodox attempts to make Jesus of Nazareth conscious of being the second person of the Trinity. . . . I propose, as a matter of history, that Jesus of Nazareth was conscious of a vocation . . . to enact in himself what, in Israel's scriptures, God had promised to accomplish all by himself" (653). For an account of early Christian exegesis skeptical of the claim that it originated with Jesus himself see Donald Juel, *Messianic Exegesis: Christological Interpretation of the Old Testament in Early Christianity* (Philadelphia: Fortress, 1988), 114-17.

2. Comment on Psalm 149 in *Expositions of the Psalms*, trans. Maria Boulding, from the *Works of Saint Augustine: A Translation for the 21st Century*, vol. III/20 (Hyde Park, NY: New City Press, 2004), VI, 494. (Hereafter this and other volumes will be cited as *EP*. As there are six volumes of psalm translations, we shall refer to these with Roman numerals I-VI). In its own con-

ence to himself, he himself is the divine source of scripture, and so ought to be taken to know best how to read it. Jesus' own practice is continued in all parts of the New Testament, most impressively by Paul, whose arguments for allegory in such places as 1 Corinthians 10:1-11, Galatians 4:21-31, and Ephesians 5:25-33,[3] made its practice a matter of course in the church for more than a millennium and a half. It would seem, on the basis of such solid christological, biblical, and traditional arguments, that the burden of proof should be on those who would deny the legitimacy of such figurative forms of exegesis.

But, of course, it is not. Generations of Christian interpreters now have been well aware of these intertextual displays of allegory within scripture, and yet have not seen fit to "go and do likewise" in their own interpretive practice. The Reformation, the Enlightenment, and modern historical critical study all brought complex argumentation to bear against Christian figurative reading, such that it is difficult now to find anyone interpreting scripture in ways that Augustine could take for granted. In the face of this now half-millennium-old triple onslaught, we must return to the basic "cornerstone," if you will, of Augustine's own exegesis of the Old Testament: his christology. I wish to show by the end of this chapter that anyone who holds to a christological orthodoxy at all like Augustine's ought also to read scripture as Augustine does.

---

text Augustine polemicizes against the Donatists who would rip the tares sown by the enemy from the field prematurely, thereby threatening the good seed. In their impatience the Donatists contravene the Lord's own word that we must "let them both grow together until harvest time" (Matthew 13:30). Augustine aims his rhetoric against anyone presumptuous enough to challenge the Lord's own reading of scripture, especially when Jesus tells his disciples explicitly what his parable means. Contemporary historians are also eager to seek out older meanings of parables than those offered by Jesus, though for historicist reasons rather than the christological and ecclesiological ones that drove the Donatists to challenge Jesus' exegesis.

3. The Pauline authorship of the Ephesians text is, of course, not unchallenged. Augustine was unaware of this debate over the "deutero-Paulines" and their authenticity. But he was not at all threatened by "errors" of various kinds in scripture, and would have had resources with which to deal with those not known to him. Because the fathers did not see scripture as a set of facts for either ascent or dispute, but rather God's word through which the church is drawn into the divine life, the proving or disproving of authorship poses no fundamental threat to their hermeneutic. In any case the exegesis in Ephesians 5 is conducted in the same spirit (Spirit?) as that in the indisputably Pauline passages of 1 Corinthians 10 and Galatians 4, and so poses no problem for us here.

## On Taking a Metaphor Literally:
## Augustine's Scriptural Christology

For Augustine, theology is nothing more (or less!) than a reading of scripture. This point is often obscured in now centuries-old debates over the emphasis on "Platonism" in Augustine. Augustine thought of himself as a biblical thinker. If he could be convinced that something he was teaching contravened Christian scripture, on his own grounds he would have to reject it. To suspicious modern readers or critics of Augustine this understanding of the nature of theology would seem to offer no strictures whatsoever on his work. How could such an avid user of allegory fail to find whatever he wanted, tucked away in Leviticus (or wherever), and so manage to smuggle all sorts of things Platonist (or whatever other negative adjective) into his exegesis, all the while calling his work "biblical"? Yet the point is crucial for understanding his christology and the reading of the Psalter that christology entails: for Augustine, Christian teaching derives from scripture, and then sends one back to scripture, for new and deeper reading. For example, Augustine's interwoven doctrines of Christ and the church as one body — *totus Christus* — originate from Paul's teaching on the church as the body of Christ in such places as 1 Corinthians 12:12-27. That exegetically based teaching sends Augustine back to such places as Psalm 21 with new skills with which to read. In turn, this christologically laden rereading of Psalm 21 affects the way Augustine reads and uses 1 Corinthians 12 and the language with which he speaks of christology, soteriology, and all the rest of Christian teaching throughout his work. We have here a sort of "hermeneutical spiral" that began with the first Christian attempts to summarize Christian teaching into a *regula*, then became (and remains) a hermeneutical rule to guide all further scripture reading.[4] Hermeneutical reflection on such spirals is well known and often commented-upon. What is less often (or at least less favorably) noted is the fascinating readings produced when Christians like Augustine return to portions of scripture not in obvious agreement with the *regula*. These are some of the most glorious portions of Augustine's work. They are akin to a skilled poet being forced into a word choice she would not have made without the need to rhyme, which choice turns out to be surprisingly beautiful. Allegory is not merely a wooden restraint that forces an exegete into awkward misreadings of scripture, if Augustine is any indication. It rather can prod a Christian exegete toward spectacularly beautiful readings of scripture, de-

---

4. Paul Blowers describes this spiral in ancient Christianity generally in his "The *Regula Fidei* and the Narrative Character of Early Christian Faith," *Pro Ecclesia* 6, no. 2 (1998): 199-228.

signed to encourage one's readers and sermon hearers into ever more delightful readings of scripture and ever more loving pilgrimage toward God. Allegory, far from being "arbitrary," has its own logic to which Augustine
faithfully attends, and its own peculiar *telos* of participation in God's work to
unite humanity with himself. There is much here from which we may learn.

## Dramatic Christology

Augustine's primary impetus to read allegorically is christology.[5] Contemporary historical scholarship on Augustine's christology lacks the sheer volume
of work dedicated to other aspects of his thought. This is for two reasons: one,
none of the crises with which he so famously dealt centered specifically on
christology. Therefore we have very few primary works, and not many letters
or sermons, dedicated solely to christology.[6] We lack here the crisp didactic
formulations that the rhetor-turned-bishop fashioned for his combat against
the Manichees, the Donatists, and the Pelagians.[7] The second reason for the
gap in scholarly attention with regard to Augustine's christology has to do
with how patristic thought is studied more broadly. The "highlights" of the
patristic era, both for its participants and for its current students, tend to center around the conciliar decisions to which orthodox Christian assent was de-
manded, such as the *theotokos* of the Council of Ephesus in 431, merely a year
after Augustine's death. Because Augustine was not personally involved in
this monumentally important christological controversy conducted elsewhere in the empire and in the evening of his life, he is not commonly remembered for making christological claims as important as those of Cyril or
Nestorius. Augustine's christology is neglected then because it is taken to be
politically and doctrinally unimportant, since it neither begins, nor ends, nor
adds to any significant ecclesial controversy.

5. Henri de Lubac shows that christology is the primary impetus to the fathers' allegorical
exegesis in many places in his work. See, for example, his section "The Action of Christ" in his
*Medieval Exegesis*, vol. 1, trans. Mark Sebanc (Grand Rapids: Eerdmans, 1998), 234-41.

6. Important exceptions of christological rigor in Augustine's work include some of his
tractates on the gospel of John (*St. Augustine: Tractates on the Gospel of John*, trans. John W.
Rettig [Washington: Catholic, 1988]), his letter 137 (in *St. Augustine: Letters*, trans. Sr. W. Parson
[New York: Fathers of the Church, 1953]), and some sermons besides those in the *Enarrationes*.

7. For example, Augustine's memorable teaching on God's immaterial nature and evil as
privation in the *Confessions* against the Manichees, phrases coined in the fight against the
Donatists like *ex opere operato*, and the fourfold variant on *posse pecare* in polemics on original
sin and predestination against the Pelagians.

Augustine's christology also draws so little scholarly attention because it looks, on the surface, so conventional. So eminent an early church historian as Brian Daley has recently said that the "most striking thing about Augustine's christology is that, to later readers at least, it appears so ordinary."[8] Earlier scholarly discussions took conventional shape. Early and mid-twentieth-century conservative French Catholics explored what they saw as the deep similarity between Augustinian and Cyrillian christology, his congruity with later Chalcedonian teaching, and the parallel contours between Augustine's work and later understandings of the "mystical body of Christ."[9] They were goaded to write by such illustrious revisionist historians as Adolf von Harnack, who attempted to show that the Platonist provenance of Augustine's thought was the source of its (alleged) crypto-docetism. William Babcock, in his 1971 Yale dissertation on Augustine's christology, summarized his teaching in a way that explains each of these twentieth-century scholarly trends.[10] He argues that Augustine, as a pre-Chalcedonian figure, did not use

8. "Christology," in *Augustine Through the Ages*, ed. Allan D. Fitzgerald, OSA (Grand Rapids: Eerdmans, 1999), 164. The rest of Daley's essay shows just how compelling Augustinian christology is! William Babcock's dissertation shows both why Augustine's work in christology is important and why it seems to us so unremarkable (*The Christ of the Exchange: A Study in the Christology of Augustine's Enarrationes in Psalmos* [Ph.D. dissertation, Yale University, 1971; Ann Arbor: University Microfilms, 1972]). It is very hard to read Augustine's christology without the categories of two nature/one person later given at Chalcedon. His christology is easily assimilable into that description, as Babcock shows. Yet in its own terms it is a highly developed "dramatic" christology that is remarkable both for its sophistication and for the readings of scripture it allows Augustine to produce. So while it may appear conventional to us after Chalcedon, in its time it represented an important moment in the development of the doctrine of Christ.

9. Joanne McWilliam, "The Study of Augustine's Christology in the 20th Century," in *Augustine: From Rhetor to Theologian* (Waterloo, Ontario: Wilfrid Laurier University Press, 1992), 183-205.

10. Unfortunately Babcock launches a typically modern criticism of Augustine's christology for its failure to grant any "independent status" to the humanity of Christ, and his allowance of an "unremitting hegemony" of Christ's divinity to reduce any genuine humanity to the mere "instrument" of the divine Word (*Christ of the Exchange*, 333). Although Augustine does better than many of his theological forebears in granting the humanity of Jesus some importance in his christology, and in devising a christology in which the two natures are genuinely united ("dramatically" so), he also leaves us with a regrettable "loss of human autonomy in motivation and decision" (340). This is because Augustine's dramatic categories leave him little place for the mere "way" of the humanity of Christ once the "goal" of his divinity has been reached. Over against this Augustinian portrait, Babcock wishes to insist that a proper christological emphasis on the humanity of Christ will maintain that "Christ himself must be depicted as one who controls and directs his own human experience" (344).

The way to respond to Babcock is to investigate his descriptions of human "autonomy," "independence," and the wished-for human agency in the verbs "controls" and "directs." For Au-

Chalcedonian categories (with the German revisionists), yet that the thrust of his christological work was also not fundamentally opposed to later Chalcedonian teaching either (with the French conservatives). For Babcock, Augustine's christology is marked by the use of strikingly *dramatic* categories, as opposed to the fixed ontological ones of Chalcedon's nature/person distinction. Augustine writes often of Christians' pilgrimage from Christ as way to Christ as goal, from his humanity to his divinity.[11] This progress is a graced pilgrimage made possible by the divine *kenosis* among us. In Christ — the mediator between God and humanity — God *gives* (again, note the active verbs) to humanity his divinity, in return for humanity's sinfulness. The site of this exchange is in the body of Christ itself, with Christ as head, and the church as the head's members. We are not surprised to see Babcock exploring the strong similarities between Augustine's teaching on the *admirabile commercium* with Eastern Orthodox understandings of *theosis,* which he finds to be deeply concordant with Augustine's soteriology. In short, Augustine's christological imagination is biblically funded (the "way" of John 14:6, the *kenosis* of the Christ hymn at Philippians 2:7, the link between *theosis* and beatific vision of 1 John 3:2, and so on), it lacks the technical terms made necessary by the polemics in other areas of Augustine's thought and elsewhere in the history of dogma, yet it remains important to the church today for its use of dramatic categories and its similarity to the eastern church's *theosis.*

I am glad simply to assume the achievement of such historical work as Babcock's, and above all the more recent work of Michael Fiedrowicz.[12] Yet I

---

gustine it is no desirable goal for *any* human to seek "autonomy," that is, literally and etymologically, "rule over oneself." Rather Augustine would wish for humans to submit their stubborn pride, their misplaced desires, and their damaged intellects, to God for healing and genuine freedom. I take this to be the anthropological vision of the *Confessions,* and one that closely aligns with the human nature of Christ described in *Enarrationes.* It can be asked back to Babcock whether the "autonomy" for which he wishes for Christ ought to include the ability to sin. If so, he and Augustine are so far apart it is little use trying to reconcile them. If not, he should see that inability to sin is, on Augustinian grounds, freedom itself. It may be that there is room for a critique of Augustine's christology and its inability to account for Jesus' genuine humanity in a way that, say, Maximus Confessor suggests later (as Robert Wilken argues in "Not My Will but Thine," in *The Spirit of Early Christian Thought* [New Haven: Yale University Press, 2003], 110-35).

11. Described by Basil Studer, OSB, in his *The Grace of Christ and the Grace of God in Augustine of Hippo: Christocentrism or Theocentrism?* (Collegeville: Liturgical, 1997).

12. Unlike Babcock, Michael Cameron, Michael McCarthy, and the present book, Fiedrowicz manages to describe Augustine's work in the *Enarrationes* without assuming it into any more all-encompassing theological project. It is difficult simply to describe what is going on in a great church figure like Augustine without concluding with a theological "moral to the story," but Fiedrowicz's work approximates that goal quite closely. The encyclopedic detail of his

would like to question some of what has become a conventional telling of the story of secondary scholarship on Augustinian christology. To say that the Donatists' mistake is ecclesiological is not wrong, but it is not sufficient, for it pretends that one can "do" ecclesiology in an Augustinian vein that is not always already bound up with faithful christology. For Augustine, Christ is always both head and members, the church is always Christ and us, with our head at the right hand of the Father, and our members spread throughout the world. As he preaches, "When you hear Christ mentioned, never divorce Bridegroom from bride."[13] The Donatist attempt to sever the body into pieces is, of course, an ecclesiological heresy, and just so, it is also a christological one, for it is an attack on the whole body of Christ, *totus Christus*, head and members. These quite good historians' description of Augustine making no contribution in the area of christology, but significant contribution in ecclesiology, owes more to modern divisions of "systematic theology" than to Augustine's own categories.

On these grounds, it is not even clear that Augustine's christological contributions fell outside of his many polemical battles.[14] Because the bulk of the *Enarrationes* were written in the middle portion of Augustine's career, after the Manichean controversies and before the Pelagian ones, most of their polemical ire is aimed at the Donatists (though plenty is left over for others).[15]

---

work, including his gathering of various scholars' efforts to date individual expositions, is indispensable. See his *Psalmus Vox Totius Christi: Studien zu Augustins 'Enarrationes in Psalmos'* (Freiburg: Herder, 1997).

13. Psalm 34 (2) in *EP*, vol. II, 59.

14. Examined in Michael Cameron, *Augustine's Construction of Figurative Exegesis Against the Donatists in the Enarrationes in Psalmos* (PhD. dissertation, University of Chicago, 1996; Ann Arbor: University Microfilms, 1997).

Part of Michel Barnes's contribution to Augustinian studies has been the argument that Augustine's polemical work ought not be seen as any less theological than any other. It seems that moderns' discomfort with the level of invective in ancient polemics, coupled with a peculiarly modern and "systematic" theological sense that theology is best done dispassionately, have caused contemporary readers of Augustine to overlook his more controversy-driven theological moments.

15. After studying the *Enarrationes*, I am struck by the complementary nature of the various stages of Augustine's polemical career. The arguments against the Manichees on the goodness of creation slide easily into criticisms of Apolloniarius's christology. These, in turn, fit naturally with criticisms of the Donatists' attempts to sever the church's head from its limbs and to tear the body apart. The description of salvation as our graced grafting into Christ's body needs no dramatic break to turn to criticisms of the Pelagians' celebration of the salvific capacities of non-graced humanity. It may be that these three phases of Augustine's polemical career are too easily and too often divorced from one another, and that christology is the unifying theme of his entire life's work. For older accounts that emphasize the changes through which Augustine's

And since, as we have said, the Donatist heresy is also necessarily a christological heresy, we might say the *Enarrationes* represents Augustine's most significant christological polemic. Further, though the work itself sprawls across six recent volumes and spans decades of Augustine's career, unified more by its biblical subject than by any intentional literary composition, we might still consider it a work unified by a christological *skopos*.[16] Augustine often feels the need to apologize for his frequent reiteration of his central hermeneutical and dogmatic principal in his expositions on the Psalms: the *totus Christus:* "As you know, brothers and sisters — and it can never be said too often — Christ sometimes speaks in his own person as our Head . . . at other times as from ourselves, his members."[17] The very repetition, and apology for its repetition, is itself didactic: he wants his congregation never to forget his central christological and hermeneutical premise. The *Enarrationes in psalmos* should be seen then as Augustine's most important christological work.

Michael Cameron's 1996 dissertation shows precisely how this is so. In it he tracks a shift in Augustine's biblical hermeneutic without which Augustine could not have written the *Enarrationes* as he did. Early in his theological career Augustine employed what Cameron calls an "anagogic" perspective in his allegorical readings — that is, he sought readings in which a temporal sign is correlated with an atemporal thing. To use the language of the *De doctrina christiana,* the *signum* of the scriptural word points to the *res* of eternal, disembodied meaning — the two are related enough that the reader can draw a connection from the one to another, but "separate by reason of their participation in mutually exclusive universes."[18] This "Platonist" move allowed Au-

---

thought progresses see Eugene TeSelle, *Augustine the Theologian* (New York: Herder and Herder, 1970), and Rowan Greer's chapter on Augustine in *Broken Lights, Mended Lives: Theology and Common Life in the Early Church* (University Park, PA: Penn State Press, 1986). It is to be hoped that the doctrinal revisionist scholarship of Ayres, Barnes, Williams, and others will yield a new theological biography of Augustine in the future.

16. Robert Wilken describes the *Enarrationes* as more satisfying in part than in whole. That is, if one tries to read them straight through in a single sitting one will not get far. They are so tied to the particular lines of the Psalter that they can more profitably be read like a commentary than like a treatise — that is, referred to in order to discern how Augustine makes sense of these words in light of their christological *skopos*.

17. Comment on Psalm 39, in *EP* II, 200.

18. Cameron, *Augustine's Construction of Figurative Exegesis*, 58. The great strength of Cameron's dissertation is its "dramatic" approach to Augustine himself — Cameron patiently displays the evolution of Augustine's approach to scripture that made his Psalm hermeneutic possible. This book can then simply assume Cameron's diagnostic work on Augustine. To use Cameron's terms, I display here a fairly "anagogic" approach to Augustine; to use modern New

gustine to avoid crudely literal descriptions of God such as those used in the Bible's many anthropomorphisms. This hermeneutic came to him as a revelation of sorts, as the *Confessions* makes clear.[19] Yet as a theory of the relationship between words and their meanings, anagogy did not suffice. Persistent, rigorous attention to the scriptures and the incarnation led Augustine to a more "dramatic" approach to allegory. That is, one rooted not in a disjunction between *signum* and an eternal *res*, but in a *conjunction* between a temporal *signum* and an incarnate *res* — Jesus.[20]

It was not long before this hermeneutical shift produced exegetical fruit. In an early *enarratio*, Augustine reads Psalm 3 straight through with reference to Christ, and then begins again from the first verse reading it with reference to the church.[21] Soon he realizes there is no need to separate these two readings — for to speak of Christ as head is also to speak of Christ as body. Cameron shows that Augustine brings to full flower a Pauline hermeneutic that would speak of Christ and the church as one "person."[22] This is also a

---

Testament terminology, a "synoptic" one. That is, I write about Augustine's exegesis in the *Enarrationes* without much attention to its evolution over the course of his career. I can do so for two reasons — one, if Cameron is right the key hermeneutical shift has already been made before Augustine writes the bulk of the *Enarrationes*, and two since this is a work of systematic theology speaking more to a contemporary conversation in theological exegesis than to historians.

19. Book VII of *Confessions* describes the books of the Platonists and Ambrose's preaching as crucial in showing Augustine a way of thinking about God as non-material. At this point in the narrative Augustine is already converted to "philosophy," but still thinks of God as "something physical occupying space, diffused either in the world or even through infinite space outside the world" (VII.1.1). Then some "books of the Platonists" allow him to read the substance "if not the exact words" of John's prologue (VII.9.13). Another conversion to the incarnation still awaits him. See *Confessions*, trans. Henry Chadwick (Oxford: Oxford University Press, 1991), 111 and 121.

20. Cameron also shows that one of our difficulties in reading Augustine on scripture is that his two most famous early works, the *De doctrina christiana* and the *Confessions*, are written before this christological turn. So Augustine's reflections on and practice of exegesis there are not as fully christologically shaped as the interpretation he would give later of the Psalms. Because we in English so often read these two works, and so seldom read the *Enarrationes*, we are left with a truncated Augustine, one whose exegesis is not yet fully shaped in the christological direction to which it would later turn.

21. *EP* I, 76ff.

22. Cameron, *Augustine's Construction of Figurative Exegesis*, 274. "Paul spoke of Christ's death not only 'for' us, but 'with' and 'in' us in such places as 2 Corinthians 5:14, 1 Corinthians 12:12-27, Romans 6:3 and 12:4-5, and following Paul Ephesians 1:22-23 and 5:21-33, Colossians 1:18 and 24. Cameron describes Irenaeus's teaching on divine recapitulation, Athanasius's and Hilary's on *theosis*, and the Donatist Tyconius's whole-scale application of the Psalter to Christ, as continuing Paul's radical identity between believers and Christ, on the way to Augustine's full exposition of it in the *Enarrationes*.

thoroughly *historical* vision of exegesis, rooted in the history of the incarnation, with every line of every psalm referring in some way to Christ, the whole Christ, head and members. Cameron speaks of the *Enarrationes* as the explication of a "christo-ecclesiological" form of exegesis, premised on the *totus Christus,* the "whole Christ," who speaks throughout the Psalter.

Michael McCarthy's dissertation assumes Cameron's work, and extends it into discussion with twentieth-century Roman Catholic doctrine.[23] He wishes to show that Augustine's *Enarrationes* can represent what recent Catholics have meant by a "fundamental theology" — that is, an apologetic project that aims to display the intelligibility of Christianity's understanding of God's revelation. McCarthy recognizes that he risks serious anachronism, since Augustine does not use such modern terms as "fundamental theology" or "revelation." Yet McCarthy seeks to place old wine in these new wineskins — to fill out these modern loci with Augustinian meaning. If revelation deals with God's disclosing of what was heretofore unknown, the *Enarrationes* indeed disclose a mystery: "God's own self, made irrevocably manifest in Christ, whose union with the church grounds the ongoing experience of God: 'the whole mystery of all scriptures is Christ and the church.'"[24] Augustine's psalm hermeneutic "locates the practice of praying and interpreting the psalms within the present and ongoing activity of God." That is, it is not just that reading the psalms like Augustine yields christological insight, it is that praying the psalms with Augustine inducts the church into the divine life itself.[25]

The most important recent scholarship on Augustine's christology pays comparably little attention to the *Enarrationes.* It comes from a group of patristic scholars *cum* theologians loosely associated with theology's recent Radical Orthodoxy movement. Rowan Williams, his student Lewis Ayres, and

23. Michael McCarthy, SJ, *The Revelatory Psalm: A Fundamental Theology of Augustine's Enarrationes in Psalmos* (Ph.D. diss., University of Notre Dame; Ann Arbor: University Microfilm, 2003).

It is striking that the most important work on Augustine in English is all in the form of unpublished dissertations (in addition to those dealt with here see also Amy Oden's *Dominant Images for the Church in Augustine's 'Enarrationes in Psalmos': A Study of Augustine's Ecclesiology* [diss., Southern Methodist University; Ann Arbor: University Microfilms, 1990], written under Babcock). That these dissertations go unpublished may be a sign that we continue to think that the fathers' "real" theology takes place someplace other than in their biblical exegesis, as though they were bound by our clumsy modern division of academic disciplines. Or, more benignly, it may be that writing *about* Augustine's exegesis is not nearly as interesting as the exegesis itself. It is surprisingly difficult to write about *anyone's* exegesis without becoming terribly tedious.

24. McCarthy, *The Revelatory Psalm,* 30, quoting Augustine's *Enarratio* 79 in *EP* IV, 141: "Christ and his Church, that total mystery with which all the scriptures are concerned."

25. McCarthy, *The Revelatory Psalm,* i.

their intellectual colleague Michel Barnes have launched an Augustinian revival of sorts by responding to what they claim is a dated and misinformed
reading of Augustine's Trinitarian theology. This misreading was born in the
nineteenth-century French Augustinian scholar Théodore de Régnon's contention that Augustine's work "begins" with an undifferentiated divine unity,
while that of the eastern Cappadocians "begins" with the three divine persons. This Augustinian starting point is allegedly due to the predominant influence upon him of neo-Platonist philosophy,[26] for which, it is often
claimed, any "difference" cannot be seen as original or primordially good.
Not only have patristic scholars continued to tell the story of the early
church's doctrine of God in this way, but theologians have whole-heartedly
adopted and retold it with ever greater enthusiasm. These have claimed that
Augustine has a non-negotiable hatred of matter that leads to a denigration
of the human nature of Christ and a correlative flattening of the triune persons into undifferentiated "sameness," with a corresponding inability to read
the scriptural narrative about God well.[27]

Williams, Ayres, and Barnes have attempted to subvert what they take to
be a poor reading of Augustine's trinitarian thought largely through counter readings of his great work *De Trinitate,* since that is the primary source
of most of the modern theological ire directed his way.[28] Yet they have also

26. Argued in Olivier du Roy's enormously influential *L'intelligence de la foi in la trinité
selon saint Augustin* (Paris: Études Augustiniennes, 1966).

27. This critique of Augustine has reached almost canonical status, but some names that
have helped it reach that point include John Zizioulas, Catherine LaCugna, Colin Gunton, David Brown, and Stanley Grenz. Barnes helpfully points out that even Du Roy's original description of Augustine is not so near-sighted as these contemporary reappropriations of his work
hold in his "Augustine in Contemporary Trinitarian Theology," *Theological Studies* 56 (1995):
237-50.

28. Barnes has offered important readings of *de Trinitate*'s books I and V in "Exegesis and
Polemic in *De Trinitate* I," *Augustinian Studies* 30 (1999): 43-59, and "The Arians of Book V, and
the Genre of *De Trinitate*," *Journal of Theological Studies* 44 (1993): 185-95. Ayres has concentrated on the christologically thick books IV and XIII in his "The Christological Context of Augustine's *De Trinitate* XIII: Toward Relocating Book VIII-XV," *Augustinian Studies* 29, no. 1
(1998): 111-39, and on book X in "The Discipline of Self-Knowledge in Augustine's *De Trinitate*
Book X," in *The Passionate Intellect: Essays on the Transformation of Classical Traditions Presented to Professor Ian Kidd,* ed. L. Ayres (Brunswick, NJ: Transaction, 1995), 261-96. Barnes and
Ayres are both purported to be working on book-length studies that systematize their view of
Augustine's great treatise. Williams's recent work has focused more on the pneumatological and
ecclesiological content at the end of *De Trinitate* in his "*Sapientia* and the Trinity: Reflections
on the *De Trinitate*" in *Collectanea Augustiniana,* ed. B. Bruning et al. (Leuven: Leuven University Press, 1990), 317-32, and his article on *De Trinitate* in *Augustine Through the Ages,* ed.
Allan D. Fitzgerald (Grand Rapids: Eerdmans, 1999).

attended to lesser-read sermons and treatises in an effort to present as broad a view as possible of his thought, and to counter the reflexive modern instinct to treat *De Trinitate* like a textbook in systematic theology, containing all Augustine would ever wish to say on the topic. Most importantly for our purposes, they have shown the inextricability of a robust christology from Augustine's teaching on the Trinity. They have argued that if we are to speak of any point of departure from which Augustine "begins," that would most properly be the pro-Nicene insistence on the inseparability of operations among the three divine persons.[29] This adage leaves Augustine in some exegetical difficulty, as he has to offer readings of biblical texts that seem to say otherwise, such as those that describe Jesus' baptism. Scripture seems patently to describe three separate operations, one by each of the three persons. How can pro-Nicene readers of scripture make sense of this? Augustine has some suggestions, and these are elaborated in fascinating ways through the course of his career.[30] The more fundamental point however is his overall approach to the question. We *cannot* finally understand the kind of divine unity scripture describes. We can point to it in better rather than worse ways through images given in scripture and taught in church, but we should be clear up front that we speak of a Mystery we cannot fully understand, but can only point toward in ways appropriate to creatures. Ayres puts to use here George Lindbeck's analogy of theology as a sort of "grammar."[31] The church's language for God instructs us in how to speak well, but we do not understand precisely how that language "refers" to its divine subject. Yet we can trust it does since it is given to us by God in

29. Ayres and Barnes use the description "pro-Nicene" as a foil to the more commonly used description of Augustine's theological heritage as "neo-platonic." The latter is not so much wrong as it is misleading, for it fails accurately to describe the intellectual source for much of Augustine's teaching (such as on the inseparability of activity among the three divine persons), and suggests his commitments lie elsewhere than defending and expositing the trinitarian grammar delineated at Nicea and elaborated upon (a modern description, not his) throughout the fourth century.

Michael Hanby, another theologian making use of this revival in Augustinian trinitarian thought, has argued that it is improper to think of any theological "starting point" in time at all, since all thought and speech about God begins and ends with God! His book *Augustine and Modernity* (London: Routledge, 2003) engages the recent work I also deal with here, before critiquing the charge that Cartesian interiority owes any serious debt to the trinitarian and anthropological work of Augustine.

30. Described especially in Ayres's "'Remember You Are Catholic' (serm. 52.2): Augustine on the Unity of the Triune God," *Journal of Early Christian Studies* 8, no. 1 (2000): 39-82, and "The Fundamental Grammar of Augustine's Trinitarian Theology," in *Augustine and His Critics*, ed. Robert Dodaro and George Lawless (London: Routledge, 2000), 51-76.

31. Lindbeck, *The Nature of Doctrine* (Philadelphia: Westminster, 1984).

scripture.[32] All of Augustine's efforts to offer "analogies" for the Trinity, to read proto-trinitarian passages of scripture, to speak of the divine nature *at all* must be understood in the context of this general apophaticism he shares with all the fathers: fallen human beings cannot understand the divine nature.[33]

What then are we given in scripture, if not ways to describe the divine nature? Not information by which to understand God, but grammar that organizes scripture's words so our language points to God better rather than worse. To use Ayres's own language, we are given in scripture a "dramatic"[34] presentation of God's action in Christ peculiarly suited to our nature as fallen creatures. Christ's two natures are intentionally fitted to human traversing of the distance introduced between us and God in the fall. This distance becomes, in the incarnation, a redemptive *dispensatio* by which we travel "through God to God," through Christ's human nature to his divinity. Ayres writes, "the logic of the Incarnation is peculiarly suited for its purpose in healing fallen humanity," offering a certain "harmony" or "fittingness" by which it matches our particular malady to repair it. For example, Christ's single death, in his body, suffices to prevent our double death, in body and soul (so book IV of *De Trinitate*). Creatures see the beauty in this divine drama, note that it is supremely "fitting" *(conveniens)* with our presently fallen state, and learn to love God well and attend properly to the scriptures. What the in-

---

32. This sentence makes a stronger claim about the referent of theological claims than Lindbeck is inclined to do, but I think it faithful to Ayres's Augustine.

33. Ayres's most important contribution here may be his specification of Augustine's quite reserved use of "analogy." Augustine never intends to offer an analogy of proportion by which we can understand precisely how the analogy corresponds to the analogand. How can we, when the subject being spoken of is God? Rather, the goal with Augustine's analogies is quite limited and specific: to help us envision how three could possibly work inseparably, for example. Augustine's grammar of simplicity serves to demonstrate that no created thing — "complex" as these are as they are made up of parts — can fully or properly demonstrate the divine nature. Further, these images are offered as part of a specifically Christian exercise of seeking to have faith grow in understanding, to imagine more faithfully that in which we participate. That is, as a "spiritual exercise" along the lines described by Pierre Hadot in his *Philosophy as a Way of Life: Spiritual Exercises from Socrates to Foucault*, trans. Matthew Chase (Oxford: Blackwell, 1995). For these two reasons — the equivocation in all analogical speech about God, and the offering of images only as part of the spiritual exercises of Christian people — modern attempts to dissect and disparage the *vestigia Trinitate* in Augustine's *De Trinitate* fail.

34. Ayres is not here borrowing from Babcock, whom he does not cite, but rather from Hans Urs von Balthasar, whom he does. Hanby carries on a rigorous theological conversation between Augustine and Balthasar with regard to their presentations of the christological drama in scripture, especially with reference to their differences over divine immutability. See Hanby, *Augustine and Modernity*, 195, 199.

carnation offers us then is not exactly more "knowledge" about God (in the common modern sense of knowledge as "information"), and certainly no ability to envision the divine unity yet. It rather offers us, in scripture and through the teaching and practice of the church, proper glimpses of holy teaching for our particular moment in the working out of salvation. The incarnation provides *scientia* of God on the way to eschatological *sapientia*, to use the language of *De Trinitate* — that is, "knowledge" appropriate to our current place in the divine economy, on the way to "wisdom" for which we hold out faith, but cannot possess yet. To use the language of an earlier work of Augustine, the incarnation gives to humanity "a sort of art," or "a system of life," that does offer right glimpses of knowledge of the Father given through Christ in the delight of the Spirit.[35] The life of the church mediates these glimpses through its catechetical and liturgical practices, from now until Christ is head of the body at the judgment. To put it colloquially, if you want analogies to the Trinity, don't look at the Trinity — you cannot now "see" the divine nature anyway. The way to arrive at such knowledge, insofar as is appropriate among creatures, is through the church's efforts to look upon Christ, which purge wrong images of God, invite new ones, and bear us from our current piecemeal and necessarily incomplete knowledge to the promised vision of God at the end, which we cannot now fathom but look forward to in faith.

The important point for us here is how crucial scripture is to Ayres's and Barnes's description of Augustine's christology, and so of his trinitarian theology. Scripture offers to those of us *in via* the limited amount of knowledge *(scientia)* of God that is possible on the way to the wisdom *(sapientia)* we receive in the eschaton. Scripture, with its unending panoply of images, is God's way of offering *scientia* to us that is sufficient for our growth toward the beatific vision. In Augustine's own words, Christians are to treat the Bible as "the face of God for now."[36] As Augustine makes abundantly clear throughout his work, the word "scripture" does not refer to a book in the hand of an

---

35. The language is from the early Epistle 11, which both Ayres and Barnes use to show that Augustine's work was rigorously christological throughout his career, from that early epistle to *De Trinitate*'s thirteenth book, written quite late. See Ayres, "'Remember That You Are Catholic'," cited in note 30 above, and Barnes, "Rereading Augustine's Theology of the Trinity," *Journal of Theological Studies* 44 (1993): 185-95.

36. Ayres does not use this quote from Augustine here, but rather in his article with Stephen Fowl criticizing the Pontifical Biblical Commission's 1991 document on exegesis, "(Mis)Reading the Face of God: *The Interpretation of the Bible in the Church*," *Theological Studies* 60 (1999): 513-28. For that document see Pontifical Biblical Commission, "The Interpretation of the Bible in the Church," *Origins* 23, no. 29 (1994): 497-524.

individual Christian, but rather to the quite communal process of slowly learning to read well, overseen by more practiced readers in the school for reading that is the church. Scripture is integral to the process of the church's growth from *scientia* to sapientia, from Christ as way to Christ as goal. For it is that which properly funds the human will to continue the pilgrimage from here to there. This is why the *Enarrationes* is such a rigorously christological work. Augustine is leading a pilgrimage of people from Christ's human to his divine nature, and the unending diversity of images in the Psalter are all part of the providential economy by which his flock can grow from the one to the other.

## Augustine's Christological Approach to the Psalms

But how could a commentary on the Psalter possibly be a christological work? Or to ask the question with roots more deeply sunk into the language of our own time and place: how is a christological approach to the Psalms defensible as anything other than dishonest *eisegesis?* Because of one of the most important instances of inner-biblical textuality in the Christian scriptures: the New Testament's use of the psalms.[37] At some of its most crucial junctures, the New Testament displays its fundamentally Jewish nature by its frequent attention to Israel's Psalter. To conduct christological debate, Psalms 2, 109 (our 110), and 117 (118)[38] are absolutely fundamental.[39] A line from the latter, "blessed is he who comes in the name of the Lord," is crucial in the Gos-

37. On intertextuality see Richard Hays, *Echoes of Scripture in the Letters of Paul* (New Haven: Yale University Press, 1991).

38. For the purposes of this study we will use Augustine's own numeration of the Psalms. His Psalm 2 and ours are the same, but his Psalm 68 is our 69 and his Psalm 117 is our Psalm 118. The numerical disjunction begins with Psalm 9, which for Augustine is a combination of our 9 and 10. It ends with Augustine's Psalms 146 and 147, which combine to form our Psalm 147. So roughly from Psalm 9 through Psalm 146 Augustine's numeration is one behind ours.

39. Psalm 2 includes the lines "You are my Son, today I have begotten you," and "ask of me and I will make the nations your heritage." This psalm is mentioned at Jesus' baptism scene (Mark 1:11; Luke 3:22), and also at Acts 13:33; Hebrews 1:5 and 5:5; and Revelation 2:26-27.

Psalm 109 is the Old Testament passage most oft-quoted in the New Testament: "The Lord said to my Lord, sit at my right hand, as I make your enemies a footstool for your feet," quoted or alluded to at Matthew 22:44 and 26:64; Mark 12:36; 14:62; 16:19; Luke 20:42-43; 22:69; Acts 2:34-35; 1 Corinthians 15:25; Ephesians 1:20; Colossians 3:1; Hebrews 1:3, 13; 8:1; 10:12-13; 12:2; among other places.

Psalm 117 includes the christologically crucial line, "The stone that the builders rejected has become the chief cornerstone. This is the Lord's doing; it is marvelous in our eyes," cited at Matthew 21:42; 23:39; Mark 12:10-11; Luke 19:38; 20:17; Acts 4:11; and 1 Peter 2:7.

pels' description of Jesus' triumphal entry.[40] Psalm 68 (69) is vital to the New Testament's description of Jesus' clash with his fellow Jews during his temple demonstration.[41] Psalms 15 (16), "you will not abandon me to the grave," and 67 (68), "you ascended on high," are key for the New Testament church's attempts to come to grips theologically with Jesus' work among them.[42] The risen Christ in Luke tells his disciples that everything written about him in "the law, the prophets, *and the Psalms*" had to be fulfilled (24:44). This list could be expanded indefinitely — the Psalter competes with Isaiah as the most oft-cited books of Israel's scripture in the New Testament. The reason is obvious: what more fundamental source for Jewish prayer — that is, commerce between God and humanity — was or is there, than the Psalter? And once Christians came to see Jesus as the greatest instantiation of the complementary movements of divine *kenosis* and human *theosis* in his own person,[43] it is not at all surprising that when these now-Christian Jews looked anew at their Psalters, they saw him there throughout. That Christians from their earliest days have seen the Psalter as a basic grammar with which to think, speak, and most importantly, to praise christologically is not at all surprising, given our Jewish provenance. As Augustine exegetes the entire Psalter christologically, he continues and extends a venerable Jewish practice stitched into the church's very fabric, canonized in the New Testament, and continued for centuries before and after him. Our modern incredulity at Augustine's psalm hermeneutic would be matched by similar befuddlement from him at our inability to allow for such exegetical practice.

### Augustine's Actual Exegesis of the Psalms

We should begin with Augustine's exegesis of the Psalm 21 (our 22), for several reasons. First, it played a key role in the earliest Christian attempts to

40. Cited at Matthew 21:9; Mark 11:9; Luke 13:35; and John 12:13.

41. "Zeal for your house has consumed me, the insults of those who insult you have fallen on me" at John 2:17 and Romans 15:3.

Another portion of the Psalm describes the vinegar given to a sufferer to drink, used at Matthew 27:48; Mark 15:36; John 19:28-29; Romans 11:9-10; and "may his place be deserted, let there be no one to dwell in it" at Acts 1:20.

42. Psalm 15 has the line "You do not give me up to Sheol, or let your faithful one see the Pit," used at Acts 2:25-31; 13:35. Psalm 67 includes the majestic words, "You ascended on high, leading captives in your train and receiving gifts from people," with noteworthy shifts from second person to third person and from receiving to giving gifts in Ephesians 4:8-10.

43. I use the language of *kenosis* and *theosis* throughout this study because I agree with Babcock's argument that it fittingly describes Augustine's christology.

grapple with the events of Jesus' death and resurrection.[44] Second, it may be the most important psalm of all for Augustine's christological and exegetical work. He returns to it frequently as a hermeneutical touchstone throughout the *Enarrationes*. Third, it has caused modern interpreters no small amount of interpretive difficulty, as it once did for ancient ones.[45] Precisely what could it mean that Jesus protests his abandonment by God at the moment of the completion of his mission and the narrative climax of the Gospels? What could this hopeless cry from the cross possibly add to Christian understanding of the nature and work of Jesus? Attending to this psalm will not only give us a grasp of Augustine's overall hermeneutic, it should also shed light on an ancient and modern exegetical quandary.

The problems for Christians interpreting this psalm may indeed have vexed interpreters before and long after Augustine, but he himself did not share their level of frustration. He has a christological solution to this puzzle; or perhaps we should say a christological compass to navigate this mystery. What should have been an exegetical difficulty — the imputation of divine abandonment to Jesus — becomes for Augustine a hermeneutical possibility so fundamental he returns to it throughout the *Enarrationes*. This, we should say, demonstrates the inaccuracy of the standard portrait of allegory as a trick for covering up doctrinal difficulty in scripture, as in the Greeks' allegorical efforts to make Homer edifying. Allegory is often taken to be a sort of exegetical fig leaf meant to allow Jews and Christians to ignore the particular textual difficulties that may compete with their already held views of God and the world. Whatever truth there may be to this view elsewhere in other patris-

---

44. See Matthew 27:35, 43, 46; Mark 15:24, 29, 34; Luke 23:34-35; John 19:24; Hebrews 2:12.

45. This is the case at least for those interpreters interested in the metaphysical questions around Jesus' divinity. For a taste of modern exegetical debate see Gérard Rossé's *The Cry of Jesus on the Cross: A Biblical and Theological Study,* trans. S. Wentworth (New York: Paulist, 1987), who argues against older, more "conservative" efforts to avoid suggestion of any ultimate divide between Father and Son by noting Psalm 22's concluding note of praise, effectively evading the difficulty of the "cry of dereliction."

Today one must turn to theologians, rather than biblical scholars, for attention to metaphysical difficulties raised by this verse. Even though they both seek to revise the church's traditional vision of divine immutability in light of biblical passages like these, both Jürgen Moltmann and Hans Urs von Balthasar suggest Jesus is actually nearest to God in his cry of dereliction than at any other time. While Augustine would disagree with them on metaphysical issues, we should recognize theirs as important efforts to make theological sense of the difficult philosophical issues raised by the scriptural narrative. Moltmann's reflections come in *The Trinity and the Kingdom: The Doctrine of God,* trans. Margaret Kohl (Minneapolis: Fortress, 1993), and Balthasar's in *Mysterium Paschale,* trans. Aidan Nichols, OP (Grand Rapids: Eerdmans, 1990).

tic literature, the *Enarrationes* demonstrate that evasion of difficult scriptural texts is not a goal of Augustine's own figurative reading of scripture. Far from using allegory to evade an awkward scriptural text that hinders his dogmatic teaching, Augustine makes more (and more creative) use of this psalm than any other text in the *Enarrationes*.[46]

### Psalm 21:2-3 in Augustine's Latin version

My God, my God, why have you forsaken me?
The tale of my sins leaves me far from salvation.
O my God, I will cry to you all day, and you will not listen to me,
And in the night, but you will not collude with my foolishness.[47]

Augustine closes off one exegetical possibility without hesitation: "God had not abandoned him, since he himself was God." Augustine needs only marshal evidence from one New Testament passage for this obvious conclusion, the prologue of John: "the Word was God," and "was made flesh, and dwelt among us." Scripture's own letter announces that Christ is God incarnate among us. It naturally follows to ask, with regard to the "sins" of 21:2b that Christ implicitly confessed by praying 21:2a, "what sins could these be," when Christ had none? As 1 Peter 2:22 makes clear, "he committed no sin, nor was any guile found on his lips." The note of despair of 21:3 and the Gospels' depiction of Jesus' anguish in Gethsemane also cannot then be taken at face value. For, Augustine writes, "a soldier is not braver than the commander-in-chief," and one such soldier in scripture — Paul — professes his total lack of fear of death (Philippians 1:23). "If Paul craves death in order to be with Christ, can Christ himself fear it?" Elsewhere Augustine uses the example of post-biblical martyrs. If so many ordinary believers have willingly gone to horrible deaths without complaint, could Christ, whom they emulate, have been frightened at the prospect? Notice what Augustine does *not* say here. He does not say it is unfitting or unbecoming to think of an incarnate deity suffering. He simply says it is not *true* that Jesus was God-forsaken, a sinner, afraid. And he bases this claim on the New Testament evidence and on observation of faithful lives in the church.

Why then does Jesus quote this psalm with his dying breath, if it does not, indeed *cannot*, literally describe Jesus' own psychological state, or metaphysical relationship to God, or religious standing before God? First, he did so to offer

46. Augustine refers to this verse dozens of times in the *Enarrationes*. These are not normally isolated references but usually include some extended exegesis, normally focused around the apparent problem of the divine abandonment of Jesus.
47. *EP* I, 229.

later readers of scripture a hermeneutical cue: "he was somehow trying to catch our attention, to make us understand, 'this psalm is written about me.'" Jesus offers this bit of self-referential exegesis so that later biblical readers would go and read likewise. Second, and far more importantly, Jesus was speaking not on his own behalf, but on "ours."[48] "What other reason was this said than that we were there, for what other reason than that Christ's body is the Church?" Augustine continues, "beyond doubt, he was speaking of me, of you, of him over there, of her, for he was acting as his own body, the Church." It is *our* God-forsakenness, our fear, our sin, and not any of his own, that Christ is representing on our behalf before God. Or better: Christ has made humanity's God-forsakenness, fear, and sin, *his*, and simultaneously has made divine Sonship, assent to the Father's will, and righteousness, *ours*. Again, Augustine: "how could he say 'the tale of my sins,' except because he himself intercedes for our sins, and has made our sins his own, in order to make his righteousness ours?"

We have here a prime instance of why Augustine's christology is so often ignored by historians. It lacks technical terms or philosophical sophistication. And it sounds so pious! Yet something interesting and important is going on here. As Babcock, Cameron, and Ayres describe so well, we have here an essentially "dramatic" christology, as Christ represents human sin and teaches humanity to represent his righteousness. Continuing the metaphor of "drama," it is tempting to say Christ "plays the role" of the sinner, inviting the sinner to play the role of divine Sonship. Lest we be tempted to make soteriology so extrinsic a thing as an ancient actor's role, we should note the essentially organic connection indicated by the corporal metaphor of the "body." Head and body are inseparable, so that even if a sin is not, properly speaking, the "head's" sin, it can be spoken of as such because of the head's inseparability from the members.[49] Finally, we should note the sacerdotal

48. The first-person plural language is meant not so much to be pious as to reflect Augustine's own theological stance that all of humanity is represented in Christ's person. It is hard to speak of the fathers' theology at all without using first-person plural pronouns.

49. This seems to me the most striking Augustinian parallel with Cyril of Alexandria's christology. For Cyril, though we cannot properly speak of God suffering, and though the divine nature of Christ cannot have suffered and died, we can, because of the unimaginable unity of the two natures into one, speak the unspeakable, and say that God suffered. To say simply and without qualification that God suffers is to collapse into precisely the sort of mythical schemes loved by modern thinkers after Hegel, in ways not owing to scripture or traditional Christian thought. To say *how* God suffers in Christ in a way that indicates its absurdity absent the union of the two natures is to speak with a properly Christian grammar. See Cyril's *On the Unity of Christ*, trans. John A. McGuckin (Crestwood, NY: St. Vladimir, 1995). For a marvelous recent defense of divine immutability see David B. Hart, "No Shadow of Turning: On Divine Impassibility," *Pro Ecclesia* 11 (2002): 184-206.

connotation of Christ's prayer. The high priest of the New Testament letters "intercedes" for us and *mediates* the exchange of divine righteousness for human wickedness (Romans 8; Hebrews 8–10). Augustine has here made sense of the words on the biblical page with what we might call an essentially *representational christology* — in which Christ represents humanity before God, and divinity before humans. That word, "representational," or perhaps more strongly and biblically, "mediatorial," should be taken to include all these dramatic, corporal, and priestly connotations.

Christ does not merely represent us before God in any way that would suggest a caricatured Reformation view of imputed righteousness — the unmerited gift of something that remains not "ours."[50] In Augustine's soteriology, Christ actually makes people righteous.[51] Or to focus on the verbs in Augustine's actual use — Christ not only "represents" us, he also "transfigures" us. We can see this with a glance at another psalm verse quoted by Jesus from the cross in Luke's Gospel. In Augustine's translation of Psalm 30:

### Psalm 30:6 for Augustine

"Into your hands I commit my spirit.
You have redeemed me, Lord God of truth."

Augustine has this verse in mind from the beginning of this *enarratio,* the first verse of which for him bears the superscription: "to the end, for David himself, an ecstasy." What could "the end" be, for Christians, other than Christ, "the end of the law" in Romans 10:4? And who is David, but the king whom the New Testament works so hard to show is the ancestor of Jesus? And what is an "ecstasy" but being outside one's mind, "beside ourselves for God, in our right mind for you" as again Paul articulates? (2 Corinthians 5:13-14). Augustine interprets the psalm title, via these lexical links to the New Testament, as a reference to the incarnation. Augustine, as a contemplative, would like

---

50. Especially as described in second-generation Reformers more than Luther or Calvin themselves. The recent Finnish school of Luther scholarship, attending in depth to such texts as *The Freedom of the Christian,* has shown the deeply Augustinian strain in Luther that makes it possible to speak of Lutheran *theosis*. See Robert Jenson and Carl Braaten, eds., *Union with Christ: The New Finnish Interpretation of Luther* (Grand Rapids: Eerdmans, 1998). Luther himself also never lost a love for allegorical exegesis that he learned as an Augustinian monk — a love Calvin never had. For a current-day Lutheran proponent of allegory see Jenson, "The Bible and the Trinity," *Pro Ecclesia* 11, no. 3 (2002): 329-39, and his more recent commentary *Song of Songs* in *Interpretation* (Louisville: Westminster/John Knox, 2005).

51. This is important to remember even in the Pelagian controversy. See Hanby's noteworthy repositioning of that latter controversy in *Augustine and Modernity,* 72-133.

nothing more than to gaze upon the mysteries of God to his own unending delight, yet the "charity of Christ compels him" to descend, and speak of these mysteries to people who cannot so easily understand them. The parallel of this *kenotic* movement to the incarnation is unmistakable, and Augustine makes sure it is so by referring to Philippians 2:6-7. There is a fundamentally incarnational shape to Augustine's allegory throughout the *Enarrationes,* one not limited to the Logos's descent among us, but one that can be imitated by preachers (or contemplatives-turned-preacher) and all Christians in their love for others. Because this incarnational motion is the central motif at the heart of the Bible, Augustine sees it everywhere, in the smallest of details and in the most remote of biblical hinterlands.

These links to the New Testament, that seem so abstract to modern eyes, are fundamental to Augustine's exegesis of Psalm 30:5. *Kenosis* is scripture's fundamental motion, whether from the *Logos* to creation, contemplative preachers to unruly congregations, or one Christian to another. These derivative *kenoses* reflect the divine *Kenosis* at the heart of things. And it is no imposition to find this movement in this psalm when Christ himself cited this place in scripture at the nadir of his own abasement. Biblical interpreters in all ages have had to make sense of the conflicting reports of Jesus' last words and do so in their own ways: historical critics as evidence of varying sources or differing narrative purposes, Christians during Holy Week as seven different topics for sermons or even levels of contemplative ascent. Augustine makes sense of the gulf between Mark and Luke, and their use of Psalm 21:2 and 30:6, as indicative of the *kenosis* and *theosis* of Philippians 2, and indeed, for him, of the whole Bible. "He who deigned to assume the form of a slave, and within that form to clothe us with himself, he who did not disdain to take us up into himself, did not disdain either to transfigure us into himself [*transfigurare nos in se*], or to speak our words, so that we in our turn might speak in his."[52] Augustine's Christ does not merely represent a guilty humanity before a terrible throne of judgment, he also transfigures humanity into his divinity. This transfiguration is not a "change," for humans remain human, their divinity always derivative, at every moment a gift, but it is indeed "theirs." "This is the wonderful exchange, the divine business deal,[53] the transaction effected in this world by the heavenly dealer. He came to receive insults and give honors, he came to drain the cup of suffering and give salva-

52. *EP* I, Exposition on Psalm 30 (2), 322ff.

53. This is one of the few inelegant English renderings by translator Maria Boulding, O.S.B. The Latin is *admirabile commercium.* Perhaps she is trying to get at the quotidian nature of the word *commercium* as the sort of thing conducted every day in the streets, rather than any more esoteric philosophical notion.

tion, he came to undergo death and give life."[54] Augustine continues to support this christological reading by extending the logic of Paul's metaphor of the church as the body of Christ: "the Head is he who is the savior of his body and has already ascended into heaven; but the body is the Church, toiling on earth." The link between the head and the body, the "neck" (shall we say?), is "the bond of charity, so close a link that Head and body speak as one." Augustine continues to knead this metaphor like dough with reference to a favorite verse, Acts 9:4: "Saul, Saul, why are you persecuting *me?*" The Christ of Saul's vision does not protest against the persecution of his saints or his servants, but against "me." Augustine writes that this is tantamount to one's tongue crying out that one's foot is being stepped on. The tongue complains on behalf of the foot, just as Christ, himself unassailable now in heaven, protests on behalf of his members still here on earth, indicating a link so close between them he can refer to them as "me."

Augustine's endeavor to offer a consistent, christological exegesis of the Psalter could be read as a constant oscillation between the cry of dereliction of Psalm 21:2 and the gentle release of spirit of Psalm 30:6. In both cases Christ speaks and acts *representationally,* so that later readers and followers will notice themselves in the story and will pray and confess accordingly. And in both Christ speaks and acts *transfiguratively,* so that those who speak these words and imitate these actions will themselves be changed into Christ. The simultaneous *kenotic* and *theotic* movement of the incarnation is the red thread that guides Augustine through all of scripture and the Christian life. It allows him to make sense of the stunning array of images in the Psalter, its byzantine twists and turns in subject and tense, its display of the full gamut of human emotion, its piecemeal accounts of Israel's history, all included in Israel's hymnal. Augustine takes each of these strands of thought in the Psalter as a means to illumine something about Christ's taking of human God-forsakenness and giving of divine righteousness. Augustine believes this biblical hermeneutic is enabled, and indeed mandated by Jesus' own exegesis of the Psalter. How could those who are "in Christ," indeed who are joined to him through charity more strongly than the parts of a body, read otherwise than in the manner of their head?

We are beginning to see the particular rules that govern Augustine's reading of the psalms. Christ's own exegetical practice at the crucial moment of his *kenosis* directs his church in how to continue to read the Psalter. Yet this is not an extrinsic instruction for others to emulate or not. This is the teaching of the head of the body of which Christians are members, the mediator be-

---

54. *EP* I, 323.

tween human beings and God, the site of the *admirabile commercium* that represents us in order to transfigure us. Christian reading habits are then a product of Christians' being taken up into the life of God through Christ and deified. It is no accident that Augustine turns so easily from christology to ecclesiology in the course of each of the expositions we have mentioned so far. Psalm 21 itself eventually turns to a note of praise — a promise that the ends of the earth will see this suffering Lord and turn to him (21:28). As Augustine comments on the line, "all the ends of the earth will be reminded and turn to the Lord," he acerbically asks, "What have you to say to me, you heretic? That it was not the ransom-price of the whole world? That Africa alone was redeemed?"[55] How could the Donatists limit the Lord's largesse to only part of the world, when the Psalter's quite literal promise is for an extension of God's kingdom to the ends of the earth? Augustine observes the movement of Psalm 21 from lament to global praise, and expects the limbs connected to this head to follow this movement. The Donatists deserve rebuke for severing themselves from this head, from this kenotic and universally laudatory exchange. That is, for an inability to see *themselves* in the psalms, and to act accordingly. Even more impressively, in a later comment on Psalm 30:12, "those who saw me fled outside, away from me," Augustine writes, "the prophets spoke more clearly about the Church than about Christ"![56] Scripture is so clear about the universal reach of the kingdom precisely because even heretics like the Donatists would not dispute Christ's headship, and so would only dare go after his body, to sever it. Foreseeing this danger, the Spirit directed scripture's absolute clarity about the nature of the church, and left Christ more obscurely prefigured.[57] If we can glance past the polemic for a moment, we can see the key point: Augustine is astonished that those once joined to the body, being transfigured to the head, could wish to be severed from its unity. Those being represented and transfigured in Christ, joined to both head and other members by charity, are learning to read like Christ. Augustine caps this

---

55. *EP* I, 238.

56. *EP* I, 341.

57. In my seminary training at a Protestant institution I learned of the significance of the Donatist controversy for church teaching about grace: the holiness of the sacrament depends on the action of God, and not on the character of the priest *(ex opere operato)*. While this is indeed an important conclusion of Augustine's polemic against the Donatists, he mentions this criticism of his opponents quite rarely in the *Enarrationes*. Instead, his claim that the church must be spread throughout the world to reflect the global reign of the Lord described in the Psalter appears much more frequently — and appeared in my seminary courses not at all! John Henry Newman noted the importance of the *Enarrationes* in his conversion, since Augustine's logic there worked in favor of the Roman Catholic Church over against Protestant "branch" theories of ecclesial unity, held to by Newman's Anglicanism.

hermeneutical argument with a classic *de maiore ad minorem* move: if Christians are willing to hold that there are two in Christ, divine and human, how much more ought they be willing to believe that two speak in one voice in the Psalter?

## The Breadth of Augustine's Argument for Allegory in the *Enarrationes*

One of the reasons allegory rings so oddly in modern ears is that we hear it performed so seldom. All of our historicist instincts inveigh against it immediately, and it dies under a hailstorm of either faint praise ("clever," "ingenious") or of patronizing dismissal ("fanciful," "absurd"). But part of the effect of reading such a great swath of exegetical material as the *Enarrationes* is the fundamental logic of christological allegory starts to seem less foreign, more familiar. Its use begins to feel less like a verbal trick of some sort, and more like a discipline for reading, which like any other has rules, strictures for identifying a misstep, and means to interpret exegetical success.[58] It is important for our purposes to show the breadth of biblical ground on which Augustine believes he stands as he reads this way in order to get a sense of the full flavor of his exegesis.

We have already seen a key verse undergirding the *totus Christus* in Acts 9:4, in which the risen Lord identifies himself with the persecuted church in his appearance to Saul. Another to which Augustine returns with great frequency is the parable of judgment in Matthew 25. This fits his purposes particularly well, since there the incredulity of both the sheep and the goats is

---

58. I take the observation that an intellectual tradition's integrity depends on being able to show when a mistake has been made from Rowan Williams in "The Discipline of Scripture," in *On Christian Theology* (Oxford: Blackwell, 2002), 44-59. It may be simply a philosophical truism, however.

I fear that the whole of this article, uncharacteristically for Williams, actually obscures matters more than it clarifies them. He argues that a text's literal sense might fruitfully be thought of as its "eschatological" sense, and that the church's search for it ought then to incorporate a posture of eschatological reserve. The patristic interpreters of scripture about whom Williams writes so lovingly elsewhere would have found this observation quite odd. Instead we should distinguish between various kinds of texts and their literal senses. Some may well be spoken of as literally indeterminate until the eschaton. Quite a few others however — not least those that, say, ascribe divinity to Jesus — have a quite discernible literal sense *now*. Further, if the patristic adage is true that the allegorical sense of a text rests on the foundation of scripture's overall literal meaning, then if we cannot find *any* text's literal sense until the eschaton, we should despair of reading scripture altogether.

matched by vehemence on the part of the king: "whatever you did for the least of these, you did for me" (Matthew 25:40). Another touchstone text is Isaiah 61:10, in which the scriptural speaker changes genders so fast, from bridegroom to bride, that Augustine can interpret the two as the same person: "'The Lord has arrayed me like a bridegroom adorned with his wreath, or a bride decked with her jewels.' He calls himself bridegroom and he calls himself bride: how can he say he is both bridegroom and bride, except because they will be two in one flesh?"[59] This is no mere "proof-text," as we moderns are wont derisively to say.[60] It is an observation rooted in a deeply scriptural logic of the joining of God to Israel, Christ to church, imaged among humans as a union after which no subsequent division can be imagined, a bodily union so close we can no longer tell where one stops and the other starts — a marital and sexual union. Jesus himself cites Genesis as he affirms that husband and wife "will be two in one flesh, so they are two no longer, but one flesh" (Matthew 19:5). And Paul applies this "great mystery" to "Christ and the Church" in Ephesians 5:31-32.[61] Ancient Christian interpreters long before and after Augustine continued to find this matrimonial metaphor in such places as the Song of Songs and Psalm 18. Augustine finds it only natural that the members of the church, whose wedding to Christ makes them into his members, should learn to think like their *own* head, to speak like their *own* tongue.

Another source of scriptural support for Augustine's psalm hermeneutic is almost too obvious to mention: Paul's own use of the metaphor of a body to speak of the church's relationship to (might we even say identity with?) Christ in such places as 1 Corinthians 12:12ff., Romans 12:4ff., Colossians 1:18, Ephesians 4:25 and 5:30, and many more. When Paul introduces his metaphor in 1 Corinthians 12:12 by saying "as a body is a unit and has many members, and

59. *EP*, I, 324.

60. I am told a helpful personal anecdote by Dr. Warren Smith of his teacher, Professor Rowan Greer of Yale, who has done important work on the distinction between Antiochene and Alexandrian biblical exegesis in the early church. In response to a claim that these two were really dramatically different, Greer replied, "What's the difference? They're both just 'proof-texting'!"

This description is often used to deride the New Testament's or the early church's citations of Old Testament texts in support of specifically Christian belief. Yet it seems to do more rhetorical (in a weak sense) work than anything else. What is the function of any citation of any biblical text in any argument, other than to "prove" something with a "text"? What else do scholars and religious people alike do with their scriptural materials? If one wishes to say that a citation is poorly used, or lacks sophistication, one can say as much without resorting to a term that obfuscates as much as it clarifies.

61. Or his school. On the question of Pauline authorship see note 3 above.

yet all the members of the body, many though they be, are one body, so too is Christ," Augustine notes that "he did not say, 'so too are Christ's members.' He called the whole entity he had spoken about, 'Christ.'"[62] Augustine is here simply laying out the logic of Paul's metaphor by his identification of Christ and church: neither now can speak nor act nor even *be* without the other. He often returns to a verse that has troubled interpreters since the Reformation, Colossians 1:24, "that I may fill up what is lacking to the sufferings of Christ."[63] Reformed readers of Paul have had to find some (non-allegorical!) explanation for the suggestion that Christ's redemptive work is somehow incomplete, requiring later addition. Augustine seems untroubled. "If you are numbered among the members of Christ, whoever you are . . . then whatever you suffer . . . was lacking to the sufferings of Christ. . . . He suffered as our head, and he suffers in his members, which means in us."[64] Augustine is here commenting on a line from his Psalm 61, "Kill me, all of you," and puzzling over how all readers of the psalm could kill a single man, unless that "man" be spread out across historical time and space as the body that the church is. He notes that the saints of the old covenant are no less "organically connected" to the head than any other part of the body, and suggests that their preceding the head is no more unusual than Jacob's hand emerging from Rebekah's womb before his head, grasping his brother's heel! (Genesis 25:26). This last example is striking for its exegetical finesse in contrast to Augustine's exegesis of the Pauline corporal metaphor. That is to say, Augustine does not have to do much *work* to demonstrate that the church just is Christ's body, head and members. Paul has not only laid the foundation for such a view, he has constructed it completely. Augustine is simply displaying a Pauline logic throughout the *Enarrationes.* He is taking Paul's metaphor literally.[65]

---

62. *EP* I, 324.

63. We should note that Colossians can make a stronger case for Pauline authorship than Ephesians (see Hays, *The Moral Vision of the New Testament* [San Francisco: HarperCollins, 1996], 56). In any case it is not the man Paul who was canonized by the church, as though anything he said were scriptural and anything that can be shown not to have been authentically Pauline ought to be discounted. Rather, the church canonized the book of Ephesians, which remains scriptural whether pseudepigraphal or not, and as such must be reckoned with as scripture. Gary Anderson makes this point over against modern attempts to come to grips with the New Testament's sexism by distancing the historical Paul from the pseudepigrapha in his "Is Eve the Problem?" in *The Genesis of Perfection: Adam and Eve in Jewish and Christian Imagination* (Louisville: Westminster/John Knox, 2001), 100.

64. *EP* III, 204.

65. A rabbi first showed me the oddity inherent in keeping the terms "literal" and "metaphorical" in isolation from one another. In a lecture at Duke, he pointed to the command in Deuteronomy 6:8 to write the law on one's hands, and bind it upon the brow. Apparently the

Augustine draws on a number of other strands in Paul's thought. These are necessarily related to the central corporal metaphor, as all of Paul's theology is, yet they refract this theological insight a bit differently in different places in Paul's work. Commenting on another lament psalm, Psalm 70, with its cry in verses 10 and 11, "my enemies . . . say, God has forsaken him," Augustine returns to his claim that God could not forsake God. In this instance, he draws on a crucial soteriological passage in Paul's thought, 2 Corinthians 5:16-21: "Did God abandon him, though 'God was in Christ, reconciling the world to himself'?"[66] All biblical readers will have to agree that scripture attributes divine abandonment to the various stages of Christ's passion. The question then is over its purpose and ongoing significance. For Augustine, it was "our voice that cried out then, the voice of our old nature," taken up by Christ with the salvific intent of transforming it into praise. Commenting on Psalm 49:2, "His beauty shines forth from Zion, throughout all nations, beginning from Jerusalem," Augustine contrasts the hiddenness of Christ's divinity with his future open eschatological manifestation. He sounds a Pauline note, that Christ took the "likeness of sinful flesh" (Romans 8:3). This passage was heavily contested elsewhere in the church's history and in Augustine's own polemical career for its potential Docetic and Arian implications.[67] Augustine notes that the "likeness" refers not to Christ's flesh, which was certainly genuine and tangible, but to "his" sin, which Paul must mean is only a "likeness" because it is not truly his, but ours. Augustine continues, "if he took on himself the likeness of sinful flesh, why should he not also take to himself the likeness of a sinful voice?"[68] Again, *de maiore ad minorem*, if Christians can confess that Christ is somehow two ontologically, both divine and human, why should they stumble over the idea of him being two "representationally," as he speaks both for himself and for us? Augustine often refers to another key Pauline notion, that of the old humanity crucified with Christ in Romans 6:6: "our old humanity has been nailed to the cross with him." The preacher-theologian makes a rather pastoral argument as he com-

---

"literal" meaning of that text is a metaphor — think on the law with the mind, put it into practice with the hands. Yet orthodox Jews have put into effect a quite "literal" interpretation of these words in the form of phylacteries. Or is it "metaphorical," if the biblical author's intention was to offer a metaphor, now being put into place "metaphorically" by "literal" practice? Pretty soon the lines between the terms begin to blur.

66. *EP* III, 423.

67. A helpful summary of patristic interpretation of this verse appears in David Steinmetz's "Calvin and Patristic Exegesis," in his *Calvin in Context* (Oxford: Oxford University Press, 1995), 122-40.

68. *EP*, II, 384.

ments on Psalm 37:22's request, "O Lord my God, do not leave me." He asks, "if he does not forsake you when you believe in him, did the Father and the Son and the Holy Spirit, one holy God, abandon Christ? No, but Christ had taken the identity of the first human being to himself."[69] If God does not forsake poor sufferers now, could he have forsaken a poor sufferer who was . . . himself? Augustine reads the Psalter as one who is convinced Paul's soteriology is true: Christ takes sinful humanity to himself, and gives in exchange divine favor. The Psalter's dramatic depictions of divine and human abasement and ecstasy take on a specifically Pauline hue for Augustine, as they cannot but do for a reader convinced that what Paul says in scripture is true, and then goes and reads likewise throughout the Psalter.

Augustine's scriptural grounding for the *totus Christus* and the *admirabile commercium* is not limited to Paul. He draws broadly on several strands in the New Testament literature for support.[70] We have already seen his use of the story of Saul's conversion, of the judgment parable of the sheep and goats, and of the matrimonial imagery of the Old Testament. Jesus' comparison of his relationship to the disciples as that of a vine to its branches in John's "farewell discourse" shows a similarly organic, inclusive relationship to Paul's metaphor of head and members.[71] Augustine also finds the dynamic of the *commercium* in several prominent New Testament soteriological images, and frequently shifts his discussion of the *theotic* exchange into new keys as the New Testament directs. For example, in commenting on Psalm 40:2, "understand about the needy and poor man," Augustine's lexical imagination is drawn to Paul's description of the divine and human *commercium* in 2 Corinthians 8:9, "though he was rich he became poor so that by his poverty you might become rich." Augustine writes, "He is rich, because that is what he is, but poor, because that is what you were. His poverty is our wealth, just as his weakness is our strength, his foolishness our wisdom, his mortality our immortality."[72] The exchange between God and humanity in Christ and the church is here run through a register of wealth and poverty, following Paul's lead and the words of the Psalter. Elsewhere a brief discussion of the "generosity" of God leads to a "non-identical repetition"[73] of the theology of the

---

69. *EP*, II, 166.

70. I use the description of "strands" in the New Testament a bit more loosely than Hays in *Moral Vision*, for whom three are of paramount importance: community, cross, and new creation. I mean here merely significant storylines, or "persistent patterns of figuration" in the New Testament (to use Ayres's language that we discussed in the last chapter).

71. *EP*, I, 324.

72. *EP*, II, 226.

73. I find this description enormously felicitous. John Milbank borrowed it from Kierke-

*commercium.* He wonders how Psalm 55:10 can speak of God as "my" God, when there is no one over whom God is not God? Is this some needless repetition? Augustine replies, "He is most properly the God of those who love him, hold fast to him, possess him, worship him. . . . What magnificent generosity God has shown us, that we should be his, and he ours!"[74] A pious note of the psalm, objected to briefly on philosophical grounds, is made intelligible again by the *admirabile commercium,* and praise is only intensified. Augustine elsewhere offers a moving meditation on Psalm 103:2, "you have clothed yourself in confession and seemliness," to describe *kenosis* and incarnation in a key of beauty and ugliness. Why do souls like the psalmist's, and ours, seek beauty? We wish to be beautiful so that our beloved, who is "fair . . . beyond all the children of men," may love us and be pleased with us in return (Song of Songs 1:2; 5:9; 8:5). Yet we cannot please such a beloved one because of our deformity and ugliness in sin. So we must first confess our deformity, so that "he who formed you in the beginning will reform you." Yet we could do no such thing had not the fair one first become deformed, as Isaiah 53 records him doing: "there was no fair form or seemliness in him." The very ugliness and God-forsakenness of the cross even caused passersby to lament Christ's deformity. Philippians 2 guides Augustine's description of Christ's exchange of his beauty for our ugliness. Just as in that key Pauline passage, *kenosis* and deformity are not the end of the story. The end, both narratively and teleologically, is the transformation of ugliness into beauty, such that Ephesians can ask of us, "'Who is this who comes up from the wilderness, made white,' so lovely, so radiant, free from stain or wrinkle?" (5:25).[75] Augustine here begins with the psalmist's words about the action of clothing with confession and honor, and uses them to tell the entire story of Christ's *kenosis* and human *theosis,* drawing on the full range of scripture, in order to give direction and delight to his listening church. For Augustine, the pattern of *kenosis* and *theosis* is present throughout scripture's breadth and depth and so ought to be seen in its every detail by attentive interpreters.

Augustine elsewhere turns to Jesus' final promise in Matthew's Gospel, "Lo, I am with you even to the end of the ages," to show that "He would not have us speaking apart from him, any more than he wants to be apart from

---

gaard to speak of Christians' lives lived in imitation of the saints, yet it works just as well to describe biblical exegesis in both continuity with tradition and difference appropriate to new time and place. Milbank uses it in several places, for example in "Can a Gift Be Given? Prolegomena to a Future Trinitarian Metaphysic," in *Rethinking Metaphysics,* ed. L. G. Jones and Stephen Fowl (Oxford: Blackwell, 1995), 119-61.

74. *EP,* III, 96.

75. Psalm 103 (1) in *EP* V, 110-13.

us."[76] Christ's promise to be present to his evangelizing church is not merely a word of comfort, it is also a hermeneutical directive: "If he is with us, he speaks in us, speaks about our concerns, and speaks through us, because we also speak in him." In the words of the psalms, interpreted christologically, members of the church's body find a language with which to interpret their lives. This is *why* Christ struggled so in Gethsemane. He did not have to, for Paul did not fear death, the martyrs did not. Surely Christ was no less courageous than they. So the depiction of indecisiveness and fear must serve another purpose: to illuminate the struggles of those (like all of us) who are weak and suffer like Christ. Christ guides, in advance, the experience of Christians who struggle, like Paul, with the "different law in my members" (Romans 7:23). Augustine says, commenting on Psalm 41–42's interrogative refrain, "why are you sorrowful, o my soul?" that "even the Lord himself deigned to prefigure all who engage in a fight like this."[77] Human discouragement is natural, even despair at death's approach, yet Christ's illumination of such experience shows that Psalm 21's despair can be turned to Psalm 30's assent and trust. Here a christological reading pushes Augustine and the church to read individual portions of the Psalter in light of the entire biblical canon. Notes of despair remind us not only of our experience, but of other psalms whose hope and even jubilation we may not now remember. We are then appropriately reminded of the shape of the entire Psalter, which begins humbly enough in its recommendation of daily wisdom, plunges intermittently into deep despair, and ends in the jubilant strains of Psalms 147–150.[78]

We see here the heart of figural reading. What resemblance does Paul's life have to Jesus'? Or even more audacious: what resemblance does Augustine's life have to either one? Yet Paul speaks of his life in terms provided by Jesus' life: "I have been crucified with Christ" (Galatians 2:19). When exactly was Paul ever *crucified?* In Paul's conversion, in his struggles with his members (Romans 7), in his trials in ministry (2 Corinthians 11), and so on. These ex-

76. Psalm 56 in *EP*, III, 104.

77. *EP*, II, 262.

78. Gregory of Nyssa writes about the canonical shape of the Psalter itself as he follows the five divisions of the psalms and attends to their overall movements theologically. See Gregory's *Commentary on the Inscriptions of the Psalms,* trans. Casimir McCambley, OCSO (Brookline, MA: Hellenic, n.d.).

Augustine is more interested than Gregory in the more detailed questions of how to interpret each scrap of the Psalter christologically. Gregory's awareness of the overall shape of the Psalter is now mirrored by much of the Old Testament guild. See for example James L. Mays, *Psalms,* in the Interpretation commentary series (Louisville: Westminster/John Knox, 1994), 14-19.

periences are now read through the cross, which provides Christians' basic vocabulary for the language of struggle and conversion. As with Paul so too with Augustine. His own angst-filled years of decision and conversion, his worries as a bishop over heresy and schism, his grief at seeing the body of Christ torn asunder, are all spoken of with language from Christ's own passion. The differences between the three lives and times fade before what each of the latter two see as their profound similarities. Yet each remains rooted in its own historical particularity. Christological description, applied now to Paul, now to Augustine, jars its readers just a bit, until we remember the theology of the *totus Christus* that makes such descriptions possible. We should ask, "When was Paul ever crucified? Was he not beheaded?"[79] And then remember, "Oh yes, he is crucified in Christ, as all Christians are, figurally speaking." And no wonder, for they are members who belong organically to their head.

These similarities and differences between the lives of Jesus, Paul, and Augustine provide a nice example of the difficulty with the modern division between "allegory" and "typology." Usually this distinction is drawn to try and make room for the kind of biblical interpretation practiced within the Bible itself while excluding what smacks as "arbitrary" or "ahistorical" allegory, with its flight from historical particularity. In this case, all three figures — Jesus, Paul, and Augustine — are rooted in quite particular histories. Yet the latter two find words borrowed from another history — that of Jesus — which gives greater meaning to their lives than any other. So they borrow its language to inform themselves and others about the christoform patterns of their lives. Is this a typological comparison — rooted in historical particularity? Or is it an allegorical one — unmoored from history? Clearly both — as long as "allegory" is not being used in a derogatory sense, but simply in its etymological root meaning of "another reading."[80]

79. It requires attentive readers to remember that Paul was not actually crucified — readers willing to ask questions about the text, to notice incongruities and wonder at them.

80. Jean Daniélou spent a career attacking allegory as a pagan and Jewish intrusion into biblical thinking and extolling typology as a more fittingly biblical hermeneutic, for example in *From Shadows to Reality: Studies in the Biblical Typology of the Fathers,* trans. W. Hibberd (London: Burns and Oates, 1960). G. W. H. Lampe and K. J. Woollcombe's book *Essays on Typology* (Naperville: Allenson, 1956) made the distinction stick for two generations of English-reading theologians. More recently and deftly R. R. Reno and John O'Keefe have distinguished "allegory" and "typology" as broad styles rather than carefully distinguished hermeneutical schools in their *Sanctified Vision: An Introduction to Early Christian Interpretation of the Bible* (Baltimore: Johns Hopkins University Press, 2005). For an important account that also blurs the distinction between the two see David Dawson's work, especially his *Christian Figural Reading and the Fashioning of Identity* (Berkeley: University of California, 2002).

Elsewhere, commenting on Psalm 53:4, "let the words I speak reach your ears," Augustine again returns to Psalm 21:1-2. He actually offers a long paraphrase of Christ's use of the Psalter there: "He means, 'even during the night I have cried to you, and you did not listen; yet your refusal to listen was not to compound my foolishness but rather to teach me wisdom, so that I might come to understand what I ought to be asking of you. Until then I had been asking for things that would perhaps have harmed me to be asking of you.'"[81] That's quite a paraphrase! Augustine's use of Christ's prayer of the psalm has shifted to a discussion of the proper subject of prayer, and a homiletical lesson not to pray for riches, but for wisdom. For Augustine, Christians look to scripture for wisdom on how to live with reference to Christ. The church's perennial experience, the words on the page, and christology all converge in every act of exegesis. As they do also, of course, in prayer.

I am drawn here to an Irenaean *iconic* image as a way to explain Augustine's christological hermeneutic. The church looks to scripture for wisdom in how to live amidst its daily struggles, as Augustine did in his own battles with the Donatists. As the church looks to the particular words of Israel's scripture, these are like so many tesserae of a mosaic that can be arranged in a remarkable variety of patterns. The heretics can arrange the tesserae in awful ways, to form the image of a dog or a fox, disgusting images that mock the exegetical task and leave the church directionless. Or, the pieces can be arranged to form the image of the king — their proper subject. The christological import of Irenaeus's image is unmistakable, and the iconic, *optic* nature of the image is just as important. As Christians look to the myriad images in the Old Testament they see the bewildering array of options for their arrangement to depict whatever manner of heresies, and decide instead to arrange the pieces to depict their king. Now this royal depiction will vary depending on the particular pieces at hand, so the image will always be slightly different from one depiction to the next, as even the narrowly restrictive canons of iconography have to allow room for variation in artists' skill and time in history. Yet all viewers will recognize the king. If they cannot, it is a bad icon.[82] To return to an audial, choral key: the words of scripture are as

---

81. *EP*, III, 47.

82. The Irenaean image comes from his discourse against the Gnostics in *Against Heresies* I.8.1-2, English translation by Robert Grant, *Irenaeus of Lyons* (London: Routledge, 1997), 65-66. Orthodoxy has long seen its icons as themselves quite complex exegeses of scripture, done by trained monks for the sake of liturgical performance. See Leonid Ouspensky and Vladimir Lossky, *The Meaning of Icons* (Crestwood, NY: St. Vladimir, 1983). Verna Harrison has similarly made this explicit in her "Word as Icon in Greek Patristic Theology," *Sobornost* 10, no. 1 (1988): 38-49.

diffuse, as full of possibility, as the great range of notes that an instrument may play.[83] An expectant audience wishes to hear the music of the gospel every time it gathers, though of course with slight variation each time. The musician has a great deal of flexibility in how she plays the gospel in any particular setting with attention to the specific audience. She and they both will necessarily be aware of discordant notes that jar instead of please because they do not belong to the song.[84] Likewise, *this* people to whom Augustine preaches has gathered to hear Christ speak from scripture to its particular life's circumstances. All three elements must be present — the people's particular circumstances, scripture, and Christ — for what else *is* exegesis but retracing the *kenotic* and *theotic* pattern of Christ's life among us, using these particular words on the page, for the sake of this particular gathering in its *Sitz im Leben?*

R. R. Reno has written compellingly about the temptation to "distance" that marks modern biblical exegesis, and modern forms of theological reflection and intellectual endeavor more generally.[85] Biblical hermeneutics has been fascinated with the problems of historical distance between current readers and the writers of scripture, trying ever more ingenious means to bridge, or leap across, the ditch between the historical record of scripture and contemporary theological reflection. Others note the great gulf between the thought of ancient writers and our own, insisting upon the irreducibility of this distance-causing difference. In either case, it is striking that these various "problems" that must be solved before any meaningful exegesis can take place all serve to keep the specifically moral and theological demands of the biblical

83. For a clear survey of recent theological use of the category of musical performance see Stephen Barton, "New Testament Interpretation as Performance," *Scottish Journal of Theology* 52 (1999): 179-208, and Nicholas Lash's article that we discussed in Chapter 1, "Performing the Scriptures," in his *Theology on the Way to Emmaus* (London: SCM, 1986), 37-46.

84. Compare Origen, ruminating on King David as a musician: "If a reader comes who has been instructed in God's music . . . he will produce a note of God's music, for he will have learned from God's music to keep good time, playing now upon the strings of the Law, now upon those of the Gospel in harmony with them, now upon those of the Prophets; and when the harmony of good sense is required he strikes the apostolic strings tuned to suit the foregoing, and, similarly, apostolic strings in harmony with those of the evangelists. For he knows that the whole Scripture is the one, perfect, harmonious instrument of God, blending different notes, for those who wish to learn, into one song of salvation, which stops and hinders all the working of an evil spirit, as the music of David laid to rest the evil spirit in Saul which was vexing him" (*The Philocalia of Origen*, trans. J. Armitage Robinson [Cambridge: Cambridge University Press, 1893], 43-44).

85. R. R. Reno, *In the Ruins of the Church: Sustaining Faith in an Age of Diminished Christianity* (Grand Rapids: Brazos, 2002).

text at a safe distance from our souls. And in truth this is the greatest problem we have with scripture. It is not the historical or metaphysical distance between us and the authors of scripture, it is a *spiritual* problem of a distance between our souls and God that we truly do not wish to see bridged. Distance is safe, undemanding, open to ironic evaluation or deconstructive play, but thankfully not a candidate to transform us in any significant way. Given Reno's insightful analysis, we can see anew the radical edge to Augustine's project. For here we have a radically *inclusive* form of biblical exegesis — one that draws Christ, the words on the page of scripture before us, and our souls ever closer. For example, commenting on one of the Psalter's many ascriptions of a Psalm "to David," Augustine writes, "Christ was present in David, but you who are well instructed in his school are used to understanding that Christ comprises head and body. You must therefore not assume that anything you hear spoken in reference to Christ himself is of no concern of yours. It does concern you, because you are members of Christ."[86] It is difficult, if not impossible, to imagine a contemporary academic expositor of scripture saying anything like the following: "Do not rubbish yourselves or despair of yourselves. You are human beings made in the image of God, and he who made you became human himself for your sake. . . . If you hold yourselves cheap in your earthly frailty, esteem yourselves precious by reason of the ransom paid for you."[87] No irony, safe distance, nor fear of piety there. Yet these sorts of comments are not mere emotivist sentiments, confidence-boosters, meant to lift up his hearers' "self-esteem."[88] They represent a profound reflection on the fundamental motif of the incarnation, in which

86. A comment on Psalm 143:1 in *EP* VI, 360-61.

87. On Psalm 32 in *EP*, I, 394.

88. Ellen Charry's project has been to show that doctrine was never conceived as removed from the goods of believers' lives until modernity. See her *By the Renewing of Your Minds: The Pastoral Function of Christian Doctrine* (Oxford: Oxford University Press, 1997), and "Is Christianity Good for Us?" in *Reclaiming Faith: Essays on Orthodoxy in the Episcopal Church and the Baltimore Declaration,* ed. Ephraim Radner and George Sumner (Grand Rapids: Eerdmans, 1993), 225-46. I worry about descriptions of Charry's that seem to render patristic thinking into the terms of modern psychological categories, as in her description of Paul's efforts to "uplift" gentiles' "self-esteem" (*By the Renewing of Your Minds,* 37). The first intention of scripture and the fathers is to tell the truth about God. Effects on the hearers, important as they are, must remain secondary. I doubt that Charry would disagree. It is difficult to talk about "experience" in anything other than corrupt terms. Perhaps the way to do so better rather than worse is to attend to the historical theologian's own psychological language as closely as possible. So when Charry describes Athanasius's efforts to "build the reader's . . . nobility by linking human *logismoi* with the divine *logos,*" the use of Athanasius's own terminology is preferable to talk of uplifting gentile "self-esteem" (90).

Christ "displayed your nature, to straighten you out."[89] Christ accepted the abasement of our God-forsakenness, to give us his divinity, and transform us back into the divine image. Augustine's biblical hermeneutic forecloses ironic distance from the biblical text because the incarnation does just that.

Earlier in this chapter we glanced at the recent history of Augustinian scholarship with regard to christology. Though thin in comparison with work in other areas, this portion of Augustiniana has filled out in recent years, with explorations of the proximity of Augustine's work to eastern visions of *theosis*, its dramatic nature and scriptural formation, and so on. No one, however, has written of Augustine's christology as validating, or even mandating, a certain sort of biblical hermeneutic. Yet this is precisely what Augustine thinks his christology does. Christ in his earthly life quoted scripture at crucial moments to demonstrate to his followers how now to read scripture. Those who are joined to him in the church as members of a body look to their head for direction in all things, not least in how to read scripture. Augustine often asks if we hold that there is present in Christ both humanity and divinity, as all Christians must, why should we not hold as a corollary that two may speak in one voice in scripture? As Augustine writes of Psalm 99, "Nothing but his own voice sounds sweetly in his ears. When we speak we delight him, as long as he speaks through us."[90] Scripture teaches us to speak like the one into whom we are being changed. Augustine often meditates at great length about what Christians learn from such texts as John 1:1-3 — to "contemplate the super-eminent divinity of God's Son, which transcends every nobility found among creatures." Yet Jesus often groans, prays, confesses, even "sins" according to the psalms. So "we shrink from ascribing these words to him, because our minds, so recently engaged in contemplation of his divinity, balk at descending to his humility." Attentive readers of scripture are in the place Augustine was in his self-remembrance in *Confessions* — desirous of glimpsing the vision of God, able to do so for a moment, but unable to sustain without an incarnate mediator.[91] Augustine the healer prescribes the following rem-

---

89. *EP,* I, 395.

90. *EP* V, 13.

91. For example, Augustine writes that he first heard most of the content of John 1 about the eternal and creative nature of the Word in the books of the Platonists. But he did not hear there that the Word became flesh and was crucified. He learned from philosophy God's grandeur but not God's mediatorial *kenosis.* See *Confessions* (VII.9.13). Or his description of his effort to glimpse the Beauty from which all lesser beauty comes: "in the flash of a trembling glance it attained to that which is. At that moment I saw your 'invisible nature understood through the things which are made.' But I did not possess the strength to keep my vision fixed. My weakness reasserted itself, and I returned to my customary condition" (*Confessions* VII.17.23). Later, after

edy: "when this happens our meditation needs to wake up and be more alert in faith, remembering that he whom we were just now contemplating in the form of God took upon himself the form of a servant." Without any change in himself, Christ "takes upon himself the creature who needs to be changed, making of us one single man with himself, head and body." Therefore,

> Let no one, on hearing these words [of scripture], maintain, "this is not said by Christ," or on the other hand, "I am not speaking in this text." Rather let each of us who know ourselves to be within Christ's body acknowledge both truths, that "Christ speaks here," and that "I speak here." Say nothing apart from him, as he says nothing apart from you.[92]

Both Christ and the Christian are always speaking in scripture. Sometimes they speak of human debasement, graciously assumed by Christ. Sometimes they speak of divine exaltation, granted to humans in Christ. Whichever it is, or whether scripture speaks of any state in between these two poles, scripture ever speaks in both a human and divine voice. For its purpose is to continue the incarnational work of transfiguring humanity into divinity.

Augustine's hermeneutical approach to the psalms answers one of the long-standing accusations still often levied against Christian figurative reading: that it is arbitrary. That there is no actual logic governing its exercise, but rather that it is a thinly veiled cipher, useful for the exegete to justify whatever exegetical flight of fancy she or he may wish to launch from the biblical text, or to validate whatever infliction of power or violence against another that she may wish.[93] This may indeed be the case in other areas of Christian intellectual history. Exegetical traditions can continue on long after their theoretical underpinnings have lost their cogency or been forgotten, and this hermeneutic is, like any

---

the fullness of his conversion, he and Monica attain to a glimpse of the beatific vision now grounded in the mediatorship of Christ. They cannot sustain it due to the weakness of the flesh, but the falling away is not now tragic as it was when Augustine tried to maintain a glimpse at divine Beauty not grounded in the flesh of Christ (IX.10.24), trans. Henry Chadwick (Oxford: Oxford University Press, 1991), 121, 127.

92. The preceding discussion is all from Augustine's work on Psalm 85 in *EP* IV, 220-21.

93. This is a common claim, but can be found explicitly in R. P. C. Hanson, *Allegory and Event: A Study of the Sources and Significance of Origen's Doctrine of Scripture*, 2nd ed. (Louisville: Westminster/John Knox, 2002), and in Gerald Bonner's "Augustine as Biblical Scholar," in *The Cambridge History of the Bible*, vol. 1: *From the Beginnings to Jerome*, ed. P. R. Ackroyd and C. F. Evans (Cambridge: Cambridge University Press, 1970). For a claim about the arbitrariness of the exegesis of Origen, to whom the entire ecclesial project of christological allegory is indebted, see Charles Scalise, "Allegorical Flights of Fancy: The Problem of Origen's Exegesis," *Greek Orthodox Theological Review* 32, no. 1 (1987): 69-88.

other, open to abuse. In Augustine's case, his many polemical contexts are to thank for his own repeated discussions of his own hermeneutic and for the ability with which he defends his exegesis. For the debates against the Manicheans, the Donatists, the Pelagians, and others against whom Augustine wrote (some of whom, like the Arians or the Apollinarians, may not have had a historical presence in Augustine's time) were all, either in part or in whole, exegetical debates. As such Augustine has continually to shore up the defenses around his exegetical apparatus. His arguments against each of these groups on creation, the church, grace and nature, and the doctrine of God are, above all, exegetical arguments. By keeping Augustine in pride of place in the church's memory we thereby enshrine his exegesis in the church's practice as well.[94]

We have seen in this chapter that Augustine defends his hermeneutic of the psalms with a fundamentally christological argument. Christ himself prays the psalms. Christians — those whose humanity is assumed in Christ's humanity and who are being transfigured into Christ's divinity — cannot do other than their head. The Psalter itself displays the great range between human deprivation and divine glory and all else in between, so humans pray each of these as part of the process of *theosis,* the ladder of ascent left in place for us in the descent of Christ's *kenosis.* For Augustine, these arguments add up to a complete certainty that Christians cannot but read the Psalter as he does. Christians must read the Old Testament, must pray the Psalter, and must do so through Christ.[95]

It is fitting to conclude with a question Augustine himself was always quick to ask: is it true? I ask this guided by two recent theologians with interests in figurative reading. First, Robert Jenson has shown that his great constructive project in his two-volume *Systematic Theology* is largely guided by just this question. He asks of the statement, "the Lord raised Jesus from the dead," whether it is "true in the dumb sense, the sense with which we all use the word when behaving normally," without any need of the kind of self-effacing retreat or conceptual "fancy dancing" to which academics are often given. If Jesus is truly "eternally begotten" by the Father, and the Spirit is eternally spirated by them both, then God is not fundamentally static, and must be re-thought as

---

94. It may be that any ecclesial hermeneutic functions best when it is at least occasionally challenged, and so has to answer for itself. Otherwise it does run the risk of simply being assumed and not having to display the logical or aesthetic purchase that it grants Christians in exegetical practice.

95. Kavin Rowe has used language borrowed from Brevard Childs to argue that the hermeneutical "pressure" of the biblical text, and the trinitarian reflection to which it gave rise, are each unthinkable without the other. See his "Biblical Pressure and Trinitarian Hermeneutics," *Pro Ecclesia* 11 (2002): 295-312.

one whose being is determined in time.[96] Jenson's project leads him far from, and into quite biting polemical opposition to, our own Augustine of Hippo. Nevertheless his question, and his manner of placing it, are instructive. Is it true that Christians are nothing other than the members of a body of which Christ is head? That, in an extraordinarily aneconomic exchange,[97] we trade with God our sinfulness for his divinity? And that the remainder of our lives is a working out of this divine *theosis* in response to Jesus' *kenosis?* If so, must we not also read in some manner quite similar to Augustine?

The second contemporary figure is Nicholas Lash, the author of several important essays on theological method and exegesis that have greatly aided the recovery of theological exegesis described in the first chapter. In a crucial essay, "What Might Martyrdom Mean?" Lash surveys the scholarly consensus in England of that time as to the question of whether Jesus of Nazareth thought he was the messiah (a dissertation mill no less impressive than Augustinian scholarship!). After briefly laying out each view on the question of how Jesus conceived himself, Lash bends the entire conversation in a fundamentally new direction. After concluding that scholars who hold that Jesus saw himself as messiah are correct, he writes, "this still leaves untouched the far more interesting question: *was Jesus right?*" Here most biblical scholars will demur that such a question is outside their field of expertise or competence, yet this will not do. For "to refrain from answering it, or to answer it in the negative, is to refrain from giving . . . the kind of trust that the authors of the NT gave, and in giving it, exhibited their intention to maintain the 'testimony of Jesus.'" That is, it is to turn away from the most important question, and presumed answer, of scripture itself. Lash then turns to the question posed in his essay's title, which he meant to reflect the sort of theological speech to which we distance-loving moderns are given. He notes that it is not the sort of question the New Testament asks. The Bible rather asks something to the effect of "what form might contemporary fidelity to the 'testimony of Jesus' appropriately take?"[98] That is, if the claim of these texts is true — that Jesus is indeed Christ and Lord — how should we live?

---

96. Jenson, "What If It Were True?" *CTI Reflections* 4 (2002): 2-20.

97. I take this term from John Milbank in *Being Reconciled* (London: Routledge, 2003), 47. His interest there is in human participation *(methexis)* in the infinite self-gift of God in the form of forgiveness as a "paradoxical attempt to economize the aneconomic." I use it here in a more general Augustinian spirit of claiming that while God's gift to us of *theosis* is unimaginably beyond our giving of ourselves in exchange, there is indeed an exchange of some sort in which we give *something* (here our sinfulness) out of all proportion to that which has been given to us (divinity).

98. Lash, "What Might Martyrdom Mean?" in *Theology on the Way to Emmaeus,* 75-92.

The writers of the New Testament held that the God of Israel's promises had indeed been fulfilled in his eschatological gathering of all nations round Israel's crucified messiah.[99] Paul works extraordinarily hard in Romans and elsewhere to show that this surprising action of God, and the large-scale rejection of God's work by "Israel according to the flesh," are both in quite literal accord with Israel's own scripture. And the more clearly Paul, the Gospel writers, and the rest of the New Testament authors looked at what was becoming the Old Testament in their hands, the more often they found this story line already present: Israel's crucified messiah and a gathering of Jews (not enough of these) and gentiles of all nations (more of these than previously imagined) around him. Further, as they came to see Jesus himself as originally and unalterably intrinsic to the identity of Israel's God, and just so as the divine agent in creation and source of Israel's scripture, it is even less surprising they would see traces, or indeed clear indications, of his presence and power throughout Israel's scripture. As Jenson and Lash show, those who share similarly Christian views of the world, who hold themselves to be (or indeed, in the "dumb sense," *are*) those assumed and now being transfigured in Christ, should not be surprised to find themselves reading scripture in ways quite similar to Jesus, Paul, Augustine, and Jenson and Lash.

Augustine's own going and doing likewise evoked his longest single theological work, a collection of homilies preached over the course of decades all over north Africa, covering the whole of his field of theological concern. Essentially he took the New Testament's and more specifically Jesus' and Paul's ways of reading the Psalter, and extended that hermeneutic to every portion of the 150 psalms. The church had long attempted similar projects, though without the great christological consistency and breadth and depth of reading that Augustine achieved. Augustine set the standard for western readings of the psalms for more than a thousand years, and continues to do so in some places of the church, though mostly his hermeneutic lies dormant now. It will hopefully be the fruit of works like this that such exegesis will be restored to a place of prominence in our exegetical repertoire.

Though Augustine thinks a christology like his mandates a hermeneutic like his, it is not exactly necessary to argue quite that. We can make a lesser claim: if we hold to a christology not unlike Augustine's, we must at least grant that a hermeneutic like his is *permissible*. To make this somewhat weaker claim would suffice. For allegory by nature allows for multiple meanings, even those that conflict with one another. Attempts to systematize the various levels of texts

---

99. I take this sort of description from Hays, *Echoes of Scripture in the Letters of Paul*, and also his *Moral Vision of the New Testament* (San Francisco: HarperCollins, 1997).

and hermeneutical approaches completely have often been forced to admit failure. Commentators often complain that Origen is never consistent with his three-leveled approach, and even when he is, he usually neglects the "soul" of the text. De Lubac demonstrates that Augustine was frequently imprecise with the terminology surrounding his hermeneutic, and varied a great deal in the precise number of levels of exegesis that he allowed to exist.[100] This vacillation continued throughout the Middle Ages. Even when specific churchmen developed jingles that attempted to canonize four levels of reading, these levels often changed, sometimes in the hands of the same writer! No matter. The point is this: allegory has room to allow for various, perhaps conflicting, levels of interpretation, and so is sufficiently expansive to include modern historical critical insights as well as figurative, christologically based Augustinian ones. It is usually not the case however that overly historicist versions of interpretation can allow for the continued existence of hermeneutics such as Augustine's. In this case, Christian exegetes' christology should trump this fairly typical policing of the church by modern forms of thought.[101] At least now we have seen that Augustinian allegory, far from arbitrary, is rooted in the deepest sense in his fundamental theological logic: his christology, and so should find a place in a renewed multivalent contemporary exegetical practice.

## Christologically Schooled Exegesis in Practice

It is fitting to close this chapter with a look at how Augustine's christological approach to the psalms looks over the course of an entire homily. We shall look at his Psalm 33. This one carries an odd superscription that plainly diverges from the narrative told in 1 Samuel: "A Psalm of David, when he altered his behavior in the presence of *Abimelech,* and forsook him, and went away."[102]

---

100. In his *Medieval Exegesis,* vol. 1, trans. Mark Sebanc (Grand Rapids: Eerdmans, 1998), and vol. 2, trans. E. M. Macierowski (Grand Rapids: Eerdmans, 2000). Michael Cameron states this problem well: "Since Augustine did use familiar terms like "type" *(typus, typical)* and "allegory" *(allegoria, allegorica),* their use in explaining his thought seems ostensibly faithful to his mind. But though they approximate certain dynamics in his thought, these dynamics were not consistently named and so the utility of the terms waxes and wanes. . . . His terminology is more often concerned with comprehensiveness than precision, a tendency which has challenged and frustrated analytical thinkers since the Middle Ages" (*Augustine's Construction of Figurative Exegesis Against the Donatists in the Enarrationes In Psalmos* [Ph.D. diss., University of Chicago, 1996], 55-56).

101. This way of putting the matter is owing to John Milbank, *Theology and Social Theory: Beyond Secular Reason* (Oxford: Blackwell, 1990).

102. *EP,* II, 13ff., italics mine, to emphasize the "mistake" on which Augustine seizes here.

In this case our English translation of Augustine's Latin translated from the Septuagint is remarkably similar to modern English translations of the Hebrew Psalms. We shall see here one kind of textual feature that will drive Augustine to christological exegesis. We have already seen the use of a psalm by the New Testament, and the use of psalms like Psalm 21 and Psalm 30 in similar christological ways. Yet we should say that Augustine does not interpret every line of every psalm christologically, despite a general christological approach to the Psalter overall and frequent christological readings of particular psalm verses. Occasionally, as we have seen, he will interpret a psalm ecclesiologically, and is convinced such a reading is entirely literal. At other times he simply reads the psalms as offering spiritual advice about avoiding wickedness and doing righteously, without great need for christological interjection. In general, however, Augustine is quick to find reason to interpret christologically,[103] and the mistaken inscription of this psalm is a prime instance.

Augustine first turns to the scriptural story of David's feigned madness before King Achis, done to head off any attempt by Achis to please Saul by harming David (1 Samuel 21). Augustine comments on the mistaken inscription, "this is something that really happened, and what happened has been written down, so that although the title of that psalm was assigned very mysteriously, it was, all the same, derived from an event that really occurred." Augustine is keen to say that the historical events here narrated indeed took place. Any figurative, christological sense to this text then rests squarely on the historical reliability of the events narrated.[104] Yet alterations such as these in the biblical text are not merely historical markers: they are shot through with mystery. "How is it possible that all this had no significance?" Augustine asks. This is holy scripture, after all, written by the Spirit to direct believers' attention to Christ. We who read this text, who hear these sermons, can hardly be edified by a mere scribal error. Augustine's ears prick up upon notice of this textual problem. He recalls Jesus' admonition to "knock, and the door will be opened" (Matthew 7:7). Biblical meaning does not lie open for all comers, it has to be worked at. Yet a reward is promised to those who do such work, as those "upon whom the ends of the ages have come" see something

---

103. Perhaps more strongly, for Augustine the Psalter simply *is* christological, without need for the exegete to "make" it so. His hermeneutic then is a matter of showing us, who are not similarly schooled in seeing Christ in the Psalter, that he is present there and how. See the section "A Surprising *Sensus Literalis*" in Chapter 5.

104. Indeed, more so than we moderns may like. As with most ancient exegetes Augustine is more convinced of the historicity of the events scripture narrates than we often are. This is the irony of the common charge that the fathers fail to attend to the historicity of the biblical text: often they do so, to a degree we would find alarmingly "fundamentalist."

new in scripture about Christ that they had not seen before (1 Corinthians 10:11). Augustine points to Paul's exegesis of the Israelites' wilderness wandering in 1 Corinthians, and elsewhere Paul's writing on the two covenants signified by the slave and free woman of Galatians 4. He concludes, "If all these signify nothing, in spite of the statement backed by apostolic authority that they happened as mysterious types of what was to come, then we are right to think that what I read to you just now about David from the Book of Kings had no further meaning either. Nor, consequently, is there any significance in the change of name when the psalm says, 'in the presence of Abimelech.'" Augustine here names our modern squeamishness about allegory with prescience, and he counters that his reading is no less rooted in "history" than is the error on the page before him, or the lives of David, Christ, and Paul, who teaches us to read Israel's history. Paul's exegesis is exemplary. The error in the text is a warning to the attentive: be alert for mystery.

Augustine prefaces his exposition of the mystery here hinted at with a christological aside. Humble David's conquest of proud Goliath (not surprisingly!) prefigured Christ, who cut down the devil with humility on the cross. He did so in just this way because humans fell by pride, and had "no model of humility to hold before us and imitate." Since we disdained humility, God himself came as one who was humble, so we would recoil from that way no longer. In any event, we could never have understood the divinity the Son shared with the Father. Try though we might, it is too much for human contemplation, too rich a meal for us nursing infants. It was necessary then for "that banquet to be converted into milk" if it were to be available to such little ones as us. "But how does food become milk, except by being passed through flesh? This is what a mother does . . . since the baby is unable to digest bread, the mother turns the bread into her own flesh, and through the humility of the breast she feeds her baby the same bread." We have here what could be called a "mammory christology"! The incarnation is the place where we can take breast milk and grow up for stronger fare, where a wisdom too high for angels can be made palatable for infants. The eucharistic overtones are unmistakable, as is the extraordinary nature of the matriarchal imagery for God.

Augustine turns to a favorite technique for interpreting this mysterious name change: nominal etymology. Coached by Hebrew readers (like Jerome), Augustine writes that Achis means "how can this be?"[105] Achis's name is ap-

---

105. Augustine is surprisingly loath to mention his literary sources, whether when working with etymologies and translations or even when mentioning previous exegetical tradition on a given verse. Perhaps since the primary home of these expositions is in preached sermons he was less careful to document his sources, as preachers are wont to be, especially before the advent of

propriate, for the Israelite king was surely baffled at David's feigned insanity. In a similar way, Jesus seemed insane to those to whom he insisted life was to be found in eating his flesh, in drinking his blood (John 6:54-56). "Indeed, does it not sound like insanity to say, 'eat my flesh.' . . . Christ seems to be mad." Yet it is only madness to the unschooled and ignorant. Christ was feigning insanity for a purpose: "by making use of apparent madness and insanity he was proclaiming his sacraments." His was a wisdom that seemed foolish to those perishing. In David's case, the feigned insanity, the wise foolishness, saved him from a king bent on doing him ill. In Christ's case, it resulted in his death, and just so his availability to others in the foolishness of the eucharist. Augustine continues, now diverted by way of the psalm's superscription to exegesis of 1 Samuel 21:15, "He was carried in his own hands, he fell down outside on the threshold, as saliva dribbled down his beard." Christ was indeed carried in his own hands as he said, "This is my body." The threshold is the place where we make our entry in faith that admits us to salvation, at the place where he humbled himself to death. And the saliva? "It represents the babbling of infants, for babies do plenty of dribbling. And were these words not like baby-talk: 'eat my flesh, drink my blood'? Yet these words masked virile strength. . . ."

How do we make a contemporary assessment of Augustine's exegesis here? It is conceivable that the superscription describing David's feigned madness before Abimelech was a mere mistake, that its presence above Psalm 33 ought to add nothing to our reading of that psalm. It is conceivable, but to a scripturally shaped imagination, unlikely. Such a misattribution is better thought of as a gift than a mistake. A wink to the fellow initiate: read closer. Augustine does, and finds stories of danger, chicanery, deliverance, and spittle. What more does he need than these cues to find the gospel retold anew, as a tale of a willful madness that leads some to death and others to life? And of a God willing to reveal himself in simple stories such as these, to be mocked by many of his creatures to demonstrate humility to others, to show them the way out of their pride through such humility as his. The result is deeper knowledge of the gospel, but more significantly, delight. More of that in the next chapter.

---

the modern concept of intellectual property. By way of contrast his *Enarratio* on Psalm 67, which was written to fill out the *Enarrationes* and not to be preached, documents his engagement with his predecessors more carefully (*EP* III, 324-63).

We should say here that it is far from an inappropriate move to interpret a story from Israel's scripture via a cue from an etymology, when Hebrew names are indeed filled with meaning, and that meaning often is a subtle (or not so subtle!) indicator of how a story is to be read. Augustine is here then simply continuing a common inner-biblical hermeneutic — though without the language skills he or we would like.

# 3  Beauty and Exegesis

Augustine's *Confessions* is a masterful account of human desire. Augustine shows that his following of wrong desires, toward what he mistakenly thought was true beauty, brought him nothing but misery. Only a conversion to true good could bring him lasting happiness, and only Christ could allow him to attain and keep that happiness. In the *Confessions*, Augustine illustrates proper human desire for Christ by describing its shadow in the form of perverse desire for blood sport. He describes his poor friend Alypius's being dragged to the circus against his will. Or at least "against his will" applies to his soul's initial state:

> When they arrived and settled themselves in what seats they could find, the whole place was heaving with thoroughly brutal pleasure. He kept the gateways of his eyes closed, forbidding his mind to go out that way to such evils. If only he could have stopped his ears too! At a certain tense moment in the fight a huge roar from the entire crowd beat upon him. He was overwhelmed by curiosity, and on the excuse that he would be prepared to condemn and rise above whatever was happening even if he saw it, he opened his eyes, and suffered a more grievous wound in his soul than the gladiator he wished to see had received in the body. . . . As he saw the blood he gulped down the brutality along with it; he did not turn away but fixed his gaze there and drank in the frenzy, not aware of what he was doing, reveling in the wicked contest and intoxicated on sanguinary pleasure. (VI.8.13)[1]

Here we have an anatomy of a perverse desire. Alypius assents to attend the circus against his will. But he cannot be present in body only, for unfortu-

---

1. *Confessions*, trans. Maria Boulding, OSB (New York: Vintage, 1997), 108-9.

nately he cannot close his ears, and what he hears excites. He determines to follow with his eyes but remain unmoved in soul. Then he likes what he sees. Each of his "interior" senses is engaged by the action, his mind is no longer aware of what he is doing, and he is "carried away with a madness" that consumes him. This brilliant account of the progressive steps of titillation, desire, and ecstasy, shows us anew that evil is a mere parody of good.[2] Each of these human capacities — bodily presence, the physical senses, interior senses, the mind, the will, desire, ascent, and so on — is only *there* as a mechanism given by the creator to lure creatures into the divine embrace. They are here engaged amiss in the raving spectacle of the circus. But they can be engaged rightly in the church's liturgy so as to incite proper desire for God.

As Augustine is about to interpret a reference in Psalm 80 to "olive presses" as a sign of the mystery of the church, he announces, "this is a wonderful spectacle: focus your attention on it. God never fails to provide us with sights to fill us with joy. Could any of the crazy things in the circus compare with a show like this? Circus shows are like the dregs, but this one is like the precious oil."[3] The problem with Alypius's attendance and delight in the circus is that he is missing the real spectacle, settling for a parody of the genuine mystery. His body, then ears, then eyes are meant for a far greater delight: attendance to the divine mysteries, chanting of the psalms, and longing and preparation for the beatific vision. The problem is not a puritanical one of desiring too much, it is an Augustinian one of settling for a far lesser satisfaction.[4]

Elsewhere Augustine goes into this comparison of the church's liturgy and human spectacles as liturgical parody in more depth. "God provides glorious sights [*magna spectacula*] for a Christian heart. Nothing could be found more

2. Some significant recent theological work has defended this view of evil as a *privatio boni*. See Rowan Williams's description of Augustine's own views in "'Good for Nothing'?: Augustine on Creation," *Augustinian Studies* 25 (1994): 9-24. For contemporary theological reappropriations of Augustine's views see John Milbank, "Evil: Darkness and Silence," in *Being Reconciled: Ontology and Pardon* (London: Routledge, 2003), and David Hart, "No Shadow of Turning: On Divine Impassibility," *Pro Ecclesia* 11, no. 2 (Spring 2002): 184-206.

3. *Expositions of the Psalms*, trans. Maria Boulding, OSB, from *Works of Saint Augustine: A Translation for the 21st Century*, vol. III/18 (Hyde Park, NY: New City Press, 2002), IV, 152. Hereafter referred to as *EP*.

4. As in the description of another latter-day Augustinian, C. S. Lewis: "if we consider the unblushing promises of reward and the staggering nature of the rewards promised in the Gospels, it would seem that Our Lord finds our desires not too strong but too weak. We are half-hearted creatures, fooling about with drink and sex and ambition when infinite joy is offered us, like an ignorant child who wants to go on making mud pies in a slum because he cannot imagine what is meant by the offer of a holiday at the sea. We are far too easily pleased" (*The Weight of Glory* [New York: Macmillan, 1949], 26).

delightful than these, assuming that the palate of our faith is truly discerning and capable of enjoying the full flavor of God's honey."[5] What precisely causes proper delight? Nothing less than biblical exegesis! Delight comes "when the prophecies are read." For these "prophecies were uttered many years ago by the lips of holy men, and now, so many years later, they have been fulfilled in the acceptance of the faith by the Gentiles." Joy comes at seeing the ancient writings now fulfilled in surprising ways, especially in the incorporation of the very gentiles hearing and singing those prophecies (that is, us) into Israel's body. In other words, joy has its source in figurative reading of scripture! These words may not appear, on surface, to refer to Jesus, or anything befitting biblical faith. Yet we gentiles have been grafted into Israel, surprising as that is. We, the church, are then quite physical proof that these scriptures are fulfilled in ways contrary to ordinary expectation. So we will search for the Lord even here, above all here, in scriptures that either literally or allegorically testify to him. And the result will be delight — a display or spectacle far more glorious than the circus. Finding Christian figurative meaning, like finding God in flesh, represents a "sane insanity, a sober intoxication."[6] No less than the friends of Alypius did to him, Christians ought also "seize all your kinfolk and drag them along to the love of God, and all your household."[7] For who would not want to find the Lord in unexpected places, to delight in such a sane insanity? "Think how the righteous old man Simeon was transported with delight when he saw the infant Jesus. In that tiny child he recognized the Great One; in that diminutive body he knew the creator of heaven and earth."[8] Delight comes from finding the Lord in unexpected places, even places we would think

5. Comment on Psalm 96 at *EP* IV, 438.

6. On Psalm 33 (2), *EP* II, 33.

7. *EP* II, 28. This sounds quite similar to Augustine's famous reading of Luke's "compel them to come in" as a justification for coercion of the Donatists by an empire aligned with the church. Even if we have no interest in defending Augustine on the appropriate use of violence to squash schism, we should note that his argument is not solely negative (ending heresy), it is also positive (showing those compelled something genuinely delightful). An appropriate response to Augustine on his own grounds would be that such coercion is likely to make such *dilectio* impossible. He would likely counter, as he often did, with stories of the gratitude expressed to him by former Donatists to the church that dragged them, initially against their will, away from their errors.

John Bowlin has written about the irony of the tongue-clucking by historians and theologians over Augustine's position on coercion, done despite their common agreement with him that some measure of violence is necessary to maintain a peaceful *polis*. They simply do not wish to see it argued for on theological grounds. See Bowlin, "Augustine on Justifying Coercion," *The Annual of the Society of Christian Ethics* 17 (1997): 49-70.

8. *EP* IV, 438.

he *cannot* be, operating under expected conditions — in gentiles, in a child, in confusing words from Israel's scripture. Yet — surprise! — there he is. The result can only be increasing ecstasy, and finally, love.

## The Beauty of Allegory as Intrinsic to Salvation

A central contention of this book is that precisely at the point at which patristic exegesis seems most strained, at which we moderns are most likely to cry "arbitrary!" and return to our historicist reconstructions, precisely there, the most interesting things are happening. That is where patristic interpreters are winking at us, and where we are failing to get the joke. But the point is not mere amusement, it is the profound motion from bewilderment, to sudden enlightenment ("ah hah!"), to a return glance at the scriptural words in which we recognize that they can indeed bear this surprising interpretive weight. This moment of discovery of christological meaning in an unexpected place delights, then teaches us, and finally arouses love in us, moving our wills closer to God. The echo of Cicero's famous tripartite description of the purpose of rhetoric — to instruct, to delight, and to move — is instructive. Augustine, the now-Christian rhetor, in his exegesis chips away at our affections like so many chisel blows, making us into new creatures as a result of having heard him. Or to shift the metaphor, the ecclesial rhetor shapes his hearers' emotions like water shapes rock: slowly, over a great deal of time, but finally successfully. For Augustine allegory is beautiful, and this is key because its use is meant to draw readers into the beauty of God. If we miss this, we miss the whole point of Christian figurative interpretation and Augustine cannot but appear "arbitrary" in the extreme. If we see it we might well be drawn into the divine life ourselves.

Such *theosis* through preaching and hearing scripture is not easy, because the Bible is not easy. These texts were written by far different people, far away, in different languages, with different interests than ours. Scripture is full of jagged edges, places where not even the greatest Hebraicist using the best manuscripts can determine its "meaning," or occasionally where if she can we wish she had not. We moderns have various ways of explaining what to do with scripture's difficulty — mostly historicist ones. Augustine is not insensitive to these sorts of moves. Yet he is also not content with them. In one place he describes the difficulty of exegesis as part of the discipline of Adam brought on by the fall itself: "so hidden and closed are all things that even if we are able by [God's] aid to arrive at anything upon which we may feed to our health, still we must eat the bread in the sweat of our face; and pay the penalty of the ancient sentence not with the labor of the body but with that of the heart."[9] Such post-lapsarian discipline, as ever for the fathers, is not merely punitive, but also part and parcel of our salvation.[10] Augustine makes this even more clear with a comment on his Psalm 146:6, "The Lord takes up the gentle, but humbles the sinners to the ground." He sees there the experience of the exegete. "Do not be over-bold and find fault with the obscurity of scripture or even allege that it is self-contradictory. There is no contradiction here. Some obscurity there may be, not in order that insight may be denied you, but so that your mind may be stretched until you can receive it." Fairly mild, basic pedagogical advice so far. Yet he continues: "When some text seems dark to you, be sure that the physician has made it so, that he may open to you when you knock. . . . As you persevere in knocking you will be stretched; as you are stretched, your capacity will be enlarged; as your capacity grows, you will receive what comes to you as gift." The difficulty of scripture is part of a specifically incarnational pedagogy.[11] Christ himself advised gentle persistence when approaching God in prayer (Matthew 7:7), and here Augustine applies that teaching to exegesis. The reason knocking is not immediately met with opening is to humble pride, increase desire, and eventually to incite love. The reading of scripture is central to God's particular way of saving us through the eradication of contented self-reliance, toward the incitement of right desire, and finally the cultivation of love. Any protest against this *theotic* way of exegesis is only evidence of the state from which God is trying to save us: "let not the sick man seek to amend his remedies. The physician knows how to temper them. Believe him who cares for you."[12] The very difficulty of interpreting a text allegorically is intrinsic to God's saving dispensation for both the preacher and those listening.

## Beauty in the Bible and in God

As ever with Augustine, the proper place to begin an exploration of desire and beauty in the psalms is with his christology. Just here a key debate has taken

9. Carol Harrison uses this passage from *Enarratio* 77.4 in her *Beauty and Revelation in the Thought of Saint Augustine* (Oxford: Clarendon, 1992), 61. The translation is hers.

10. Gary Anderson shows how this is true generally in patristic exegesis of Genesis 1–3, and in different ways also in ancient Jewish interpretation of Eden, in his *The Genesis of Perfection: Adam and Eve in Jewish and Christian Imagination* (Louisville: Westminster/John Knox, 2001).

11. I borrow this description of a "pedagogy of the incarnation" from Karen Jo Torjesen's work on Origen's exegesis, *Hermeneutical Procedure and Theological Method in Origen's Exegesis* (Berlin: Walter de Gruyter, 1986).

12. From comments on Psalm 146 in *EP* VI, 431.

place among Augustinian scholars. There are those who see in the Augustinian theme of training desire a sort of undigested Platonism masquerading as Christianity. Does not scripture itself rarely mention "beauty," while Platonists place heavy emphasis upon it? Augustine's earlier, more obviously "philosophical" works seem more optimistic about the intertwining of platonic themes of beauty with Christian reflection, whereas his latter, more scriptural concern with human fallenness seems to lessen his enthusiasm for speaking of beauty as a means to draw persons to God. He seems to sound later less like Plato and more like Paul, as it were. The early Augustine had planned an elaborate course of writings on the liberal arts, designed to sharpen readers' senses sufficiently to allow them to contemplate divine rationality. He never got far in this endeavor, and instead became more pessimistic about the usefulness of the rhetorical practices in which he had been so invested. Yet even when Augustine laments Christian use of rhetoric, and insists on a plain, unvarnished presentation of the truth, untainted by pagan rhetorical skill in selling the false as true, he speaks with an extraordinary degree of rhetorical flair. Robert O'Connell has famously argued that in this, as in most things aesthetic, Augustine remains even more deeply indebted to his Platonic intellectual heritage than he lets on. Because Augustine continues to hold that human souls are pre-existent and have fallen from an original beauty beheld in contemplating the forms to the prison-like existence of embodied materiality, he can have no place for a genuinely incarnational vision of beauty that holds human flesh, material creation, art and language as potentially vessels of divine meaning. O'Connell sets out to correct Augustine's "disincarnate epistemology," with a more world-affirming aesthetic befitting a Christian doctrine of the incarnation.[13]

Carol Harrison's dissertation dramatically attacks this contention head-on. While a small army of scholars had already critiqued O'Connell's suggestion that Augustine believed in preexistent souls, no one had yet reworked our view of Augustinian aesthetics accordingly. O'Connell tries to provide for a union between seen and unseen realms, material and spiritual, historical and eternal, that his unreformed Platonist Augustine failed to do except in limited areas and degrees. Harrison sees in Augustine a profound union between "realms" given "by the theological doctrines which give structure to the whole of Augustine's thinking as a Christian theologian and Bishop: Creation *ex nihilo*, man created in the image of God, Scripture as the word of God, and most especially the incarnation."[14] She reviews Augustine's early works and

13. Robert O'Connell, *Art and the Christian Intelligence in Saint Augustine* (Cambridge, MA: Harvard University Press, 1978).

14. Harrison, *Beauty and Revelation*, 36-37.

finds even there a specifically Christian ingredient lacking in the Platonism Augustine had inherited: a positive evaluation of creation, scripture, and especially the flesh of Christ incarnate. For even there it is precisely God's own entry into materiality in the incarnation that allows his creatures not just to disparage the frailty and vicissitudes of created life, but to use them as gifts left for us to make our pilgrimage possible.

Christ is consistently both the way and the goal in Augustine's christology, his humanity the means to participate in his divinity. Augustine's way of talking about salvation indeed shifts over the course of his career — his earlier, more Platonic, other-worldly emphasis gives way to a more specifically scriptural vocabulary with which to speak of salvation as he spends a pastoral career meditating upon and preaching from scripture. So earlier speech of Christ as the "supreme measure," as the "measure of the soul," as "supreme Truth, Unity, Form, and Number" relents some before specifically scriptural descriptions of Christ as incarnate Wisdom, foolish to our senses initially, but whose human life offers us the very knowledge *(scientia)* of God and whose divinity is the very Wisdom *(sapientia)* of God. Yet despite this shift in terminology, the heart of his christology remains consistent. Harrison cites Goulven Madec's work with its insistence that early works like the *Confessions,* the *Beata Vita,* and the *Contra Academicos* present a christology and concomitant aesthetic that is fundamentally coherent with those of such later texts as *De Trinitate*'s books IV and XIII.[15] Harrison sees what O'Connell cannot: Augustine has scriptural texts to wrestle with that stress both God's incarnation and human *theosis,* divine abasement and human growth toward something more than mere ungraced creatureliness. Such stately texts as John 1:1-5 rest alongside such mundane ones as those about John the Baptist in the rest of the Johannine prologue; such depictions of divine *kenosis* and human *theosis* as Philippians 2:1-11 are each incomplete without the other. Augustine's early emphasis on Platonic otherworldly escape rests alongside later emphases on divine abasement and human sanctification because both are present in scripture and so must be accounted for in any scriptural christology. As in Augustine's christology so in his aesthetics. Part of our problem as creatures is that we overestimate the importance of the glimpses of earthly beauty we can see and mistake these for all the beauty there is, when they are meant to lead us to the true beauty of God, whose beauty is veiled in the form of Christ's ugliness. Augustine sees the Psalter as a continuation of the work of the incarnation in rehabilitating us out of devotion to a false beauty and into the true — that of the incarnate God.

---

15. Harrison, *Beauty and Revelation,* 210. She cites Madec, "*Christus, Scientia et Sapientia nostra,*" *Recherches Augustiniennes* (1975): 77-85.

While O'Connell was part of an older generation of Augustinian scholars who saw Augustine's Platonism as a prison from which he could not finally part, Harrison is part of a newer generation of historians-*cum*-theologians who see Augustine as not only falsely maligned, but also as a positive remedy to the disincarnate devaluing of creation by modern philosophers. In another frontline of this battle, Michael Hanby disputes the philosophical link between Augustine and Descartes made so strongly by Charles Taylor and almost canonical by his readers.[16] Hanby not only attributes the purported link to a misreading of Augustine, he even identifies it with a heretical Stoic philosophical position actually attacked by Augustine! One can only find Descartes' *res cogitans,* the individual unencumbered by historic specificity or human community as the measure of all truth *by planning to find him there* and reading bits of Augustine in isolation from the whole. Such a misreading has become common with the fracturing of academic guilds that allows us to envisage a "philosophical" Augustine in isolation from such theological themes as Trinity and ecclesiology. Yet this does great violence to Augustine's own work. For as Rowan Williams shows us there is no Augustinian "inwardness" or "individuality" that is not always already bound up with such "exterior" themes as christology and church.[17] Williams argues that while the various alignments of such complex human processes as "memory, reason, and will" in *De Trinitate* are indeed interior to a single human person, and so can lure a careless reader into seeing Augustine as a sort of proto-Cartesian, such a reading would be merely a superficial skimming of the surface of Augustine's thought. Toward the end of *De Trinitate,* Augustine makes clear that the soul is only rightly related to God and others when infused with *caritas,* which is, for Augustine, the very love between the Father and the Son that *is* the Spirit. There is no exploration of such "inner" themes as the memory, reason, and will, which is not also simultaneously an exploration of such "outer" themes as politics, friendship, and the good work of redemption in the world. That is, the distinction between "inner" and "outer" is artificial at best, misleading (as it is to contemporary Augustinian critics) at worst. No one then should hear the themes of Augustinian "inwardness" sounded in this chapter and think in Cartesian terms, since for Augustine the soul being healed is always already radically turned outward toward God and others.

Hanby's work represents a convergence of the most important recent Au-

16. In Taylor's *Sources of the Self: The Making of the Modern Identity* (Cambridge, MA: Harvard University Press, 1989).

17. *"De Trinitate,"* in *Augustine Through the Ages,* ed. Allan D. Fitzgerald (Grand Rapids: Eerdmans, 1999), 845-51.

gustinian historical and theological research. He argues that the best way to present the "historical" Augustine is to do Augustinian theology anew: "By Augustine's own lights, the best literal reading of Augustine's theology would be a new Augustinian theology."[18] That is, Hanby receives the crucial work done on Augustine's trinitarian theology by Ayres, Williams, Barnes, Robert Dodaro, and others and fully digests it into a full-blown Augustinian theology. For Hanby's Augustine, being as such is doxological. The Son is the image and likeness, the *forma* or beauty, of the Father who eternally begets him. The Father delights in his Beauty and gives this delighting to his Son who in turn gives this delight or Love back. That mutual giving of delight and love is itself, as Spirit, a *persona* no less than the Father and the Son. Creation itself is an expression of this inner-trinitarian beauty and delight. The incarnation then is not more or less than an intensification of the unfolding of trinitarian communion in creation, and sets up among Christ's fellow creatures a two-part economy of love and knowledge. Christ discloses the eternal Trinity whose three *personae* are inseparably present in the man Jesus. The disclosure of the triune God in Christ allows us to draw closer to God in love and knowledge. Yet his flesh also veils his divinity, making explicit an *aporia* in our approach to God that incites desire for us to know and love more. This horizontal oscillation between knowledge and love and their lack is the "space" opened up in the incarnation for human sanctification. For our progress is "through Christ to Christ," from Christ as way to Christ as goal, from Christ as *exemplum* to him as *sacramentum*, from him as human to him as divine. Since our very being as such and that of the whole cosmos from the beginning is not less than an expression of the inner-trinitarian delight in divine beauty, this christological growth into that beauty as part of the church is not less than an intensification of our very being. "Only the saint truly *is*," Hanby quotes Gerhart Ladner as saying, in a deeply Augustinian description.[19]

Hanby does not limit himself to the *De Trinitate* as he unfolds Augustine's trinitarian theology and accompanying doxological ontology. He also uses the *De doctrina christiana*'s exposition of human sign-making. When we make signs or words we naturally reflect the sign and Word of God who is Christ, just as the love required for humans to know anything properly reflects the Love of God that is the Spirit. The "space" opened up between the two natures of Christ for human participation in the divine life is also a

18. Michael Hanby, *Augustine and Modernity*, Radical Orthodoxy Series (London: Routledge, 2003), 17.

19. Hanby, *Augustine and Modernity*, 68. He cites Gerhart Ladner, *The Idea of Reform: Its Impact on Christian Thought and Action in the Age of the Fathers* (Cambridge, MA: Harvard University Press, 1959), 279.

hermeneutical space, one filled with signs that draw us further into the life of God. Hanby continually notices what many Augustinian scholars miss or dismiss: Augustine's love of specifically scriptural language. Where most of us with our modern hermeneutical ears tune out when Augustine turns to quoting scripture, Hanby's attention picks up. Yet Hanby himself pays little attention to Augustine's own biblical exegesis in his role as bishop. He does quote the *Enarrationes,* often following Harrison's work on it, but rarely with an eye to how Augustine's preaching puts his aesthetic commitments into practice "on the ground," as it were, in an actual church's life. Yet this is crucial. If Augustine sees Christ as drawing us into the very beauty of God which he *is,* we must pay attention to how Augustine conducts this drawing, how he directs his church's attention to the divine allure. If we fail in this we risk keeping Augustine's work at the level of ideas only, which Hanby is rightly so keen not to do.

Harrison and Hanby have successfully restored our attention to the role of beauty in Augustine's theology, or better put, of the aesthetic nature of the divine way opened up to humans in Christ. The question to ask now is this: how exactly does the gospel display the beauty of Christ so that a preacher's hearers can be drawn to the beatific vision of Jesus, as part of the community of love called by the Spirit to be the body of which Christ is head?

## The Beauty of Augustine's Preaching on the Psalms

It is striking how seldom Augustine speaks directly of trinitarian theology in the *Enarrationes.* Even in places where Christian preachers normally find "proof texts" for trinitarian doctrine, such as Augustine's Psalm 32:6 ("by the word of the Lord the heavens were established, all their strength comes from the breath of his mouth") and 50:15 ("strengthen me by your original spirit"), Augustine passes on the chance to do so.[20] Why? Principally because his attention is on Christ in the Psalter, through which attention his hearers are drawn in to the triune life.[21] The complexities of what we can know and what

---

20. Psalm 32:6 is in his comments on Psalm 32 (3) in *EP* I, 410-11, where he says nothing on the Trinity; on 50:15 he says, "Some have understood this to be a reference to the Trinity in God. . . . This may be correct. Alternatively the psalmist may have meant the upright spirit in a human being. . . . Neither opinion is heretical" (*EP* II, 425).

21. Augustine here stands in sharp contrast to social trinitarians like Miroslav Volf ("'The Trinity Is Our Social Program': The Doctrine of the Trinity and the Shape of Social Engagement," *Modern Theology* 14, no. 3 [1998]: 403-23) who mine trinitarian thought about divine "persons" for cues on human relationship generally, as opposed to attending to what God has

we cannot about the Trinity he saves for a work like *De Trinitate*. In his actual preaching he takes pains to exposit in detail what we can know of the *res* of Christ through the *signa* of these words. The goal is to change the "affections" of his hearers — to have them love and shun the right things rightly.

## A Mirror for Our Affections

It is first a vitally anti-Apollinarian move to insist that Christ himself had "affections," lest he be thought to be a divine Word who has merely invaded the shell of a human being. In this way Augustine exemplifies the Irenaean adage that "what is not assumed cannot be saved." Augustine writes of Christ that "he had affection. But what is it to have affection, or be affectionate? He had compassion on our infirmities."[22] Because he himself had affections — certain loves and aversions — and because as our creator he gave us our affections that we might seek him, he wishes to direct those affections aright. That Christ had human affections is not only logical corollary of his full humanity, it is actually crucial to the entire redemptive economy. For Augustine, God is always ecstatic self-outpouring, always going "outside" himself in kenotic love, first *in se*, then toward creation. Indeed, as we have seen in Hanby one divine *persona* for Augustine is the mutual love outpoured between Father and Son, in whom the church itself becomes deified. A proper human response to trinitarian divestment and inner-personal self-giving is human divestment in ecstatic self-outpouring back toward God and to others. In a theme from ancient physics that Augustine famously develops in the *Confessions*, "weight is like a force within each thing that seems to make it strain toward its proper place." Just as a stone strains downward out of its desire to rest on the ground, or as oil will not consent to remain underneath water but strains upward, so Christians strain to follow their "foundation," ahead and above them, into heaven. This is no mere "spiritual" ascent, in the minimal way that term is often used to the exclusion of bodies and politics, it is rather quite a physical one (or a "spiritual" one in the inclusive way ancients used that term), as Augustine's metaphors of rock and oil imply.[23]

---

actually given us to know of the divine life through the incarnation. See by way of contrast the essays in Sarah Coakley, ed., *Re-Thinking Gregory of Nyssa* (Oxford: Blackwell, 2003). Volf's more christological (and brilliant) work in *Exclusion and Embrace* (Nashville: Abingdon, 1996) and *Free of Charge* (Grand Rapids: Zondervan, 2006) represents a better way forward in trinitarian doctrine.

22. Comment on Psalm 33, in *EP* II, 20.
23. *EP* II, 309-10.

Elsewhere, in a particularly moving exploration of desire in scripture, Augustine comments on the first verse of Psalm 41, "as a deer longs for springs of water, so does my soul long for you, O God." He asks a standard prosopological[24] question with which he often opens expositions: who is speaking here? The answer is that it is "within your power to be yourself the answer to the question" — the speaker is the "one" who has just chanted this psalm. But that "one" is not an individual, but "a single body, the Church, which is the whole body of Christ." The speaker here is everyone throughout the world who has tasted the sweetness of the Lord, who sings here with a unified voice. Augustine notes that this passage is customarily sung by or for catechumens, those "hurrying toward the holy, grace-giving bath," in order to "arouse in them a longing for the fountain of forgiveness." Baptism cannot be the stopping place for the passionate use of this psalm, for Augustine "cannot believe that a longing of such intensity is satisfied" even at baptism. That we continue to sing it implies both a certain lack and its frequent fulfillment. The interplay between desire and satisfaction, longing and love, will continue throughout this pilgrimage. So Augustine sings: "brothers and sisters, catch my eagerness, share my longing. Let us love, all of us together, let us burn together with this thirst, let us run together to the fountain of understanding."[25] Scripture incites desire in more people than just initial catechumens. It does so in all who long for the heavenly city. Just so, figurative exegesis is essential to the entirety of the Christian life.

This description could suffice for any religious community that sees beauty in its scriptures, and so grows in longing for the divine. Yet we must see the particularly incarnational logic here, the "christo-logic" by which figurative reading of scripture is mandated. Augustine sees this logic at work in a bit of Psalm 103, "you have clothed yourself in confession and seemliness."[26] We readers of this psalm seek beauty, as all creatures do. Specifically Christian readers seek beauty in him who is "fair beyond all the children of men"

---

24. Michael Fiedrowicz describes "prosopological" exegesis as that which first asks the key question of who is speaking before interpreting a bit of scripture accordingly ("General Introduction" to *EP* I, 50-51, a translation of part of his *Psalmus Vox Totius Christi* [Freiburg: Herder & Herder, 1997], 238ff.). Augustine and other patristic figures learned this sort of interpretation from classical readers of Homer and Plato. Though here as in all things allegorical the application of this hermeneutic to Christ made for hermeneutical approaches and readings that their forebears could not have anticipated. The pioneer in work on prosopological exegesis is M. J. Rondeau, *Les commentaires patristiques du Psautier (IIIe-Ve siècles)*, vol. 2 (Roma: Orientalia Christiana Analecta 220, 1985).

25. All the preceding is from Psalm 41 in *EP* II, 239-40.

26. Psalm 103 (1) in *EP* V, 110-11.

(Psalm 45:3), for whom maidens long with love (Song of Songs 1:2). Yet we cannot please him, because we are deformed, ugly, because of our sin. Augustine now turns to a crucial metaphor in the *Enarrationes* to describe how we heed our ugliness: the "mirror" of scripture. Often this "mirror" is specifically associated with the "purity of heart" Jesus says is necessary in order to "see God": "See whether you are one of the pure-hearted it mentions, and grieve if you are not yet like that; grieve in order to become so."[27] Seeing our deformity, we must accuse ourselves and grieve appropriately, as a first step toward beauty. That first step would be useless, and indeed impossible, had not the one we desire, who is "fair beyond all the children of men," himself "come to the ugly one to make her beautiful. And that is not all; I will say something more daring still, since I find it in scripture: to make her beautiful he became ugly himself." Augustine points to Isaiah 53's description of the lack of comeliness in the savior, and to Matthew 27's description of passersby mocking the deformed Christ on the cross. He argues that Christ himself willed this deformity, this lack of comeliness, as part of a fundamentally *kenotic* and *theotic* logic, shown above all in Philippians 2. As a result of his voluntarily deformity, we who were deformed become "most beautiful among women" (Song of Songs 5:9; 8:5). We are those who come "up from the wilderness, made white" as we emerge from baptism (Song of Songs 8:5 [LXX]; Ephesians 5:27; Revelation 7:13-14). This exchange should not shock us, for it is the heart of the incarnation: "If the lowliness he accepted for her sake astounds you, you will be less amazed by the eminence [the church] enjoys because of him." The Lord indeed clothes himself with both confession and honor, for "he clothed himself in the church," which in its own life ascends from deformity to beauty in imitation of his descent from the latter to the former. Augustine sees in the entire Psalter a vast pedagogy of the incarnation, by which Christ himself shapes human desire and affection away from ugliness toward beauty in a process that itself is *theosis*, is our very salvation. As Augustine writes elsewhere, Christ is

> beautiful wherever he is. Beautiful as God, as the Word who is with God, he is beautiful in the Virgin's womb, where he did not lose his godhead but assumed our humanity. Beautiful he is as a baby, as the Word unable to speak, because while he was still without speech, still a baby in arms and nourished at his mother's breast, the heavens spoke for him, a star guided the magi, and he was adored in the manger as food for the humble. He was beautiful in heaven, then and beautiful on earth: beautiful in the womb, and

27. Psalm 103 (1) in *EP* V, 110, citing Matthew 5:8.

beautiful in his parents' arms. He was beautiful in his miracles but just as beautiful under the scourges, beautiful as he invited us to life, but beautiful too in not shrinking from death, beautiful in laying down his life and beautiful in taking it up again, beautiful on the cross, beautiful in the tomb, and beautiful in heaven.[28]

And, we might add in a similar vein, beautiful when he takes us up in our ugliness, to make us beautiful in him.

What scripture is *for* is the conversion of human affection. Again, this should not be taken in a reductive sense, such as for theologians after Friedrich Schleiermacher who surrender such possible fields of theological meaning as history and metaphysics to retreat to the psychological. For Augustine this affective emphasis rests on historical accounts he presumes to be true and a christological ontology he largely works out elsewhere. On those bases, we can say that scripture is written just so for the conversion of its readers' affections. We have already seen elsewhere that the scenes of Jesus' temptation only took place, and were recorded as they stand, to help Christians who suffer now.[29] As Augustine comments on Psalm 56:2, "have mercy on me, for my soul trusts in you," by saying, "you hear your teacher praying, so learn to pray. He prayed *for this very reason,* to teach us to pray, just as he suffered to teach us to suffer, and rose from the dead to teach us to hope for resurrection."[30] Augustine has here a ready explanation for the emotional breadth of the psalms: "if the psalm is praying, pray yourselves; if it is groaning, you groan too; if it is happy, rejoice; if it is crying out in hope, you hope as well; if it expresses fear, be afraid. Everything written here is like a mirror held up to us."[31] In Augustine's hands this image of the "mirror" does more *work* than our ordinary mirrors do. Scripture does more than show us what is the case about our face — it directs us, tells us how to feel anew, gathers up our affections and converts them. Augustine's mirror *gives* us our faces. We might say that this is a mirror that acts in reverse of normal mirrors, for here the reflection does not simply mimic the person standing before the mirror. Here the image *leads.* As Augustine says elsewhere on Psalm 107, where again the people of God sees itself as it ought to be: "Let us consider, then, the lessons this psalm offers us about what should give us joy and what evoke our groans, from whom we should expect help, why we are abandoned and how we are to be rescued. Let us see if it can teach us anything about what we are of our-

28. Comment on Psalm 44 in *EP* II, 283.
29. Chapter 2, pp. 71-73 above.
30. *EP* III, 108.
31. Comment preceding Psalm 30 (4) in *EP* I, 347.

selves and what through the mercy of God, about how our pride is to be shattered and his grace glorified."[32]

## Expanded Vocabularies

We cannot overstate how important this theme of the conversion of the affections is in Augustine's exegetical work, or indeed how important it is to understanding ancient Christian figurative reading more generally. This approach to exegesis did not assume the primary purpose of reading scripture was to acquire new information previously unknown. Rather, it was to re-learn what was already known in a new way. It is often noted that Christian figurative reading cannot add anything new to Christian teaching that was not already present in literal form elsewhere in scripture.[33] Otherwise we would have a gnostic approach to scripture, in which a creative genius could find whatever she or he wished lurking wherever she wished in scripture. No Christian teaching can rest merely on allegorical exegesis for its foundation — it has to be present somewhere in scripture in a clear, literal fashion.[34] What allegory did was allow the exegete to interpret puzzling words, or unclear ones, in light of already held Christian teaching. Augustine himself, commenting on the frequent poetic device of repetition (with slight variation) in the psalms, makes theological cash out of it in this way: "repetitions of this kind are frequently used to drive home the meaning of God's utterances. Sometimes the same words are repeated, sometimes the same idea in different words. Such repetitions are especially common in the psalms, and in any other type of discourse that aims to arouse the affections of the spirit."[35] Psalm exegesis, like, say, the singing of hymns, is not meant to add new information, though it is meant to teach. It's not meant to say something not already present in scripture elsewhere and codified by the creeds. It is meant to

---

32. *EP* V, 223.

33. This is such a conventional comment largely because Augustine asserted it so clearly in *De doctrina christiana* in his argument that any *signa* that cannot be literally applied to the *res* of love of God and neighbor ought to be read figuratively. Following Michael Cameron's work, we can read the *Enarrationes* as expanding on *De doctrina*'s argument with a less formal and abstract description than "apply these words to love of God and neighbor," offering instead a more specifically christological hermeneutic. The words of the Psalter are to be ascribed to Christ, both head and members, and that "ascription" can include showing what the body of Christ now needs to grow more deeply toward its head.

34. Though what precisely we mean by "clear" and "literal" is naturally up for dispute.

35. Comment on Psalm 71, "commit your judgment to the king, and your justice to the king's son," in *EP* III, 453.

celebrate that which we already know, to show it to us anew, and so, to delight us more deeply into love of God. Elsewhere, commenting on the promise of the psalmist that the wicked will be "disposed of like melted wax," Augustine argues that this is a poetic restatement of common Christian teaching that sin is its own perilous reward in this life. He almost apologizes for giving such a quotidian reading of this verse: "I am bringing out for inspection things you already know, but when I bring them out from a place where you had not yet seen them, it will make previously known truths seem to you delightfully new."[36]

What allegory *does* is to expand greatly the language with which its practitioners can describe the Christian faith.[37] This is crucial for anyone who has ever stood in a pulpit, like Augustine, and had to expound on strange words to a congregation that has long since been catechized.[38] For every time the church opens its doors, there they all are again, waiting to hear more. What such people need is not another tired repetition of what they already know, but to hear the truth of what they know again in a new way, with greater profundity, so as to grow not just in knowledge, but more importantly, in love. This purpose of allegory — to expand the language with which the gospel is retold — also accounts for an important feature often lacking in contemporary biblical exegesis: humor. When Augustine comments on his version of Psalm 148:7, "Praise the Lord from the earth, you dragons and all the depths," he asks, "What? Are we to imagine dragons forming a choir to praise God? Of course not, but when you think about dragons you are reminded of the dragons' designer, the dragons' creator. When they fill you with amazement you reflect, 'How great must be the God who made them.'"[39] Like the rabbis who read in similar ways, the fathers knew their task of delighting their audience anew in biblical knowledge already held would often require humor. This is not meant merely to entertain, but to avoid ennui, and to love more deeply

---

36. Comment on Psalm 57 in *EP*, II, 140.

37. As Robert Wilken writes, "Having the New Testament in hand, Christians saw terms take on different hues, certain images spring to life, persons and events privileged, and everything woven together in a tapestry imprinted with the face of Christ. . . . As its words took up residence in the minds and hearts of Christian thinkers, it gave them a vocabulary that subtly shaped their patterns of thought." So Christ could be spoken of in all the "different hues" offered by the breadth and depth of Israel's scripture, and in turn exegetes have their imaginations shaped in particularly scriptural ways (*The Spirit of Early Christian Thought* [New Haven: Yale University Press, 2003], 76).

38. Even if perhaps poorly. To use a common homiletical metaphor, allegory may be most important for those who have received just enough Christianity to be "inoculated" against the real thing.

39. *EP* VI, 484.

that which is already known.[40] The result is not the staid environment of a contemporary classroom, but rather nothing less raucous than, say, a soccer stadium in which the crowd is delighted at multiple successful passes upfield and responds with a resounding chorus of "olé!" Or to return to a liturgical setting, the result is not unlike a *shul* during an appropriately raucous and joyous debate over *Torah*. After one particularly stirring allegory Augustine notes in passing, "These shouts of·yours, this is evidence of your joy — what prompts them? Your delight, obviously." He then proceeds to weave their delight back into his allegorical exposition. They are pleased, but more than entertained, they are moved. If Augustine had stuck to the Ciceronian rules of ancient rhetoric he could have stopped when they had been informed, delighted, and moved.[41] Christian rhetors' use of the same goal takes on new contours. Their goal is to delight and move in particularly *biblical* ways. Allegory does not expand the language with which we may speak of the gospel in an arbitrary direction, it expands such language in a specifically biblical way. In Robert Wilken's example, the word "hyssop" takes on a particular *gravitas* when used to speak of confession and purgation because it is a peculiarly biblical word.[42] The priest who holds the fractured host aloft and says, "Behold the lamb of God," uses words that echo through Isaiah, John's Gospel, and Revelation, and so take on a particularly *biblical* depth that draws the hearer into a form of delight and love shaped by the peculiar words of scripture and the great story it narrates.

This process often takes place in scripture's hearers as initial frustration, confusion, or even boredom, gives way to recognition of something familiar here seen in a surprising new shape, in even *these* words, with a surprise that yields delight and greater love. One is tempted to say it should not surprise if we already expect to find Jesus everywhere before we even begin! Yet it seems to, largely, because of the exegetical skill of Augustine and his contemporaries. For he manages to find verbal or theological connections between the text of scripture at hand and christology such that the interpretation is not merely

40. William H. Willimon has written about the importance of humor to pastoral ethics in his *Calling and Character: Virtues of the Ordained Life* (Nashville: Abingdon, 2000).

41. Augustine uses Cicero's threefold description of the purpose of rhetoric in *De doctrina* IV — it is to inform, to delight, and to move — though of course Christians will do those things differently than pagans since their *teloi* in particularly Christian rhetoric is different.

42. He uses this example in the classroom. In his most recent work he writes that Christians will be attracted to biblical metaphors more than, say, Plotinian ones: "The point is not that 'living water' expresses things better than 'inexhaustible infinite' or 'boiling over with life.' What is significant is that 'living water' is found in the Bible and would always be found in the Bible" (*The Spirit of Early Christian Thought*, 77).

extrinsic or question-begging, but turns out to be surprisingly succinct — if you grant the terms on which he does exegesis. That is, that scripture is a unified book with a common *skopos* articulated in the *regula fidei* and then in the church's creeds, and that the purpose now of reading scripture is not to find out what it says as though unaware, but rather to see anew truth already held in delightful new ways. Further, to use the terms of modern biblical scholarship, the connections Augustine makes are not surprising when one realizes that the New Testament writers themselves thought, wrote, and indeed lived within a biblical idiom that saturated all *they* wrote with the cadences of Israel's scripture. It is fitting then that Augustine finds Christian teaching throughout the Psalter when the New Testament itself, and that generations of ecclesial interpreters before and after him did as well.

## Exegesis and the Conversion of the Affections

Because allegory is meant to delight, rather than to prove anything, it is also meant to sit lightly. Augustine often concludes an interpretation by humbly submitting that if what he has said "pleases," then it suffices and he can move on to the next verse. Or, he can offer several interpretations of the same passage, some seemingly contradictory of others, because each will serve different purposes in the lives of hearers and so can be allowed to stand alongside each other. Finally, if Augustine could be shown that an interpretation he offers is indeed "arbitrary" or even contrary to Christian teaching, he would be the first to give it up. For anything that comports ill with the church's dogma or that hinders rather than aids the growth in virtue of his hearers should indeed be rejected.

It is important to look at the way Augustine himself examines the process by which his listeners hear and digest figurative interpretations of scripture. As he closes his introduction to an exposition on Psalm 96, Augustine offers this injunction: "may the Lord our God himself stir up in us the expectant delight proper to such a great matter. May he also adapt our discourse to your hearts, so that whatever exultation our heart feels at such sights may be communicated to our tongue, and thence to your ears, to your hearts, and eventually to your actions."[43] As in his former rhetorical career, the goal in speaking is here not merely to inform nor to entertain, nor even to persuade another of one's position, but to *move* speaker and hearers both toward a specific *telos*. Here, it is to move a congregation to re-embrace the truth of the gospel to

43. *EP* IV, 441.

which they are already committed. In another place Augustine gives a more thorough anatomy of desire. Just as a powerful emperor issues orders and the entire empire proceeds into instant commotion, so does a person act on the orders of her heart. "It is impossible for anyone who entertains good thoughts to commit bad deeds, for deeds proceed from thoughts. A person cannot do anything, or move his limbs to perform any action, unless his thoughts first issue the order. . . . Not only must your tongue and your voice praise God, but your conscience must praise him too, and your life and your deeds."[44] The goal is not merely to pass on information, nor to touch up seemingly heterodox scripture so it will pass orthodox muster, the goal is to move hearts, to sharpen desire, to increase love. Figurative reading is essential to that process.

Augustine here is in dialogue with an ancient philosophical conversation about the four principal "passions" — desire, joy, fear, and sadness — and what the wise person ought to do about them. Much of this ancient tradition Augustine finds useful, as all patristic writers find things among the treasures of the Egyptians that should be plundered for use in God's temple. It is a tidy description to say that joy is the possession of what is desired; that sadness is the possession of what is feared. Yet much in ancient philosophy must be rejected. An ancient Stoic version of *apatheia* would have such motions of the soul to play little or no part in human affective life. The late Augustine of *City of God* is quite critical of such a view: "If *apatheia* is to be defined as a condition such that the mind cannot be touched by any emotion whatsoever, who would not judge such insensitivity to be the worst of all vices?"[45] Citizens of the heavenly city indeed feel fear and desire, sadness and joy, but "in a manner consistent with the Holy Scriptures and wholesome doctrine." We feel *sadness* in the present time as we groan inwardly, awaiting the redemption of our bodies. We feel *fear* now of sin and temptation. We feel *joy* now in the hope of resurrection, and in the *desire* for good works that please God. Of these four cardinal passions only two will survive the present age: eternal life "will exhibit a love and a gladness . . . and will contain no fear or pain at all."[46]

The *City of God*'s discussion is mostly a polemic against other philosophical visions of the passions, one that is slightly mechanical in its insistence that proper knowledge of God brings the correct alignment of the passions. By contrast, the *Confessions'* brief discussion of the impact of the psalms on Au-

---

44. Comment on Psalm 148 in *EP* VI, 477.

45. *City of God* XIV.9, trans. R. W. Dyson (Cambridge: Cambridge University Press, 1998), 600.

46. *City of God*, 597-601.

gustine's conversion is drenched with emotion: "How loudly I cried out to you, my God, as I read the psalms of David, songs full of faith, outbursts of devotion with no room in them for the breath of pride!"[47] The psalms here do not simply reflect passions properly ordered by right doctrine, they are rather themselves the engine firing both emotion and intellect aright. Augustine offers here a quick exegesis of Psalm 4. The psalmist's question, "Why love emptiness and chase falsehood?" suggests to Augustine that he had indeed loved wrongly, causing him to "bewail many an episode among painful memories." The charge to "let your anger deter you from sin" fires Augustine's own anger against any memory of his sinful past that could spark present imitation of it. As he prays with the psalm's longing for joy in the right things and anger at wrong desire, Augustine makes the psalm his own. The praying of the psalm becomes a therapy for his affections, allowing it to affect not only his knowledge of God but also his deepest feelings toward God. His whole self is aligned properly with God. Affections are not then taken away, as with the Stoics, they are straightened out — toward God.[48]

We might even say that, for Augustine, learning to read the Psalter aright *is* salvation. "Play psalms to God's name, so that your name may be immovably preserved with God," he writes.[49] Augustine worries that without the psalms rightly read, pilgrims may lose heart and cease to ascend. So he preaches "with an eye to the spiritual weariness that can afflict us. God has no other song to teach us than the song of faith, hope, and love," which must be repeated skillfully anew to keep pilgrims' feet moving.[50] The reading of scripture is only an essential part of this earthly dispensation then, and has no need to continue in the eternal city, where no Gospel or epistle is read, but rather all persons "are directly nourished by the Word of God."[51] Some

---

47. *Confessions* IX.4.8, trans. Boulding, 175.

48. I am dependent here on Fiedrowicz, in his "Introduction" to the *EP*, I, 37-41.

49. On Psalm 91, *EP* IV, 348.

50. On Psalm 91, *EP* IV, 345.

51. On Psalm 93, *EP* IV, 379. Telford Work explicitly (if somewhat whimsically) rejects Augustine's contention in *De doctrina* that the use of scripture will discontinue in the eschaton (and can, theoretically, be discontinued by those who love sufficiently now): "When the prophets and apostles toast at the final banquet, their words will remember the events that led to the occasion" (Work, *Living and Active: Scripture in the Economy of Salvation* [Grand Rapids: Eerdmans, 2002], 312). Work decries as Augustine's "overdetermining Platonsim" his view that says scripture is for humanity's rehabilitation now, for our growth in faith, hope, and love in this age, until another age when we see Jesus "face to face." The difference between Augustine and Work is actually a difference in scriptural teleology. For Augustine, scripture is a mystery through which God's people grow in knowledge and love of God and one another until the beatific vision when faith gives way to knowledge, hope to reality, and love remains. For Work, whose al-

amount of progress continues even then however, for there human voices are permanently transfigured, ever in concert with angels' "amens" and "alleluiahs," in a "vision unclouded, love without satiety."[52] Until then Christians are on pilgrimage, a people on the way, and as pilgrims are wont to do, we are to "sing as [we] go. This is what wayfarers do to lighten their fatigue. You do the same."[53] Without such singing the pilgrim collapses; with it she is born to the heavenly city.

The psalms depict a broad spectrum of human emotion and affection because all of this is useful in the church's ascent. Human beings have the ability to grieve, to fear, to dread, or more positively to rejoice, to hope, to trust, and to love as capacities meant to lead us in our *theotic* ascent. Starting at the bottom: those who are not in the body will be surprised at all Christians have to "groan over." We might think Augustine is speaking of angels or some other disembodied spirit, but he is not, he is speaking of the church. Ecclesial life is no escape to ease, as anyone who has set foot in an actual church building knows. Life in the church requires much groaning, as Paul himself testifies (Romans 8:23). Let the surprised one "be incorporated, and he will feel the same."[54] When the psalmist asks, "How long will sinners gloat, oh Lord?" Augustine explains the particular therapeutic approach being taken: "the psalm grieves with you, and asks questions with you . . . anyone who wants to console someone else acts like this: unless he grieves with the other, he cannot lift him up."[55] Even a vice such as greed can be turned to a good use: "however greedy you are, God is enough for you," if your desire is properly changed by the psalms to seek the right thing rightly.[56] Other vices though, such as pride, "natural" though they may seem, are merely destructive and must be rooted out.[57] Everywhere Augustine describes how affections must either be bent to

---

most Qur'anic view of scripture keeps him from seeing its dispensability once we are face-to-face with Christ, scripture cannot ever be done away with. It is not only "the face of God for now," as with Augustine in Sermon 22.7, but remains the face of God even when we may behold the (actual) face of God.

52. On Psalm 85, *EP* IV, 231. Augustine not infrequently invokes an infinite growth in love and praise of God for the saints in the eschaton. While his is not as philosophically explicit as Gregory of Nyssa's, I wonder if his positive invocation of the description "infinity" casts doubt on Ekkehard Mühlenberg's famous thesis that Gregory was the first ancient writer to give a positive intellectual view of "infinity" (*Die Unendlichkeit Gottes bei Gregor von Nyssa: Gregors Kritik am Gottesbegriff der Klassischen Metaphysik* [Göttingen: Vandenhoeck & Ruprecht, 1966]).

53. On Psalm 66, *EP* III, 316.

54. On Psalm 54, *EP* III, 55.

55. On Psalm 93, *EP* IV, 385.

56. On Psalm 55, *EP* IV, 98.

57. On Psalm 59, *EP* IV, 183.

divine service or extirpated, he also insists that his hearers must "condemn what you are so as to deserve to become what you are not."[58]

In other places, Augustine seeks to turn more patently "positive" human affections to divine service. In a comment on "you have become my hope," Augustine writes that God has become our hope precisely in the passion and resurrection of Christ: "in him you see mirrored both your labors and your reward."[59] Much of the *Enarrationes* is taken up with reassuring hearers that their current labors are their participation in Christ's labors; their promised resurrection, demonstrated in Christ, is as assured as their current suffering. Often Augustine insists that his congregation should rejoice, as the psalmist says to rejoice, especially at the end of lament psalms, most of which turn to praise by their conclusion. Or, in contrast, occasionally Augustine will insist that his congregation follow a psalm's downward descent, from joy to anguish, as in Psalm 94: "we began with intense joy, yet the psalm closes on a note of sheer terror, 'to them I have sworn in my anger, they shall never enter my rest.'"[60] Even when we are allowed good things in this life over which we are right to rejoice, God is not so careless as to let us think these are ultimate goods. For they fall to the unjust as well as the just, and can easily be mistaken as ultimate goods in themselves, undirected to any higher good.[61] This is why "God infuses bitter troubles into what is sweet but harmful in this life, to teach us to seek other things that are sweet and salutary."[62] Eventually God intends to change human desire through our prayer of the Psalter and the prac-

58. On Psalm 99, *EP* V, 16.

59. On Psalm 60, *EP* IV, 195.

60. *EP* IV, 421.

61. Augustine is still often clumsily accused of "dualism." This is true if one means by "dualism" what Paul meant — that even as our outer form is wasting away, our inner selves are being renewed day by day (2 Corinthians 3–4). But it is mistaken if it indicates that, for Augustine, the body is bad and the soul good — he is at pains after his break with the Manichees to insist that they are two goods. The body is good as all created things are good in reflection of the beneficence of their creator, yet it is not an ultimate good that can be loved for its own sake. Likewise his concern about romantic love and human sexuality is not simple disparagement. In *The Excellence of Marriage* and other places Augustine finds a good role for marriage and sexuality (more limited than we might like perhaps), without calling them ultimate goods. His words of condemnation of flesh and sex echo scripture's own concern that these can easily be taken as goods in themselves and worshiped without reference to God. There are dualisms and then there are dualisms. See "The Excellence of Marriage," in *Marriage and Virginity,* trans. Ray Kearney, vol. I/9 of the *Works of Saint Augustine* (Hyde Park, NY: New City, 1999), 33-61.

62. Comment on Psalm 43, *EP* II, 266. I am struck by the parallel to Gregory of Nyssa's *On Virginity.* He writes there that for those who marry "pain is inseparably bound up with their existence," so that even its profound beauty must be seen as temporary in the face of God's eternity (in *Nicene and Post-Nicene Fathers,* vol. 5 [reprint in Grand Rapids: Eerdmans, 1994], 346).

tice of having our affections converted. He wishes that his hearers would soon "find it intensely pleasurable to love your enemy," and insists frequently that the martyrs were right to prefer their deaths to any other pleasure.[63] What we have here is a version of ancient philosophical *eudemonism* thoroughly reworked on Christian grounds. The particularly rigorous demands of the gospel, such as loving enemies or being martyred, become strange pleasures for Christians, while fear and anger and guilt are retrained to allow the church to shun sin.[64] Augustine imagines his hearers "blurting out a mouthful of requests" if the emperor offered to do for them whatever they wished. Their problem, he says, is that they must "widen" their desire. For the God of heaven and earth has offered whatever they wish — the earth? The sea? All the beauty of the sky? As marvelous as these are, they only attest to the beauty of their maker, who is the very source of all their beauty and is Beauty itself.[65] In Christianity, Augustine maintains, pleasures "are changed, not taken away."[66]

## What If Augustine Fails to Delight?
## Training the Spiritual Senses

So far we have seen that Augustine sees scripture as a display of the beauty of God that draws its hearers more deeply into the divine life. Figurative reading displays the Lord's beauty in such a way as to work on its hearers, reorder their desires, and lead them by means of these converted affections toward God. Yet there could be a problem here, or even a host of problems. Most basically: what if someone hearing Augustine's exegesis simply objects that she does not find it "beautiful"? Or even that it strikes the reader as absurd, or even worse, that it scandalizes? This is no trifling objection, since the very *point* of Christian figurative exegesis is to delight its hearers more deeply into the divine life, and since the scholarly opinion of this exegetical practice tends to oscillate between patronizing approbation and furious indignation. One of the reasons for modernity's continuing relegation of aesthetics to the private sphere is for just this reason — people of radically different political and intellectual commitments will have correlatively discordant views of the sublime. It seems

---

63. On Psalm 39, *EP* II, 216.

64. Gerald Schlabach has helpfully wrestled with the specifically Christian eudemonism of Augustine in his *For the Joy Set Before Us: Augustine and Self-Denying Love* (Notre Dame: University of Notre Dame Press, 2000).

65. On Psalm 34 (1), *EP* II, 55.

66. On Psalm 74, *EP* IV, 38.

preferable then to leave aesthetic questions to the mall of individual choice than to allow them a place in the already contested arena of public discourse. Further, it seems supremely question-begging to recommend Augustine's exegesis because of its "beauty." If we follow the order of Kant's three critiques and say that metaphysical questions are no longer up for debate, moral ones are, and aesthetic ones hardly matter, we would be hard-pressed to say how an aesthetic claim can win an argument about what is most true.

The most important and substantial recent theological work in this area has suggested that Christians cannot abandon the aesthetic so readily as this, if for no other reason than that our forebears built much of their theological work on the foundation of the aesthetic.[67] For Augustine the beauty of Christ and the refracted beauty of his figure in scripture are crucial to right interaction with human desire and growth toward *theosis*. This is, of course, no modern description of "beauty" without preexisting intellectual commitment — corporate art or Muzak that offends no one and just so strikes no one as beautiful. For something to be beautiful the beholder must recognize that it is indeed "fitting," *conveniens*, with the truth. It sits in a certain proper proportion with the contours of already held Christian teaching.[68] Yet it also explores those contours in a way that initially surprises because it seems discordant and out of proportion. Only when the exegete shows that these words indeed accord with the *regula* and the figure of Christ can the beholder see scripture's fittingness, its beauty, and just so have love increased. An example: very little of the polemical literature against the Donatists explores exactly

67. This is why Hans Urs von Balthasar famously rolls up the order of Kant's three critiques with his own three-volume work with a theological aesthetic in the first and most important place, a theo-drama focusing on the divine act in Christ in the middle, and a theo-logic reserved for the end. John Milbank, David Bentley Hart, and Michael Hanby follow in this tradition of seeing beauty as the heart of Christian thought and practice, with "reason" only following in its train.

68. In *Confessions* Augustine rebukes his early self for attempting to understand even God according to Aristotle's *Categories*, with its ten questions designed to group objects according to physical properties (IV.16.28). At the time he still thought of God as being in some way spatial, and could only recognize a proper view of God when he could conceive of a "spiritual substance," a "form not formed." Yet even later in his career he hardly abandons "fittingness" as a criterion for determining truth. After his conversion he can evaluate whether something "fits" with the creed because that is the true word about God entrusted to the church in pilgrimage to the City of God. In other words, his earlier attempts to perceive God direct and unaided foundered on God's immateriality, but his later attempts to see the beautiful conformity of scripture and Christian teaching follow the pattern of God's own appearance to humanity in the incarnation, church, sacraments, and scripture. The former is rejected as a failed human attempt to reach God (as any search for a physical deity will necessarily miss an immaterial God), the latter practiced as appropriate to God's *kenosis* in Christ.

*why* it is so harmful for someone to be rebaptized. The basic theological reason seems to be a lack of trust that God has done what he said he would do in baptism the first time, as well naturally as the rejection of the catholic church and the efficacy of its sacraments. In the *Enarrationes* Augustine adds an even more basic, exegetical reason the Donatists' practice of rebaptism must be wrong. In Jesus' confrontation with the authorities in the temple, he makes clear that soon no stone will be standing upon any other (Mark 13:2).[69] The stone, or rock, as Paul makes clear, is Christ (Romans 10:4). Therefore anyone who attempts to "put on" Christ a second time when she or he already has "put on" Christ in baptism before is stacking one stone upon another — a clear defiance of the Lord's own plain words.[70] Case closed! This is the kind of exegetical argument that ruled the day in the ancient Christian world, and yet that seems self-evidently absurd and laughably preposterous to our ears. But we are the ones who miss out here. For this way of arguing lends ancient Christian polemics a deeply biblical resonance that our debates often lack. It allows, and indeed demands, that these conversations draw on the full breadth and depth of scripture. It taxes the lexical and memory skills of even the best exegete. And most importantly, for those involved, it brings delight. Augustine says elsewhere, "I contemplate the saints more pleasantly" when I imagine them as teeth tearing off people from their errors and allowing the church to digest them and make them part of its body (Song of Songs 4:2).[71] This pleasure is, of course, premised on Augutine's *a priori* acceptance of Christian teaching, his practice of reading scripture for links between passages and life, and his desire to see scriptural ambiguity solved by the display of surprising continuity with the *regula* and Christ's *figura*. If someone does not see the beauty, does not "get the joke," as it were, Augustine is not stopping to explain it to them. That is to say, he will not here step out of the discourse of figurative exegesis to explain himself in plain terms; he will continue to provide figures of Christ from the tesserae of the Old Testament, in hopes that eventually his critics will see the beauty.[72]

---

69. *EP* IV, 424, "If anyone who is baptized in Christ puts on Christ, then who is engaged in putting one stone upon another? Surely the person who piles baptism upon existing baptism."

70. Citing Galatians 3:26 and its baptismal formula.

71. Augustine, *On Christian Doctrine* (II.6), trans. D. W. Robertson (Upper Saddle River, NJ: Prentice Hall, 1958), 37.

72. I am struck by the frequency with which figural readers of scripture turn to visual aesthetics, as with Gary Anderson's book on Genesis, with its lovely exposition of Michelangelo's Sistine Chapel paintings, *The Genesis of Perfection*. Similarly I am struck by the great sophistication of the exegesis of scripture offered in the iconographic tradition. For descriptions of iconography that are at once profound and accessible see Rowan Williams, *Ponder These Things:*

One Augustinian response to our concern about those who do not see the beauty in his work is his comments on the developing tradition of the "spiritual senses." Often the Psalter, and scripture more generally, speaks in metaphorical terms of human perception of God as a certain seeing, hearing, touching, tasting, smelling, or some combination of all these. "Taste and see that the Lord is good," the psalmist says. And for Christians these terms take on a multiplicity of meanings. Of course God in himself cannot be approached by physical human senses, since God is not a body. Yet God did himself become tactile, visible, audible, *sensible* for us in the incarnation, to train us who cannot properly perceive God how to do so (1 John 1:1). This divine tangibility continues for the church in her worship, where Christians can taste the sacraments, behold the divine mysteries, hear the sermon, and physically touch those who are also members of Christ's still-physical body.[73] These physical encounters with God now however are not sufficient in themselves. They must train our "inner" senses to perceive God "spiritually," with an "eye," or "ear" more profound than merely our physical senses. We must progress from "seeing" Christ in the flesh, which alone is not sufficient, to "seeing" his divinity, which can be accomplished only at the beatific vision. These "spiritual senses" are not non-material, since Augustine firmly holds to the resurrection of the flesh into a transfigured materiality in which we are capable of "sensing" God. In fact, for Augustine, the materiality of the church and the immateriality of the divine nature are inseparably and eternally joined in the two natures of Christ, between which our sanctification takes place.[74] In the meantime, we are left with a dramatic interplay between seeing and not-seeing, sensing and not sensing. Some of those who "saw" Christ in his flesh crucified him (1 Corinthians 2:8), others saw him in faith yet were promised some sort of future seeing of him (John 14:21), those who await such vision "see" him now in his pluriform body in the church, the sacraments, each other. Augustine actually paraphrases Jesus' words in John, "whoever loves me will be loved by my Father and I will love him and show

*Praying with Icons of the Virgin* (Franklin, WI: Sheed and Ward, 2002), and *The Dwelling of the Light: Praying with Icons of Christ* (Grand Rapids: Eerdmans, 2004), and Michel Quenot's *The Icon: Window on the Kingdom* (Crestwood, NY: St. Vladimir's, 1996). These show that the icons are complex *exegetical* displays, as well as objects of devotion meriting the church's *doulia*.

73. For an example not so much about Augustine but about early Christian physical interaction see Edward Phillips, *The Ritual Kiss in Early Christian Worship* (Cambridge: Grove, 1996).

74. Lewis Ayres shows the "space" of our salvation is that between the two natures of Christ — *per ipsum pergimus ad ipsum*, "through him we travel to him" — in "The Christological Context of Augustine's *De Trinitate* XIII: Toward Relocating Books VIII-XV," *Augustinian Studies* 29, no. 1 (1998): 111-39.

myself to him," saying, "It was as though he said, 'You see the form of a servant, but the form of God is concealed. With the one I am wooing you, but the other I am keeping for you; with the one I am nourishing you now while you are still children, but with the other I feed you in your maturity.'"[75] This interaction between seeing in one's spiritual senses on the way to a seeing that is not non-physical in the beatific vision incites desire on the way to hoped-for full vision (1 John 3:2; 1 Corinthians 13:12).

Similar dynamics to this are at work with regard to other "spiritual senses," such as taste, and even smell. In a comment on "my bruises have rotted and festered," Augustine writes, "You only need a healthy sense of smell in spiritual matters to be aware how sins fester. The opposite to this reek of sin is the fragrance of which the apostle says, 'we are the fragrance of Christ offered to God. . . .'"[76] Christians are those more repulsed by sin than by physical rotting flesh; more drawn to God than to any lovely fragrance in creation. As with any metaphor, the terms of comparison *matter* and are not left behind — Augustine here counts on his hearers' own experience of repulsion and attraction to various smells. In an incarnational faith these are not merely to be discounted in pursuit of spiritual allure (as the early Augustine may have thought), they are rather gathered up and used liturgically to draw believers (e.g., through incense), and eventually will be brought to the fullness of their created purpose in the transfigured materiality of the heavenly city. Grace does not destroy nature, nor does it leave it alone, but transfigures it.

Similarly, "taste" is a spiritual sense that must be developed in order properly to attend to God in the world. We only *have* a sense of thirst at all to draw us toward our greater thirst for God, satisfied as this is for now in the exposition of scripture, until it will be satisfied in full at the eschaton. Augustine often speaks of "Iduthin," a character to whom several psalms are devoted, translated as "leaping across" and interpreted as such in the *Enarrationes*. The central inspiration for Iduthin's leaping is scripture itself. As the deer pants for water, so Iduthin leaps, for "droplets of divine dew were falling on him from the scriptures, arousing his thirst to run like a hart to the fountain of life."[77] Elsewhere, commenting on the psalmist's "our soul was crushed down in the dust, our belly stuck to the ground," Augustine's mind is drawn to Revelation's comment that the book the seer is given to eat "was sweet in my mouth, but bitter in my stomach" (10:10).[78] What can this mean? "Surely" it

75. On Psalm 43 in *EP* II, 274.
76. On Psalm 37:6 in *EP* II, 153.
77. On Psalm 38 in *EP* II, 175.
78. On Psalm 43 in *EP* II, 278.

refers to the "highest precepts," which "spiritual" persons can accept but are "unacceptable to the carnal," and can "only give the carnal indigestion." The prime example is Christ's command to sell all you have and give to the poor. "How sweet is that command in the Church's mouth! All the spiritual have obeyed it." But ask a sensual person to do the same, and he will walk sadly away, as the rich man in the Gospel. "Why does a carnal person walk away? Because that book, so sweet to the mouth, is bitter in the belly." Notice that the image is premised on the spiritual and carnal being one body, such that the carnal can be the distressed stomach and the spiritual the sweetened mouth. And notice the attempt by Augustine at conversion here. He is trying to lure his hearers into *being* the spiritual, to having this difficult command not only taste good but settle well in the stomach. Talk of the spiritual senses is also talk of the conversion of the affections, a rhetorical attempt to train hearers into seeing a certain beauty, tasting a sweetness that remains sweet and does not cause indigestion.

Sometimes the spiritual senses can run together, as when Augustine prepares his hearers to hear a "sweet mystery" in the designation of many psalms that they were written "for the sons of Korah." He has been told that the word "Korah" is translatable into Latin as *calvus*, that is "bald," such that the sons of Korah are the sons of Calvary — the place of the skull. He anticipates this explanation by promising a "special sweetness, as you ruminate on things you have heard already, but now think about once more as we remind you." In the Lord's commands about animals that chew in certain ways, we are taught "by this reference to rumination that each of us should consign what we hear to our hearts, and not be slow to mull over it afterwards." By these words on spiritual hearing and chewing we are led to "delicious new flavors in what we already know, enticing us to listen to them again with delight, for when the idiom is diversified, the ancient truth seems ever new as it is presented differently."[79] Those who hear these words about spiritual hearing and tasting could not but also hear references to a Word now spoken anew in liturgy and preaching, a saving mystery available in tasted sacraments, and correlatively in holy feasts and fasts. Those who allow their spiritual senses to be appealed to through figurative reading of scripture will have these senses honed, enhanced, on the way to a plenitude of spiritual (again, not non-physical) apprehension in the beatific vision. Augustine, like any preacher, is not unaware that he has to convince his hearers to see beauty where they may not immediately see it, and so with other senses physical and spiritual. The aesthetic is contested territory, then and now. Augustine hopes to show them the beauty

---

79. Comment on Psalm 46 in *EP* II, 324.

he himself now sees, the fullness of which he anticipates. He is worried about the problem that others will not see it, so he works tirelessly to show them the beauty he now contemplates on the way to apprehension.

Undoubtedly for Augustine the most important spiritual sense is that of vision. Arguably, at least, this is because the most important spiritual sense in scripture is that of vision. Augustine loves such verses as John 14:9, in which Jesus asks, "Have I been with you so long and hast thou not known me, Philip?" Obviously Philip has "seen" Jesus in one way, but in another and more profound way, he has not. On one hand, Christ is indeed "fair beyond all humankind," the bridegroom for whom the bride longs in Solomon's canticle. Yet on the other hand, and more obviously, he "has no fair form or comeliness," and the ugliness of the cross is rightly derided. For Augustine, this dynamic between seeing and not-seeing continues in the church and until the judgment, because Christ remains both present and absent, both visible and not. "The bridegroom to whom we have been wedded is absent, in a sense. He gave us his Holy Spirit as his pledge, but he is absent in himself." In a similar way, he was "absent" to those who murdered him, for these "lacked the eyes to see Christ's beauty." His disciples lacked the eyes too until Pentecost, as Philip demonstrates. For these "eyes first need to be cleansed to enable them to see the light, but even when gently touched by its splendor they are enkindled with love and a longing to be healed, and at last they are illumined." This interplay between seeing and not seeing is meant to bring about love, which is God the Spirit himself: "charity falls in love with charity! He loved us in order to win our answering love, and to empower us to love him in return he came to us in his Holy Spirit. He is beautiful, but he is absent. His bride must question herself, if she is chaste," as she awaits his coming.[80] The incarnation has set up among us a pedagogy of alternation between presence and absence, between desire, love, and anxious waiting, all meant to grow us toward that Love that is God himself, now pledged in earnest to us, later to be given in full.

It would be difficult to overstate the importance of this theme — of God's beauty, human desire, and the growth of the latter toward the former — in Augustine's exegetical work. The entire purpose of biblical interpretation is to *move* those who attend the liturgy to love of God. The active verb — move — is important, for those present are all pilgrims on the way somewhere, and need to be helped along. Augustine tries to do this by showing his hearers the beauty of God refracted through the seemingly ordinary words of scripture. Those listening must have, to begin with, some expectation that what will be said is important. What is being read and

80. All comments on Psalm 127 in *EP* VI, 104-5.

exposited is the very word of God, the saving oracles, written by the very finger of God (Exodus 31:18).[81] If it confuses or offends the problem is not with scripture, but with its hearers — the interpreter must make plain precisely how these words bear witness to the *totus Christus*, to both the head and members of the body of Christ. This also requires an interpreter of some skill. Like Origen's horticulturalist, working in the garden of scripture to mix herbs into the right medicine for a particular ailment, the interpreter must be able to mix scripture in just the right way to help his hearers.[82] Such ability in the interpreter, and such basic interest from one's hearers, are both presumed. What happens next is as difficult to explain as is beauty itself. Augustine notes a point of exegetical puzzlement, enlightenment takes place, and his hearers are surprised to see the faith they already hold newly illumined by these strange words. As this continually happens the church's hearers develop spiritual senses able to perceive Christ even here, and so grow toward the love of God that is both journey and destination in this pilgrimage of Christian discipleship. Proper accounts of divine beauty and human desire are then absolutely crucial to a particularly Christian biblical hermeneutic. In an exposition delivered in Augustine's late and anti-Pelagian period, he preaches that "every part of holy scripture commends to us the liberating grace of God, to the end that we may commend ourselves to grace. . . . The Lord will help me to conceive in my heart worthy ideas on the subject, and also to bring them forth in a way that will be useful to you. It is the love of God and the fear of God that chiefly bring home the truth to us." Grace, and the proper loves and fears that it brings, is a hermeneutical issue. Without proper longings, always given as gift by God to direct the recipient aright to God, no psalm can be read well.[83] Else-

81. Commonly in patristic exegesis the "finger of God" of Exodus 31:18 is equated with the "Spirit of the living God" of 2 Corinthians 3:3 since Paul says it is he who has "written not with ink" and "on the tablets of human hearts."

82. "As every herb has its own virtue whether for the healing of the body, or some other purpose, and it is not given to everybody to know the use of every herb . . . the saint is a sort of spiritual herbalist, who culls from the sacred Scriptures every jot and every common letter. . . . Just so you may regard the Scriptures as a collection of herbs, or as one perfect body of reason; but if you are [not] a scriptural botanist . . . you must not suppose that anything written is superfluous . . ." (from St. Basil of Caesaria and St. Gregory Nazianzus, *The Philocalia of Origen*, trans. George Lewis [Edinburgh: T&T Clark, 1911], X.2, 52.

83. Comment on Psalm 70 (1) in *EP* III, 112. Both Stanley Hauerwas and R. R. Reno echo this Augustinian theme when they argue that the primary difficulty with scripture is not its words, its historical distance from us, or any other abstract "problem," but rather with the spiritual condition of its hearers, with our lack of holiness, and our opposition to the God there making claims upon us. Hauerwas and Reno are both here indebted to Karl Barth's description of "eth-

where, after a promise of great mystery in words just read, Augustine insists his congregation must help him unfold the mystery to them: "we must search for the spiritual sense in everything the psalm has said. Your desires will help us in Christ's name as we seek it out."[84] Without their longings properly ordered, Augustine's exposition will necessarily fail. Without scripture their desires will not be properly ordered. The loves, ears, longings, in short, affections, of a congregation are essential to its hearing and living the word correctly — that is to say, beautifully.

## Examples: Zoology and Numerology

This emphasis on beauty in biblical interpretation explains two related features of patristic biblical exegesis often lampooned even by sympathetic historians of Christian thought: his penchant for seeing Christian meaning in faulty ancient zoology, and his love of numerology. Both of these are meant to bring about delight, not at Augustine's expense, as commonly happens now, but the delight of seeing Christian meaning displayed in a surprisingly new way that accords with faith and so increases love. Commenting on the "deer" that "pants" in Psalm 41, Augustine notes that deer are thought to rest their heads upon one another's backs, allowing the weak to be supported by the strong, and all to "bear one another's burdens" (Galatians 6:2). Innocent enough. He also inquires precisely why the deer are so thirsty, and answers "a hart kills snakes, and . . . he burns with more intense thirst than before." Naturally snakes represent vices: "put the snakes of your iniquity to death, and you will long more keenly for the font of truth."[85] For Augustine the psalmist cannot simply be giving zoological information, nor even speaking of God or humanity in prettily poetic terms — he has to be bearing witness to the incarnation and right human response to it. Here a contemporary zoological tradition about deer allows him to do that.

In several places in the *Enarrationes* Augustine draws on an ancient zoological tradition about eagles. This held that elderly birds were kept from eating by excessive growth in their beaks. By necessity, then, an old eagle

---

ics" as a traditional Christian way of avoiding the command of God. The relationship between Augustine and Barth has been too seldom explored. See Hauerwas, *Unleashing the Scriptures* (Nashville: Abingdon, 1993); Reno, *The Church in the Ruins* (Grand Rapids: Brazos, 2003); and Barth, *Church Dogmatics* II/2 and III/4, trans. G. W. Bromiley et al. (Edinburgh: T&T Clark, 1957, 1961).

84. Comment on Psalm 103 (1) in *EP* V, 107.
85. Psalm 41 in *EP* II, 241-42.

smashed its beak against a rock, so as to be able to eat and return to health. Augustine expresses a note of agnosticism about the biology: "Now, I do not know, brothers and sisters, whether the reports about the . . . eagle are true, or are only old wives' tales, but it does not matter. The truth is in the scriptures, and scripture has its own good reason for putting them before us." Scripture's purpose is to have "you" be "the sort of person whose youth can be renewed like the eagle." This is done by smashing the overgrowth of desire remembered from life before conversion, and its confining memories, against the rock that is Christ (Romans 10:4). Augustine is unworried whether the particular analogy satisfies: "you do not find this particular image helpful? Very well, take another; the point is you must act on it."[86]

The most developed zoological image to which we will attend is that of Psalm 101, "I have become like the pelican that lives in solitary places, like the owl in ruined walls. I kept watch, and was like a sparrow alone on a roof."[87] The pelican is a solitary bird, Augustine is told, like a Christian among pagans. The owl in the ruined walls is like a Christian among the lapsed. The sparrow that sits on the roof is a Christian among Christians who have become lukewarm — in Augustine's lexical imagination, he represents one tempted to descend from the rooftop instead of staying to meet the Lord at the end of time (Matthew 24:17). Such a one should remain on the rooftop and announce from there the gospel (Matthew 10:27). Not very revealing so far. Then Augustine asks why so much is made of these birds, and, sure that scripture must edify, he turns to identifying *the Lord* with each bird. Pelicans, he is told (for they do not live in the preacher's or hearers' part of the world) slay their young in the nest, mourn them deeply, and then the mother wounds herself to pour her blood over her young, which then revive. The christological image is clear in the pouring out of life-giving blood. Christ has a motherly love for his church, like a hen over chicks (Matthew 23:37), just as Paul is both motherly and fatherly to his churches (1 Corinthians 4:15; Galatians 4:19). The parallel between the pelican's and Christ's life-giving blood is obvious enough, but Augustine asks about the initial slaying of the young in the mother's own nest. "But does her killing of her chicks fit into that picture? Yes, it does fit, for he declares, 'I will kill, and I will give life; I will strike, and I will heal' (Deuteronomy 32:39)." Just as Saul of Tarsus had to be wounded before being revived, so do the pelican's young. The solitude in which the pelican dwells refers to Christ's virgin birth, a birth without the companionship of another, and more generally to the loneliness of the wil-

86. Comments on Psalm 66 in *EP* III, 322-23.
87. *EP* V, 52-55.

derness and the passion of Christ. Returning to the other birds, the pelican's solitude refers to the temptation in the wilderness, the owl in the ruins to his passion and its destruction of the temple that is his body, and the sparrow on the rooftop to his ascension, after which he crows in prayer for us. Again, as before, the analogies sit rather lightly with regard to the zoology textbooks: "This report may be true or false; but if it is true, observe how apt a symbol it is of him who gave us life by his own blood." He does indeed wish to be biologically correct, yet that is quite obviously a matter of much less importance. It is more important that his exposition *fits* with the words on the page, the truth of Christian teaching, and the needs of his hearers at the time. Notice the effects of this exegesis as well: readers will now associate pelicans with Christ, as is appropriate, since he is their creator; all creation, if viewed aright, indeed bears witness to him.[88] Further, any later time that one hears mention of a pelican (how often? Perhaps not until the church's lectionary returns it to this passage) one will remember this allegory, think of Christ, and be delighted anew. Not so much that the biology is correct, for as we have seen Augustine's biological certainty rests lightly. But rather that even this odd animal the preacher has never seen bears witness to the church's Lord. Augustine's exegesis here is *fitting* then with the words on the page, with Christian teaching, and with the goal of propelling his hearers more deeply into the divine life. The last goal remains paramount.

Augustine's love of numerology does not figure in the *Enarrationes* as often as in some other prominent works. Yet it does appear — as when he puzzles over the number of psalms in his comments on Psalm 150, noting that the number fifteen represents the conjunction of the Old and New Covenants, the former symbolized by its seventh day Sabbath and the latter by its eighth. Or that the number 50 suggests "a week of weeks," and the number 7 is important both in Isaiah's and in Revelation's discussions of the Spirit.[89] Did not the Spirit come fifty days after the resurrection? That number 50 is simply multiplied by the 3 in the Holy Trinity to arrive at 150.

Augustine also wonders elsewhere over Psalm 89's promise of seventy years of life, eighty if we are strong. Have not many lived far less, and others

88. Translator Boulding notes that Augustine here influences medieval iconography and hymnody: "it is referred to in the Eucharistic hymn *Adoro te devote,* attributed to Saint Thomas Aquinas: *Pie pellicane, Iesu Domine,*" as commonly translated, "Oh pelican divine." If one is in a part of the world in which pelicans live, such as Egypt for Augustine or North Carolina for us, to see the bird is to see a christological marker in creation, that is, to see the sign quality of the creature called pelican for what it was created to be — a reference to the *res* that signifies no other, the triune God.

89. *EP* VI, 508-9, referring to Isaiah 11:2-3 and Revelation 4:5 and 5:6.

lived far more?[90] There must be something more than just a factual recording of years here. Seventy reflects the temporal benefits of the Old Testament, since the temporal world was created in seven days, and eighty years represents the eternal benefits of the new, befitting a Christian understanding of the resurrection as the eighth day of creation. Yet, scripture says, "any more than these are labor and sorrow," which would seem to auger against a view of the 80 referring to eschatological bliss. Not to worry. The days are still "labor and sorrow" for those under the New Covenant, for we still groan as we await the redemption of our bodies. Augustine hopes the exegesis will match Christian teaching, the words on the page, and the need to spur the affections of his hearers at that particular moment in time.

Elsewhere the numerical observations grow a bit more elaborate. Augustine shares the patristic age's fascination with the 153 fish that are caught when the risen Lord orders the disciples to cast their nets one more time in John 21. As a good reader of John, Augustine is keen to look deeper than the surface, for numbers and events and dialogue in John more often than not take on multiple meanings, as only poor readers could fail to see.[91] The number cannot refer to the full number of saints, or those who remain in the net untorn, as opposed to the heretics whose escape from the catholic church and so from the Lord. It cannot mean this, for there have been more than that many martyrs in the very town (Massa Candida) in which Augustine is preaching! No — the number must mean something more. A good beginning is the number 10 — a key number in scripture, here referring to the number of the commandments. Another is 7 — in this case taken to mean the sevenfold gift of the Spirit in Isaiah 11:2-3 by which God enables Christians to follow the divine law. Now, if you add up the numbers between one and seventeen, $1 + 2 + \ldots 17$, guess what result you get? 153. The lesson in John is that Christians know "nothing fulfills the law except the charity which is poured out in our hearts through the Holy Spirit."[92] Further exercised by the problem at hand — precisely how many will be at the judgment, when the Lord promises only twelve thrones for those who are to judge Israel (Matthew 19:28) — Augustine notes that 12 appropriately stands for the whole of God's people, as it stood for the tribes of Israel, and now can be seen as the full number of those called from the 4 winds by the 3-fold God: $4 \times 3 = 12$. So "12" is not a limit, but a sign to be mirthfully explored. The exegesis fits with the

90. *EP* IV, 308-9.

91. See, for example, Craig Koester, *Symbolism in the Fourth Gospel: Meaning, Mystery, Community* (Minneapolis: Fortress, 2003).

92. On Psalm 150 in *EP* VI, 510.

words on the page and the teaching of the church, and throws further light on faith already held, inching love higher. And it makes its hearers laugh — not in mockery — but in seeing that which they already hold true depicted anew in ways that delight.

If we moderns were to object, "No, that's arbitrary!" or "You can make anything you want out of that number!" Augustine might reply, "Go ahead — what other point of faith might 12 or 153 illumine?" Faces would turn toward us, expecting to be enlightened and delighted. We might demur, as modern biblical scholarship often has about the *significance* of numbers in scripture. One contemporary commentator on John's Gospel, after summarizing Augustine's own efforts to explain 153, protests, "such proposals hardly commend themselves to the modern mind." Gerard Beasley-Murray is more impressed with Jerome's suggestion that the number represents all the species of fish then thought to exist in the world, so that the 153 merely points to a universal number. There is scant historical evidence for that use of the number however, so we can only hold out hope that "one of these days some ancient writing will come to light containing a comparable tradition to the varieties of fish attested by Jerome." Beasley-Murray prefers to "allow the secret of 153 to remain, yet acknowledging its attestation to the greatness of the sign it emphasizes."[93] Augustine's auditors would have been either puzzled or disappointed. To say 153 adds to the greatness is to say nothing — we knew already the miracle was great. And it contends against the spirit of John's Gospel, which propels good readers to find christological significance in all things, not least in numbers. Further, no delight has been enhanced, no love forwarded. Just so, for Augustine, *scripture has not been read at all.*

My point here is not necessarily to recommend ancient zoology or what seems to us the parlor game of playing with numbers. It is rather to say that Augustine offers a remedy against the malady that strikes contemporary biblical exegesis, namely that it is boring. Not always, nor in all hands (for many contemporary exegetes have their own greatness that Augustine himself lacked). Rather it is their premise that is so frequently dull. The goal of discovering the intention of an original author or redactors, while bearing an antiquarian interest that will captivate the few, cannot feed the many whom the gospel seeks to attract. These want to hear about God, about creation, and about the salvific work of the incarnation that bears the one to the other, now illumined anew by the preacher from the particular words of today's lection. To offer theories about proto-Q or the community of the beloved

---

93. *John*, Word Biblical Commentary 36 (Waco, TX: Word, 1987), 401-4.

disciple will be, in many cases, to offer a stone when bread is what the children need (Luke 11:11-12).

This is hardly to say that modern critical study corners the market on boring exegesis. On the contrary, Augustine himself is often tedious reading on the psalms, belaboring a point long since made, continuing on seemingly just to cover each verse of a psalm rather than to illumine or delight. His polemics against schismatic and heretical groups grow more tiresome the longer one reads. The strain of the Pelagian controversy in particular in driving Augustine to find unmerited grace on every page of the psalms can be simply somnambulant. This is often a difficulty with ancient Christian figurative exegesis: knowing in advance that any interpretation must match the *regula fidei*, must illumine the figure of Christ, can indeed serve as a sort of imaginative straight-jacket (Jesus again — surprise!). Yet even here Augustine outflanks his modern rivals. For with Augustine we have tools that allow us to say why exegesis has failed: it is not sufficiently beautiful. So when Augustine is tedious or belabors a point or fails to show the shimmering newness with which the scriptures are meant to shine, we have grounds on which to complain. In short, Augustine's exegesis has not only a christological foundation, as we explored in Chapter 2. It has also a christological *telos,* a goal of showing the beauty of God anew so as to convert anew the affections of his hearers on their way in pilgrimage to the heavenly city. If an act of exegesis fails in that task, we at least have tools with which to explain its failure. Whereas exegesis without telos lacks adequate theological means to display a mistake.

Here I turn a common attack against allegorical exegesis on its head. It is commonly claimed that if figurative exegesis is allowed then a clever interpreter can claim to find anything present in scripture, and so may give to whatever previously held intellectual or political conviction, on whatever other arbitrary ground, a supposedly biblical approbation. It is important to be able to ask of any intellectual tradition precisely when it has made a mistake.[94] Without the ability to answer that question a tradition of enquiry can hardly be deemed intelligible. There are indeed Augustinian grounds for determining the success of an act of exegesis — namely, whether it is beautiful. By this we mean whether it is "fitting" with the words on the page, with the figure of Christ, and with the need of the congregation present to have its af-

---

94. See Chapter 2, p. 77 n. 58 above. This can almost be stated as a philosophical truism, but I first saw it stated this way in Rowan Williams's essay "The Unity of Christian Truth": "It is when we know what a mistake is — in *any* sort of discourse — that we know we are responsible to something other than individual taste or will; if you want to know what sort of truth-claims a certain discourse is making, ask what, if anything, it means by a mistake and how it identifies it" (*On Christian Theology* [Oxford: Blackwell, 2000], 17).

fections redirected aright once more. If one wishes for a more "scientific" appraisal of the success of exegesis than that, such as conformity to the original intention of scripture's authors, I submit that they have merely chosen their own standard of beauty, their own criteria of "fittingness," and that there is no neutral ground on which to decide which to prefer it to Augustine's. Those committed to a vision of humanity and its destiny similar to Augustine's however should choose the grounds for exegetical criteria of divine beauty and human desire.

## An Augustinian Pause in Reading Like Augustine

This leads to a further question about Augustinian "fittingness" and beauty in interpretation: the question of a text's "working effects," its impact on previous traditions of readers as an indispensable aspect of interpretation for today.[95] A great deal of my own interest in ancient Christian allegory is a trust that a millennium and a half of an exegetical tradition that served the church well cannot have been wholly aberrant. This sense is furthered by contemporary historians' success at throwing new light on ancient church figures by examining previously ignored tomes of exegetical work.[96] But my primary concern is a pneumatological one: the Spirit led the church to interpret scripture in these ways for a great deal of its history. The witness of the majority of the church's saints is to practice exegesis in ways similar to Augustine. The fruits of Augustine's exegetical labors were long codified as essential reading for ecclesial exegetes by his presence in the *glossa ordinaria* — a quite *physical* insistence that one could not read scripture without also reading the saints' readings of scripture, as well as their readings of previous saints' readings.[97]

Yet there are at least two problems here. One, Augustine himself does not read with anything like a gloss in front of him. He is in fact reticent even to

95. The description of course comes from Hans-Georg Gadamer's *Truth and Method*, trans. Joel Weinsheimer and Donald G. Marshall (New York: Continuum, 1999).

96. David Steinmetz's work on Luther and Calvin consistently returns to their biblical exegesis of specific passages in order to show their theological positions with greater clarity and accuracy. His *Calvin in Context* (New York: Oxford University Press, 1995) and *Luther in Context* (Grand Rapids: Baker, 1995) shed such light on those figures precisely because they examine their biblical exegesis in particular instead of making broad generalizations about their work.

97. I take this point from Peter Candler. See his *Theology, Rhetoric, Manuduction, or Reading Scripture Together on the Path to God* (Grand Rapids: Eerdmans, 2006).

say when he is leaning on previous exegetical tradition, or even on others for linguistic or manuscript help. My recommending Augustine as a gloss through which we should read the Psalter is not, in fact, a particularly Augustinian thing to do, historically speaking. Further, if it is crucial that biblical exegesis demonstrate scripture's refraction of God's beauty, then it remains a legitimate protest to say that one does not find Augustine's exegesis beautiful! My gesturing above to Augustine's theology of the spiritual senses is merely a sign that as a preacher he was aware that aesthetic claims are debatable, and that he has work to do to show his hearers how the beauty of Christian faith shines through the Psalter's words. For our part we can say that if the very thing meant to convert our affections in fact hardens them, contorts them, turns them against God, then a proper remedy for our spiritual malady has hardly been applied. There might in fact then be times when an Augustinian approach to biblical exegesis would have to withhold Augustine's own exegesis from contemporary hearers of scripture. Chapter 4 will provide an example of precisely this with regard to Augustine's treatment of the Jews. To use a musical metaphor, if a hearer of scripture has become accustomed to a score present in contemporary scholarship, such as modern success in rapprochement between Jews and Christians, a score not sufficiently present in Augustine's work, how can we expect her to find delight in Augustine?

Here again, an ancient multivalent approach to exegesis can absorb this question in a way that modern critical approaches typically cannot. If Augustine's own work fails to delight, fails to convert affections, in such a way that another approach may be more successful, then an Augustinian response would be to let the other approach do its work. The hope would be that eventually Augustine, or an ancient Christian vision of exegesis more generally, might also aid in such a reader's ascent to the beatific vision even if it cannot now. Conversely, modern critical approaches to scripture have no room to allow for Augustine's approach except in the odd circumstance that what he has to say happens to comport with a historical critical approach. It is, once again, an ancient Christian vision of exegesis that can allow multiple approaches to the biblical text, including those that seem to be antithetical to it, whereas modernist approaches normally cannot.

## Augustine Verse-by-Verse

A final task for this chapter will be to display a bit of Augustinian exegesis in detail. The goal will be to see how Augustine pulls on his hearers' desire in an attempt to draw them toward God in an ordinary exposition. We shall look at Augustine's Psalm 61:

**To the end: Iduthin's song for David himself.**

Shall not my soul surrender itself to God?
For my salvation comes from him.
He is my very God, my savior, my protector, and I shall waver no more.
Let not the foot of pride come near me.
How long will you pile your loads on one man?
Kill me, all of you. Press on me as a leaning wall or a shaky fence.
Yet they thought to refuse me honor.
With their mouths they were blessing, but cursing in their hearts
     all the while.
All the same my soul will surrender itself to God.
To God will my soul be subject, for my patience comes from him.
He is my God and my salvation, he is my refuge, and I shall never leave him.
In God is my salvation and my glory,
He is the God who helps me, my hope is in God.
Hope in him, you whole assembly of the people.
Pour out your hearts in his presence, for God is our ally.
What liars the children of men are, with their scales!
Intent on deception, in their empty pursuits they are as one.
Do not set your hope on iniquity, or your desires on robbery.
If riches flow in abundance, do not set your heart on them.
Only once has God spoken, but these two things have I heard:
That power belongs to God, and to you, O Lord, mercy;
For you will requite each one according to our deeds.[98]

"All the utterances of God are to us a delight," Augustine begins. "The sweetness that we find in his word is to us an inducement to speak, and to you to listen, so that with the help of him who grants us such exquisite enjoyment, our land may yield its fruit." The psalm is ascribed to Iduthin, which Augustine reminds his hearers means "one who leaps over them." Yet this already presents a problem: how does one who makes progress in the spiritual life, who successfully "leaps over them," avoid pride at the achievement? Iduthin himself, the speaker of the psalm, worried over this very thing, for "he had heard the warning, 'anyone who exalts himself will be humbled. . . .'" Precisely how Iduthin had "heard" Luke 18:14 is unclear! Yet the theme of shunning pride and seeking humility was a biblical one long before Jesus or Luke's

98. From Psalm 61 in *EP* III, 202-28.

Gospel. We see here the sort of exegetical problem that Augustine's own hermeneutical strictures place upon him: how does scripture encourage spiritual ascent while shearing spiritual pride? The psalmist already has an answer in the further prayer, "let not the foot of pride come near me." The shearing of pride is *itself* ascent, as the literal and spiritual progress of the psalm indicates. Augustine adds a theological gloss to explain how ascent and humility can coincide, and indeed be too intertwined to separate: "however near I draw to him, however high I soar, however far I leap over others, I shall be below God, not a rival to God." This ascent represents no competition, since there is always ever more of God toward which to ascend, and the comparative calculus that measures one against another is ruled out both by the psalm text and by the non-competitive nature of God.[99]

Augustine then turns to the complaint, "How long will you pile your loads on one man?" and suggests that the psalmist's opponents pile their load by insults, ambush, and persecution. These are enough trouble to deter anyone who might be praying the psalm as part of a false ascent of pride. Then Augustine asks a question of the verse, "Kill me, all of you," which is, "How could there be enough room in a single human body for that person to be killed by 'all'? The words would make no sense without the Church. We must then understand this person as ourselves, as the person of our Church, the one person that is Christ's body." The *totus Christus* is (are?) "two in one voice, two in one passion, and when iniquity has finally passed away, they will be two in one rest." Again we see Augustine's description of twoness and oneness in Christ in more dramatic than ontological terms, though the former is certainly not exclusive of the latter. He cites Colossians 1:24[100] for support here, and then is drawn to discuss the way in which the *totus Christus* actually preceded Christ's historical life, as Jacob's hand came out of his mother's womb before his head did! "Before his coming in the flesh he sent ahead of him certain of his members; and after they had foretold his advent he came himself, organically connected with them." We see here the manner in which Augustine's approach to the literal text of scripture works in conjunction

---

99. Kathryn Tanner makes the non-competitive nature of God's relationship to his creatures key in her *Jesus, Humanity and the Trinity: A Brief Systematic Theology* (Minneapolis: Fortress, 2001). Hanby's discussion of the Pelagian controversy in *Augustine and Modernity* rightly notes that many misreadings of that part of Augustine's polemical career happen because historians treat God's grace and human merit as two things opposed to one another, as though a good deed is not always already enabled by God's own goodness (that is, they make the very mistake Augustine accuses his Pelagian opponents of making).

100. In which the writer hopes "that I may fill up what is lacking to the sufferings of Christ in my own flesh."

with his christology of participation in Christ's body. We also see his conception of the unity of God's saving work in history. There is no difference in substance between the Old and New Covenants, but only in people's ability to discern Christ under each. The saints could perhaps see him before his incarnation; now all can. Yet it is one and the same Christ to whom both testaments refer. The psalmist's first-person plural voice, his complaint of murderous oppression, and the church's historical, "organic" connection across time and space as recorded in scripture all cohere in this christological reading.

"Yet they thought to refuse me honor" — Augustine notes that no one now can actually be killed for being a Christian, so the opponents of the church can only deny honor to it by disparaging it quietly to one another. The mention of "honor" and of "one man" killed by all seem to have drawn Augustine's lexical imagination to the story of Joseph, one man denied honor and left for dead by a mob, only later to be redeemed. For, Augustine says, "a reversal of fortunes has come to Christians like that which befell Joseph, by whom they were spiritually prefigured." He then tells that story, concluding with the present-tense description, "no longer is he helpless in the hands of brothers who sell him; now he is handing out grain to these same brothers in their hunger." Christians' urge to curse their enemies should give way to the peaceable activity of feeding them, difficult as it is, for "we must hope that good may come to them, even though they hope for evil."

Augustine is then drawn to another grammatical detail — the second-person plural address of "kill me, all of you." He concludes that just as there is one city, Jerusalem, with Christ as its king, so there is one city in opposition to it, Babylon, with the devil for its king. Augustine's working out of the relationship between these Cities famously runs to thousands of pages in the *City of God.* Here their relationship draws him to a story that he confesses disturbs him — that of the man thrown from the wedding banquet for failing to appear in wedding clothes (Matthew 22:1-14). The conclusion of that story is what is puzzling, for how can Christ say "many are invited but only a few are chosen" when only one man has been excluded? As Augustine wrestles with these details he concludes that *in* the one thrown out, many more must be included. The excluded man is a gross parody of the one body that is Christ's, whose members are clothed properly in the wedding gown of his righteousness.

We may think we are a good distance here from the text of the psalm. Yet we must remember that for Augustine the purpose of exegesis is to throw particularly christological light on both our life's circumstances and the words on the page. Here, Christians' ongoing experience of antagonism with enemies is illumined by the psalmist's complaint against his would-be killers, Joseph's reversal vis-à-vis his brothers, and the *totus Christus*'s grotesque mirror image in the form of a perverse head and members. We should also note that this is a surprisingly literal reading of this psalm! The basic contours of the psalm have been followed here, if indeed elaborated in a specifically Christian direction. Yet that direction is not obviously antithetical to the overall thrust of the psalm nor to the words on the page. Augustine, as if anticipating our concern with allegory, describes both his own hermeneutical procedure and the members of the heavenly city at the same time: "all whose taste is schooled to the things above, who ponder the realities of heaven, who live with circumspection in this world . . . all these belong to the one city whose king is Christ," these will be separated from the city of the wicked only at the end. In the meantime they will see themselves in such words as these in the scriptures — their true self, joined in Christ's flesh to Christ's divinity, marching as part of his body to the heavenly city.

"Concentrate now, brothers and sisters, I beg you, for I want to say a little more to you about this sweet city. I love talking about it." Augustine, perhaps noticing some drowsy parishioners, perhaps with hopes that his own inflamed desire will allow theirs also to catch fire, continues to expound on the differences between the two cities. "One homeland we have, one homeland most dear to us, only one homeland, and compared with that whatever we have now is nothing but a journey." The purpose of their gathering is to grow toward that homeland in their desire, to put distance between themselves and the wicked city, all under the guidance of scripture and its churchly interpretation. Augustine is interested in the fact that Cain's wicked city preceded Abel's in time, that God promises the "elder will serve the younger," contrary to expectation and ancient convention (Genesis 25:23). He warns, "You must be alert to the profound mystery concealed in these events, and keep in mind what I said to you earlier, 'it is not the spiritual that comes first. The animal body comes first, and what is spiritual afterward'" (1 Corinthians 15:46). In a similar way, the site of the city of Jerusalem was previously inhabited as a place called Jebus, and the new city, the vision of peace, was built only after Jebus's destruction. Here is the mystery concealed in this crucial biblical theme: "no single one of us born from Adam immediately belongs to Jerusalem." We all die in Adam; even so in Christ shall all be made alive. It is as though a thoroughly Pauline theology of the old and new humanity is here providing the baseline along with which the musical notes of these particular words in the psalm are being played. Pauline themes of Christian life as a representation of Christ's death and resurrection, so important in places like Romans 5–6, 1 Corinthians 15, Colossians 3, and Ephesians 5 are on constant display as Augustine ponders the two cities in opposition, and the righteous one denied honor who is redeemed by God at the end. A Pauline epistolary template is placed over the Psalter, but the result is not less literal (or beautiful) for those in Christ.

Augustine then turns to a political corollary of the inextricability of the two cities in time. Certain persons who belong to Babylon will be in control of affairs of Jerusalem, and vice-versa. "That sounds like a puzzling statement I have proposed to you, doesn't it? Be patient, though, and I will clarify it by examples." He reminds them of Paul's hermeneutical premise in 1 Corinthians 10:11, that the things that happened in the history of Israel did so "'with symbolic import, for they are written down as a rebuke to us, upon whom the climax of the ages has come.'" There were, patently, bad kings who reigned in Jerusalem. "This is a well-known fact; they are listed and named." Likewise, citizens of Jerusalem have often wielded authority in Babylon, as Nebuchadnezzar's affairs were looked over by the three young men in Daniel. Similarly, Christ himself told his hearers to "'do what they tell you, but do not imitate what they do'" (Matthew 23:3). The scribes and Pharisees had charge over the affairs of Jerusalem, but were themselves citizens of Babylon. In the odd (but distinctly biblical) case that Augustine's church finds itself in, Jerusalemites in charge of the affairs of Babylon must serve cheerfully, and Jerusalemites under Babylonian authority must behave no less cheerfully, so as to fulfill Christ's injunction, "'if anyone obliges you to go a mile, go freely with him two miles more.'" The political working out here of the relationship between the cities is familiar, sounded often throughout Augustine's work. What is interesting is what has led him to enunciate it in this case: a complaint psalm, spoken by one in mortal danger. The church does not now find itself in mortal danger, but rather in a place of having to bear pacifically with its intertwining with (or even indistinguishability from) the earthly city. Here the current circumstances of Augustine's church produce a reading quite at odds with the words on the page. Is it, perhaps, precisely the sort of discordant note that disqualifies beauty?

On the other hand, perhaps it is a quite understandable change in the circumstances of the covenant community that requires new reflection on the words at hand — at least if the goal of exegesis is progress in pilgrimage, growth in desire of God. Since the churches are now full of those who also "fill the theaters on Babylon's high days; yet they serve, honor, and pay homage to Christ," because no one is now trying to kill the church, the church's goal in contest with the world is patiently to bear even these silent antagonists along, to coax even them into pilgrimage, and this requires less shouting and more subtle goading. Augustine is reminded of an earlier psalm, "I ran thirstily," and imagines Christ's body constantly longing to draw opponents in. He remembers Moses' commanding the people to drink their ground-up idols as an image of this: "the impious are dissociating themselves little by little from the body to which they belonged . . . conspiring together, they hate; broken apart, they love." When Christ asked the Samaritan woman for a drink, what he meant was that he longed for her, to drink her into his body. When he told his tormenters he thirsted, he meant "he was thirsting for them," but they unfortunately reached for old wine, not the new wine of the gospel. The church now likewise thirsts for all people to join, and not just in body by baptism, but in affection. Just as the hemorrhaging woman was the only one who "really" touched Christ, though many touched him physically, so the church now seeks to have all people "really" touch him, and not to "bless with their mouths, but curse in their hearts all the while." That line of the psalm explains Augustine's view of the previous verses. The church does not now struggle against martyrdom. But its struggle with internal, unspoken curses, the very thing the psalm complains about, is all the greater.

"In God is my salvation and glory," means for Augustine that in God I am being changed from "an impious person to a just person." The memory of that change allows the plaintiff of the psalm to bear with his opponents with hope, to avoid repaying them evil with evil. For "Iduthin is thirsting for these very people." As Iduthin preaches to his people and Augustine to his, each turns to the unjust means by which people make great gain. Clearly Augustine thinks Christ still thirsts even for these in his hearing, that the line between righteousness and wickedness proceeds through each of his hearers, as it does through him.

"Only once has God spoken, but these two things have I heard." Augustine is puzzled, and he asks his hearers to thresh out this verse's meaning with him. God clearly spoke many times in the history of Israel, as scripture makes plain (Hebrews 1:1). Far more than once, or even twice. There must be a deeper mystery here. "This man had leapt a very long way to arrive at that place where God spoke only once." The answer is this: within himself, God spoke only once, "because God begot one Word." Iduthin has leapt high enough to see the one Word, "the very beginning, the Word who is God-with-God, he found the unique Word of the unique Father, and he knew then that God did indeed speak only once." The psalmist, and those who pray in his wake, have had to climb quite high to make sense of this verse. Yet he has heard "two things." The psalmist continues, "that power belongs to God, and to you, O Lord, mercy." These two things, power and mercy, become the keys in which Augustine retells the whole gospel, for "almost all of scripture is summed up in these." The *theotic*, contemplative ascent to the Word ends here with a *kenotic* return to God's work for salvation in the world, of dispensing power and mercy both.

Augustine then puzzles over "power" and "mercy" in a rather philosophical vein, pondering Plato's old question (now in a new key) of whether God does a thing because it is good, or if something's goodness follows because God does it. He leans here toward the latter: "from the very fact that God did it, be sure that it is just." Damnation to hell for the wicked is then no injustice on God's part. Augustine continues to ponder the justice of God in the great *theotic* tradition of scripture, and concludes that "you may believe . . . [that] God acts in accordance with his plan even if it is hidden from you." Divine justice may not look like justice, but we must trust it is. Why? Because the redemptive economy has been arranged among us for therapeutic reasons. Christ's saving work took the form it did precisely to convert our affections, to change our loves and fears, to draw us into the divine beauty. Augustine's exegesis here, indeed the whole of his theology, is directed toward this goal. Christ's "example of patience was needed, and the example of his humility; the sign of the cross was needed to subdue the devil and his angels. We needed the passion of our Lord." The *need* here is for a patience that bears with the intermingling of the two cities in anticipation of a perhaps far-off *parousia*. Look, after all, at the patience of the Lord, and God's creative bringing about of salvation out of the worst intention of evil. "His mortal flesh was killed, but by its death it slew death, gave us an example of patience, and modeled in advance our resurrection." As Iduthin leapt across those who wished to kill him, and Christ was indeed killed, the church can now bear with its *not* being killed (but only whispered about!) with a patience born of conviction that even this is working out salvation for us.

Augustine's final note is jarring: "the thirsty Church is longing to drink in this man too, the man you see here!" Augustine has spotted an astrologer in the assembly's midst, one who pretended to be a Christian before, all the while providing astrological advice, for a fee, to fellow "Christians." Now, however, he is penitent, and Augustine asks his people to "commend him to your eyes and your hearts . . . take care of him. Look at him, make sure you will know him again, and wherever he goes, point him out to our brothers and sisters who are not here today. This watchfulness is a mercy." The man has brought his astrological books to be burnt: "once they have been thrown into the fire, he will pass into a place of cool refreshment." Clearly, church in north Africa cannot have been dull! Just as clearly, preaching was not unrelated to ecclesial discipline. Augustine's rhetorical acumen from the pulpit did not mean it was divorced from the most mundane of churchly matters.

Augustine is in the same place any preacher is in when it is time to preach. How shall these words be made lively for these people once more? To use Augustine's terms, how do I convince these people they must leap across pride and silent antagonism, to follow the two words spoken by the Word? If he fails, we have means to say why: we are not more delighted in God than we were before. If he succeeds, the affections of not only an astrologer but all of us will be converted anew to fear the right things and to love the right things rightly. For what other purpose would anyone ever read holy scripture?

## Return to Augustinian Beauty

Augustinian Christians are not the only ones now attempting to recover something of a Platonic and Christian vision of beauty. Elaine Scarry has recently written an aptly beautiful book on aesthetics that stands within the Augustinian tradition without subscribing to its most important theological claims. Beauty is generative. It bears children. It is naturally linked then with thoughts of eternity, as a glimpse of beauty sends the mind into its memory for traces of similar glimpses in the past, and keeps one vigilant for future sightings as well. It can be defended against modernist critiques that beauty distracts from the search for justice, that an appreciative gaze fetishizes and does violence to its object, and that a search for beauty as such is necessarily religious (it is not for Scarry). For our purposes her most important contribution is as a secular reminder of the generative power of beauty. A glimpse of beauty incites, "even requires" the act of replication. Wittgenstein says when his eye catches beauty his hand must draw it. The idea of a Source of beauty that is eternally fecund "sponsors in people like Plato, Aquinas, Dante the idea of eternity, the perpetual duplicating of a moment that never stops." Painters see beauty and follow it in a daze, almost required to paint it. Writers wax lyrical about it and are also ensnared to its reproduction. These responses to beauty are visceral, physical, as we have realized since Plato that beauty bears offspring. "An act of touch may reproduce itself as an acoustical event or even an abstract idea, the way whenever Augustine touches something smooth, he begins to think of music and of God."[101]

We have already seen in Michael Hanby's work that beauty is close to the heart of Augustine's trinitarian theology. The Son is the *forma*, the image, the splendor of the Father, who delights in the Son who is his image. He gives to the Son not only his delight but also his delighting, which mutual delight simply is the Holy Spirit. This inner-trinitarian beauty and delight is different than the Platonic heritage from which it comes, since its Source is eternally

101. Elaine Scarry, *On Beauty and Being Just* (Princeton: Princeton University Press, 1999), 3-5.

triune, and one of the Trinity empties himself in incarnation and divinizes in himself his church. Creation then is not just the bottom of an ever-declining set of degrees of reflection of original beauty. It is rather a fitting reflection of the mutual delight of the triune God, which delight becomes a creature to hallow creation. In the incarnation Christ sets up a "space" between his human and divine natures, a landscape for a pilgrimage from him as way to him as goal. The Christian life is an alternation between longing for that homeland and so pushing forward, and finding sustenance on the way so as not to despair. The Christian preacher then points out each of these features of scripture: those that encourage and those that challenge, as well as the full range of scriptural emotions that direct faith, hope, and love aright. Christians' way into the triune God is a pilgrimage marked with the signposts of scripture, which preachers like Augustine are trained to point out.

A return to an Augustinian vision of beauty in exegesis then would not mean just that preachers should preach more beautifully (though that would, of course, be nice). Christian aesthetic claims are not injunctions to work harder, to be more flawless or to imitate an extraneous beauty. They are calls to participate in the beauty of God. Or better, to show the beauty of God always already present that we reflect more fully as we grow in Christ. Such a creative reappropriation of an Augustinian exegetical aesthetic would do the following:

(1) It would pay lavish attention to the words of scripture. The Psalter is already beautiful long before Christians read it or Augustine interprets it. Scripture as such is a gift from God, almost an "extension" of the work of the incarnation, if that word did not sound too physical for Augustine. He has no need to "update" scripture to make it pass theological muster. At its worst his hermeneutic looks like one that has to perform radical cosmetic surgery on the Bible before he can call it beautiful. Yet this is not so. Even Augustine, the most consistently christological interpreter of the Psalter among patristic exegetes, has long stretches of simply luxuriating in the text of the psalms. Retelling the stories, praising the beauty of the words, reading them as simple prayers and inviting his congregation to do likewise. It is a love of the actual words that drives his frustration with competing manuscripts and language difficulties. And it is primarily this sort of lavish attention to the beauty of the words that the modern exegetical tradition continues. No one could put in the trouble to learn Hebrew language, history, and poetry to read these psalms without a deep love for words, difficult words that require expertise to read. Historical critics' lavish attention to texts is what enables them to spot the fissures that make for historical questions, and to spend careers doing the hard work required to read such hard texts. They and Augustine alike are ex-

emplary in putting forth the sort of effort that the church's preachers and members would do well to imitate.[102]

(2) It would recognize the generative effect of commentary. The ascertainment of beauty is at the heart of education. As Scarry writes, "One submits oneself to other minds (teachers) in order to increase the chance that one will be looking in the right direction when a comet makes its sweep through a certain patch of sky."[103] For Scarry, today's arts and sciences are still about granting greater clarity, about refining and directing the urge to reproduce brought on by contact with beauty. It is no accident then that the previous commentators on whom today's commentators rely will be sources not only of "information" but of formation — they will shape both what the exegete says and how she says it. It is for this reason that this work commends Augustine as an exegetical partner and hermeneutical exemplar. Preachers who turn to Augustine will write like Augustine — if not as beautifully, at least with the same goals. They will take part in his project of learning from the saints how to read scripture for the sake of the cultivation of further saints. Notice this hardly means that other sources cannot be consulted, for they have their own beauty. It is rather to say that our exegetical work will be generative in ways that good teachers encourage. Whatever the modern academy's exegetical strengths, its primary project is not to produce and encourage saints. Whatever Augustine's weaknesses, his project is. Extended reading of Augustine's exegesis will allow the reader to imagine an Augustinian interpretation before she sees it, and even more hopefully, to produce one for the sake of her own work.

(3) An Augustinian aesthetic in exegesis will show its deepest fruition in increased charity in the church. Exegetical debates can be among our most acrimonious. The other side always seems to be reading a passage out of context, allegorizing away one's own beloved text, or laboriously insisting on the application of a minor verse from Paul to mandate behavior of a certain sort.

---

102. After a book that is quite critical of historical criticism, Fowl recommends the modern historical critical guild as an exemplar in his own project of post-critical reclamation of the Bible as Christian scripture: "Christians need to become much more well-versed in the skills, habits, convictions, and practices attendant upon Christian interpretation of scripture. Surprisingly, in this regard, the profession of biblical scholarship may have more to teach Christian communities than it does in regard to questions concerning any particular biblical text" (Fowl, *Engaging Scripture* [Oxford: Blackwell, 1997], 187). He offers the guild's extraordinary technical expertise, and its members' ability to sift through the avalanche of available material to pick out the arguments that matter and reformulate them in their own words, as examples of biblical *phronesis* (practical wisdom) that the church would do well to emulate in its own ways (187-90).

103. Scarry, *On Beauty and Being Just,* 7.

Churches, from the denominational hierarchy to the smallest parish, struggle not only to agree on scripture's meaning but also with how to argue about it charitably. Scholarly works like this one are noticed or rewarded in greater proportion when they score polemical points against other scholars or ecclesial bodies. In every contemporary institution, whether sacred or secular, it is difficult to find exegetical charity.

Yet for Augustine charity is no marginal matter. On the contrary, *caritas* is nothing less than the very love between the Father and Son that *is* the Holy Spirit. Augustine frequently quotes Romans 5:5 in pneumatological and ecclesiological contexts: "the love of God is poured into our hearts by the Holy Spirit who is given to us." The church is drawn into the love between the Father and the Son by the infusion of the Spirit at Pentecost, in baptism, and continually in the epiphanies wrought in preaching. The conversion of the affections of which Augustine speaks in more hermeneutical moments in the *Enarrationes* is the process by which persons in the church are drawn into the divine life. Its measure of success then is the degree of charity in an ecclesial body. The person of the Godhead most appropriately identified with love, the Spirit, is present for our holiness to the degree to which persons are tied together in charity and evince this tie in their common life.

This is not to say that everyone must agree with everyone else's interpretation. The church's ability to disagree well is part of its being drawn toward God and one another.[104] Neither is it a plea for greater sentimentality in the church. Augustine's form of "love" for the Donatists is to "compel them to come in"! For the astrologer above it is to point out his sinful life publicly and admonish the assembly to help him leave its every vestige behind.[105] It is to say that the church is an exegetical school devoted to the conversion of our affections for the sake of imitation of the *kenosis* and *theosis* of the Son of God. Exegesis that leads us into greater cruciformity then is to be celebrated; that which does not is not. Further, as we shall see in greater detail in Chapter 4,

---

104. Rowan Williams offers a reading of *De doctrina* that emphasizes the importance of Christian community to Augustine's hermeneutics in his "Language, Reality and Desire in Augustine's *De Doctrina*," *Journal of Literature and Theology* 3 (1989): 138-50.

105. Stephen Fowl presents Augustine as an exemplar of "interpretive charity" in his "Vigilant Communities and Virtuous Readers," in *Engaging Scripture*, 91-95. It is ironic to make use of this patch of Augustine's career, since his famous "compel them to come in" opened the floodgates to use of imperial power against the church's schismatic enemies. Yet Fowl shows that the particular way Augustine argues is to show that "love" is defined in Augustine as a willingness to bear with a church from which one would prefer to break away in protest. Love is a sort of suffering-with, rather than proud self-separation. Augustine's position is made possible by his listening to his opponents and then incorporating the strengths of their argument at its best into his own position.

the church carries on the christological work of the converting of God's enemies into God's friends. How else can enemies become friends than by listening carefully, growing in ability to enunciate an opponent's arguments to
their satisfaction, hearing one's own weaknesses publicly displayed and one's
interlocutor's strengths as well. The beauty of exegesis is, like all things Christian, the beauty of transfiguration of lives into the divine image. Those devoted to it will pursue such transfiguration in themselves and others above all
else.

Admittedly Augustine is not always the preferred model for exegesis that
brings the interpreter to repentance and shows interlocutors in the best possible light. Neither, we must admit, are we, whoever the "we" in question is. Yet
an Augustinian aesthetic in exegesis will allow us to see that the beauty we
seek is one of a gracious community of interpreters, displaying enemy-love
and cruciformity of spirit in our common life and toward those who do not
now share it.

(4) An Augustinian aesthetic in exegesis would shift interpretive debates
from simply being about the rightness of one's words according to the letter
and toward the promotion of the flourishing of lives. For all of Augustine's
intensity of interest in getting the letter of scripture "right," a misstep in that
regard is not nearly as important as one that deforms lives, that produces ugliness. Notice that this solves no exegetical debates right away. It simply
repositions them. For example, we should still imagine the church's need to
fight out whether God is calling it to bless gay unions and ordain homosexu-
als, for example. The question would simply be whether that form of life is a
genuine form of flourishing, and one that shows fittingness with the words
on the page of scripture. If modernity was secure in its confidence in finding
the "correct" or "objectively true" interpretation of a given passage, post-
modern reacquisition of ancient wisdom will have no such singular confidence. It will rather seek to show that its readings display conformity with the
words of scripture, with the lives inspired by it, and by the Lordship of the
one who is our judge and redeemer. A christo*telic* approach to scripture will
seek to show its conformity, its fittingness, its beauty in relationship to the
words on the page, the flourishing of human lives, and the beauty of the one
who reflects the Father's beauty and shares that beauty with us in the Spirit-
drawn body of Christ.

I have been surprised when I have lectured on aesthetics as a standard for
exegesis how eager those in favor of liberalizing church teaching on homosexuality seem to be, and how nervous conservatives on that issue seem. I suppose I should have anticipated that people who would wish to get around the
stricture imposed by the handful of biblical verses condemning homosexual-

ity should find in a celebration of allegory resources with which to do just that, and their opponents should be nervous about them receiving fresh ammunition. This is a ramification of my line of argumentation I did not expect and do not wish to encourage. My own inclination is for a high respect for the letter of scripture, one informed by Augustine and fitting with centuries of church practice. That letter is only to be contravened in cases where it does not obviously attest to the truth about God or virtuous living, as Augustine makes plain in the *De doctrina*. Efforts to use allegory to avoid biblical passages one does not like seem to be an appeal to ethics in the mode Barth rightly condemns — as a shield against the lordship of Christ.

However, I must admit that fittingness as a final criterion for exegetical success might shift the argument about homosexuality in ways I did not anticipate. If it could be shown that the flourishing of specific lives could happen only in same-sex relationships — in essence an anthropological argument that the following of Christ of particular persons is furthered rather than hampered by such unions — then the church should see fit to bless them.[106] I am not now equipped to say how such persons would argue that this practice is in conformity with the words on the page of scripture, but I imagine that such readings may be possible. My goal here is not to close this debate but to open it in new ways, ways more in line with Augustine's hermeneutic.[107]

(5) An Augustinian aesthetic in exegesis will be aware that it cannot control the object of its exegesis. That is, it will be aware of its own creaturely limitations, and the nature of exegesis as ever-dependent on divine gift. Genuine

---

106. See Eugene Rogers, *Sexuality and the Christian Body: Their Way into the Triune God* (Oxford: Blackwell, 1999).

107. A fruitful place for reflection here is the difference of opinion between Stephen Fowl and Richard Hays on homosexuality. Fowl in *Engaging Scripture* (97-127) promotes an analogy that Hays opposes (in *Moral Vision of the New Testament*, 379-406) in comparing the inclusion of gays and lesbians in the church to the inclusion of the gentiles in Acts 15. Such an inclusion would have been anathema according to the scriptures and Jewish practice before the pouring out of the Spirit upon the gentiles made Peter see that the water for baptism could not be withheld. With Hays I would argue this exegesis is suspect. The reason is that the early Christians could look back on Jewish scripture and see, after the fact, a narrative logic by which the gentiles were intended from the beginning to be included in the covenant community with the dawning of the eschaton. There is no similar scriptural logic for the inclusion of lesbians and gays into the covenant community at the eschaton. If one could argue scripturally that the dawning of the eschaton with the church as its earnest should mean that homosexual persons (to be clear: those unrepentant of their sexual practices) should stream to Zion like gentile worshipers of the Lord, then the analogy can hold. As it stands, it seems the argument fails to be fitting with the words on the page of scripture.

beauty stops us short, catches our breath, makes us aware of the presence of something we did not create and cannot perfectly imitate, though we are indeed drawn to try. It is appropriate to speak of such an encounter as frightening, or even terrifying. It is Moses before the burning bush, Elijah in the face of earthquake, thunder, and wind, Jesus transfigured upon Mount Tabor. For beauty is a sign of the greatness of God. To try and explain God's nature is, in a famous Augustinian (but pseudepigraphal) image, to try to place the ocean in a bucket. To gaze on his beauty is to be summoned outside of oneself, to be made literally *ec*-static, in a glance that cannot be sustained but only longed for, as the *Confessions* make clear. This jealous God will tolerate no rivals, will overlook no sin, will demand only perfection and the fullness of faith, hope, and love. A God better "spoken" of in silence than in speech will give exegetes and preachers pause, at the very least.[108] Those who read his scriptures best will tremble, at least a little, upon every opening of their covers.

(6) An Augustinian aesthetic in exegesis will be truly fecund. Because those reading scripture are gazing on the beauty of God, and longing for others to be drawn into that gaze, they will produce readings of scripture that are beautiful, that grow out of their participation in the divine beauty, and that announce the compelling nature of that beauty to the world. An Augustinian allegorical approach will then be profoundly evangelical. This effort to produce new readings that conform to Christ, new saints who bear his image, will not then suffer under the negative connotation of words like "conformity" in modernity. For the One who is the beauty of God will ever be generative of more interpretations, more saints who are not the same but each reflections of a beauty that cannot be captured. The flux of created time for Augustine is a gift — a creaturely participation in the timelessness of God. *Inability* to plumb the divine depths, to be an image of God in the way Christ is, will inspire our efforts to create further likenesses in our own life, our church, our enemies, and all the world.

For attention to one specific community that will likely find such language threatening, that can hardly find Augustine, his exegesis, or his God compelling in quite these ways, we turn to Augustine and the Jews in the next chapter.

---

108. On this see "Attending to Silence," in Nicholas Lash's *Holiness, Speech, and Silence* (Burlington, VT: Ashgate, 2005), 75-95.

# 4 Allegory and the Jews

The central argument of this book — that we should now read again like Augustine — has an obvious and important rejoinder. What of all the awful things Augustine says about the Jews? Would not a return to allegory, and indeed a return to Augustine, also mean a return to the sort of state-sponsored and religiously inspired hatred of Judaism that was sown in the ancient church and reaped in modern times in the cataclysmic harvest of the *Shoah*?[1]

This is a serious charge that cannot be simply dismissed. One does not have to search hard in the *Enarrationes* to find the sort of comments about the Jews that make one's blood curdle, and that make pro-Augustinian apologists either contort or fall silent. What is worse is that Augustine's derogation of the Jews is not limited to thoughtless offhand comments, though there are plenty of these. It is rather theologically worked out with a rigor that would remain throughout western Christendom, though of course it did not begin with him. What is worse still for our project is that the very exegetical approach for which we have praised Augustine — allegory — is often precisely the one turned upon the Jews in his polemic. For example, he reads Psalm 18's proclamation that "night to night" proclaims knowledge as a sign of the turning over of the Lord Christ by one carnal person, Judas, to other carnal per-

---

1. I choose to focus on this topic, not because there are not other areas of Augustine's thought and practice with which we could take issue, but because this one arises with extraordinary frequency in Augustine's Old Testament exegesis especially and is of crucial theological and historical import for later centuries. It is also of particular importance today, as Christian theologians and biblical interpreters continue to reevaluate past attitudes and look to forge new ones. Finally, as I will argue below, there are resources in Augustine to suggest how things might have gone differently, and indeed how the church might live more faithfully today.

sons, the Jews.[2] Jesus' promise that even a mustard seed–sized faith can move a mountain into the sea (Matthew 17:20) is glossed allegorically as a sign that Christ, the mountain, will go to the sea — a representative of the unruly gentiles — and will "abandon the Jews."[3] That allegorical motif recurs often in the work. Other recurring tropes along this line include Gideon's fleece (Judges 6:36-40). It was first miraculously wet compared to the dry ground around it, then dry compared to the miraculously wet ground around it. Just as one small patch of the world — Judea — was once blessed and the rest dry, so now the reverse will happen. Another such reading is the portico in John 5:1-8 where the crippled wait in hopes of a cure, like the multitudes of lame people whom the law could not heal before the coming of Christ. Augustine describes the Jewish dispersion after 70 AD as "a sign of their shame."[4] The description in John 11:48 of an intentional Jewish decision to kill Jesus in order to keep the Romans from destroying the land and scattering their nation is lamented: "what stupidity, what crass lack of good sense." As a result the Jews have lost both their territory and their nationhood — the very things for which they were willing to give up Christ. This is why there are in that land no Jews in Augustine's time — it was given over entirely to Christians.[5] Augustine sees such an end as fitting for those who desire only carnal, material rewards for their religion rather than enlightened, spiritual ones: they lose both. The psalmist's acclamation to "shout with joy to God all the earth" is taken as a salvo "against the self-satisfaction of the Jews," who arrogantly thought only they could praise while all other people should stay in darkness. In contrast, the church munificently invites all peoples to praise. Catholicity itself here is hammered out against an anvil of perceived Jewish parochialism.[6] The psalmist's request to God to "save me from the blood" is read in light of the chilling curse of Matthew 27:25, "his blood be on us and on our children," when the New Testament claims the Jews not only accepted responsibility for Christ's blood but actually also "offered it to their descendents to drink."[7] Not content only with destroying Christ, the Jews also turned to persecuting the church, filling her with martyrs.[8] We see here a terrifying portrait of later

---

2. Comment on Psalm 18 (2) in *Expositions of the Psalms,* trans. Maria Boulding, OSB, from the *Works of Saint Augustine: A Translation for the 21st Century,* vol. III/15 (Hyde Park, NY: New City Press, 2000), I, 208. Hereafter cited as *EP.*

3. On Psalm 45 in *EP* II, 314.

4. On Psalm 52 in *EP* III, 34.

5. On Psalm 52 in *EP* III, 39.

6. On Psalm 65 in *EP* III, 286.

7. On Psalm 58 in *EP* III, 151.

8. On Psalm 78 in *EP* IV, 126.

Christian anti-Judaism: that their stupid materialism led them to reject the spiritual claims of Jesus, to betray and murder him and accept responsibility for their crime, only to be repaid in the Roman destruction of their land and temple as they deserved, in perpetual wandering of the earth, and eventually in eternal perdition. It is little wonder that so many Christians reading such descriptions have been so willing to help actual Jews on the way to their eternal punishment.[9]

Recently Christian biblical scholars, theologians, and church leaders have done much to attempt to repent of the traditional ecclesial stance of "supersessionism," in which the church simply takes the place of the Jews in God's favor. This is as it should be. But we should note here Augustine is not merely presenting a supersessionist portrait of God's dealings with the world, in which the church unseats Israel. It is actually a theology of wholesale indictment against a people, a curse both this-worldly and other-worldly, owing to their rejection of God's messiah and murder of him and his followers. Perhaps we have recently seen less repentance of this sort of position than of supersessionism because a full-blown teaching of contempt so little resembles residual ecclesial attitudes, at least at an official level. We tend now to be thoughtlessly supersessionist but more rarely vindictively violent anymore (despite how often Christians have been in the church's history).[10] This sort of exegetical material is also so painful to read that we are hard-pressed to do the work necessary to respond to it. Yet we must respond to these parts of Augustine's thought here. They are seamlessly interwoven with a theological exegesis that I am claiming is not only worthy of emulation, but is actually a cure for what ails modern theology and church practice! How does Augustine's explicit anti-Judaism not make this prescribed therapy into a poison pill?

This chapter will struggle with this question. It will answer it not with evasion or apology for Augustine, but with an Augustinian category: confes-

9. Paula Frederiksen argues that Augustine's anti-Jewish polemical comments are fairly conventional, and that it is only in his more positive constructive place for a theology of Israel that he shows innovation. He is, by comparison, far kinder in his comments on Judaism than such predecessors as Justin Martyr and Tertullian. Such "kindness" still makes for excruciating reading for us. The ancient world was also much more given to explosive rhetorical attacks on enemies than ours is. We can see better perhaps than they that rhetoric matters, and can matter in unintended and tragic directions. See Frederiksen's "*Excaecati Occulta Justitia Dei:* Augustine on the Jews and Judaism," *Journal of Early Christian Studies* 3, no. 3 (1995): 299-324. See also Frederiksen's book-length study on this topic, *Augustine and the Jews: The Story of Christianity's Great Theologian and His Defense of Judaism* (forthcoming from Doubleday, 2008).

10. Whether this shift in most official church teaching has "trickled down" to those in the pews is another matter however.

sion. Our own inclination here as modern readers of Augustine is simply to look away and do otherwise in our own reflection on the Jews and conversation with actual Jewish people. Lectionaries skip over the Bible's most bitterly polemical passages. Modern translators debate whether to tidy up John's description of Jesus' enemies as "the Jews." Church history courses give token attention to historical anti-Judaism before moving on, leaving the perception this attitude was not rampant or widespread, which of course it was. It is easier simply to look the other way. Yet an Augustinian answer, which Augustine himself did not make on this issue but we now can, would be honestly to face sin, name it as such, and provide resources with which to do otherwise. We shall be surprised to see that there are in Augustine's *Enarrationes* resources with which to respond to traditional Christian anti-Judaism, even as he himself does not make use of them. For when Augustine reads the cursing psalms or reflects on what an "enemy" is in Christian parlance, he offers some of his most glorious exegetical descriptions of enemy love and the desire to turn opponents into reconciled friends. I shall argue that we can read Augustine against himself. We can turn some of the most crucial insights of his christology into an argument against Augustine's own anti-Judaism in a way that is genuinely confessional for Christian readers — that is, that causes us to examine the church's historic sins honestly, to rehabilitate out of that sin and into righteousness, so as to relate to contemporary Jews in far more faithful ways than Augustine or his community or those after him did. Finally we shall argue that Augustine's prime exegetical instinct that we have defended in this book — allegory — actually offers resources for dealing with the Bible's own anti-Jewish elements that can be lacking in historical criticism.

## Augustine Contra Iudaeos

Occasionally, Augustine can both surprise and disappoint within a short span of time in his theological approach to what Paul called Israel "according to the flesh" (e.g., Romans 9:3). He does make great use of some key New Testament motifs that are more favorable to Israel than those normally cited by more violent supersessionists and proponents of a vindictive theology against Jews.[11] For example, he thinks of John 4:22's claim that "salvation is from the Jews" when he reads the Psalm line, "you drew me up out of the womb," ac-

---

11. These latter include John 8:31ff., when "some Jews who believed in him" argue with Jesus and are eventually told they belong to their "father, the devil," and 1 Thessalonians 2:14-15, "the Jews, who killed the Lord Jesus and the prophets and also drove us out. . . ."

knowledging that Christianity came from Judaism as a child from her mother.[12] He does attend regularly to the gospel tradition of Jesus' teaching of love for enemies.[13] He is clear that those who crucified Jesus only thought they were executing a man, since only those who are practiced in *scientia* and are advancing toward *sapientia* could know this is God incarnate (1 Corinthians 2:8). Murder is serious, but it is less serious than intentional deicide. He frequently cites Paul's midrashic wrestling with God's faithfulness to his people in Romans 9–11, including Paul's blunt warning against gentiles grafted into the promises of Israel who would look down on those "branches" broken off to make space for them on the tree, and Paul's promise that "all Israel will be saved" (11:26).[14] Another Augustinian favorite is the description in Ephesians 2:11-22 of the breaking down of the dividing wall between Jewish and gentile peoples and bringing peace in place of enmity, since he can use the glowing description of trans-national unity in polemic against the Donatists. In places like these, Augustine draws from similar New Testament texts as those on which recent theologians have, when they have tried to offer a more constructive theology of Israel for the sake of a church trying to repent of violence and antagonism against the Jews.[15]

Yet in almost the same breath with which he makes these claims, he can return to an even more bitter attack on Jesus' religious and ethnic brethren. After citing John 4:22 about salvation's source in the Jews, he blasts anyone who trusts for salvation in such material observances as Sabbath and such practices as circumcision, accusing them of being in "Jewish darkness" from which they should be plucked. His reflections upon Jesus' teaching of enemy-

---

12. Psalm 21 (1) in *EP* I, 223.

13. E.g., Psalm 30 (4) in *EP* I, 347.

14. Psalm 65 in *EP* III, 290-91.

15. In addition to the examples listed in Chapter 1, note 18, see also the symposium on Michael Wyschogrod's work in *Modern Theology* 11, no. 2 (1995): 175-227; Robert Jenson, "Toward a Christian Doctrine of Israel," *CTI Reflections* 3 (2000): 2-21; Bruce Marshall, "Do Christians Worship the God of Israel?" in *Knowing the Triune God: The Work of the Spirit in the Practices of the Church,* ed. James Buckley and David Yeago (Grand Rapids: Eerdmans, 2001), 231-64; and George Lindbeck's work on the "Israel-like" nature of the church in such places as *The Church in a Postliberal Age,* ed. James Buckley (Grand Rapids: Eerdmans, 2002). See also such ecclesial documents as the Presbyterian Church (USA)'s "A Theological Understanding of the Relationship Between Christians and Jews: A Paper Commended to the Church for Study and Reflection by the 199th General Assembly" (1987), at www.pcusa.org/pcusa/wmd/ep/country/xnjewpaper.pdf, and the Roman Catholic Church's "The Jewish People and Their Sacred Scriptures in the Christian Bible," by the Pontifical Biblical Commission (2004), at http://www.vatican.va/roman_curia/congregations/cfaith/pcb_documents/rc_con_cfaith_doc_20020212_popolo-ebraico_en.html. This small sample is simply a pointer to the depth of work being done on this issue.

love are tempered by infamous comments about the occasional necessity of love acting physically to restrain, deter, or punish another, to "compel them to come in" if they would not come into the catholic church voluntarily.[16] Such correction is perfectly in line with love of enemy for Augustine, if only it is administered in a loving spirit. Augustine also reflects that Christians do not instigate violence, but if attacked they are willing to wage war back — the posture of the innocent victim that can rhetorically serve to justify almost any level of bellicosity.[17] Augustine's seemingly hopeful reflection on the Jews' inability to see the divine nature is followed by a claim that Jesus' Jewish killers not only crucified him but also jeered at him in his dying moments. Augustine's use of Romans 9–11, cited above, comes just after he has launched the stock accusation of "deicide" against the Jews. His extended use of Ephesians 2's description of the breaking down of the dividing wall is closely followed by a barrage against the Jews for thinking God's favor is only for them, for seeking a visible kingdom, and for being deceived by the devil into slaying Christ. The search for more positive depictions of the Jews in the *Enarrationes*, or almost anywhere in classical Christian literature, can be a deflating experience. Even if we think we have found a place where the demon of anti-Judaism has been exorcised, if we read on, we usually find seven more.

This is made all the more grievous in contrast to Augustine's glowing comments about the Roman Empire. Psalm 3's exultation that God "*has* broken the teeth" of his enemies is appropriately spoken in the past tense, since the church reigns even now throughout the world.[18] Augustine is thrilled that the world is indeed filled with converts to the cross — a sharp contrast to his dark insistence that the kingdom has been taken from the Jews, abandoned as they are by God.[19] He is happy that laws have been instituted against heretics in the empire.[20] The day of evil rulers has clearly passed for the church, and its now-baptized kings are good and holy. Rulers have faith — the jewel of Christ — on their forehead now rather than any earthly treasure.[21] The cross

16. For example see his Letters 87, 93, and 220 — the last of which is commonly called his "Treatise on the Correction of the Donatists," in which he argues from such biblical texts as Luke 14:23, "compel them to come in," that there is a place for Catholic magistrates to use civic force against the Donatists. It is worthy of note that this argument deals specifically with Christian heretics and not with the unbaptized, such as Jews, for whose protection Augustine specifically argues (see below). The letters may be found in *The Political Writings of St. Augustine*, ed. Henry Paolucci (Chicago: Gateway, 1962), 190-240.

17. Psalm 119 in *EP* V, 509.

18. Psalm 3, *EP* I, 82.

19. Psalm 66 in *EP* III, 320-21.

20. Psalm 59 in *EP* III, 181.

21. Psalm 32 (3) in *EP* I, 414.

has passed from being an instrument of torture in the hands of emperors to one of worship marked on monarchs' foreheads. It has gone from the butt of its enemies' ridicule to the crowns of kings.[22] Clearly the bulk of the strictly political reflection in the *Enarrationes* precedes the shift in Augustine's later thought to a more sanguine view about earthly political authority as expressed in the *City of God*. In any event, these words of praise for Caesar, now converted to a friend and even prized member of the church, are poignant in their contrast to his words of condemnation for the Jews, whose ignominy fills Augustine's words and world.

These sorts of anti-Jewish reflections are all the more painful to read in our own day, with the extraordinary paradigm shift in biblical studies and a parallel shift in systematic theology in Christian attitudes toward Judaism, both biblical and contemporary.[23] Christians have rightly been chastened by the fruit of two millennia of unrelenting supersessionist and vindictive anti-Jewish preaching in the form of the Nazi holocaust, which was only the culmination of a long history of violent persecutions. We have learned from several generations of biblical scholars now that the anti-Jewish roots of Christian preaching and teaching go "all the way down," as it were, into the depths of Christian scripture and the earliest ecclesial dogmatic teaching. We should not dismiss too quickly Rosemary Radford Ruether's radical claim that Christian anti-Judaism stems from christology itself.[24]

For the most part, the writers of the New Testament saw themselves not simply as rejecters of Israel, but as Jews who see that the messianic age has dawned with the death and resurrection of Jesus, such that the gentiles can be gathered in to worship Zion's God, as the prophets predicted.[25] Christians have slowly and begrudgingly come to see that it is not only modern liberal tolerance toward religious others that dictates respect for traditionally perse-

22. Psalm 36 (2) in *EP* II, 107, and Psalm 54 in *EP* III, 66.

23. One minor way to express the paradigm shift in Christian attitudes toward Jews is to note the change in Christian use of the adjective "Jewish." When we use it now, as I do in Chapter 1 note 6, it is normally as a compliment — I rhetorically position allegory as a practice similar to Jewish exegesis in order to defend it. Ancient Christians used the adjective in precisely the opposite sense. Something "Jewish" was despicable on Christian grounds. As John O'Keefe writes, to accuse an exegete of being too "Jewish" was "a stylized way of saying that the interpretation is not very good." Perhaps the thoughtlessness of this rhetorical equation of "Jewish" and "bad" shows just how deeply Christian anti-Judaism runs ("'A Letter That Killeth,'" *Journal of Early Christian Studies* 8, no. 1 [2000]: 98 n. 33).

24. Ruether, *Faith and Fratricide: The Theological Roots of Anti-Semitism* (New York: Seabury, 1974).

25. I take my cues here from Richard Hays, *Echoes of Scripture in the Letters of Paul* (New Haven: Yale University Press, 1989).

cuted minorities like Jews, we have also seen that our own biblical sources mandate ongoing concern about Israel "according to the flesh." If Jesus himself had no mission to anyone other than his fellow Jews, and Paul himself could wring such exegetical sweat as we see in Romans 9–11 out of his worry about the apparent infidelity of God to his covenant with Israel in the Jews' rejection of Jesus, then biblically attentive Christians have no choice but be similarly concerned about the ongoing place of non-Christian Jewry in the working out of God's covenantal promises. This process of coming to see strands of our own scriptures that inveigh against longtime sinful practices only shows those practices to have been all the more sinful, for it suggests that history could have been otherwise. Had Christian attitudes through time been more deeply Pauline, and less deeply anti-Jewish . . . who knows? Sin is not mitigated in its seriousness by the realization that the possibility existed for avoiding it, it is rather then shown in its sharpest relief.

This is precisely where Augustine surprises with resources we did not expect to find. For Augustine, no less than the New Testament, has portions of his work that suggest to us that things could have been different with regard to western Christian attitudes toward non-Christian Judaism. To summarize what is to follow in this chapter: Augustine's reflections on the cursing psalms, and on the Psalter's words about Israel's enemies, can be helpful for thinking about his theology of Israel. Augustine also offers the most "positive" vision for ongoing non-Christian Jewry anywhere in ancient Christianity (whether we ourselves can find much use for it or not). Finally Augustine's christology — the foundation upon which this entire work rests — suggests a particularly Christian way forward past his own anti-Judaism. Often modern scholars like Ruether who seek *rapprochement* with Israel both as a theological category and as a living, breathing, people, have been willing to discard rather central tenets of Christian faith to do this, such as christology itself — for understandable reasons. Augustine's work may show us something counterintuitive however: that the way past such anti-Judaism as Augustine's is to enter more deeply into a christology like Augustine's. To say this a bit more historically, if Augustine had taken his own christology with sufficient seriousness, he would have been unable to say the things he said about Jews.

## Augustine on Cursing and Enemies

As part of my argument for allegory in this book I have maintained that individual portions of the Bible must be read in light of the church's creedal summaries of the whole content of the faith. I have argued against textbook accounts that hold allegory to be only a cosmetic cover placed over embarrassing scraps of scripture that would seem to inveigh against an ecclesial position. In Augustine's actual use allegory becomes the rhetorical exercise of making particularly Christian sense of words that would seem, on first glance, to admit of no such thing. So the cry of dereliction from Jesus' cross is actually an expression of sinners' divine abandonment healed in Christ's *kenosis.* Allegory is interesting then not only in its display of the exegetical nimbleness Christians show in turning troubling passages to their use, but also in the extraordinary beauty of the readings they offer. It is not only impressive to make the cry of dereliction a touchstone of christology, it is also a compelling and theologically defensible reading of scripture.

When Augustine turns to the many psalms of malediction we see something similar at work. He has read, and often commented upon, Jesus' prohibition of vengeance against enemies. How then is a reader committed to the central tenets of Christian teaching able to attend to these particular lines that would seem to discount that teaching, specifically on the issue of the contradiction between one strand of the Bible that curses enemies and another that blesses them?

When the psalmist prays, "Lord, lead me onward in your justice, because of my enemies," Augustine immediately thinks of Jesus' admonition in the Sermon on the Mount to love of enemies. As we saw in Chapter 2, it is important to have a concrete, verbal link to make an allegorical reading possible. Here Augustine has one in the form of the word "enemy," which has driven him to explore the difference between one strand of biblical teaching that would condemn enemies and another that would bless them. The *signum* "enemy" cannot simply be taken by Christians to refer to someone deserving curses, though that may be the meaning of the word for those whose language is not disciplined by all of Christian scripture. The *res* to which this and every word of the Bible attests is that of the triune God, whose love for his enemies was demonstrated in dying to reconcile them to his Father. So Augustine must discern some "other sense" to this word than that which it normally takes — literally an allegorical sense — read properly in light of the nature of the Christian God while fittingly making sense of the words on the page. As we have seen this is precisely where Augustine gets most interesting. In this particular instance he has no explicit curse to wrestle with, just the simple mention of the word "enemy." The resource to which he turns for help is Psalm 7, which speaks of a villain who digs a hole for another and falls in it himself. Augustine can now conclude, "when God punishes sinners, he does not inflict on them his evil but abandons them to their own evils." Augustine here does not quote Paul but is clearly in accord with the writer of Romans' description of God "giving them up" to the false gods they have chosen for themselves (Romans 1:24, 26, 28). For Augustine has known since his first dis-illusionment with the Manichees that God cannot do or choose evil.[26] God inflicts on sinners no "evil from himself, but [drives] them out toward that very thing they have chosen." This is in stark contrast to human beings' typi-cal posture of seeking quickly to repay evil "with an evil intent."[27] There is no emotion in God, let alone a biblically condemned one like the desire for re-venge. Divine justice and judgment merely take the form of God relegating those who have chosen against God to the nothingness they have chosen.

Augustine also reflects on the interweaving of Christian evangelism and liturgy in his attempt to change his hearers' attitudes toward cursing and ene-mies. Christianity is a relentlessly missionary religion. Even at its most estab-lished, its adherents hear regularly in their New Testament reading of the early church's aggressive attempts to proselytize and of their spectacular successes.[28] Augustine turns this basic Christian evangelical stance against the letter of the cursing psalms. He insists we must not think "bad people are in this world use-lessly."[29] They are there to offer chastening to good people, so these will grow in humility and faith and away from pride. More importantly for us, Augus-

---

26. G. R. Evans's book on Augustine's theodicy, *Augustine on Evil* (Cambridge: Cambridge University Press, 1982), shows the relationship between Augustinian biblical interpretation and his views on evil. She is specifically interested in the famously inflexible view of the mature Au-gustine against lying. Is not allegory, in which God purports to say one thing in scripture but ac-tually says another, a kind of divine lie? (78). Augustine extricates himself from this problem as follows: scripture intentionally offers an abundance of images of God that are meant to drive readers between desire for the God they cannot know and love for the God they can. Her sources here are early Trinitarian material like Epistle 11, the *Enarrationes,* and the later *De Trinitate.* At the beginning of our pilgrimage we cannot imagine how to speak well of the rela-tionships between the triune persons. Yet as we progress in this oscillation between knowing and not-knowing God, we become able to say a bit more about the Trinity than we could have otherwise. Our not-knowing God becomes less based on sheer ignorance and more on God's difference from humans. We progress from *scientia* to *sapientia,* from Christ to Christ. We have offered a similar description of Augustine's christology in Chapter 2.

Evans' book seems a good primer on Augustinian views of evil. Yet I fear she confuses the *privatio boni* with the claim that evil simply isn't there and must be ignored. She shows well how Augustine maneuvers out of troublesome biblical passages in the Psalms. Yet her description of an Augustinian conundrum in the face of what could be taken to be a divine lie seems to indi-cate a problem of hers, rather than Augustine's. Augustine himself does not seem troubled that scripture speaks in images and allegories. It is our own modern distrust of allegory that sparks that particular question rather than Augustine's own reflections.

27. On Psalm 5 in *EP* I, 98-99.

28. To cite examples from just one biblical book, see Acts 2:41, 47; 4:4; 5:14; 6:1, 7; 9:31, 35, 42; 11:21, 24; 14:1, 21; 16:5; 17:12.

29. Psalm 54 in *EP* III, 56.

tine insists that such people "might be converted, and then tried along with us!" Therefore "we must not hate them," lest, as Christians often have, we end up "unwittingly" hating one who in the future will be "a brother or sister." Here Augustine combines his insistence that the church is a *corpus permixtum* with a humility about human knowledge before the eschaton to say that everyone is a potential sister or brother in the church, and so cannot be hated. He also draws on either a real (in his case) or rhetorically constructed (in some lifelong believers' cases) "memory" of pre-conversion life to adjust attitudes toward enemies: "The road to a devout life must not be barred after you have traveled along it." Augustine draws not only on Christian habits and stories of evangelism but also on liturgical practices, especially praying the Lord's Prayer. "Consider your situation. You will say, 'Our Father. . . .'" He quotes a bit, "so far, so good. You continue," then just before the line about sins he draws attention: "and then — here it comes." After the line about forgiving those who sin against us, he asks, "so what are you going to do, when you and this verse meet here head-on?" What else, if we are to be those who not only pray this several times a day, but act upon it? The most basic of Christian practices — proclamation of the faith to outsiders and praying the Lord's Prayer — militate against seeking vengeance. We must find some other way to read such lines in the Psalter than simply to proclaim their literal imprecation.

Augustine also builds his case for allegory here from basic Christian catechesis. Christians learn among their first lessons in the Christian life to avoid seeking revenge, just as they learn early to live for God, to despise the world, and to give up the desire to be rich.[30] This is no esoteric or high-flown Christian teaching — it is basic church pedagogy. A psalm of imprecation, like our Psalm 88 or 137, must mean more than simply an expression of anger with God. Augustine posits that a cursing psalm can be taken in the way the Old Testament's prophets' warnings should be read: as a forecast of coming disaster promised *unless* those listening change their ways. If they do as, say, Jonah's hearers in Nineveh did, the withholding of divine punishment is no indication that the prophecy was untrue. On the contrary, it has then most profoundly fulfilled its purpose.[31] Augustine reads the cursing psalms with a similar hermeneutic. When we hear the *vox Christi*, present as it is throughout the Psalter, praying against its enemies, we can see his words as a pro-

---

30. On Psalm 48 (2) in *EP* II, 371.

31. See Jonah 3:6-10. As the use of an Old Testament exemplar makes clear, the hermeneutical issue here is not simply the New Testament's stance of enemy love versus the Old Testament's of vengeance. It is rather complexly interwoven strands of New Testament and Old Testament scripture, some of each of which promote sacrificial enemy-love, others of which set forth destruction of enemies.

phetic warning meant to bring about *conversio*. In Augustine's own words, "when he seems here to be praying for calamities to fall upon his enemies, it is not to be thought that he does so out of malevolence." Such curses are not unlike Jesus' woes pronounced over towns like Bethsaida and Korazim that will not listen to him: "he does not pray out of malice, but foretells the disasters that will fall upon them."[32] Elsewhere Augustine even seems to apologize for how frequently he must make this point: "We have often remarked on this distinction, and you must remember it; otherwise what is uttered by a prescient mind in the Spirit of God would seem like a malevolent imprecation."[33] So when Psalm 68 asks that evildoers' ill deeds "become a trap for them," we cannot take the Spirit's[34] words to be expressing divine hope for such a fate, but rather to be predicting what will happen unless there is repentance. Augustine goes further to note that scripture records such sentiments as warnings to *us*. When we see demonstrated the natural fruit of unjust actions, "our enemies do us a good turn" by showing us scripture's prophetic warning against sin being enacted. Augustine here attends loyally to the inner logic of the gospel, which promotes not the self-satisfied condemnation of one's enemies but the amendment of one's own and one's community's ways in light of scripture's prohibitions against hatred and pride.[35]

Augustine also attends to the saints who are held up in the church's liturgy for emulation, whose story shows that "cursing" cannot be the last word in Christian parlance. When Psalm 58 insists that God "show no mercy to any who deal unjustly," Augustine hedges a bit: "yet God did show mercy to Paul." Despite his brazen persecution of the church, Paul became someone who would later testify that though he had acted unjustly, yet "I received mercy" (1 Timothy 1:13). How then can we read the psalm's description of God's mercilessness? It can be read as a word against defensiveness over one's sins and in favor of repenting from them.[36] Augustine also has Old Testament exemplars

---

32. On Psalm 27 in *EP* I, 291.

33. On Psalm 68 (2) in *EP* III, 390.

34. I wish I could say more about this pneumatological description of scripture's authorship, but Augustine does not say more. He will often speak of scripture as having been authored by the Spirit, as well as by its human authors, but he does not elaborate on the significance of his view of inspiration in the *Enarrationes*. Robert Jenson has recently seen the lack of a robust doctrine of biblical inspiration as a lacuna in his own two-volume *Systematic Theology*. See his "A Second Thought about Inspiration," *Pro Ecclesia* 13 (2004): 393-98. It may be important to have some such doctrine, yet a "proper" theology of inspiration often does surprisingly little to arbitrate exegetical debates.

35. I am influenced in my comments here by Rowan Williams, *Resurrection: Interpreting the Gospel* (Harrisburg, PA: Morehouse, 1982).

36. Psalm 58 (1) in *EP* III, 161.

who show there to be another biblical word that overcomes condemnation. Nineveh was indeed "overthrown," as Jonah threatened. It was thrown down with respect to its evil deeds, and was built up in goodness.[37] Most importantly Augustine inveighs against the letter with the counter-example of Jesus, whose own practice and teaching about enemy love must be regnant for any specifically Christian consideration of scripture. When the author of Psalm 7 asks God whether he has indeed paid back evil for evil, Augustine can reflect on the specifically and oddly Christian teaching of rewarding good for evil. That is the exchange singled out for the highest praise in Jesus' own teaching about perfection in faith (Matthew 5:45-48). He then boldly paraphrases the Lord himself saying, "it was for you, ungodly sinner, that I endured my betrayer in deep silence and inexhaustible patience, so that your iniquities might be washed away by the shedding of my blood. Should you, then, not imitate me and, in your turn, refrain from rewarding evil with evil?"[38] Christ makes his own the very voice of his tormenters when he protests the Father's abandonment, in order to attempt to secure for them and all salvation. No reference to "enemies" can be the same once run through this christological filter.

Augustine can also bring concrete church practice to bear against the letter of scripture in favor of a christologically disciplined reading of a cursing psalm. When Psalm 70 asks God to "rescue me from the hand of the sinner," we know well enough to ascribe this prayer to Christ, the whole Christ, *totus Christus*. The voice of the head is here speaking on behalf of his body, filled as it is with sinners and saints both, who will remain inextricable from one another until the judgment. Christ's praying of this prayer is then not unlike Paul's lament in Romans 7 that he fights with another law in his members. Salvation has not meant the eradication of sin, but the patient bearing of it on the way to the eschaton: "until the end of the world there will be this one person crying out to be set free from his sins."[39] Neither the psalmist nor the Christian praying the psalm can yet be physically rescued from the hand of the sinner without a Donatist-like flight from the catholic church into a schismatic body of super-saints. Sinners and sin remain in this world, and Christians should know as well from Paul and from Jesus to bear with their weaker members in patience, just as God bears with them. As Augustine writes, "Once saved from your own iniquity, have regard also to the iniquities of others, among whom you are obliged to live until life

---

37. Psalm 50 in *EP* II, 420.
38. Psalm 7 in *EP* I, 115.
39. Psalm 70 (1) in *EP* III, 419.

comes to an end."[40] One can almost hear Augustine sigh as he thinks of the mountain of quotidian tasks facing a bishop in his day, all of which press with equal fervor, few of which seem directly related to the gospel. Yet all of this — bearing with enemies, abiding tedious churchmanship — demonstrates that Christians cannot simply be done with difficulty if they are to be disciples in this world. Rather, such difficulty, termed "cross-bearing" in some later Christian traditions, is the very condition of the possibility of faithfulness. Donatists need not pray to be rescued from the hands of sinners, for they already have been in their flight from the church. Catholics need this prayer, and praying it they learn of the importance of enemy love for their own growth.

When the psalmist asks God that his opponents be "covered with shame and embarrassment," Augustine insists that we not think scripture is being vindictive. He muses here on Stephen's description of his enemies as "stiff-necked people, uncircumcised in heart and ears, forever resisting the Holy Spirit" in Acts 7:51. Stephen sounds almost "as though his soul had been provoked into fighting." Yet this cannot be — Stephen is a saint, one who follows in the way of Jesus as the archetypal martyr, who could have no such hatred for his antagonists. Rather, we must read these words, and the words of the psalmist, in light of Jesus' interaction with and prayers for his murderers. Stephen here was treating his attackers "like dangerously delirious patients," trying "to restrain them with his words."[41] Like the Hebrew prophets, Stephen criticizes only to restore. Augustine's Stephen uses words that cut like a surgeon uses a scalpel — only to heal. Elsewhere Augustine turns with extended attention to one of the Psalms' most bitter maledictions: "may the outpoured blood of your servants be avenged among the nations before our eyes." Slaughter them, and let us watch. He uses his normal hermeneutical move on this passage, arguing that it has to be a prophecy meant for deliverance, and not an ironclad future prediction. Then he argues, cleverly, that it is a sort of "retribution" for the church's enemies to watch her grow in numbers and in grace. But then he turns up the heat — he notes the New Testament's restrictions on vengeance are not limited to Jesus' words, but include Paul's (Romans 12:19) and Peter's (1 Peter 3:9).[42] Yet other portions of the New Testament suggest a lust for vengeance no less passionate than the psalmist's, as when the martyrs under the altar in Revelation 6:10 ask God "how long" until

---

40. *EP* III, 419.

41. *EP* III, 426.

42. For problems concerning the authorship of latter New Testament epistles see Chapter 2 note 3. The reflections there about deutero-Pauline epistles apply also to the Petrine literature.

their blood is avenged.[43] We cannot think that the saints themselves wish to be avenged — the Bible itself rules out not only retributive violence but even ill thoughts toward enemies! What do we make of a wish like that in Psalm 78 or Revelation 6? Augustine sees a difference in the way the righteous and the wicked would pray a prayer like this. The righteous offer prayers of cursing against their enemies in hopes of seeing them corrected, rather than punished. They wish to see wrongs put to right. And if a sinner winds up ruined instead, the righteous exult not in prohibited vengeance, but in the lesson given about divine chastisement, and the hope others will see and be edified. Even then, their satisfaction must come not from seeing the punishment of the wicked, but from "the goodness of the judge."[44]

This may sound like cold comfort to those who were on the receiving end of "correction" from the hands of Augustine. We may indeed be left with words of serious critique for Augustine's own manner of interpreting correction, or compulsion, against the Donatists.[45] The more pressing point for now is this: Christians cannot curse, nor take joy in vengeance, nor even wish to see wrongs against themselves avenged. When they come upon such sentiments in scripture, these must be signs that God wishes them to read deeper. We who are praying this psalm must be cursing the wrongs done, not the persons doing them — for whom we only wish good. The aim of any such "cursing" must be *metanoic:* its goal must be a turning from darkness to light, for both the other and ourselves. Augustine is clear that church life will be full of difficulty, especially in relating to covert sinners and hidden enemies within the *catholica.* No Christian can presume her own innocence. Here again we see some of Augustine's greatest hermeneutical gifts, in turning phrases that would seem to make his view impossible into those that enhance it. The psalmist's repeated request that God "turn my enemy back" is a request for an act of mercy — where should someone wish to be but behind Jesus, following him?[46] His prayers that his opponents would be "confused" can come true in

---

43. Whatever problems Augustine has, he does not subscribe to the facile conclusion that the Old Testament God is one of wrath and the New Testament one of mercy — he reads his Bible too carefully to be unaware that the old covenant is resplendent with figures and stories of grace, and the new with frightening displays of violence. Job is a dear and favorite figure in these pages; New Testament stories like Revelation 6 do not escape his gaze.

44. Psalm 78 in *EP* IV, 136-37.

45. William Cavanaugh has recently tried to show that Disney is a more effective coercive power in our day than Augustine was in his, largely because Disney's opponents (fundamentalists involved in the Baptist "boycott" against Disney in the early 1990s) are resigned to defeat in a way that Catholics' opponents in Augustine's day were not. Cavanaugh, "Coercion in Augustine and Disney," *New Blackfriars* 80 (June 1999): 83-90.

46. Psalm 9 in *EP* I, 150.

an instance like that on the Damascus Road, in which Paul was indeed confused in his rush for punishment, knocked to the ground, and made to follow (Acts 9:1-8).[47] Prayers about God's avenging foot being "dipped in blood" can be turned around in Augustine's hands. What are the Lord's feet but his preachers, who announce good news (Romans 10:14-15)? And with what blood do they drip but their own? This is clearly a prayer for martyrs, not for warriors.[48] A Christian's hope is to suffer, not to inflict suffering. Just as mercy triumphs over judgment in Christian thought and practice (James 2:13), here mercy triumphs over judgment in Augustine's psalm hermeneutic. However we assess the success of Augustine's own political practice in this regard, we should say his hermeneutic allows a degree of flexibility that we can only wish the church could have put to better use.

### God's Love of Enemies

Augustine's observations about the meaning of such *signa* as "cursing" and "enemy" are, as ever, determined by the *res* of the triune God. The *kenotic* and *theotic* exchange between God and humanity in the mediator Christ forces a rethinking of all biblical and extra-biblical reflection on how to interact with enemies. Christ, we're told, came "to receive insults and give honors," to receive all of human sin and divine abandonment and offer in return divine blessings, sonship, and indeed the divine nature itself.[49] We need not focus on the *admirabile commercium* in detail here since we did so in Chapter 2. We simply need to note that Augustine is not oblivious to the way language about the "wonderful exchange" affects Christians' interactions with their enemies now. How could it not? These are the very members of the body of Christ, whose head acted in quite specific non-retaliatory ways toward his enemies in offering them salvation in exchange for rejecting and killing him. Just as Christians cannot read other than the way *their own* eyes and mouth do, as we argued in Chapter 2, so they cannot relate to enemies in any way other than their head does. Augustine paraphrases Christ's own words: "I bestowed honors, they insults, I medicine, they wounds." As we participate in this exchange we "are taught to pray that even our persecutors may be brought back to spiritual health and righteousness."[50] Those who are being transformed from one

---

47. Psalm 69 in *EP* III, 404.
48. Psalm 67 in *EP* III, 352.
49. Psalm 30 (2) in *EP* I, 323.
50. Psalm 34 (2) in *EP* II, 60-61.

degree of glory to another (2 Corinthians 3:18), who are growing from *scientia* of Christ's human nature to the *sapientia* of his divine, have a blueprint for how to respond to enemies: without retaliation, with unearned love, all in reflection of the God toward whom we are all being drawn.

In reflecting on the psalmist's description of God as "our helper in the terrible tribulations that have come upon us," Augustine thinks of the crowd at Pentecost as described in Acts 2. Peter preaches to them a stern sermon of rebuke and they recognize their complicity in killing God's messiah: "let all Israel be assured of this: God has made this Jesus, whom you crucified, both Lord and Christ" (Acts 2:36). The crowd is "cut to the heart" and asks what it should do, and is told to repent and be baptized so as to receive the Holy Spirit. Augustine paraphrases the crowd's desperate realization of its guilty status: "he whom we killed has proved to be so great, and now what is to become of us?" Surely such murderers deserve no mercy, and normally in this world have no chance of receiving it. They are like patients so sick that they kill the doctor sent to care for them. What punishment could be too severe? Augustine, like Paul, is impressed with the victimizers' ability to recognize themselves as sinners. "You have recognized your physician, though belatedly. Now that you have received this assurance, drink the blood you shed." The eucharistic overtones are unmistakable, as is the enormity of the forgiveness offered: "if that can be forgiven, is anything unforgivable?"[51] Augustine has no hesitation in delivering the same sort of harangue to his congregations gathered in north Africa as had Peter to the Pentecost crowd in Acts. If we can paraphrase: you yourselves have murdered your physician, and are now offered reconciliation in the chalice you have filled with his blood. This is the fundamental logic of sin and grace for Augustine — the recognition of culpability, the desire for conversion, and the openness to a new eucharistic fellowship and way of life.

Augustine makes clear that Christ's own response to evil was to offer good in exchange. He cites broad New Testament support for such a view, including the Sermon on the Mount, Jesus' mediatorial prayer from the cross, and the injunctions against revenge in the Pauline and Petrine epistles. He also shows that the possible responses to evil we can make are like a ladder, progressing upwards from least like Christ to most, up which believers must climb. He offers six possible responses to another's actions: (1) to render good for evil; (2) not to render evil for evil; (3) to return good for good; (4) not to return good for good; (5) to give evil in exchange for good; (6) not to give evil for evil. Christians ought indeed return good for good, and refuse evil for

51. Psalm 45 in *EP* II, 313.

evil, but these are responses to be expected even of "mediocre" people. The Lord does not denounce such behavior, but "he does not want his disciples to remain stuck there." Christ showed in his own actions the best way to respond to any human interaction is to repay good for evil. "While hanging on the cross he did not display his strength in the face of those detractors whom he could have annihilated . . . this restraint was meant to give us an example of patience. It was more profitable for us. . . ."[52] We see here another example of the pedagogy of the incarnation, spoken of in Chapter 2, now applied to Christians' interactions with their enemies. The shape of Christ's incarnate life is such as to offer models for how his followers ought to relate to enemies. Augustine offers Christ first as a warning against the worst responses, then moves to encourage somewhat better ones, and finally offers Christ as the utmost model of reconciliation for his followers' emulation. This pedagogy is as slow and gradual as the course of a long life in Christ. It begins simply — with the confession of sins and an intentional attribution of any good deeds to God, and not to oneself. Then, "something is still missing. What does he still need? He needs to beware of arrogance with regard to others who do not yet live as he does."[53] This is *why* God became human — to teach humility to those who need to be made holy. It is for this reason that pagans mock Christianity, but Augustine suggests, "if it is beautiful in your sight, Christian, imitate it." Grow toward a God who loves and dies for enemies, who sends sunshine on just and unjust, who reconciles bitter foes. "Grow gentle, then, believer, if you have been trained by God's law."

It is surprising to find Augustine so insistent on the importance of patient enemy-love, first by God and then by disciples growing toward God. This church father is normally, and not unjustly, depicted as the forerunner of theological justification of state violence against religious non-conformity for his begrudging willingness to have the imperial sword fall upon his Donatist enemies. Indeed it may offer cold comfort to historic foes of Augustinian Christianity to hear of enemies being "turned into" friends, if the Donatists be examples of that sort of forced conciliation. Nevertheless, it is important to note that Augustine sees it as a mark of the divine character (and just so as a possible human response enabled by the incarnation) to reach out to enemies and seek reconciliation — "a bad person has harmed you: very well, forgive him, or there will be two bad people."[54] Christians cannot abide revenge, nor even desire it. They cannot think of evil-doers anything other than that

52. Psalm 108 in *EP* V, 244.
53. Psalm 93 in *EP* IV, 391.
54. Psalm 54 in *EP* III, 68.

they are a gift meant to chasten our pride and hasten our humility, on the way to what we hope will be their inclusion in Christ also. All of this has a deeply christological shape, as an emulation of a savior who offers his murderers his blood to drink as he creates a fellowship of forgivers from an assembly of former sinners. Whatever poor political uses Augustine may have turned his theology toward, and whatever promising ones he may not have been aware of, we can see here the seeds of what could have been a profound theology of grace, of patient cross-bearing, and of suffering love of enemies. Perhaps it still can be all that.

## Israel in Augustine's Theology

These promising reflections on enemy-love in the *Enarrationes* are not explicitly brought into correlation with Augustine's theology of Israel. Nowhere does he say he has Jews in mind as those with whom his listeners must patiently bear in hopes of bringing about reconciliation. His theological engagement with Israel as an intellectual category, and with actual Jews, draws on different scriptural and theological resources.[55] His writings *contra Iudaeos* are always painful for post-Holocaust ecclesial readers like us, especially those of us who wish to promote Augustine's thought on many theological topics other than this one.

Augustine's version of the Psalter mistranslates a frequent psalm superscription as "not to be tampered with." This is verbal link aplenty to lead Augustine to think of Pontius Pilate's insistence that his sign above Jesus' cross is to be left as he wrote it, "Jesus of Nazareth, King of the Jews" (John 19:19-22). This, in turn, leads Augustine to reflect on the significance of the crucifixion for Israel. We are not surprised to find a standard supersessionist statement, "Now, it is evident that if he who was crucified was King of the Jews, and if the Jews crucified their own king, they did not so much destroy him by doing so as make him king of the Gentiles."[56] Augustine relates this standard ecclesial charge against the Jews to another: Israel was always obsessed with "carnal," "worldly" things rather than spiritual. They failed to see that the earthly promises in the Old Testament "were fraught with symbolic meaning, and the people did not understand what lay hidden under these signs." This

55. Frederiksen argues against the dean of Augustinian scholarship on Judaism, Bernhard Blumenkranz, that Augustine probably did not have significant interaction with actual Jews and instead writes of them as a biblical and theologically imagined category of people. See her *"Excaecati Occulta Justitia Dei,"* 320-24.

56. Psalm 58 (1) in *EP* III, 148.

desire for the wrong things, or even to see properly spiritual and carnal things for what they are, was a "very pernicious" one that "arose in the heart of the synagogue, one which sent its feet slithering and all but slipping off God's path."[57] They slid to the point where they could make the most foolish bargain imaginable. John's Gospel records a deliberation in a Sanhedrin meeting that leads to a decision: "if we leave him alive, the Romans will come, and sweep away our land and our nationhood" (John 11:48). Augustine acidly observes, "They wanted to kill Christ in order not to lose the earth, and they lost the earth by killing Christ." The result is that their land is "emptied of Christ's enemies, but filled with people praising Christ."[58] Augustine then ascribes a psalm line, that "they shall become the prey of foxes," to the Jews. Christ had called Herod "a fox" (Luke 13:32). The Jews violated their own scripture's commands to have no king but the Lord, and proclaimed instead "we have no king but Caesar" (John 19:15). Augustine writes, "they rejected a Lamb and chose a fox, so they deserved to become the prey of foxes."[59] The destruction of Jerusalem and the temple, the slaughter of the Jews at the hands of foreigners, their current wandering of the earth — all these are fitting punishment for a people who behaved in such dastardly ways. Augustine is not surprised. What else could one expect of "the hapless Jews" who so "clutched at their earthly blessings" in their demonic bargain to save their land by rejecting their king that "in that place where they slew Christ, they themselves were slaughtered"?[60]

Now, when Augustine hears the word "Israel," or any number of crucial names and theological concepts in the psalms, he immediately thinks of the church. Normally this is done with an etymology — that Israel means "one who sees God," that is, those progressing toward eschatological vision of Christ's divine nature. Occasionally he does stop to counter the reading that the word "Israel" in the Psalter could refer to Israel according to the flesh. He can ask, "Are they still to be called 'Jews' then?" The answer is not difficult: "No, they are not . . . the real Jewry is Christ's Church."[61] The best that can be said for fleshly Israel now is that it sings the same psalms as the church. This is a praise without deeds. The words remain, like so many dead leaves, but there is no fruit, as in the tree that Jesus cursed (Matthew 21:19).[62] "No one must say, 'I am not a child of Israel.' In case you are inclined to think like that, in

---

57. Psalm 72 in *EP* III, 476.
58. Psalm 62 in *EP* III, 245.
59. Psalm 62 in *EP* III, 245.
60. Psalm 73 in *EP* IV, 17.
61. Psalm 75 in *EP* IV, 55.
62. On Psalm 138 in *EP* VI, 271.

case you are tempted to assume that, while the Jews are children of Israel we are not, I will say something daring to you, my brothers and sisters: they are not, but we are."[63] Augustine ascribes the words of Israel's prophet against her: "these people honor me with their lips, but their heart is far from me" (Isaiah 29:13). He can often ascribe such words of warning to the church, but only in a temporary sense, intended to turn its course of action or thought around. It seems here permanently hung on the neck of the Jews.

In none of this is Augustine original. Indeed, some of his most stringently anti-Jewish material comes from the New Testament itself, and that material was only hardened in the oven of inner-Jewish polemic over Jesus' claimed messiahship, and then inter-community conflict between church and synagogue after these two became distinguishable entities. It is not reviewed here as though it were anything new. Rather, it is offered in a spirit of confession. Here is what Augustine said and passed on to his readers, who for a millennium and a half insisted that we should do as the saint and father did — a claim this book also makes. As Augustine never tires of saying in *Confessions,* what is good comes from God, what is not from Augustine.

Yet could there be anything of God in Augustine's reflections on Israel? Perhaps, in an area in which Augustine does offer some innovative reflection. He reflects on a description of God as "the God of Israel" and insists that his hearers not say to themselves, "'I am not Israel.'"[64] For the God of Israel is the "God of the younger son, the God of the junior people," citing Paul's favorite line from Genesis 25:23 that "the elder shall serve the younger." Augustine attempts to ground his reading of the church's status as "Israel" in a reading of Israel's scriptures — one learned from Paul. While he is certainly more overtly supersessionist than the Paul of Romans — in the same breath that he warns his hearers not to think of themselves as excluded by the term "Israel," he writes that "it would be truer to say that the Jews are not Israel" — he still recognizes that Christians have to offer a convincing reading of Israel's scriptures to demonstrate their claim about their relationship to Israel's God. Augustine does this by describing the Jews in this way: "Consider, brothers and sisters: the Jews serve us now; they are like slaves [*capsarii*] carrying our satchels; they carry books for us, the students. Look how the Jews are like slaves to us, and deservedly. . . . The prophets and the law are cherished among them, and in the law and the prophets Christ was made known." Augustine may be working here with Paul's description of the law as a pedagogue to Israel meant to discipline Israel until Christ came (Galatians 3:24).

63. On Psalm 148 in *EP* VI, 490.
64. Psalm 40 in *EP* II, 238.

He extols the Jews' reverence for their and our scripture. Most importantly, he cites the Jewish provenance of scripture as useful in polemical argumentation with "pagans": "if they suspect we have forged these prophecies, and written them up after the event as though they purport to refer to something future, we bring forward the books of the Jews. This is all the more convincing inasmuch as the Jews are our enemies, so our opponent is convinced by our enemy's documents." This is the most impressive instance of a patristic thinker making positive theological use of Jews as Jews that we have: as proof against pagan scoffers. That may not be saying much! Yet it is noteworthy that Augustine here can make reference to the synagogue as an ally, even if in a quite limited and patronizing sense. This has been called Augustine's "witness" doctrine — that the Jews unwittingly bear independent witness to the truth of Christian faith against non-believing pagans that Israel's scriptures were not written *ex post facto* to match Christ's life, but rather that Christ's life fulfilled prophecies written long ago and proved by the guardianship of these books by Jews who are Christians' "enemies." The significance of this doctrine is often commented upon, not least because it had a hand in leading quite bitterly anti-Jewish governing authorities in Christendom in later centuries to offer some protection of Jews for reasons appealing to their own Christianity.[65] For our purposes it says something more profound: that Augustine is convinced that Israel's scripture bears such patent witness to Christ that unconvinced outsiders will be convinced by it, if only they can be shown that the books indeed date to an antique age long before Christ. And of course, such proof will be allegorical! The witness doctrine is an indirect claim about allegorical exegesis, demonstrating that Augustine did not take this hermeneutic as esoteric or question-begging — he rather than it offered a compelling witness to the truth of Christianity that could wield evangelical power over non-committed readers.

Now, to be sure, the witness doctrine could be brought to bear against the Jews in bitter terms. In another exposition Augustine describes the Jews as "book bearers" in much harsher terms than in the one cited above. They are like "slaves who are accustomed to walk behind their masters carrying their books, so that while the slaves sink under the weight, the masters make great

---

65. Frederiksen cites previous work indicating that Augustine's prestige meant his argument here allowed the Jews "an immunity from religious coercion enjoyed by virtually no other community in post-Theodosian antiquity" (*"Excaecati Occulta Justitia Dei,"* 300). His influence continued in later centuries, for example encouraging Bernard of Clairvaux to call for the protection of Jews in the Crusades, and Thomas Aquinas to insist on the protection of Jewish property (Michael Signer, "Jews and Judaism" in *Augustine Through the Ages,* ed. Allan D. Fitzgerald [Grand Rapids: Eerdmans, 1999], 470-74, 473).

strides through reading. Such is the shameful position to which the Jews have been reduced . . . that they can read this verse like blind people looking into their own mirror."[66] Clearly this teaching can be easily combined with standard polemic about Jewish obstinacy and blindness. If we are looking for a positive traditional Christian doctrine to bring to the inter-religious dialogue table today, this is not likely to be it! The witness doctrine is as deeply enmeshed with thoughtless, or worse, well-thought-out, anti-Jewish sentiment. Yet it does represent an instance in which Christian theology claims to need Jews who remain Jews. And it does so based on what Augustine takes to be a compelling reading of Old Testament scripture as a witness to Christ. Augustine's exegesis regarding the Jews, and his biblical hermeneutic generally, were situated in an era that treasured rhetorical debate. Church leaders no less than other ancient rhetors had to offer compelling oratory that expanded on foundational texts in aesthetically pleasing ways.[67] For us to rebut Augustine on his own grounds would be a rhetorical *riposte* in spirit with Augustine's age. If Augustine offers the best Christian teaching on Judaism available in the ancient world, he encourages us to offer the best in ours: the bearers of our books can themselves pass judgment on the readings of them we offer. That is, if Christians cannot offer exegesis of Israel's scripture that can pass muster with those who carry our books, then we must reexamine our own exegetical conclusions.

Augustine thought Christians offered the best reading of Israel's scripture possible — one that would appeal to pagans who did not yet hold those books to be religiously foundational, just ancient. How much more ought we be able to argue exegetically in honorable ways with Jews who share a zeal for these books? To the point that if they cannot admit the feasibility (not necessarily truth) of our arguments, then our own claim to truth can be called into question? "They hold the books in which Christ was foretold, and we hold Christ."[68] However effective this claim may have been in polemic against pagans in Augustine's day, it now offers a challenge to Christians who care about dialogue with Jews: can we demonstrate our theological claims exegetically from Israel's scripture? And if not, what right have we to be reading it? I offer this question against a now rampant unthinking Marcionism in the church — one that has lost the Old Testament due to years of thoughtless neglect and patronizing dismissal in mainline Protestant churches, what Ellen Davis calls the

---

66. On Psalm 56 in *EP* III, 110.

67. Joseph Lienhard shows the importance of Augustine's rhetorical training and of his culture's love for rhetoric generally in his "Reading the Bible and Learning to Read: The Influence of Education on St. Augustine's Exegesis," *Augustinian Studies* 27 (1996): 7-25.

68. Psalm 58 (1) in *EP* III, 166.

"loss of a friend."[69] Yet I also offer it against opponents of allegory. I do not think Augustine's claim can be demonstrated without allegorical exegesis. The lament psalms, the suffering servant, the prophecies that the New Testament and later Christians hold point to Christ who cannot be taken to do so on mere literalism divined by historical criticism alone. *Of course* Psalm 22 or Isaiah 53 or Malachi's prophecy about Bethlehem do not "refer" to Jesus of Nazareth in their original context — who could claim they do? Yet Christians cannot give up these sorts of crucial biblical and theological claims and remain Christian. The only hermeneutic that allows us to continue to make these sorts of claims is an allegorical one. By that same hermeneutic the entirety of Israel's scripture can be taken to witness to Jesus. Nothing less than that will do if we wish to continue to claim our faith to be a living thing, passed down "in accordance with the scriptures" (1 Corinthians 15:4), centered on the Christ to whom Moses and all the scriptures testify (John 5:39, 45).

Augustine famously describes the church's relationship to non-Christian Judaism with the story of Cain and Abel. Commenting on a psalm verse about God's preference of mercy over sacrifice, Augustine reflects on the end of the temple and Jewish oblation.[70] He insists that no one should find fault with Jews for having sacrificed in the past, and that those sacrifices are suitably ended, presumably as punishment for rejecting Christ. "But," he insists, "something has remained to them that they can celebrate, so that they are not left entirely without a sign." Just as God mercifully provided a mark for Cain so he would not be killed in Genesis 4, "the Jewish nation likewise has survived." Their "mark" is their cultural distinctiveness. While other peoples under Roman rule share its laws without distinction, "the Jewish people remained unaltered with its sign, the sign of circumcision and the sign of the unleavened bread; Cain was not killed." Not that Cain's future is enviable: "But he was cursed and banished from the earth that had opened its mouth to receive a brother's blood . . . it cries to the Lord, but the one who shed it is too deaf to hear, because he does not drink it." The Jews are like Cain now — left wandering, but not killed. Yet they are different in one significant way. They are unaware that their survival is granted by Christ: "what has remained to them like Cain's mark has achieved its purpose, but they do not know it," whereas Cain clearly was aware of his "mark." Augustine does not draw extended attention to this difference. He merely wishes by the exegetical move to insist on the God-given prerogative for the Jews to continue as a wandering and cursed, but not killed, people.

69. Davis, "Losing a Friend: The Loss of the Old Testament to the Church," *Pro Ecclesia* 9, no. 1 (2000): 73-84.

70. Psalm 39 in *EP* II, 209.

This allegory of Augustine's and its comparison of the Jews to Cain is often commented upon.[71] What is less frequently attended to is the fact that Augustine's theology of Israel is dependent on an allegory. We can add now that Jewish readers of scripture should have every opportunity to challenge with exegesis of their own, with self-description in their own voice, an opportunity they do not receive from Augustine. The granting of a rationale not to be killed must be cold comfort to a people long accustomed to being marked by outsiders for having been "murderers," and the prohibition against killing them has often proved flimsy. Yet it is interesting to note Augustine can here find something positive to say about Jewish distinctiveness. The "mark" that mercifully keeps them alive is an identity rooted in circumcision and Passover. Augustine himself has to explain exegetically how Christians can themselves justify not following these observances. With Paul he insists that Christ is our Passover, celebrated with the unleavened bread of sincerity and truth (1 Corinthians 5:7-8). Again, Christians have to be able to argue exegetically as to why they can claim to be a continuation of Israel without observing Jewish practices.[72] It is a thin thread that connects ongoing Christian identity to Israel's scripture — the thread of allegory. We usually unwittingly sever it. Paul and Augustine still felt the force of that exegetical necessity in a way far surpassing churches in our day.

It is also deeply important to Augustine to show what sort of continuity exists between the church and Israel, between gentiles who worship Jesus now and Jews before the incarnation. He writes on Psalm 77's recounting of the history of the Exodus that "our psalm tells the story of what befell Israel's ancestors long ago. But it does so to warn a later Israel, the Israel of the psalmist's own day, to beware of proving ungrateful to God."[73] The church can only claim this text because it likewise claims to be a "later Israel," to be in organic continuity with the community that experienced this history and with the psalmist who re-recorded the events for the sake of Israel's praise. The psalmist's request to "open my mouth in parables" leads Augustine to think of Paul's exegesis of the Exodus in First Corinthians, where he discusses continuity and discontinuity between Israel and church: "all our ancestors walked under the cloud, and all crossed the sea, and all were through Moses baptized in cloud and sea; all of them ate the same spiritual food and drank the same spiritual drink, for they drank from the spiritual rock that followed them, and the rock

71. For example in Signer, "Jews and Judaism," in Fitzgerald, ed., *Augustine Through the Ages,* 471-72.

72. As Michael Wyschogrod says baptized Jews should. See his "Letter to Cardinal Lustiger," in *Abraham's Promise,* ed. Kendall Soulen (Grand Rapids: Eerdmans, 2004).

73. Psalm 77 in *EP* IV, 90.

was Christ. Yet God was not pleased with all of them" (10:1-4). Augustine announces, "In a mysterious way their food and drink were the same as ours, but the same only with regard to their meaning, not the same in kind." With Paul he must claim the Exodus generation really did participate in baptism and eucharist, but in a way different than Christians do, since we have seen the "rock," Christ, in flesh, in a way they did not. Augustine notes that Paul's description that "God was not pleased with all of them" implies there were indeed "some with whom God was pleased." He preaches that this is not unlike the church — where not all who are baptized receive grace, though some do.[74]

It is important to stop and notice what is taking place here. Augustine is glossing Paul glossing Exodus as each deals with issues of identity in Israel. The key point is that Augustine feels he must show the church's narrative continuity with Israel from Israel's scripture — a burden that later supersessionist Christians in the *ad verseos Iudaeos* tradition felt less need to do. He also works hard to show the same continuity with Israel for which the writer of Ephesians argues. Christ's death has broken down the dividing wall between Jew and gentile so that both may now worship Israel's God. Christ is a cornerstone that unites the two "walls," one Jewish, one Gentile, around the worship of Israel's messiah. As Augustine says, "let us not have regard to the diversity of these peoples whose origins were so far apart, but to their close kinship as they embrace in Christ."[75] Augustine is here clearly counterposing the "unity" of Jew and gentile spoken of in the Pauline epistles to the separation espoused by the Donatists — these heretics can have no house, for they are like a free-standing wall, unconnected to the cornerstone or any other wall. A door in such a house is a door to nowhere.[76] Elsewhere he writes, "It is not with the Jews that we should be angry, for they at least jeered only at a dying man, not a reigning king."[77] Augustine reserves his deepest antipathy for heretical and schismatic catholics rather than Jews. In fact, in places like these he explicitly contrasts the greater sin of the heretics with the lesser one of the Jews. For Christians must demonstrate their continuity with Israel — a continuity that today's Jews fail to see but from which they nevertheless enjoy protection — whereas Donatism or Pelagianism are sheer dead-ends. Heretical groups can be thanked for showing Catholics things in their own scripture they would not have seen otherwise, but they have no ongoing purpose in catholic thought, while non-Christian Jews clearly do.

74. Psalm 77 in *EP* IV, 90.
75. Psalm 94 in *EP* IV, 417.
76. Psalm 95 in *EP* IV, 426.
77. Psalm 21 (2) in *EP* I, 227.

Augustine frequently returns to the Pauline theme of the inability of the Jews to see Christ's divinity, since they could not have crucified him had they done so (1 Corinthians 2:8). He compares the incarnation to God's physical appearance before Moses on Sinai — God's hand covers Moses' face until God passes by, lifting the hand, so that Moses can see his back only. It was *God's* doing that the Jews could not see Christ's divinity, but only his "back parts," his humanity, which they crucified. Why? "'For if they had known, they would never have crucified the Lord of glory,' and if the Lord had not been crucified, his blood would not have redeemed the world."[78] Jewish rejection of Christ is here taken to be divinely mandated as somehow necessary for the salvation of the gentiles. Augustine goes so far as to suggest the psalmist wishes for Israel's survival *as Israel* so "that through its survival the multitude of Christians might increase."[79] In its context in the *enarratio* this is a reference to the witness doctrine. Yet it also seems an echo of Paul's description in Romans 11:25-26 of Israel being intentionally hardened by God until the full number of the gentiles can come in, at which point all Israel will be saved. Augustine ties the two Pauline verses together not infrequently to demonstrate that God holds back Israel to allow the gentiles to come in before a final, eschatological conversion of "all Israel."[80] He asks Paul's rhetorical question elsewhere — "now that he is glorified, will he abandon the Jewish people?" The answer is also Paul's: *me genoito*.[81] The psalmist demonstrates the order of things when he has God exclaim, "I will be exalted among the gentiles, and exalted on earth" — earth signifies the Jews, as opposed to the unruly sea that stands for the gentiles. Augustine quotes Romans 11:25-26 to leave no doubt. The full number of gentiles will come in, then all Israel will be saved. He compares Israel's eventual salvation to Moses' diseased hand returning to his bosom to regain its original color: "God's inheritance, his own people, became unclean when thrust out away from him. . . . Call it back; let it regain its proper color and acknowledge its Savior."[82] This will indeed happen eschatologically, as Augustine reads Paul. In the meantime he can say that "both Jews and Christians" hope for the second coming of the Lord — though the Jews mistakenly think it will be the first.[83]

This Pauline notion of an eschatological conversion to Christianity is not one that often gives much comfort to Jews who wish to live as Jews. It rather

78. Psalm 138 in *EP* VI, 263.
79. Psalm 58 (2) in *EP* III, 168.
80. E.g., Psalm 81 in *EP* IV, 175.
81. Psalm 45 in *EP* II, 323.
82. Psalm 73 in *EP* IV, 24.
83. Psalm 9 in *EP* I, 139.

sounds like the stuff of *Left Behind* literature and Southern Baptist mission pronouncements. We might judge it an impoverished view of difference, to say it may remain only temporarily until our interlocutors convert to our viewpoint. Nevertheless, it is not nothing to say that Jews do have a future share in the kingdom, even if it is within a particularly Christian kingdom. Such a view could inveigh against standard Christian *ad verseos Iudaeos* thinking and the strands in Augustine's own thought that lay only blame and retribution at the Jews' feet. Further, it may cut out any room for theologically repristinated blame of Israel for rejecting Jesus, if Israel was made to do so as part of the grander salvific purposes of God. Augustine's work here shows how bizarre the historic Christian claim of "Christ-killers" has been against Jews: not only was it *our* sins that killed Jesus, but if he were not killed, where would the church's salvation be? Augustine says it in his own poetic fashion: "They did not slay life; all they slew was death. Death was snuffed out in him as he died, and life rises from the dead in him as he lives."[84] Later in the same sermon, Augustine announces, "His blood was poured out among the Jews, and for the Jews it availed to salvation; but it availed also for the salvation of all who would be converted."[85] That's not a bad description of the *ordo salutis* in traditional Christian thought. It would also suffice as a historically sensitive description of the progression of the gospel among peoples: "for the Jew first, and then for the Greek" (Romans 1:16).

Perhaps the most impressive metaphor for the relationship between Jews and gentiles in Augustine is that of an estranged family. Commenting on the call to arms, "gird your sword upon your thigh, mighty warrior!" Augustine thinks of Jesus' claims to bring a sword rather than any peace (Luke 12:51). Then he reflects on Jesus' promise to divide family members, especially mother-in-law against daughter-in-law (12:53). Christians of gentile origin can be called a daughter-in-law of their mother-in-law, because they marry Christ, the bridegroom, who "was a son of the synagogue."[86] Augustine insists, "This is not some fancy of mine" but is attested by the apostle's christological reflection on marriage in Ephesians 5:32. Christ did leave his Father in a certain sense, in his *kenosis*. Similarly he left his mother, "by leaving the Jewish race, as represented by the synagogue." This is taken as the significance of the event in Mark 3:35, in which Jesus denies that his biological kin is his true family in the same sense as those who hear his word. "Think about it: aren't the Jews standing outside like that even now, while Christ is

---

84. Psalm 58 (2) in *EP* III, 170.
85. Psalm 58 (2) in *EP* III, 174.
86. Psalm 44 in *EP* II, 291.

teaching the Church? Now, who is the mother-in-law? The Bridegroom's mother. And the mother of our Bridegroom, our Lord Jesus Christ, is the synagogue."

This exegetical insight opens up doors through which Augustine himself does not walk, but we may. The Son did not leave the Father, despite scriptural and pious language to that effect: "not that he was ever separated from him, but in that he took human flesh." Similarly we might say that Christ only "leaves" his mother in an apophatic sense — that they are only apparently separated but more profoundly united. If the parallel holds, Christ has not actually left the synagogue. Augustine has no lack of reverence for Jesus' mother Mary. If the synagogue is to be so closely united with Mary as this, we can say that the division in Mark 3 is eclipsed in the greater unity expressed by Jesus from his cross in John's Gospel: "Woman, here is your son" (John 19:26). Elsewhere Augustine builds on this metaphor of estranged family by including the Pharisees' comment from John 9:29, "we do not even know where he comes from." Augustine asks on Jesus' behalf, "How did it happen? Why did they not know me? Why did they regard me as a stranger? How did they dare to say, 'We do not know where he comes from'?" That seems the sort of genuinely open questioning that Christians ought to be doing in reflecting scripturally on these problems. How did this condition of estrangement arise? It is an anomaly, impermissible and incomprehensible theologically, to which we must attend. Nothing less than our own standing as church in continuity with God's covenant with Israel may be at stake.[87]

What we have seen in this section are components of Augustine's thought that collectively add up to the possibility of Christians assigning a more positive role to Israel in their own theology. The Jews carry our books and so are an important witness against pagan adversaries. Like Cain they are cursed to wander, but not to die. The church must show its exegetical continuity with Israel or risk being cut off from salvation itself. It was actually God's doing that Israel did not recognize its messiah or his divinity, as part of a providential plan to include the gentiles in Israel's promises, and then finally to include all Jews as well eschatologically. We have seen what we take to be his most promising biblical image for describing the relationship between Jews and gentiles: that of estranged brethren. We do not offer these strands of Augustine's thought to lessen his or anyone's culpability in historic Christian anti-Judaism, far from it. If anything this rather serves to say that Augustine was sensitive enough to biblical material that could have produced a more positive theology of Israel than anything even he approached, though his was in-

---

87. Psalm 68 (1) in *EP* III, 379.

deed better than many other patristic figures. More importantly, these parts of Augustine's thought can be developed now in more profound ways to say how the church should conceive of itself and of Israel and their relationship to one another in Augustinian ways that press beyond Augustine himself.

### Augustine against Augustine for Israel

Due to Augustine's own reminiscences in the *Confessions,* we often think of his early difficulties with scripture as having been solved by his learning of allegorical exegesis from Ambrose.[88] Thereafter Augustine had an "out," a *deus ex machina* device to rescue his theology from awkward biblical passages. He then displays this Teflon-like hermeneutic in the final four books of that great work, which are often taken to be so out of sorts with the previous nine autobiographical books that it must have once been some separate work, or a poorly thought through addendum that compromises the greatness of the work as a whole. More recent scholarship on *Confessions* has suggested that the final four books, with their elaborate allegory of Genesis, are an intentional and fitting conclusion to the work.[89] *Confessions* appropriately progresses from attention to Augustine's inner self to attention to God at the end.[90] It turns away from exploration of his sins and distance from God toward interest in God in his own right. The engine of this gradual conversion is scripture: first the psalm verses that function like so many rungs of a ladder that Augustine ascends, from the first verse of a psalm throughout its course. Then also the first chapters of Genesis, exegeted christologically, give a vision of all creation as caught up in the praise of the triune God. Whatever moderns may make of allegory, it should be seen as central to Augustine's own understanding of his work, himself, and indeed of all creation.

The common portrait of *Confessions* is then wrong in its basic thrust. Yet it is also wrong in the point of detail with which this section opened: the claim that allegory solves Augustine's difficulties with scripture. He continues to struggle with the Bible and its interpretation throughout his career. Alle-

---

88. "I listened to him straightforwardly expounding the word of truth to the people every Sunday, and as I listened I became more and more convinced it was possible to unravel all those cunning knots of calumny in which the sacred books had been entangled by tricksters who had deceived me and others" (*Confessions* VI.3.4, trans. Maria Boulding, OSB [New York: Vintage, 1997], 100).

89. James J. O'Donnell, *Confessions/Commentary,* 3 vols. (Oxford: Clarendon, 1992).

90. This is a matter of emphasis more than anything, of course — God is the primary subject throughout *Confessions.*

gory does not solve difficulty, it simply offers a different set of difficulties.[91] This is no accident. God has intentionally arranged for scripture to be difficult so that its readers can grow in humility and reliance on others in order to learn to read it aright: "There would be no way for love, which ties people together in the bonds of unity, to make souls overflow and as it were intermingle with each other, if human beings learned nothing from other humans."[92] Throughout the *Enarrationes* Augustine comments on the difficulty of a biblical text at hand. "Let none imagine that because they understand the scriptures properly they are therefore already in that light which we shall enjoy in the future, when we have passed from faith to sight, for in the prophets and in all the preachers of the divine word there is obscure teaching."[93] As a preacher who has had to struggle to find homiletically edifying commentary on every line of the Psalter, he knows better than to allow anyone to presume scripture's easy perspicuity in all cases. Further, that lack of clarity is a function of our current place in God's providence: on the way to the vision of God, proceeding from *scientia* to *sapientia,* but hardly able to claim arrival, wisdom, or vision, yet. Elsewhere he insists that "whatever we understand now, we perceive only through enigmas. An enigma is an obscure parable that we understand only with difficulty. However carefully we cultivate our hearts, and withdraw into ourselves to understand what is within, as long as we see only through corruptible flesh we see only in part."[94] No one can claim full knowledge of the scriptures, and those with greater knowledge of them, such as Au-

---

91. Much as I admire Rowan Williams's work as a theologian and patristics scholar, his methodological work on scripture is occasionally problematic. For example, in a recent essay, he defends modern historical criticism of the Bible as a way to keep Christians from ignoring the fissures in a given biblical text. Yet Williams's own work on the fathers has shown well that they are often quite sensitive to the problems a given biblical text presents. They are simply interested in different sorts of "fissures" than we moderns — more often properly theological ones rather than simply historical ones. See his "Historical Criticism and Sacred Text," in *Reading Texts, Seeking Wisdom: Scripture and Theology,* ed. David Ford and Graham Stanton (Grand Rapids: Eerdmans, 2003), 217-28.

92. *De doctrina christiana* I.6, trans. R. P. H. Green (Oxford: Oxford University Press, 1997), 5-6. In its own context, Augustine seems to be arguing against those who would claim it possible to live a Christian life without use of scripture. While Augustine must grant that such a thing is theoretically possible, and indeed a few saints have so grown in love as no longer to need scripture, it is uncommon. Yet the quote also shows something important for our purposes: Augustine's hermeneutic is not simply a way out of sticky biblical problems; it is also, crucially, a means to build up the church as members wrestle with one another over how to read well. I owe this reading to Rowan Williams, "Language, Reality, and Desire in Augustine's *De Doctrina,*" *Journal of Literature and Theology* 3 (1989): 138-50.

93. On Psalm 17 in *EP* I, 191.

94. On Psalm 48 (1) in *EP* II, 355.

gustine, can see this lack all the more clearly. For scripture is intentionally difficult — a hard road given so pilgrims might not only make progress, but might be exercised along the way. Commenting on the psalmist's line, "God's words are smoother than oil, but they are like javelins," Augustine insists that the places in scripture we find most offensive are precisely those inviting us to harder exegetical work and greater piety. "Some of the sayings in scripture used to seem hard while they were still obscure; but once explained they are gentle and tender." He points to the mass desertion of Jesus by many disciples in John 6 when they are told they must drink the flesh and eat the blood of the Son of Man. Then he praises Peter's resolve to stay, since Jesus alone has "the word of eternal life." Augustine comments, "Take this to heart, we beg you. Be like little children and learn childlike piety. Did Peter understand then the mystery concealed in that saying of the Lord? No, he did not yet understand it, but in his childlike docility he believed. If some saying is hard, then, and not yet intelligible, let it be hard to the unbeliever but tender to you because of your piety. When eventually it is made plain it will be to you like oil, soaking right into your bones."[95]

Scripture is also unclear because the God on whom we long to glance through its pages is himself Mystery whom mere humans cannot claim to comprehend. We have seen his repeated insistence on St. Paul's point that Jesus' executioners could not see his divinity, else they could not have "crucified the Lord of glory" (1 Corinthians 2:8). Yet he also insists that the "God of gods was hidden not only from those among whom he walked about, and from those who crucified him, and from them before whose eyes he rose again, but from us too, who did not see him walking this earth but believe he is enthroned in heaven."[96] This is why the Ascension takes on such importance for Augustine — it is better *not* to be able to see and touch Jesus and to believe than it is to have seen and touched him physically and yet not believe (John 20:29). Even those who knew him personally had, like us, to progress from faith toward sight, from his flesh to his divinity, from his nature as a man to his nature as God. That hiddenness of Jesus' divinity remains for us now. None can claim to look upon God unmediated. Scripture's enigmatic quality is appropriate for those who cannot claim to see God fully or directly.

Now, this is not to say that Augustine is anything less than confident that God is who he says he is. Augustine is far from the modern version of apophaticism that suggests humans cannot claim to know the divine nature

95. On Psalm 54 in *EP* III, 76-77.
96. Psalm 49 in *EP* II, 385.

and so no one "religion" can claim to have grasped the truth.[97] Rather, Augustine is convinced that the God of gods has become incarnate in Christ, and that salvation is nothing less than growth in and toward this God. He is also convinced that the divine nature revealed in Christ remains greater than creatures can comprehend, so that these cannot claim to know him, even as they progress in and toward knowledge and love of him. Elsewhere, in a theodical context, he comments, "it is quite possible for God to do something for which you do not know the reason, but quite impossible that he should do anything inequitably."[98] That is to say, we are quite sure that this one, revealed in Israel, Christ, and scripture, is God. And precisely for that reason we cannot claim to plumb God's depths.

Given this basic apophatic perspective, it is appropriate that Augustine believes human beings, created in the image of this God, to be mystery to one another. "You should think of everyone as your neighbor," the preacher insists, "even before he or she is a Christian, for you do not know what that person is in God's sight, or what God's foreknowledge of him or her may be."[99] Further, since the body of Christ is itself mixed, since the tares cannot be uprooted without damaging the wheat, we do not know who among those who are in the church might actually *not* be elect, not a sibling. This lack of human knowledge and foresight suggests for Augustine that everyone must be treated like a neighbor, like a potential fellow saint. How can we presume to do otherwise, based on our fragmentary knowledge and self-serving desires? Elsewhere Augustine extends this lack of knowledge to ourselves. No one can claim any sort of full knowledge even of her or himself: "we are for the most part an unknown quantity to ourselves."[100] He goes on to explore the theodical point that trials are a God-given means for training and self-discovery in this world.

We can see in Augustine's insistence on our lack of full knowledge of scripture, God, ourselves, and one another, a possible theological stance from

97. Verna Harrison helpfully distinguishes between theologically fruitful and empty forms of "apophaticism." The claim for the fathers and the Orthodox is that apophaticism is a statement about God's infinity and human creatureliness and the path of sanctification between the two. It is not a claim of despair that seeks to call in question all human speech about God. It is rather a theological insistence that distinguishes between true and false speech about God. Vladimir Lossky is Harrison's exemplar for Orthodox apophaticism, Sallie McFague for modernist apophaticism. See Harrison's article "The Relationship Between Apophatic and Kataphatic Theology," *Pro Ecclesia* 4, no. 3 (1996): 318-32.

98. Psalm 61 in *EP* III, 223.

99. Psalm 25 (2) in *EP* I, 258.

100. Psalm 55 in *EP* III, 82.

which to reorient Christians' self-understanding with regard to the Jews. The same Augustine who so frequently and without hesitation insists that the Jews have had their place in the divine favor usurped by Christians and been sentenced to wander the earth, accursed for now and possibly eternity, can also make the kinds of humble apophatic comments that many biblical interpreters and preachers now find themselves driven to make. He saw no contradiction here. Yet we might suggest several. First, the Jews whom Augustine regularly attacks ought to benefit from the kind of openness to future events Augustine suggests should make Christians treat everyone as a neighbor. Who's to say that any Jew, or any person, might not come to recognize Jesus as messiah? Augustine might be most open to this suggestion, though it would likely fail to impress many Jews now — to be treated well only in hopes of their abandoning their Judaism! Second, we might suggest that the obscurity of scripture could lead to the possibility of openness on the question of whether God's covenant with Israel "according to the flesh" should still be adjudged as valid by Christians. Augustine wishes to maintain with Paul an eventual, perhaps eschatological, conversion by "all Israel" (Romans 11:26). Paul cannot imagine precisely how God will deliver on covenantal promises made to Abraham, but he envisions the fulfillment of those promises not just in the death and resurrection of Jesus and calling of the gentiles, but also in an eschatological event of some sort in the future.[101] If that is so — if there is still work to be done on non-Christian Israel as a people — then can we not conclude that God still *recognizes* that people as a people, and an obligation to them as the God who first called them, whatever their failings? Or even that God's own integrity depends on a future confirmation of his fidelity to Israel? Finally, does not an apophatic insistence on the mystery of God allow us to claim that we cannot understand God's purposes with regard to Israel? As things stand, two communities make a claim to be "Israel," the church and the synagogue. Each of those communities, in turn, is splintered into so many claimants to the title "church" or "Israel" that few observers or participants can keep them all straight. Can we then hold open the question of who pre-

---

101. N. T. Wright has lodged a now-famous disagreement with this view, noting that it is a rare place where fundamentalists and mainline Christians agree. He himself cannot imagine that Paul is speaking of anything other than the eschatological inclusion of the gentiles in the covenant community that has already taken place in the church as the referent for the inclusion of "all Israel" in Romans 11. His is a minority position, one not strengthened by its inability to account for Paul's aghast marveling at the end of that chapter (11:33-36). Why would Paul be newly surprised at an inexplicable work of God when he has already described that work with striking detail for eleven previous chapters in Romans? See Wright's *The New Testament and the People of God* (Minneapolis: Fortress, 1992).

cisely is "Israel," given each of our communities' tragically divided states, and relegate any complete certainty about each community's status before God to the judgment? I think I can ask this question without any surrender of the particularity of Christian truth claims, especially since church division already may belie the very truth of the gospel.[102] Christians are those who live in awareness of a pending judgment, who hope and pray not to be those who will be told, "away with you, you evil-doers" (Matthew 25:41). An Augustinian openness before the mystery of God could pry open a space for Christians to lend a more deeply biblical doubt (and just so, hope) about their own salvation, and openness to the salvation of other claimants to God's promises to Israel. Augustine wants to insist that "Christ will reign for all eternity in his saints. God has promised this, God has said it; and as though that were not enough, God has sworn it."[103] He speaks in admirable terms of the differences between Jews and gentiles in Christ, as the two walls joined at the corner by Christ, in the terms of Ephesians: "the former wall has a special claim on God's faithfulness, the latter on his mercy."[104] Yet as one who wants to insist on the reliability of God's promises to the saints, might there not be room in an Augustinian theology to suggest that the faithfulness of God to his covenant with Israel requires further divine work to be completely fulfilled?

Perhaps even more promising for the construction of an Augustinian reevaluation of Israel than this combination of divine mystery and election is Augustine's own understanding of justification, grace, and humility. Augustine comments on the psalmist's description of God, "he bowed the heavens and came down," in a normal christological fashion: "God 'bowed the heavens' in making the Just One so humble as to come down to the weakness of men and women."[105] Augustine's soteriology is inextricably bound up with his understanding of the shape of the Christian life — in fact, there is no difference between the two. The incarnation is a tonic peculiarly suited for humanity's ailment of pride. The lowliness of God's bending downward is meant to foster human humility in response. This is no extrinsically awarded grace, unrelated to how any recipient might act after its reception. Later Protestants often enlisted Augustine for such a view, based on Pauline comments like Augustine's description of "God's glorious grace, by which we have been saved despite our unworthiness."[106] This is only half of Augustine's

---

102. See Ephraim Radner, *The End of the Church: A Pneumatology of Division in the Christian West* (Grand Rapids: Eerdmans, 1998).

103. Psalm 88 (1) in *EP* IV, 277.

104. Psalm 88 (1) in *EP* IV, 275.

105. Psalm 17 in *EP* I, 190.

106. Psalm 18 (2) in *EP* I, 207.

soteriology, and a conclusion that can only be arrived at by "proof-texting" him. The incarnation is rather the offering of a graced life of humility, descent into which leads one to God. "God," he preaches, "chose the weak things of this world to put the strong to shame; and so he did not use an orator to win a fisherman, but used the fisherman to win the orator, and the fisherman to win the senator, and the fisherman to win the emperor."[107] Never mind that an advocacy of humility is here used to promote a pro-imperial theology! Augustine is adamant that God's grace is undeserved, that the only appropriate or even possible human response is humility, the inability to presume one's own righteousness, and the ascription of every good in oneself or others only to God. Augustine writes that we sinners have a way of overlooking our own sin. Salvation, in contrast, is just a hard look at one's own wickedness: "if he looks at it, God will overlook it," and if not, then not.[108] In later sermons, preached in an anti-Pelagian context, Augustine insists on the sheer gratuity of grace, and the inability of humanity to "add" anything to God's goodness. We are like incurably sick patients, in need of an omnipotent doctor. Not only that, but we also run from the doctor, and he compels and allures us to return for care. We are entirely passive in this exchange — we bring nothing but our illness, and our desire to run from care. Augustine writes that the psalmist calls God his "mercy" because that word covers every good any human can have: God is the giver of our very existence, of any goodness we have in us, and of salvation itself. "All that I am, absolutely everything that I am, comes from your mercy," he proclaims.[109] In the incarnation, we are told, Christ came "not to assess our deserts but to forgive sins. You did not exist, and you were created: what did you give to God? You were evil, and you were set free: what did you give to God?" It would be absurd to speak of someone "earning" their creation — who was there before they were there? So, Augustine suggests, would it be no less absurd to speak of earning redemption.[110]

Augustine's soteriology also bears directly on his understanding of the Christian life and how to treat other people — in short, on ethics. That life is one of imitating Jesus' willingness to respond to insults with honor, to wickedness with forgiveness, to sin with grace. He implores his parishioners to "look at [suffering] with Christian eyes" — and to recognize, with the martyrs, that "better [is] the grief of someone suffering wrong than the joy of someone doing wrong."[111] An ethics based on participation in Christ's divine life would

107. Psalm 36 (2) in *EP* II, 114.
108. Psalm 31 (2) in *EP* I, 377.
109. Psalm 58 (2) in *EP* III, 176.
110. Psalm 43 in *EP* II, 272.
111. Psalm 56 in *EP* III, 116.

suggest it to be better to suffer violence than to commit it. Elsewhere, he writes that Christ himself passed through tribulations first, and offered grace in response, so that Christians would do the same: "the physician drank the medicine first, that the patient might not fear to drink it."[112] Christian life there is understood as almost synonymous with suffering, confession, and martyrdom, in imitation of Jesus and his saints, who forgive wickedness rather than retaliate. In one instance Augustine directs his comments along these lines to a particular Christian community — the monastery. There people wish to get away from sinners. Yet Augustine asks pointedly: "is there nothing in you that anyone else has to bear with? If there really is nothing I am amazed. But if there is nothing, that means you must have all the more strength to put up with other people." He then returns to a familiar theme against religious smugness directed at the church's outsiders: "are you going to hack down the bridge, just because you congratulate yourself that your feet have been so swift at crossing it?"[113] Augustine's christologically shaped understanding of the necessity of responding to wrong with grace reaches all the way down to petty nuisances in the monastery, and of course also in other parts of the church.

The point of this last section on Augustine's understanding of grace in relationship to the Christian community is not to suggest he is some sort of proto-Mennonite — clearly he is not, as his elaborately constructed theological defense of imperially sponsored violence for the furtherance of the church's goals makes clear. It is rather to say that there are resources in Augustine for support of a "christo-form" vision of patient suffering in response to enemies — though these may be overridden in other contexts in his work where some other need is deemed to be more pressing. Here in the *Enarrationes,* Augustine's daily sermons to ordinary lay people, one has a sense that God's unmerited forgiveness of humanity mandates a matching unmerited forgiveness from God's people to one another and outsiders. Anything less would be pride, presumption of one's own righteousness, and effectively self-exclusion from the community of grace.

It is a short step to see how this could apply to a theology of Israel. Few topics in traditional theology bring about what the Bible calls "pride" more than the church's relationship to non-Christian Jewry. Precisely here all these Augustinian instincts against pride, for humility, against presumption, and for forgiveness are immediately lost. Israel is excluded and cursed; the church is triumphant and blessed. In contrast, we can see here how an Augustinian theology of grace (that goes beyond Augustine himself) could inveigh against

112. Psalm 98 in *EP* IV, 468.
113. Psalm 99 in *EP* V, 20.

this Christian teaching. Christians are those who recognize that their mercy from God is wholly unmerited, that any good within us is no more earned than our own creation, and who therefore grow accustomed to offering unmerited mercy to those who deserve it no more than they. Augustine very rarely brought his understandings of grace and of Israel into direct correlation with one another. In one place, at least, he does. "Let us, then, hold firmly to humility, charity, and piety, my brothers and sisters, for while [the Jews] have been rejected we have been called; so let us learn a lesson from their example, and beware of being proud."[114] I am suggesting against Augustine that it is Christians who have more often than Jews presumed their own righteousness at the expense of any sort of Christo-form humility. An Augustinian theology of grace brought to bear on a newly reevaluated Christian vision of Israel could bear terrific fruit — precisely the sort of humility and patient preference to forebear rather than to blame or avenge that has almost entirely been lacking in Christian relationship to Israel.

A final Augustinian point to be made against Augustine and for Israel. Occasionally Augustine takes the Bible's prophetic warnings against Israel not as justification for Christian arrogance against Jews, but rather as warnings against the church itself. Often the Bible's prophetic tradition, with its preference for mercy over sacrifice (Hosea 6:6; Micah 6:6-8), or the New Testament writers' dismay over so many Jews not recognizing Jesus as messiah, have been turned into easy anti-Jewish fodder. But the prophetic strands of scripture are meant as warnings against the community of faith, rather than weapons for it to use against its enemies or outsiders in general. Augustine himself sees this plainly enough with his commentary on "enemies" and the cursing psalms, examined above. He also insists occasionally to his hearers that the Bible's prophecy is meant to arouse fear of judgment in the Bible's hearers *in hopes of future penance.* God does not relish any permanent state of misery or perdition. Jonah preached to Nineveh that she would be overturned, yet her conversion obviously made that "prophecy" obsolete, since its true purpose — conversion — had come to pass. In one place Augustine makes the sort of offhand anti-Jewish remark that so rightly worries us: "What strenuous efforts Pilate made! How hard he tried to dissuade them!" In Jesus' trial, that is, Pilate tried to avert the "Jews' hatred of our Lord." He failed, obviously. Yet Augustine keeps this discussion from being a total disaster by turning to its true point. His hearers are not to treat iniquity "as though it were some foe outside yourself. . . . Make no mistake; it originates within yourself."[115] The point of accusa-

---

114. Psalm 46 in *EP* II, 334.
115. Psalm 63 in *EP* III, 252-53.

tions and blame, the point even of Christian preaching and thinking generally, is accusation of oneself and repentance. The Jews here are, unfortunately, merely a cipher for that larger and still true point. After another accusatory comment against Israel, Augustine asks, "Can we suppose brothers and sisters, that the house of Israel was the Lord's vineyard, but we are not? Hardly. We must see that it was said to the Jews, but we too must listen with fear."[116] Christian discourse is meant to arouse our fear before God, not self-justification and derogation of others. Elsewhere Augustine turns Paul's lament over Israel, that it has "a zeal for God, but it is not informed by knowledge" (Romans 10:2) against his Christian hearers — "Remember what the apostle said about people who wanted to boast of their own righteousness: 'I bear this witness against them: they have a zeal for God. . . .'"[117] So occasionally Augustine does read biblical prophecy and judgment as a divine word of reproof meant to turn the Christian community back, rather than a warring word against outsiders. This reading of the Bible by the church "against itself" rather than against anyone else is a salutary word for the church in this or any age, and it is frequently present in Augustine's work[118] — just not frequently enough nor in respect to all matters, or especially with regard to Israel.

No one should take this presentation of more promising aspects of Augustine's thought as an attempt to exonerate Augustine himself. If anything it is the reverse — a demonstration that Augustine had theological resources at his command that could have allowed him to say something different with regard to non-Christian Israel than he did. The presence of these motifs in his works marks all the more strongly his failure, one we should have to confess for him as we attempt to correct the church's stance toward Israel and speak a faithful word to contemporary Jews. The point is here that we actually can return to Augustine himself in order to learn how to do this. We can bring to bear his comments on the mystery and unknowability of God, ourselves, and scripture, on our theology of Israel. We can turn his theology of grace and humility into a way forward for dialogue with others, not presuming our own blamelessness nor their perdition. We can similarly turn his use of the Bible's prophecy as a community's self-correction in its proper direction — against us — rather than against any others. This way forward in Christian conceptions of Israel and conversation with Jews is to be preferred over efforts that would simply ignore our historical doctrines and documents and attempt to

---

116. Psalm 103 (1) in *EP* V, 121.

117. Psalm 142 in *EP* VI, 348.

118. The language is Bonhoeffer's from *Letters and Papers from Prison*, ed. Eberhard Bethge (New York: Macmillan, 1972).

start from scratch, with our language purged of anti-Jewish references and our attention directed elsewhere than scripture. For Christians, if we are to remain Christians, are part of a church whose thought and practice is "handed over," from Jesus to the apostles through the ages to us (1 Corinthians 15:3). We cannot simply start over. Nor should we wish to. For we cannot confess our sins, both as a means to be forgiven by God and others and to rehabilitate out of sinful practice into virtue, if we simply bypass our historical documents from such figures as the church fathers. This slow process of reexamining our own tradition, of following it avidly when it proves faithful and repenting when it does not, should be seen as part and parcel of our growing out of sin and into grace. It is what people are called to do as part of being changed from God's enemies into God's friends.

Augustine frequently suggests that another could read scripture better than he. In one of the longer of these asides, he says, "Some other person may produce a better interpretation, for the obscurity of the scriptures is such that a passage scarcely ever yields a single meaning only. But whatever interpretation emerges, it must conform to the rule of faith. Let us not be jealous of those with more powerful minds than our own, nor despair because we are so small. I am expounding to you, beloved ones, whatever seems right to us, but I do not want you to close your ears to others, who may perhaps have better things to say."[119] Preaching is hard. Allegorical interpretation is even harder. By nature it must be open to emendation and correction. For it is the preacher's aesthetic opportunity with which to lure his hearers more deeply into the divine life. It can be used poorly or flatly, and so it must constantly be tried anew, tested against other readings, measured against the plumb line of the *regula fidei*, checked to be sure it furthers the flourishing of life in its hearers. In the case of many of Augustine's readings of Israel, and those of subsequent centuries built upon him, we can say that what he has produced is simply ugly. His own appeal to be improved upon must be heeded. Yet as he makes clear this is no abandonment of tradition — it is a deeper entry into tradition's very life, to speak to our forebears as living voices who can be wrong or right, who can be argued with and tweaked, just as we wish them to do to us.

It is outside the scope of this study to tackle the larger question of whether the original Christian sources are themselves fundamentally anti-Jewish. Some biblical scholars and theologians have said yes. If that were the case, I imagine we should no longer look to these sources for direction toward God. In short, that we should no longer be Christian if our sources are inherently violent or destructive. Whatever the answer, and it would require exhaustive

119. Psalm 74 in *EP* IV, 50.

work, allegorical exegesis provides the best tools with which to counter it. If John 8's terrifying description of Jesus' words to some "Jews who believed in him" (8:31) that they "belong to your father the devil" (8:44) is inherently anti-Jewish — and it is hard to read it otherwise — then no amount of historical criticism or reading according to a theological *sensus plenior* is going to extract us from the problem it lands us in. Rather, only a reading according to some other sense, in line with the *regula* and attentive to the words on the page for the sake of the edification of those hearing, will do. Even when we most disagree with the content of some of Augustine's work, even most of it on a topic such as Israel, we can insist that the form of it offers some material that can help today's church and academy to rethink our theology of Israel. Augustine himself is not enough in this regard. But an Augustinian theology can go beyond Augustine himself.

## Where to Now?

Any effort to push Augustine's best insights past Augustine's own blindness — and the church's in his train — must wrestle with the extraordinary theological work currently under way that seeks to articulate a non-supersessionist Christian theology. Kendall Soulen's book *The God of Israel and Christian Theology* is a major contribution to this effort. He integrates some of the late Bonhoeffer's fragmentary insights with Michael Wyschogrod's theology of election to describe the redemption of the nations in Jesus without eclipsing the election of Israel according-to-the-flesh. His key move is to speak of God's work of redemption as secondary to God's work of consummation. Christianity is not primarily about the redemption of persons after the fall, as Bonhoeffer showed us. When that is the center of theology, then the election of the Jews becomes moot after the coming of Jesus, and Israel according-to-the-flesh should disappear into the church as a river does into the sea. Rather, Christian theology ought primarily to be about the consummation of God's work in creation to bless all nations through an economy of difference. God's particular way of blessing all creatures is through his choice of a particular people — Israel — to be his people in the world. "The necessary correction is a frank reorientation of the hermeneutical center of the Scriptures from the incarnation to the reign of God, where God's reign is understood as the eschatological outcome of human history at the end of time."[120] Christians and Jews

---

120. R. Kendall Soulen, *The God of Israel and Christian Theology* (Minneapolis: Fortress, 1996), 138.

now await this eschatological consummation in God's creative purpose of blessing within an economy of difference. Some of those Jews are still Jews as they follow Jesus, in keeping with Wyschogrod's insistence that the church make a place for Jewish observance for those who "convert" to Christianity, lest God's provision for difference amidst blessing be eclipsed into a supersessionist "sameness." The church is a genuine innovation: God's in-gathering of Jews and gentiles around the crucified messiah, without the distinction between the two disappearing. Most Jews, however, do not recognize the church's claim about Jesus' messiahship. And they will not, even in Paul's eschatological in-coming of "all Israel," for they will be saved "trans-ecclesiologically," without need of conversion to Jesus or church.[121]

Soulen is quite right to seek a way in which God's election of Israel is not superseded in God's work in Jesus. Augustine would naturally worry over Soulen's description of Jesus as the "center but not the totality of Christian faith."[122] But then if there is a doctrinal weakness with Augustine's biblical hermeneutic it is that his christology does more than determine his exegesis. It dominates it. There is actually a much wider variety of dogmatic teaching to which Augustine could also attend as he reads, from creation to election, from Mary to the saints, from prophesy to the eschaton. There is one note in the *Enarrationes*, and it is a beautiful note — Christ and his church joined in praise — but it is not the only note in the church's score. Soulen offers a corrective to Augustine here that we would be wise to take into account. He also offers a model for collaboration between Jewish and Christian thought with his engagement of Wyschogrod that allows us to do more than learn: we can also imitate him.

Soulen does not want merely to be integrated with Augustine's theology. His more radical desire is to reconfigure Christian theology as such by re-thinking it on the basis of God's economy of consummation and election of Israel. He avoids treatment of the trinity and christology by attending to the "theologically more basic claim [that] the God of Israel has acted in Jesus Christ for all."[123] Likewise, Scott Bader-Saye seeks to ask not merely how Christians can do theology as we have always done, just more politely. He wants to rework Christian theology after the Holocaust and the end of Christendom with the election of Israel as its foundation, to "re-Judaize" the church's doctrine of election.[124] The church's "Israel-forgetfulness" (Soulen's

---

121. Soulen, *The God of Israel*, 174.

122. Soulen, *The God of Israel*, 156.

123. Soulen, *The God of Israel*, xi.

124. Scott Bader-Saye, *Church and Israel after Christendom: The Politics of Election* (Boulder: Westview, 1999).

terminology) left a political void that was quickly filled by Christendom. Now, with the loss of state power for the church, we are in a position to recognize what we ought never have forgotten: that salvation is only through the election of Israel, into which gentiles are grafted by Christ. Bader-Saye charges Soulen with an insufficient and "adoptionist" christology[125] and attempts over against him to articulate a fully trinitarian theology of election, marked by the visibility of Son's flesh and the public and political ingathering of the nations by the Spirit. In an ironic reversal of Paul's hope that the church's in-grafting would make the Jews "jealous," it is the Jews' embodied and political life together sustained without weapons or land for most of its history that is now a model for the church after Christendom.[126] He uses Daniel Boyarin's suggestion that Israel's social location is a crucial determinant of whether its doctrine of election will be peaceful or not. That is, as long as Israel is in a minority posture, then election will not become a means to "consolidate and justify" domination of others.[127]

Another Christian theologian who engages with Boyarin is David Dawson, whose book turns to Christian figural exegesis much more explicitly than do either Soulen or Bader-Saye. These two practice intense and rigorous exegesis of the apostle Paul and other New Testament exegetes of the Old in their attempts to articulate a non-supersessionist Christian theology. But neither attends to the places where Paul reads Israel's scriptures allegorically, such as Galatians 4, 1 Corinthians 10, or Ephesians 5. Neither do they offer extensive exegesis of the Old Testament, let alone to the question of the degree to which we can imitate Paul's hermeneutics. Both write admirably lean books offering correctives to the church's historical sins. Yet Dawson digs more deeply into how Christians ought now read Israel's scripture, without supersessionist violence to Jews, but also in concert with previous Christian history's allegorical tradition. His primary counterpart is Origen rather than Augustine, but his engagement with Boyarin, Erich Auerbach, and Hans Frei shows us a way in which Soulen's and Bader-Saye's insights can be integrated with our portrait of Augustine.

Dawson's project is to explore the degree to which Christians can read their Old Testament figurally "while respecting the independent religious identity of Jews, and, more broadly, the diverse identities of all human beings."[128] Boyarin's charge that Paul replaces "specific, historically and socially

125. Bader-Saye, *Church and Israel*, 83.
126. Bader-Saye, *Church and Israel*, 110.
127. Bader-Saye, *Church and Israel*, 137.
128. Dawson, *Christian Figural Reading and the Fashioning of Identity* (Berkeley: University

determined meanings (e.g. 'circumcision' or 'Israel')" with universal and spiritual generic ones is an ideal place to begin.[129] Dawson counters that Paul is not primarily interested in the "meaning" he might "construe" in Israel's scripture — if he were, he would indeed be the worst sort of supersessionist, and the genuine ancestor of Christianity's worst anti-Jewish heirs. He is rather interested in the "intelligibility of a divine performance." That is, the God of Israel has done something new in grafting gentiles into the covenant with his elect. Paul, and allegorical readers after him, are not inventing their figural readings, they are discovering their presence in light of this new action of God in Christ. Not only that, but Christian readings of Israel's scripture are not non-bodily or a-historical, as Boyarin claims. To say they are is merely to reintroduce the sort of binary opposition between body and soul that we should all now be eager to avoid.[130] They rather *are* bodily, historical, in a different and surprising way — one that transfigures the old without obliterating it. This can be seen above all in Origen's biblical commentaries. In reading allegorically the reader is actually transformed, bodily, historically. So, for example, Origen does not read the Passover primarily with reference to Jesus' passion, but rather "the ancient Passover continues to be celebrated in the allegorical reading of Scripture, which is not a disembodiment through interpretation but instead a consumption of a body through reading."[131] This is no more disembodied or a-historical than a reader discerning the figure of Christ, whom the church consumes in the eucharist, as she is transfigured in love of the one who joins her to Israel's promises. Allegory is "not nonliteral," as it "extends without supplanting the former Jewish meanings."[132]

Dawson's important book does no more than what this chapter also attempts to do. It shows that Pauline and Origenic styles of reading do not *have* to be supersessionist or violent to Jews. They certainly can be: Dawson appreciates Boyarin's portrait of Paul as a reminder of what Christians have done at their worst. But it is possible to read Israel's scripture with Paul, Origen, and

---

of California Press, 2002), 4. Dawson draws a distinction between "figural" exegesis, which he applauds, and "figurative" reading, which is "based on a conception of language as a series of tropes in which nonliteral meanings replace literal meanings" (15). This may simply reprise the distinction between "allegory" and "typology," which seeks to distinguish "good" readings from "bad" simply with a distinction in terminology. In this book we have avoided such terminological distinctions, for there is no way around the hard work of determining whether an individual reading is faithful or not to the words on the page, the reality of God, and the community's spiritual needs.

129. Dawson, *Christian Figural Reading*, 6.
130. Dawson, *Christian Figural Reading*, 45.
131. Dawson, *Christian Figural Reading*, 71.
132. Dawson, *Christian Figural Reading*, 15, 217.

Augustine without falling prey to some of their worst impulses, in concert with their best. And this way is to attend to God's new work in Christ in light of these words on the page of Israel's scripture, and vice versa. Neither Dawson's book nor this chapter should be taken as any sort of guarantee against misreading or the sin of anti-Jewish thoughtless rhetoric or outright violence. There is no absolute guarantee, as Steve Fowl argues, just constant repentance, with a social location outside of the levers of power, as Boyarin recommends.[133] To read not only about Jews but also with them is another crucial practice. We can see how difficult such faithfulness is in Soulen's and Bader-Saye's efforts to renegotiate the literal sense of scripture with a wholly non-supersessionist theology. It is not easy, especially since Christian reading habits historically have run the other direction. Yet we must hope that it is possible, else we Christians should simply admit that following Jesus makes us anti-Jewish and give up our claims about the presence of the peaceable kingdom in Christ. Dawson shows that this renegotiation of the literal sense can work with an allegorical hermeneutic that also need not be super-sessionist. For what could more be more important for Christian exegesis than to show that the new can be integrated with the old without the eclipse of either?

---

133. Even this is no guarantee: non-Constantinian Christians are not exempt from violent readings or actions within their own spheres of power.

# 5 Augustine's Theology of Scripture

## Psalm 98: Scripture as the School of Christ

It is not immediately obvious why Psalm 98 ought to be read allegorically. There is nothing here that should scandalize any biblical reader, whether Jewish or Christian. The psalmist's jubilant notes of praise should resound with profit for any reader on a quite literal level. There is indeed mention of a king, but even Augustine does not bother to read this reference christologically. It would seem that by Augustine's own exegetical rules — that whatever does not lead to the twin command of love of God and neighbor within the context of the church's *regula fidei* ought be read allegorically — this psalm could be left well enough alone.

Yet Augustine himself reads Psalm 98 allegorically. His first rationale in doing so is ecclesial. He coins an image for the church here much loved by later Augustinians, especially Protestants: "You are the children of the Church, beloved ones, and well-instructed in the *school* of Christ by means of all the writings of our fathers from ancient times."[1] The teacher in this school is not the learned *magister,* not Augustine himself, it is not even in this case Christ. It is, collectively, the writers of the Old Testament, who were "seeking the welfare of all of us, who were destined to believe in Christ today." It was fitting that many heralds come before so great a judge as Christ, even before his first coming in humility. Yet before that first coming, the writers of scripture "spoke in such a way as to conceal their meaning under certain figurative

---

1. *Expositions of the Psalms,* trans. Maria Boulding, OSB, *Works of Saint Augustine: A Translation for the 21st Century* III/18 (Hyde Park, NY: New City Press, 2002), IV, 466. Referred to hereafter as *EP.*

signs. The veil which covered the truth in the books of the ancient writers was to be stripped away only when truth in person should spring up from the earth." After Christ's coming, we who are Christ's body can see that the teaching of the psalmist was meant to prefigure Christ: "when we listen to a Psalm, or to a prophet, or to the law, all of which were set down in writing before our Lord Jesus Christ came in the flesh, our whole endeavor must be to find Christ in what we hear, and to discern his presence in it." Augustine reassures his hearers that this search will not be in vain. Those who seek him are given scriptural promises that they will find him (Matthew 7:7), and comfort from the recognition that those who first found him had not even been seeking him! "He will not abandon us who long for him, since he redeemed those who were careless about him."

We see here implicitly themes that this book has already visited in some depth. Augustine can assume an account of the church as the body of Christ, learning to speak like its head, since he has worked so hard to establish that christo-ecclesiological foundation for such exegesis throughout the *Enarrationes*. He can assume an account of desire operative in the oscillation of the scriptures between openness and hiddenness: the former to teach, the later to exercise, both with the goal of enticing believers into the divine life.[2] In this chapter we shall see how Augustine envisions theological exegesis that rests on this foundation, that is carried out toward this *telos*, as performed on the psalms. We want now to ask this question: what precisely is Augustine's theology of scripture? As ever, we are carrying out this investigation with an eye to contemporary systematic concerns: what precisely is scripture's literal sense? On what grounds, if any, ought we be allowed to read "past" that literal sense to something allegorical? What, if any, should be the "controls" on such reading-past? How exactly do we relate dogmatic concerns, such as christology and Trinity, with exegetical ones? More boldly, what would a christologically and trinitarianly shaped biblical hermeneutic look like? In short, Augustine will help us get at the driving question of this book: how should Christians read their scripture? We shall see, by the end of this chapter, that the answer is summarized in the book's title: *Praise Seeking Understanding*. Christians are those people who are always already praising God with the

---

2. Augustine's comment on Psalm 140 is particularly apt on this theme: "You need look for nothing else in scripture, and let no one lay upon you any other command. Wherever there is any obscure passage in scripture, charity is concealed in it, and wherever the sense is plain, charity is proclaimed. If it were nowhere plain to see, it would not nourish you; if it were nowhere concealed, it would not exercise you. This same charity cries out from a pure heart in the words of the Psalm and from hearts like his who prays here. And who this is, I can tell you in a word: it is Christ" (*EP* VI, 303).

psalms. Now, how shall we understand these words we have just offered liturgically as part of our life of being drawn in Christ to the Father?

The rest of this exposition on Psalm 98 has an ecclesial focus, in keeping with the psalmist's proclamation that "the Lord is great in Zion." Augustine mentions an ascetic practice of fasting on the festival days of the pagans: "while they are making merry, we groan on their behalf."[3] As he examines the psalmist's claim that the Lord is "most high over all the peoples," he remembers the way the church has often overcome its persecutors by praying for them. Now the pagans' fury is subsided and the Christians indeed "reign." Augustine exults later as he asks whether there is "any nation that has not heard the name of Christ?" Yet because pagan festivals continue, Christians continue to fast and pray for people's conversion. He hopes that, like their pagan forebears, those who still keep these festivals will be "eaten by the church." The pagans of old cannot now be found because they have been devoured: "look for them in the church which has eaten them, and there they are, in the church's gut." He echoes here the story of Peter being told to "slaughter and eat" the unclean animals in Acts 10:9-16. What interests me here is the close, threefold connection made between a specific churchly practice in fasting, with the church's evangelical desire to convert outsiders, and its scriptural exegesis. The church fasts in hopes of "eating" more pagans, just as Peter was taught that the church must indeed be willing to "eat" unclean gentiles in Acts 10. There is here no clean distinction between the "physical" and the "spiritual," between the "literal" and the "figural," between exegesis that draws out what scripture meant and eisegesis that sees in scripture only our own historical circumstances. These easy modern distinctions blur together in Augustine's hands as he carries out a radically *participatory* vision of exegesis.[4]

Augustine's psalm hermeneutic is no panacea against interpretive problems. Rather it creates for him problems that we later modern readers would not have encountered on our own.[5] The psalm's fifth verse, "worship his footstool because he is holy," raises a grave problem for Augustine, since Isaiah

---

3. *EP* IV, 470-71.

4. More on this description below.

5. This is the problem with Rowan Williams's contention that historical criticism must be protected by theologians because its loss would lead to an inability to see the fissures in biblical texts that were so often papered over by patristic exegetes. No doubt the fathers missed cracks in the text that we see better and that we must deal with. Yet clearly they also see fissures that we miss, dealing with which leads to some of their most beautiful exegesis. See also Chapter 2, note 58, and Chapter 4, note 91, above. Rowan Williams, "Historical Criticism and Sacred Text," in *Reading Texts, Seeking Wisdom: Scripture and Theology,* ed. David Ford and Graham Stanton (Grand Rapids: Eerdmans, 2003), 217-28.

66:1 identifies the Lord's "footstool" as *the earth*. Can the psalmist actually be recommending the worship of the earth, that is, idolatry? "In my uncertainty I turn to Christ, for he it is whom I am seeking in this Psalm, and then I discover how, without idolatry, the earth may be worshipped."[6] The answer to this literal conundrum is, not surprisingly, christological. We have known this *res* for some time, for seeking it is the reason we listen to this sermon. The "surprise" comes in seeing precisely how Augustine will apply these *signa*, these words, to this *res*. He does so as follows: "He took earth from earth, because flesh comes from the earth, and he received his flesh from the flesh of Mary. He walked here below in that flesh, and even gave us that same flesh to eat for our salvation." The psalmist's words about "the Lord's footstool" point to the flesh of Christ — that part of creation that he takes to himself to bring about creation's redemption. It is no sin to worship this "earth." Augustine can even say, "we should sin if we do not." Yet no flesh, not even the flesh of Christ, is an end to itself. The psalmist immediately adds "because he is holy" lest his readers' thoughts "remain fixed on the flesh" to the detriment of the Spirit who gives life in it (John 6:54). That was the mistake of Jesus' non-discriminating hearers in John 6, who thought "the Lord meant to hack off small pieces of his body to give them, so they objected, 'This is a hard saying.'" Yet they erred, for it was "they who were hard, not the saying," Augustine says. Instead of being hard they ought to have been docile in response to the Lord's saying, and to have said to themselves, "there is some holy mystery [*sacramentum*] here." Augustine is so bold as to paraphrase the Lord's words from John's Gospel: "you are not asked to eat this body that you can see, nor to drink the blood that will be shed by those who crucify me. What I have said to you is something mysterious, something which when understood spiritually will mean life for you." Much could bear comment here — Augustine's attempt to enunciate the Lord's presence in the sacrament in a way that is not crudely literal, his boldness in paraphrasing Jesus so liberally, the light this statement throws on the two-stage christology we discussed in Chapter 2, and more. For now we should simply note that what was a textual difficulty for

---

6. *EP* IV, 474-75. I say this is no problem for moderns because we would not be ineluctably driven to identify the Psalter's use of "footstool" with "earth" because of the textual link with Isaiah. Further, a history-of-religions approach, which would see the description of the Lord's footstool as "just" so much religious rhetoric premised on the majesty of an ancient near eastern royal court, would bend the exegesis of this psalm in quite a different direction than Augustine does. In response to this suggestion I think of Professor Joel Green's statement to me that biblical scholars ought never to use the word "just." The kind of rhetoric we use matters. After its use, it subsequently takes on a life of its own once added to the tradition and is used for worship for centuries.

Augustine became a christological opportunity: a chance to see the incarnation in a new light by a description of it given in new words.

Augustine later follows the psalm as it turns to the "punishment" God doled out to his servants Moses, Aaron, and Samuel.[7] With regard to Moses it is easy enough to find scriptural warrant for talk about his punishment (Deuteronomy 32:52), yet this is less the case for Aaron or Samuel. So Augustine must extrapolate: "every day they had to put up with people who argued with them, every day they had to tolerate those who led wicked lives, and they were forced to live among people whose conduct they had to rebuke." Just as his hearers begin thinking this is small punishment indeed, Augustine, a bishop exercised in just these sorts of endless pastoral and administrative activities, thunders: "anyone who regards that as a light matter has not advanced very far." The notion of "progress" in reading is key to any figural hermeneutic — readers must advance from the childish place that can read only what is clear and simple to the more advanced steps on which they can discern the Lord's mystery more readily. What is even more crucial here is the fact that such progress is so deeply anchored in an unflattering portrait of church life. The polemical aim of this sermon is clear. It was likely preached sometime between 410 and 414, well into the Donatist controversy in which Augustine "bore with" not a few people whom he found quite difficult, to say the least.[8] Yet Augustine is also saying something pastoral, even "spiritual" here, designed to help his hearers live in their current setting more faithfully. He preaches, "You may be conscious of a desire to keep bad people at a distance from yourself, yet . . . you cannot remove them to a distance; you have to put up with them." As charity grows within a Christian, she or he will feel sadness at the sins of fellow Christians more deeply. Yet both are part of the body of Christ. And precisely *that* body has Christ as its head, and is the flawed-yet-graced people without whom we cannot be saved, and which we cannot leave.[9] Those who leave a compromised church for a more perfect one have little reason to pray with the psalmist for help in putting up with difficult people. To pray this line both demonstrates and demands further spiritual progress *toward,* and not away from, others in the church.

7. EP IV, 479-80.

8. Michael Fiedrowicz's *Psalmus Vox Totius Christi* (Freiburg: Herder, 1997), 436, has a chart that lists each psalm and when each of the historians who has done critical work on the *Enarrationes* reasons that Augustine wrote about it. So for Psalm 98, H. Rondet suggests that it was preached in 411, La Bonnardiere says 410, and S. Zarb opines it was between 411 and 413.

9. As Stephen Fowl nicely shows, Augustine's argument is that the Donatists fail in charity — because they would leave a church with which they are frustrated rather than staying. See his "Vigilant Communities and Virtuous Readers," in his *Engaging Scripture* (Oxford: Blackwell, 1997), 62-96.

We see here the heart of Augustine's psalm hermeneutic: even when the *totus Christus* or human desire are not central topics in an *Enarratio*, they are implicitly present, guiding his comments. More pressing for our concerns now, we see here a rigorous attention to the letter of scripture — one that, far from papering over cracks or "allegorizing them away," rather focuses intense attention upon them in an effort to wring every drip of christological meaning from each line of the Psalter. We see here that allegory is not an abstract hermeneutic, much less a clever trick for insulating dogma from the particulars of the biblical text. In contrast, it is offered amidst quite earthy practices of fasting, praying for outsiders, and bearing with difficult fellow church members. It is, in short, wedded to a way of life that seeks to inculcate charity here and now, amidst these difficult people and words, all as part of Christ's bending our desire aright. We shall see more of these features throughout this chapter. By the end of it I hope to have shown that Augustine demonstrates remarkable foresight in addressing many of our modern concerns with allegory in ways more theologically satisfying than we might have guessed. Further, Augustine presses questions and concerns we tend entirely to overlook. In short, Augustine's approach to the text of the Psalter is "superior" to ours, and the church in our day should re-learn, at the school of Christ, to read like Augustine.[10] We shall revisit these claims at the end of the chapter.

### Laus Quaerens Intellectum

It is fortunate for our purposes here that Augustine is relentless in describing and defending his biblical hermeneutics throughout the *Enarrationes*. Few psalms go by without a description of the *totus Christus* and the impact of this teaching on exegesis, or mention of God's therapeutic use of the psalms to straighten human desire. Theory and practice are here inextricably intertwined as Augustine speaks about reading scripture while also reading more scripture. He does this because the controversies in which he is constantly engaged are largely *exegetical* controversies. Any cursory reader of Augustine knows that his fights with the Manichees turned precisely on figural exegesis

---

10. I borrow this description from David Steinmetz's classic article, "The Superiority of Pre-Critical Exegesis," in *The Theological Interpretation of Scripture: Classic and Contemporary Readings*, ed. Stephen Fowl (Oxford: Blackwell, 1997). By it I do not mean that modern methods and insights should be left behind. Nor, indeed, does Steinmetz mean that. Rather, on central issues ancient exegetes are to be preferred to modern — especially in their active attempt to discern God's voice as part of exegesis. We shall say more below about the place of modern exegesis in the sort of ecclesial reading we advocate here.

of the Old Testament.[11] The *Enarrationes* demonstrate that the Donatist and Pelagian controversies also represent disagreements over hermeneutics and its intersection with competing ecclesiologies. Do biblical appeals to perfection and purity in the community win out over Jesus' hints of a mixed body? Do the same appeals for sinlessness trump Pauline descriptions of the ongoing struggle between sin and grace? Recent historical work in the patristic period has demonstrated that theology in the early church was largely a fight about proper "grammar" for speech about God — a way to integrate problematic biblical texts into a larger whole that most adequately explains its parts.[12] The Catholic Church finally triumphed over the "Arians" because its exegetical grammar could readily explain biblical descriptions both of Christ's human weakness (as pointers to his *kenosis*) and of his divinity, whereas its opponents could not so readily make sense of the latter set of claims.[13] So too with Augustine's polemics here. The *Enarrationes* shows that Augustine can more readily read the entire breadth and depth of scripture than his opponents, both its central story (the creed) and its most extraneous details. As he himself says, he wishes to avoid being "accused of shameless curiosity if we seek hidden meanings where perhaps it might have been said that the story is simple and straightforward and conceals no mysterious depths."[14] Augustine is consistently careful to make his particular hermeneutical christo-logic transparent.

There is no text written without a context. Augustine's work makes this modern truism abundantly clear. A biblical psalm has *several* "contexts." The most obvious one is that of a worshiping church that reads scripture as part of liturgical practice. Augustine, contemplating why such an unsavory event as David's adultery and murder of Uriah is mentioned in holy writ and read about in God's assembly, muses, "since God wanted the matter to be written about, he does not mean us to hush it up. What I am going to say, therefore, is not what I want to say, but what I am forced to" — as a bishop speaking to

---

11. See, for example, his exegesis on Genesis, in *On Genesis,* in the *Works of Saint Augustine* I/13 (Hyde Park, NY: New City, 2002).

12. See here also Chapter 1, 40-44 above, and Chapter 2, 64-68 above. Ayres borrows from George Lindbeck the description of theology as a working out of a "grammar" with which best to read both sympathetic and conflicting biblical texts. See Lindbeck's *The Nature of Doctrine* (Philadelphia: Fortress, 1984).

13. For a lucid explanation of Gregory of Nazianzen's success in offering a successful grammar over against Homoian opponents see Frederick Norris's introduction to Gregory in his *Faith Gives Fullness to Reasoning: The Five Theological Orations of Gregory Nazianzen,* trans. Lionel Wickham and Frederick Williams (New York: E. J. Brill, 1991).

14. A comment on Psalm 143 in *EP* VI, 360.

those who are seeking God in that part of the liturgy in which scripture is read publicly.[15] Just after the chanting of Psalm 18, the preacher suggests, "We ought to find out what this means, because we want to use our human reason as we sing, not merely to sing like parrots." Scripture itself insists that "blessed [is] the people that understands the reason for its joy," so Augustine maintains, "We ought to know and perceive with clear hearts what we have sung together with harmonious voices."[16] Just before tackling the longest psalm of all, Augustine explains his rationale: Christians are "accustomed to enjoying the sound of [Psalm 118] when it is sung, as they do with other Psalms." The goal of this homiletical exposition is to see that "congregations will not be denied comprehension" of that which they enjoy.[17] Christians are those people who are constantly chanting the psalms in the daily celebration of the liturgy. The preacher's job is to help the people to understand that which they have enjoyed chanting. For Augustine, exegesis of scripture is nothing less than "praise seeking understanding": how do we make specifically Christian sense of these words we have just chanted in the liturgy?[18]

The psalms are different from the rest of scripture in that they are, themselves, praise.[19] Other passages may, perhaps, be read non-doxologically, but the psalms' very genre demonstrates that non-doxological readings run contrary to their obvious purpose. A non-doxological reading would violate the letter of the psalm. This is not merely a phenomenological observation. It rests on the highest foundation of Christian teaching: trinity and christology. In the psalms, God himself speaks — "who has so tempered the expression of his praise in this Psalm that both strong and weak can make it

15. On Psalm 50 in *EP* II, 411.

16. Psalm 18 (2) in *EP* I, 204.

17. From the prologue to the exposition of Psalm 118 in *EP* V, 342.

18. With this title I intentionally echo St. Anselm's quite Augustinian description of the theological task. Augustine is fond of quoting the old Latin version of Isaiah 7:9 in the *Enarrationes:* "unless you believe, you will not understand." Yet I worry that descriptions of that sort can become, in our hands, narrowly epistemological. To cite Anselm's *fides quaerens intellectum* can be merely an attempt to defend the rationality of theological discourse without sounding like (too much of) a fideist. To speak of Augustinian biblical interpretation as *laus quaerens intellectum* situates Augustine, and his biblical hermeneutics, more squarely in the church's liturgy and makes abundantly clear that we speak here of no abstract discussion of epistemology, but of a specifically liturgical activity in exegesis.

19. This point is pressed relentlessly by Michael McCarthy in his 2003 Notre Dame dissertation, *The Revelatory Psalm: A Fundamental Theology of Augustine's Enarrationes In Psalmos* (Ann Arbor: University Microfilm, 2003). St. Athanasius also claims the uniqueness of the Psalter within the biblical canon in his "Letter to Marcellinus," trans. Robert Gregg, in *Athanasius,* Classics of Western Spirituality (New York: Paulist, 1980).

theirs."[20] The very doxological nature of inner-trinitarian "speech" is here opened "outward" to invite human participation. The form of such divine opening to creatures, of God's invitation to participation in the divine life, is of course, incarnational. God himself has sojourned with humanity in the incarnation. Augustine can therefore pray, in a paraphrase of Psalm 16's request that "my footprints may not be obliterated," asking, "may the signs of my journey not be removed, those signs which have been impressed like footprints on the sacraments and the apostolic writings, so that people who want to follow me may discern and observe them."[21] The Psalter's work on its readers is a reflection, or even extension, of the work of Christ. As Augustine insists each time he lays out his christological hermeneutic for the Psalter, Christ accepts our human words, and then gives us divine ones of praise in return. Augustine, reflecting on Psalm 93, admonishes his hearers, "The Psalm took on your words, so now you take on the words of the Psalm."[22] Elsewhere he writes of the single Word of God, present throughout scripture: "we should not find it surprising that to meet our weakness he descended to the discrete sounds we use, for he also descended to take to himself the weakness of our human body."[23] *Kenosis* is the character of divine speech to humans — a giving over of the divine self to weak human words for the sake of the *theotic* speech that is salvation.

The psalms' unique dialogical character does not mean Augustine's hermeneutic here is inapplicable to the rest of scripture. Rather, Augustine sees the psalms as unique in the same way Ambrose and Origen see the Song of Songs as unique: we see there in its most intense focus the divine and human interaction that marks the whole of scripture.[24] Augustine's psalm hermeneutic of "praise seeking understanding," learned from a christological reading of the Psalter, is meant to apply to all the rest of scripture, since it is all read liturgically as part of a people's ongoing sanctification. Commenting on Psalm 90, Augustine speaks of the close unity between scripture, the Chris-

20. On Psalm 134 in *EP* VI, 195. In its context this is referring to human inability to see God in himself, or at least to sustain such a glance, so that God has deigned to come to us in a form we can look upon on the way to the not-yet-visible beatific vision promised in scripture. Of course this beatific vision is nothing other than a gaze upon the divine essence, which the persons of the Trinity eternally share in by nature, and which in the incarnation creatures come to share in by grace.

21. *EP* I, 185-86.

22. *EP* IV, 405.

23. On Psalm 103 (4), *EP* V, 167.

24. The analogy to Ambrose's writings on the Song of Songs is Michael Cameron's in *Augustine's Construction of Figurative Exegesis Against the Donatists in the Enarrationes in Psalmos* (Ph.d. diss., University of Chicago, 1996; Ann Arbor: University Microfilms, 1997).

tian life, and the incarnation: "from that city whence we are still exiles letters have reached us; these letters are the scriptures . . . but why speak merely of letters? There is more than that: the king himself came down and made himself the way for us on our pilgrimage." That pilgrimage includes activities like chanting psalms and searching diligently for Christ on every page: "pay close attention, beloved, for it is the discipline and teaching of our school, and it will empower you to understand not this Psalm only but many others, if you hold onto this rule. Sometimes a Psalm — *and indeed not only a Psalm but any prophecy* — speaks of Christ in such a way that it clearly refers to the head alone. . . ."[25]

The Psalter functions in a way analogous to Christ. It not only depicts, but also *effects*, the divine *kenosis* and human *theosis* that is at the heart of scripture. It is not only the case that God speaks in the psalms, though that is true enough. Augustine holds that God speaks not only in scripture, he actually speaks *as the preacher preaches:* "God never tires of addressing us. If he speaks to us no longer, what are we doing? What is the point of our holy readings, our sacred songs?"[26] Augustine takes these already strong claims one step farther. In the Psalter, Christ speaks continually in a way that allows the working out of hearers' salvation as they grow in understanding and love of the words with which they praise. As Christ speaks in both head and members, those members grow in their ability to reflect on the gathering up of all creation in Christ to the Father that is taking place in the liturgy. The chanting of psalms is a central working out of salvation. Augustine can even *quote* Christ from a psalm: "in a Psalm he said, 'I will tell of your name to my brothers.'"[27] Augustine can admonish his hearers to "listen to him in this Psalm."[28] He can even speak of the psalmist as having "heard" the New Testament![29] Listeners are to

25. *EP* IV, 330-31. The rest of the passage cited describes the *totus Christus* in typically Augustinian terms.

26. On Psalm 130 in *EP* VI, 153.

27. *Enarratio* on Psalm 44, citing the christologically important Psalm 21. *EP* II, 301.

28. Psalm 56 in *EP* III, 103.

29. Psalm 61 in *EP* III, 202. It is difficult to spell out precisely how much Augustine thinks the psalmist *knew* about the realities to be revealed only in Christ. We have comments from him such as that explored in Chapter 2 about how the psalmist spoke more clearly of the church than of Christ (discussed on pp. 76-77 above, drawing upon Psalm 30 [3] in *EP* I, 341). Yet even this can be explained, for Augustine often speaks of the psalmist "concealing" that which he knew of revelation under signs for the delight of us who have to decipher them. Occasionally he can speak of something the psalmist could *not* see, such as the mystery of the unity of Jews and gentiles in the church (Psalm 73 in *EP* IV, 19), though normally he speaks of divine inspiration allowing the psalmist to know a great deal about the mystery of Christ, the *res* he then conceals behind his *signa*. The issue of inspiration, of precisely how much the bibli-

hear themselves also, for "in him we too are Christ . . . because in some sense the whole Christ is Head and body."[30] Life in the church is the growth of the body toward its head, and its intellectual and exegetical activity is centrally an explication of scripture's description of that *theotic* growth. Psalm interpretation, and derivatively the interpretation of scripture as a whole, is a matter of praise seeking understanding.

We can see this further in the homiletical use Augustine makes of words from the communion liturgy. Speaking of the psalmist's promise that "I will keep a firm eye on you," Augustine describes Christians' ability to lift their eyes to God now that their sins are forgiven. "There is good reason for the exhortation you know well: 'Lift up your hearts,' because they may go bad if you don't."[31] Elsewhere Augustine cites the *sursum corda* again in a theodical context: "one who firmly believes in God and hopes in the world to come rather than in this earth and this life, one who hears to good purpose the exhortation, 'Lift up your hearts!,' then, I say, this Christian derides and pities those who complain about God's justice."[32] Commenting on the psalmist's lament that "I am afflicted with miseries and bowed down to the very end," Augustine thinks of Luke's description of the healing of the bent-over-woman, and preaches, "Since that woman found the Lord and healed her, let everyone with this infirmity hear the invitation, 'Lift up your hearts!'"[33] Elsewhere Augustine comments on the Lord's Prayer, "We must pray, then; we must speak the truth in prayer; and we must pray as he taught us. Whether you like it or not you will have to say every day, *Forgive us our debts as we forgive our debtors.* Do you want to say it safely? Then act in accordance with what you say."[34]

Psalm interpretation is a matter of trying to catch up intellectually with those words with which the church has just offered its praise. The Christian life is not narrowly intellectual — it is first euchological. It is an attempt to live out those words with which we have always already praised God from scripture. Augustine then can often speak of a faithful life as the best exegesis of a psalm. He tries to worry business people that their buying and selling will

---

cal authors know, matters to some degree for how we speak of allegory, for if the psalmist knew Christ and then concealed his mystery beneath the words of the psalm, then biblical interpretation runs counter to the words of the psalm, but not to the intention of their author! It is a key instance in which Augustine divides that which modernity attempts to conflate: the literal sense and authorial intent.

30. Psalm 26 (2) in *EP* I, 275.
31. Psalm 31(2), in *EP* I, 382.
32. On Psalm 93 in *EP* IV, 375.
33. On Psalm 37 in *EP* II, 153, commenting on Luke 13:10-17.
34. On Psalm 103 (1), *EP* V, 129.

lead them to blaspheme when they suffer some loss. "Consequently the Psalm verse will not be true in your case: 'I will praise your name all day long.'" That is, the *life* of the worshiper can render a psalm untrue![35] The preacher's hearers are often encouraged to live out a psalm as they "write it on your hearts and in your conduct," and by "ordering your lives in conformity with it."[36] Christian life is nothing other than a lived-out response to the psalms. The psalms offer Augustine a detailed anatomy of salvation, a medicine for anything that ails any person, a trade route for the divine commerce of salvation for sin. Just so, their chanting is central to salvation itself. Christian life for Augustine is a continual effort to make christological sense of the words we have just offered to God in praise.

## A Surprising *Sensus Literalis*

Augustine's psalm expositions attend strictly to the literal sense of the text. That is not to say the *Enarrationes* are not a robustly christological reading of the psalms, as we have seen they very much are. Rather, it is to say that Augustine's intensely theological reading of the Psalter is also a deeply literal reading of it — at least as he understands the word "literal." In this section we shall see how Augustine tends to treat the "letter" of scripture before turning to his treatment of other senses of the Bible in the next.

When Augustine brings an explicitly Christian theological reading to bear on a psalm there is almost always a literal link between the psalm and a New Testament theme, story, or idea that directs him to make that interpretation.[37] Allegory cannot take place without a verbal or narrative cue, a "wrinkle" in the text, as it were. A most common one for him is when he comes across the superscription above the psalm, "to the end." What is the "end" in a specifically Christian lexicon? It is, according to Paul, "Christ," the "end" of the law, in the full sense of the Greek word *telos* — the law's goal and its conclusion (Romans 10:4). Augustine then has literal license to read the rest of the psalm in light of a Christian understanding of the law.[38] To

---

35. The quote is from Psalm 70 in *EP* III, 429. I intentionally echo here George Lindbeck's famous formulation in *The Nature of Doctrine* that a crusader's cry *"Dominus Jesus"* is rendered *untrue* if pronounced while cleaving the skull of an infidel, because from this bit of exegesis it sounds like quite an Augustinian claim.

36. From Psalm 93 *EP* IV, 408.

37. A point frequently made in Robert Wilken, *The Spirit of Early Christian Thought* (New Haven: Yale University Press, 2003).

38. To cite only one example, Psalm 31 (2) in *EP* I, 321.

cite another example from a psalm superscription — Augustine's Latin translations often include the anticipatory announcement that the psalm is "not to be tampered with."[39] He calls this "a title about a title" — the one that hung over Jesus' cross, which Pilate insisted was not to be altered. Augustine then has a literal warrant for reading the psalm in light of Christ's lordship over Jews and gentiles alike, signified by the Hebrew, Greek, and Latin languages in which "King of the Jews" was written over his cross.[40] Augustine can also focus on a curiosity, or even a mistake, in the superscription above a psalm as a divine hint that astute readers should discern a certain mystery there. When the psalmist speaks of the temple that is presently "being built," anyone who knows anything about biblical history cannot possibly think he refers to Solomon's temple, since it was both built and destroyed long ago. Rather, a good reader will know the psalmist to be referring to that temple now being built in the preaching of the word — that is, the church — referred to with quite literal New Testament description as the temple in such places as 1 Corinthians 3:17, 1 Peter 2:5, and elsewhere.[41] In another example of his need for a verbal cue to read allegorically, Augustine often seizes what we might call a "frayed edge" of a psalm title. The psalmist dedicates a psalm "for the olive presses," and then says nothing more about them. This absence is a "fact that hints more clearly at the mystery," and sends Augustine off on a description of the squeezing of persecution that yields the fruit of faithfulness.[42] Augustine clearly glories in reading the psalm titles! Like other patristic interpreters of scripture he senses these have special significance to the meaning of the entire psalm. They are like a sign on the front of a building, careful attendance to which allows entry without misstep.[43] Or more elaborately, "it is customary for scripture to announce the mysterious

---

39. I struggle somewhat with the issue of accuracy in translation here. Are these christological moves simply enabled by bad translation from Hebrew to Latin? Yet this translation, "not to be tampered with," is not dissimilar from modern translations of the Hebrew that read something like "do not destroy." This is a closer approximation than that between Augustine's "to the end" and our "to the choirmaster." Yet Augustine could have read the latter option christologically without difficulty. Augustine himself craved more accurate translations (though he was famously upset by Jerome's *Vulgate* at first for its contravention of the *sensus fidelium* of those who had worshiped with older translations for years). He would not have been frustrated in his overall hermeneutic by better modern translations from Hebrew as opposed to his worse ones from Greek into Latin. Allegory is always more exegetically nimble than modern hermeneutics.

40. On Psalm 58 (1) in *EP* III, 148.

41. Comment on Psalm 121 in *EP* VI, 16.

42. On Psalm 80 in *EP* IV, 152.

43. Psalm 53 in *EP* III, 41.

content of the psalms in their titles, to adorn the façade of a Psalm with sublime indications of the sacred truth it contains."[44] The contrast with modern neglect of the psalm titles or superscriptions could not be more marked. Yet for our present purposes the point is that Augustine's comments on the psalm inscriptions are, in their own way, quite literal observations. They attend with rigorous detail to the letter of the psalm being read, and then travel through the entirety of the Bible for verbal connections to the word in question — "end," "trample," "temple," or whatever. To borrow a phrase, these observations are "not non-literal," or even more strongly, they ought to be considered as claimants to a literal reading of the psalm.[45]

Augustine finds quite literal rationale for explicitly Christian reading of psalms not only in their titles, but also throughout the body of their text. As early as the first line of the first psalm, Augustine sees a verbal link to Jesus. For who is he who is "blessed" for having "not gone astray in the council of the ungodly"? None other than "our Lord Jesus Christ, the Lord-Man." For he "most certainly came in the way of sinners by being born as sinners are, but he did not stand in it."[46] Here again the exegesis can be described as not non-literal — who indeed can be spoken of as "blessed" for shunning sin in a particularly Christian parlance? When Augustine reads Psalm 31's benediction upon those "in whose mouth there is no guile," the word *guile* leads him to think of Jesus' greeting of Nathaniel, as a true Israelite without guile (John 1:47).[47] For even the early (pre-Pelagian controversy) Augustine, no one is without guile except by special divine action. Augustine sees that in Christ's miraculous glimpse of Nathaniel while under the fig tree — an image for all humanity as guilty (under a fruit tree), yet gazed upon in mercy, made guileless by Christ.[48] In Augustine's reading of Psalm 138, with its unforgettable lines of intense introspection, such as "you search me and know me, you know when I sit down and when I rise," we find a full-blown christological

44. On Psalm 58 in *EP* III, 148.

45. The phrase is David Dawson's from his *Christian Figural Reading and the Fashioning of Identity* (Berkeley: University of California Press, 2002).

46. *EP* I, 67. Augustine only uses the description "Lord-Man" of Jesus in the *Enarrationes* on the first thirty-two psalms, until he came to deem it christologically inadequate for its insufficient ascription of divinity to Christ.

47. It is worth noting how hard it is to write about Augustine without constantly citing scripture, just as it is hard to read him without an open Bible. This difficulty shows the fallacy in the claim that the fathers' allegorical approach to scripture causes them to lose the letter of scripture. On the contrary, to read the fathers' allegories well requires a masterful grasp of the breadth and depth of scripture. Robert Wilken often speaks of how he learned the Bible simply through years of reading patristic literature.

48. *EP* I, 371-72.

reading that is also not non-literal. Augustine sees the psalm as a prayer addressed to the Father by the Son. We can see the rationale for this — between what two people is there such intimate mutual knowledge as this psalm describes? Who may speak with God with such familiarity, but one whom the New Testament describes as *knowing* the Father? Augustine answers: "he who sits, humbles himself. The Lord then *sat* in his passion, and rose up in his resurrection." Because of the *totus Christus* we may take these words that properly describe the head, and attribute them to the members. "We sit down when we humble ourselves in repentance, and we rise up when our sins have been forgiven, for then we rise up toward the hope of eternal life."[49] Augustine sees the ascending and descending motifs of this psalm as descriptions of the incarnation, and just so of our life in Christ. This quite verbal link between psalm words about rising and Christ's resurrection or ascension recurs throughout the *Enarrationes*. When Psalm 67 exults, "Let God arise, and let his enemies be scattered," Augustine can simply observe, "This has already happened."[50] When the psalmist asks God to "return on high," Augustine hears an echo of the ascension, after which believers can only behold Jesus in faith. Yet christological references for Augustine are not at all narrow or exclusive of other meanings. For example, he also sees here in descriptions of the Lord's rising a description of biblical exegesis! "By this is meant, 'become difficult to understand once more.'"[51] For as ever in scripture, difficulty arouses desire, it demands exegetical maturity, it guards scripture's mysteries from the immature, and grows the saints in holiness. Again, we see a deeply literal, verbal link that allows this sort of christological reading of a psalm. We might speak a bit more broadly of Augustine finding a parallel *movement* between the psalm and a theological theme — from arising to Christ's arising, from returning to Christ's returning. Augustine is ever alert to any parallel contour or motion between the psalm's words and the broader Christian story, and when he finds such a parallel he delights — for God has left it there for the church to find, with difficulty, and so to grow in delight and love.

Other links between the psalm and Christian interpretation are authorized for Augustine by the broader narrative of scripture alongside of which the Psalter is canonized. Such links are not less literal than those we have seen already. Psalm 37 is read in light of what Augustine takes to be its *skopos*, verse 19: "I will proclaim my iniquity aloud, and take serious thought for my sin." He thinks immediately of the Canaanite woman who does not deny Jesus' de-

---

49. *EP* VI, 258-59.
50. *EP* III, 325.
51. On Psalm 7 in *EP* I, 119.

scription of her as a dog, but professes her iniquity aloud.[52] Augustine sees the parallel between these two confessions and their quite similar pattern of admission of wretchedness, and so reads the entire psalm in light of a particularly Christian understanding of confession. When the title of Psalm 56 remembers "when David fled into a cave from Saul's pursuit," Augustine is led to ask "whether flight into a cave has any relevance to the new David."[53] On a quite literal level the New Testament works hard to establish Jesus' Davidic ancestry and speaks of him in messianic terms that cannot be thought of biblically without reference to David.[54] Augustine then has his license to read the pursuit into the cave as an allegory for the incarnation. A person in a cave is covered over by dirt, just as Jesus went about "carrying earth," keeping the "majesty of his godhead covered." Augustine shows his listeners the narrative parallel between David the refugee king and Christ's voluntary, *kenotic* surrender of power. These and similar links are based on the continuity of the story Christians tell between David — the psalms about or attributed to him — and the story Christians now inhabit. Christians hold that the promises held out in Old Testament scripture have been fulfilled: "when the Psalms were originally spoken and written this petition was made with prophetic import, but if we consider it from the standpoint of our own times, it is clear that the Lord has now shown his mercy to the Gentiles. . . ."[55] These observations rest on the historical continuity the church claims to have with Israel and her God — though notice they are not for that reason any less "literal."[56]

In the last paragraph I have spoken of literal links seen through the lens of

---

52. In *EP* II, 146, speaking of Matthew 15:21-28.

53. *EP* III, 106.

54. For example in Matthew 21:9; Mark 10:46-47; 11:10; Luke 1:32-33 — often in the context of the triumphal entry.

55. On Psalm 84 in *EP* IV, 204.

56. I like very much Graham Ward's description of a "letteral" sense of a text. "Christianity needs, then, to read the spiritual, the universal in such a way as not to denigrate or dissolve the historical and concrete. . . . The letteral (though not the literal, which is already an interpretation), the written, in its materiality is affirmed." No one can speak of the "literal" sense of scripture without already doing interpretation (normally for us in a historical-critical vein), hence to speak of a "letteral" sense is to insist more strongly on attention to the words on the page. It is not an attention to the words without interpretation, for such a thing would be impossible, but rather attention to the words without a preconceived notion that a "literal" reading must necessarily mean non-christological interpretation. As Augustine shows in the *Enarrationes,* a literal (or better "letteral") approach to a psalm can include a deeply christological reflection without leaving the letter behind. Eugene Rogers is after much the same thing when he speaks of the literal sense as "the way the words go." See Ward, "Allegoria: Reading as a Spiritual Exercise," *Modern Theology* 15, no. 3 (1999): 271-95, and "How the Virtues of an Interpreter Presuppose and Perfect Hermeneutics: The Case of Thomas Aquinas," *Journal of Religion* 76 (1996): 64-81.

the narrative continuity between the church and Israel. Yet I temporarily left off those links that lead to theological readings that are made by the New Testament itself. When Psalm 18 speaks of the heavens — "their sound went forth throughout the world, their words to the ends of the earth" — that language is applied to the preaching of the apostles in Romans 10:18.[57] Augustine can simply ask, and just as simply answer, "Whose words would that be? The words of the apostles, of course."[58] Similarly Psalm 77, with its rendition of Israel's history in the Exodus, is poured through the filter of Paul's words in 1 Corinthians 10:1-11, which directly apply the events of Israel's history to figural reading.[59] Another psalm that is dedicated "for Solomon" might properly be read by Christians, for both narrative and etymological reasons, with reference to the "peacemaker" described in the New Testament in such places as Ephesians 2:14-16.[60] Commenting on Psalm 94's promise that "the Lord will not reject his people," Augustine insists, "We have no authority to impose any meaning on the text, because these words have been commented on in advance by the apostle."[61] And not just any apostle, but one whose conversion shows the greatness of God's grace, no less than the grievous nature of an illness shows the skill of the physician who heals it. Paul's harder work than any other apostle makes him a particularly apt teacher of exegesis (1 Corinthians 15:10). Augustine even insists that the churches to which Paul wrote flourish more than others.[62] "Others who have written, have neither written so much, nor with so great grace. Since then he had great grace . . . what did he say?"[63] Elsewhere Augustine can hint at his deepest rationale for figural reading. In context he is polemicizing against the Donatists as he describes the apostles' request to Jesus to exegete his parable of the sower: "if the Lord had expounded a parable . . . would anyone have the temerity to assert that he ought not to have expounded it in the way he did?"[64] Paul and Jesus and the New Testament as a whole privilege certain approaches to reading the Old, which Augustine cannot imagine later readers contravening.

57. As Paul explores the question of whether Israel is culpable for its lack of belief, he asks, "Have they not heard? Indeed they have, for 'their voice has gone out to all the earth, and their words to the ends of the world'" (NRSV).

58. Psalm 18 (2) in *EP* I, 205.

59. *EP* IV, 91. See 1 Corinthians 10:11: "These things happened to them to serve as an example, and they were written down to instruct us, on whom the ends of the ages have come" (NRSV).

60. Comment on Psalm 71 in *EP* III, 452.

61. *EP* IV, 415, alluding to Romans 11:2.

62. Comment on Psalm 130 in *EP* VI, 144. That is one argument we might not be able to use now!

63. *EP* VI, 145.

64. Psalm 149 in *EP* VI, 494.

Another impetus to figural reading comes from Augustine's setting in the church. Augustine wonders at the disjunction in Psalm 30, in which the psalmist thanks God for "guiding my feet into open spaces," and then demands "mercy, for I am in distress." The reason for such a quick shift is that one single church speaks in the psalm, and in some places and times there is in the church "a sense of spacious freedom, while others are squeezed and confined."[65] Here the quick, often dizzying emotional swings in the psalms are explained as a reflection of the church's catholicity — for surely there are some places where it is unhindered and others where it is oppressed at any given moment. Psalms that sing of pilgrimage are not difficult to transpose into an ecclesial key: "O you children of grace, children of the one Catholic Church; walk in the way, and sing as you go. This is what wayfarers do to lighten their fatigue."[66] Mentions of water often turn to descriptions of baptism — not more spectacularly than when the psalmist praises God for being he who "shattered the heads of the dragons in the water," and Augustine can say that "through baptism you set free the people who had been the demons' prey."[67] This sort of liturgical link between the psalm and a Christian interpretation may occasionally have been lost on some hearers, for not all would have been baptized. Their perplexity, coupled with the fervor in response of those who have been baptized, combine in an evangelical appeal in one instance. Augustine reads a description of the crossing of the Red Sea, links it to Christian baptism, and then says, "When I remarked on that just now, many people understood and shouted their agreement, but the rest stood there dumb, because what they heard was speech unfamiliar to them. Let these latter hurry up, let them cross the sea."[68] The liturgical season itself can drive a theologically explicit reading of the psalm, as when Augustine is to pray on one of the church's many commemorations of the martyrs. That liturgical focus regularly becomes a homiletical *skopos* for Augustine the preacher. In another liturgical connection, Augustine responds to a mistake by the cantor! He apologizes to the congregation, for he had planned to preach a short sermon on one psalm, but then by some mistake the cantor led the church in singing a different one. Augustine took this mistake to be a divine suggestion as to the psalm from which he ought to preach. So the congregation ought not complain to him about the length of what they were

---

65. Psalm 30 (3) in *EP* I, 334.

66. On Psalm 66 in *EP* III, 316.

67. On Psalm 73 in *EP* IV, 25.

68. Clearly, allegorical readings of the psalm about the sacraments and Pentecostal-style interaction with the preacher were not inimical to one another in Augustine's day. Psalm 80 in *EP* IV, 158.

about to hear.[69] In short, an (unplanned) liturgical event inspires allegorical exegesis.

Liturgical blunders are not the only mistakes that drive Augustine to a particular sort of reading. Scriptural ones often drive him to read allegorically — as they had done to Christian readers of scripture for centuries. We have spoken before about the "error" of misattributing a story in the superscription of Psalm 33.[70] Yet perhaps we should say this was no error, but a divine hint that he should read deeper, as in Augustine's comments on a similar "mistake" in Psalm 51: "the change in name alerts us to the mystery. Without it, you might simply concentrate on an historical episode and ignore the sacred veils that conceal the meaning."[71] When a superscription relates as historical an event Augustine cannot find in the biblical account of that story, he finds another clue: "clearly the 'David' who is meant is Jesus Christ."[72] When the psalmist swears "I will be a lodger in your tent forever," he cannot have intended to suggest he would live forever — who will? Yet the church has its existence promised through all ages.[73] Sometimes the psalm will mention a "historical" incident in Israel's history that is not recorded in the Bible's historical narratives, as when Psalm 67 records that God "leads forth the fettered in fortitude, and . . . those who dwell in the tombs." Augustine responds: "but this cannot be right," for what shackled persons or tomb dwellers were among the slaves brought forth from Egypt? The historical "addition" must be a clue to read spiritually.[74] Or words can be "added" to a psalm that are not historically incorrect, but are simply superfluous. Why should the psalmist have said that "God smashed the teeth *in their mouths*"? What "teeth" are not in someone's mouth? We should look deeper, and will be rewarded by finding Christ in such extra words.[75] These sorts of "problems" in the letter of scripture that point to Christ could be multiplied indefinitely in Augustine's exegesis. And these are precisely the sort of literal connections that often dismay modern critics of Augustine — what is he doing here but fabricating reasons to find

---

69. On Psalm 138 in *EP* VI, 257. Augustine's ability to preach a long sermon without previous preparation does not only suggest his rhetorical training before his conversion. It also indicates a profound familiarity with the central story of the gospel to which he returns in every sermon, a collection of important themes to which he returns frequently enough to repeat them orally and in public, and practiced skill in moving those themes as befits the specific words in a given psalm.

70. In Chapter 2 above, pp. 93-96.

71. Psalm 51 in *EP* III, 17.

72. Psalm 55 in *EP* III, 83.

73. Psalm 60 in *EP* III, 197.

74. In *EP* III, 330-31.

75. In Psalm 57 in *EP* III, 133.

Augustine lurking under every rock?[76] We can agree that for Augustine the "default" of any psalm is Christ — any frayed edge in a psalm, any historical question or grammatical problem, any "wrinkle" in the letter, anything not immediately transparent at all is a license to read the psalm christologically. Yet as this book has tried to show, the place to criticize Augustine is not in the specific verbal links or mistakes that drive him to allegory. It is rather in his christology, as developed in accordance with the New Testament and the pro-Nicene tradition, and the account of desire that rests upon it. For if the interpreter and her community are being drawn in Christ to the Father, and if they read scripture to hone their desire for their homeland, then to have Christ as the subject suggested by any textual wrinkle is a perfectly coherent hermeneutic — and nonetheless quite literal. For Augustine needs a material, *textual* reason to offer a christological reading — a mistake or error or puzzle — precisely in the letter of the text before him. Augustine's work here challenges a common assumption of modern readers regarding allegory: that it is inattentive to the letter of scripture, that it is arbitrary, or that it "allegorizes away" the particular words on the page. In contrast, Augustine needs a pointer from the particular words on the page before he will read this way. The fact that he finds one frequently is no argument against his procedure.

The last several examples we have seen show Augustine responding to what we might call a "wrinkle" or a "chink" in the letter, such as a historical mistake or extraneous words. In these cases it is not that the psalm is morally or theologically repugnant such that the letter must be discarded, as is so often the case with, say, Origen. Rather the letter has a reminder in it — like a surprise left by a friend or lover — meant to warn the assiduous reader to read more deeply. In other cases Augustine can find a more deeply rooted "fault" with the letter of scripture that should cause an entire psalm to require christological reading, more like the procedure of Origen mentioned above. To be more specific about it, we should say that Augustine is driven by the letter of scripture in some places in the canon to read *against* the letter in the psalms. Even here then we may describe his procedure as "not non-literal." For example, the psalmist cries out, "show no mercy to any who deal unjustly."[77] Augustine worries, "This certainly strikes fear into us. Who would not be frightened by it?" The implication of innocence certainly does not square with Augustine's

---

76. A significant New Testament scholar in America responded to my work with this question: "why should we attempt to find Christ hiding under every rock in the Old Testament?" Augustine's answer: because for Paul the "rock" is "Christ" (Romans 10:4) — so a good Pauline reader of the Israel's scripture will indeed find Christ not just under every rock, but in every mention of that word. If we keep silent . . .

77. Psalm 58 in *EP* III, 159-60.

own hamartiology. Yet this is no extra-biblical concern of Augustine's. Indeed, profound attention to the letter of scripture in one place drives its good readers to attend differently to the letter in another.[78] This a concern expressed elsewhere in the psalms, as Augustine cites Psalm 129, "If you, Lord, keep a record of our iniquities, who, Lord, will withstand it?" Further, "God did show mercy to Paul," who was among the most notorious of sinners. So the letter is here theologically and literally suspect, precisely for biblical reasons. Augustine can think of two exegetical responses to this problem. One, that all sins are either repented of or avenged by God: "either you punish [your sins] or God does." Two, that there is some category of sin that cannot be forgiven, namely the proud defense of one's own misdeeds.[79] We should note that both of these readings are attentive to the letter of scripture in a way that accords with its letter elsewhere and with Augustine's general theology of human sin and divine mercy. It is, in its own way, surprisingly literal.

Occasionally Augustine can point out that scripture's letter could lead to a ridiculous literalism for those unwilling to grant any sort of figural reading. When the psalmist calls on "dragons and all abysses" to praise the Lord, Augustine asks, "What? Are we to imagine dragons forming a choir to praise God?"[80] Surely not. Yet all creatures, no matter how fantastic, should lead Christians to praise their Maker. Surely a figural reading of a figural verse is here a proper literal reading of it, as any reader of poetry should be able to see. We see other instances of this sort of literal figure when the psalmist praises God that "never have I seen a just person destitute, or a child of righteous parents begging for bread." Any casual glance around at the world will prove otherwise, and more strongly, the just beg for bread *in scripture*. Abram and Paul each begged for bread, and were surely just; in the latter case Paul's very justice led him to beg for bread rather than take money from the church.[81] Clearly the bread that the just do not lack must be the word of God — a literal link for which Augustine has license from Jesus himself (Matthew 4:4).[82] More broadly Augustine has to "save" this psalm from his Donatist op-

---

78. It often seems to me that those inclined to allegory are those who attend most obediently to the words in the entire canon of scriptures. Many Christians simply do not attend to the vast bulk of their Bibles called "Old Testament." Allegory may represent an obedient attention to the whole span of Christian scripture.

79. That is how much of the patristic tradition reads the dominical description of blasphemy of the Holy Spirit as an unforgivable sin. See Matthew 12:31 and parallels.

80. On Psalm 148 in *EP* VI, 484.

81. Abram is hungry due to a famine in the land and goes to Egypt in Genesis 12:10. Paul mentions his going without food in a litany of (non-!) complaints in 2 Corinthians 11:27.

82. Psalm 36 (3) in *EP* II, 130-32.

ponents, who clearly celebrated its insistence that the just are rewarded and the wicked punished as evidence for the need to separate from a compromised church. So he turns here again to his well-worn use of Jesus' parable of the threshing floor, and his defense of the dignity of the bishop's chair, as opposed to that of the man who occupies it. In another case he must save the labyrinthian Psalm 118 from Pelagian exegetes. There the psalmist makes such breezily confident claims as "those who break his law have not walked in his ways." Augustine cites a bevy of scripture to show that Christians indeed sin, and uses Romans 7 to argue that Christians both walk in God's ways and yet continue to falter.[83] Later in another sermon on the same psalm Augustine glosses the request to "pay back your servant" by arguing that God confounds human patterns of giving by returning good for evil.[84] In these instances we see that Augustine has reread the psalm at hand over against heretical groups whose cause would seem to find support in it. He is driven to do so precisely by the letter of scripture in other places. This is a literalism that pays attention to the letter of the entire canon of scripture — and sees that letter transfigured in light of Christ.

We have been focusing upon problems with the letter of scripture, whether minor ones that serve as gentle reminders to careful readers to seek Christ, or more severe ones that mandate a reading against the letter of the psalm. Yet Augustine more often than not has no difficulty reading a psalm in a literal sense. In fact, he often takes the literal sense of a psalm simply to *be* christological as it stands. In a sermon on Psalm 18, he announces that "the Psalm is sung about Christ, as is abundantly clear from a line in it, 'He is like a bridegroom coming forth from his tent.'"[85] With this christological link Augustine is able to read the "speech" that does not go unheard as the preaching of the apostles (as in Romans 10:18), the heavens as the saints, and the sound going forth as God's gift of mercy. There is no indication here that Augustine thinks he is reading against the letter. Rather, the letter of the psalm couples with the letter of the New Testament to produce a sort of *christological literalism*. Speaking of Psalm 23's words that "the King of glory will enter," Augustine can simply say that it is "abundantly clear that Christ is the king of glory." He cites 1 Corinthians 2:8 in his defense, where Paul describes Jesus as the "Lord of glory," and then explains that the difficulty with this psalm is not seeing Christ in it, but rather in seeing the church. He sets out to respond exegetically to that difficulty. Again, the literal meaning of "king of glory" is

---

83. Psalm 118 (2) in *EP* V, 347-50.
84. Psalm 118 (7) in *EP* V, 368-70.
85. In *EP* I, 204-5.

here simply christological.[86] Elsewhere, when the psalmist asks, "Show us, Lord, your mercy, and grant us your salvation," Augustine states, "'Your salvation' means your Christ. . . . Let us echo it: Grant us your Christ."[87] For Christians the words "salvation" and "mercy" are inescapably christological, so Augustine needs no further warrant to read these words both literally and christologically. The clearest example of an Augustinian christological literalism that recurs throughout the *Enarrationes* is his polemic against the Donatists, who fail to understand the psalms' many descriptions of the Lord's reign over all the earth. When the psalmist exults that "their words went forth throughout the world," Augustine can ask, "What is clearer, what more obvious?" than that the church's reach must extend beyond north Africa?[88] Augustine insists that the Donatists insult the Lord of all when "instead of the whole earth, they merely offer him Africa."[89] When the psalmist sings that God has "summoned all the earth," Augustine speaks to his home: "Let Africa rejoice then, at being within that unity, and not grow proud in isolation."[90] These examples of the Donatists failing to read the letter of the psalm well could be multiplied indefinitely. The point is this: they fail to see the psalm's literal description of the church as Christ's body throughout the earth, and instead offer the Lord only Africa. The letter here is always already christological for Augustine. As he announces elsewhere, "Christ . . . shouts in every place, through the law, through the prophets, through the psalms, through the apostolic letters, through the gospels."[91] One need only read them aright to see Christ's speaking in the letter of the psalms. As Augustine says elsewhere, "Obscure, veiled mysteries in the books of the Old Testament are sometimes unveiled by those ancient books themselves." He then gives a long quote from Micah about the gentiles seeing the Lord's marvels and licking the dust (Micah 7:15-19). On Old Testament passage drives him to read another Old Testament passage allegorically! Augustine concludes, "You can see here, brothers and sisters, that sacred mysteries are being opened in a

---

86. Though he speaks here of Psalm 23, the *Enarratio* is properly that on Psalm 47, whose inscription is "for the second day of the week." Augustine then remembers a psalm assigned to the first day of the week — Psalm 23 — with its first verse about the king of glory (*EP* II, 335).

The christological literalism of Psalm 23 would be reinforced especially in Orthodox liturgy, in which the proclamation of the "king of glory" breaking down the closed gates and trampling death is especially important in the Easter vigil.

87. On Psalm 84:8 in *EP* IV, 210.

88. Psalm 18 (2) in *EP* I, 208.

89. Psalm 21 (2) in *EP* I, 228.

90. Psalm 49 in *EP* II, 382.

91. On Psalm 100 in *EP* V, 44.

quite unambiguous way." The letter of scripture is here already christological as it portrays the repentance of the gentiles the world over.[92]

What we see in Augustine's treatment of the letter of scripture is what recent Augustinian scholars have described as a search for a grammar for God.[93] The description of a divine "grammar" is felicitous because it suggests how scripture and the *regula fidei* work for Augustine. Various verses of the Bible must be arranged according to the *regula* for particularly biblical speech to make sense, just as words in a language must be arranged according to its grammatical rules for communication to take place. In this case the particular words and themes of the psalms are arranged in accordance with the *regula*, no less than in Augustine's explorations on the doctrine of God. Augustine also arranges his psalm exegesis according to the particular *skopos* of a psalm being worked on. This *skopos* is chosen in each case in accordance with a specific christological link in a psalm — a word or motif or mistake or liturgical event, as we have been describing. Then every other word or narrative contour in a psalm is arranged accordingly. So in this case a christologically aligned *skopos* becomes the "grammar" of the psalm, and the rest of the psalm's various parts become the "words" to be arranged in accordance with that grammar. The "grammar for God" that has worked well to describe Augustine's theology at a "macro" level here functions on a "micro" level in his exegesis of particular psalms.

For example, in his exposition of Psalm 105, Augustine pauses to remind his hearers of his biblical hermeneutics. "Consider this carefully, whoever you are who read this. You recognize the grace of God by reading of it in the apostolic letters but also by searching the prophetic oracles, where you encounter that same grace whereby we are redeemed unto eternal life through our Lord Jesus Christ." Grace is learned about from the New Testament, but then, reading retrospectively, we come to recognize its presence throughout the scriptures. Next comes a famous Augustinian dictum: "You perceive the New Covenant veiled in the Old, and the Old Covenant revealed in the New." He then reminds his hearers of several key New Testament themes he finds in the psalm — in this case sayings from Paul and John about the nature of the devil. "With all this in mind, turn your attention back again to the Old Testament, and consider what is sung in the Psalm. . . ."[94] Augustine then proceeds to read the psalm in question as it refers to the *skopos* he has identified, signaled by the words of the psalm, informed in fullness by the New Testament,

---

92. Psalm 113 in *EP* V, 306-7.
93. See note 12 on p. 200 above.
94. *EP* V, 219.

then read back throughout the whole Bible with understanding. More briefly, Augustine elsewhere quotes the apostle Paul from Philippians, and then explains what Paul was doing there was "helping us to understand this Psalm."[95] This Augustinian theological grammar is drawn primarily from Paul and John, the most thoroughly dogmatic writers in the New Testament, and then this grammar is used to arrange the words and narrative contours of the psalm. Augustine is a Pauline and Johannine psalm interpreter.

Psalm 62 describes itself as being by "David himself, when he was in the desert of Edom," and its third verse for Augustine proclaims, "My soul is athirst for you."[96] Edom, Augustine rightly says, was a wandering desert tribe, often pejoratively described in scripture. Then his mind wanders to such New Testament descriptions of thirst as Jesus' promise that those who "thirst for righteousness" shall be satisfied. The *enarratio* then becomes one about right human desire for God. As opposed to our neighbors, "we are Christians for the sake of a different felicity," as we wander in the desert thirsting for righteousness, now partially satisfied, partially not, as we continue to long for eschatological satisfaction only in God.[97] The rest of the commentary here fixes on different images — sleep as an image of sin, seeing as an eschatological promise of beatific vision, uplifted hands as a signal of the cross, glue as a description of charity that keeps one attached to Christ, and so forth. Yet the overall *skopos* of right desire remains in place, refracted through a variety of images throughout the psalm. In another instance, Psalm 70, the *skopos* is more consistently fixed to a single theological motif of grace. Augustine announces from the beginning that "every part of holy scripture commends to us the liberating grace of God."[98] A bit further, "it is for this reason that we had the passage from the apostle read beforehand, for in it Paul most especially commends God's grace to us." The passage was one of Paul's various descriptions of himself as the worst sinner, and just so as the recipient of the deepest divine mercy.[99] "In our Psalm God commends the same grace to

95. Psalm 93 in *EP* IV, 377.

96. *EP* III, 231.

97. *EP* III, 234.

98. Psalm 70, *EP* III, 412.

99. "I am not worthy to be called an apostle, because I persecuted God's Church" (1 Corinthians 15:9). Shortly after, Augustine quotes 1 Timothy 1:13-16, "I received mercy because I acted in ignorance. . . . It is a reliable saying, and worthy of full acceptance, that Christ Jesus came into this world to save sinners, among whom I am foremost. I received mercy so that Christ Jesus might give proof in me of his long forbearance toward those who will believe in him unto eternal life" (*EP* III, 413). It is interesting that Augustine leaves off Paul's description in 1 Corinthians of how much harder he worked than the other apostles and turns to 1 Timothy with its description of unmerited grace.

us. . . . I judge this to be the gist of the Psalm, the message that resounds from nearly every syllable in it." The rest of the exposition is a lavish attention to the psalm's *signa,* showing precisely how they refer to the *res* of Christ. Later in the Psalter an entire genre of psalms is read according to a particular grammar of christological and liturgical ascent. In reading the first of the ascent psalms Augustine is clear that no spiritual climbing would be possible were it not for "a certain descent that occurred first, a descent right down to our level, without which no ascent would have been possible for us."[100] In response, Christians speak to one another the words of Psalm 121, "Let us go to the house of the Lord," as on a holy day when excitement is passed from one pilgrim to another like wildfire. Such people "going up" for such worship ascend both physically as pilgrims attending church, and in their hearts, by good desire, by clinging to him who descended to them. The rest of the ascent psalms' every word falls into place in accordance with this grammar.[101]

To sum up this section's analysis of Augustine's reading of the letter of scripture: only rarely does he express repugnance or dismay at the letter of a text, as Origen does so much more often. When he does so, he is driven to by the letter of another text. Yet more often he sees a frayed edge, a wrinkle, a gentle suggestion that one ought to read more deeply. Elsewhere a liturgical event spurs him to read in a deeper sense. In many cases the letter of scripture is simply already christological for Augustine, a procedure already announced in the *De doctrina christiana.* He is cued by a New Testament word or motif to a verbal or narratival link in the psalm to read the words there according to a particularly Christian grammar. This summary of our observations here opens up a peculiar question: in what sense is it possible to speak of Augustine as reading *allegorically* at all? In what sense is a Christian reading "another sense" than a literal one, if Augustine uses what we have called a "christological literalism?" If the letter of the Psalter is always already about Christ, what is there left for allegory to do? It is to this question we turn in the next section.

## What's Left for Allegory?

Augustine uses the description "allegory" with decreasing frequency as his career progresses. The reason could have been quite quotidian and rooted in his own historical context: "Be careful not to seize on the mention of allegory

---

100. On Psalm 119 in *EP* V, 499.
101. See Psalm 121 and following in *EP* VI, 13ff.

and think I am talking about music and dancing on the stage."[102] The word *allegoria* itself connoted theatrical performance, which Augustine elsewhere is keen to discourage his hearers from attending. Robert Bernard argues cogently that Augustine shifts toward using the word "figure" and the description "figurative" with greater frequency later in his career. Yet Augustine has no fear of using the word here in a positive sense alongside this warning. This sermon is dated to the late middle portion of his career, somewhere between 410 and 413.[103] His audience may have had the same theological concern as many readers in other historical ages of the church's life, including our own: that allegory signifies a play-acting that disguises textual truth. Augustine defends the term because of its biblical use (Galatians 4:24), and then describes what he means by it: "an allegory is a figurative mode of speech, so the figurative representation of a sacred mystery is an allegory."[104] In truth it is maddeningly difficult to get a hold on Augustine's technical language for his biblical exegesis — Henri de Lubac famously threw up his hands in despair at the effort. The decisive issue is not so much what Augustine described himself as doing in his exegesis as what he *did*.

We have already seen instances in which the letter of a text suggests for Augustine that he should read more deeply — either by a link with the New Testament, or by being patently impossible to read as it stands.[105] These, we have argued, perhaps against the grain of most scholarship, are in fact *literal* readings; that is, attempts to take the letter of scripture seriously (even if Augustine does so in ways we would not today regard as "literal," such as using the letter of the New Testament to make sense of that of the Old). In the cases that follow, Augustine often leaves the letter of the text in front of him behind for other biblical resources. We shall see the reasons he chooses to do so and attempt to make theological sense of them.

We spoke in Chapter 2 of Augustine's startling claim that scripture speaks more clearly of the church than of Christ. He sharpens this anti-Donatist polemic by giving an example from elsewhere in scripture. The story of the sacrifice of Isaac is a "symbol" of Christ, but an obscure one. Isaac is a dearly beloved only son, and he carries the wood for his own sacrifice. Both sonship and wood are obscure pointers to Christ. The ram is another symbol of

---

102. Psalm 103 (1) in *EP* V, 122.

103. Robert Bernard, *In Figura: Terminology Pertaining to Figurative Exegesis in the Works of Augustine of Hippo* (Ph.D. diss., Princeton University; Ann Arbor: University Microfilms, 1984). In discussing the date of this sermon, Fiedrowicz (*Psalmus Vox Totius Christi*, 436) lists Zarb's guess of 412, Rondet's of 411, La Bonnardiere's of 409, and Perler's of 411.

104. Psalm 103 (1) in *EP* V, 122-23.

105. Pages 6-77 above.

Christ, for "to be held fast by the horns is like a crucifixion."[106] Yet when the Abraham story speaks of the church, as in prophecies about his seed spreading to all the earth and blessing all nations, scripture "discards figurative language."[107] The Donatists should know better than to limit the geographic location of the church to Africa and thereby miss the Bible's literal insistence that the covenant community must be seen as ultimately universal. For they have the same Bible as the catholics, with the same clear witness to the worldwide reach of the church. This passage represents a pattern for Augustine's more strictly allegorical readings, whatever technical language he himself uses to describe his procedure hermeneutically. He often finds allegorical significance especially in *narrative* portions of scripture, such as the story of Abraham and Isaac. He will then point to ways the story "figures" Christ or "symbolizes" him, or whatever. Often he is cued to speak of such narratives by the psalms themselves, with their frequent mention of specific events in Israel's history. Other times, as we have seen here, he steps outside the bounds of the psalm and into a biblical narrative for a moment to illustrate a larger theological issue. The point to notice is this: with narrative portions of the psalms Augustine more readily speaks of the "obscurity" of scripture's representation of Christ, and the counterintuitive or allegorical manner in which scripture attests to him. The "obscurity" that Augustine confesses to in his christological reading of Genesis is a clue that he knows one must read this text in some "other sense" than the letter in order properly to see Christ there, and that such readings will be marked by obscurity.

Examples of allegorical readings of narrative portions of scripture abound in the *Enarrationes,* for the psalms frequently refer to narrative portions of scripture. For example, Cain and Abel appear in the *Enarrationes* in a fashion that would be greatly expanded in the *City of God* — as representatives of two

---

106. On Psalm 30 (3) in *EP* 341-42.

107. It is difficult to be clear linguistically here. In this book I have freely spoken of "allegorical" exegesis as any reading that would strike us moderns as a departure from the letter. I have tried to offer it as a term of approbation rather than of disdain. I myself use "allegory" more than "figure," the more preferred term now, simply because I think the word has been unnecessarily abused. I mistrust the effort to carve out a new word that is "good" over against a word commonly deemed "bad," as another effort scientifically to designate the viability of a hermeneutic in advance of seeing its fruit in actual exegesis. Yet as we saw in the subsection above, Augustine himself was often unaware he was reading allegorically when he offered christological readings. He was simply seeing the pattern of Christ in the letter of scripture. Here Augustine himself is more up front that he is offering readings of "obscure" letters of scripture that point to Christ. If he is unaware that he is being allegorical when he attends to the letter christologically in other places, here when he attends to narrative he is aware of the need to read "allegorically" and tells the reader he does so.

cities. Augustine lights on the fact that Cain after his banishment built a city that preceded the building of the holy city of Jerusalem by many years. There is a "profound mystery concealed in these events," one enlightened by Paul's teaching about the spiritual coming only after the physical in such places as 1 Corinthians 15:35-49.[108] All this is inspired by reflection on a psalm line that says simply, "yet they thought to refuse me honor." Augustine is clearly aware that he has to view this line through some sort of allegorical lens to read it in this way, as he points to the obscurity. Yet he thinks of another narrative connection to this obscure verse in the story of Joseph. The church has experienced a profound "reversal of fortunes" as it has passed from disrepute to honor in the empire — a reversal that was "spiritually prefigured" in the Joseph story.

Elsewhere, Abraham appears again as part of Augustine's reflection upon Christ's physical ancestry. "What was the meaning of that gesture when Abraham, about to send a trusty servant to find a wife for his only son, required the servant to swear to him and, in administering the oath, ordered the servant, 'Place your hand under my thigh, and so swear'?" This strange gesture is a reminder of the promise to Abraham that all nations would be blessed in him, and that his physical progeny would be the source of the world's blessing. Augustine is led to think of this story by a line that reads, "The hymns of David have failed." He follows with an exploration of Paul's understanding of Jews and gentiles in Romans 9–11.[109] In another instance, the psalmist's description that "your God has anointed you" reminds Augustine of the story of Jacob, and his anointing of a stone after seeing a vision. This event "prefigured" Christ, but obscurely — Jacob did not return to the area regularly to sacrifice, for example.[110] The odd story of Lot's wife being turned into a pillar of salt is linked by an imperative from the psalmist of "do not delay," which leads Augustine to remember that the original story was told "to season you, she was made an example for your sake, so that you may take courage and not linger tastelessly on the road."[111] An inscription "to David himself against Goliath" becomes a full-blown allegorical reading of that story, one that includes not only Christ but also Augustine's immediate hearers. David laid aside his burdensome armor and took five stones, as Christ laid aside those portions of the law that pointed to him, but "did not discard the law itself," symbolized in the number 5 for the books of the Torah. Hitting Goliath in the forehead with the one stone suggests the place where pagans have not the sign of the cross that the baptized have, and

108. Psalm 61 in *EP* III, 209.
109. On Psalm 72 in *EP* III, 470-71.
110. Psalm 44 in *EP* II, 297.
111. Psalm 69 in *EP* III, 411.

the single stone suggests the unity of the law that is love. Finally David cuts off Goliath's head with his own sword, just as the devil is undone with by his own malice. The title was full of "mystery," now laid bare.[112]

How does this sort of exegesis differ from that which we have described as "christologically literal" above? It is keyed by attention to the narrative portions of scripture that Augustine then opens up for christological reading. He knows these references are more "obscure." In these instances Augustine momentarily leaves behind the letters of the psalm before him and reads from some other portion of scripture. This departure is often cued by some detail in the letter or narrative contour of the psalm. Having made his point from this other text, he returns to the rigorous attention to the letter of the Psalter we have come to expect from him. Properly speaking, "allegory" here refers to an offering of a sense that is other than what the words read in isolation might suggest. In contrast, literal exegesis continues to attend to the particular words at hand, even as it gives them a christological sense. Notice what this definition of letter and of allegory does as opposed to more conventional ones. It implies no denigration of allegory — if anything the word here means something like "homiletical excursus," or a temporary break from expository preaching, for which every preacher hopes to have some license.

Here I call "allegorical" moves in Augustine that might normally be called "typological," especially in the wake of Jean Daniélou and of R. P. C. Hanson.[113] Both of these authors see allegory as a particularly non-Christian thing, though for different reasons. In contrast to it, typology is taken to be rooted in the historical particularities of salvation history. The examples we give here are indeed rooted in Israel's history, from Abraham down to David, as these stories obscurely figure the mystery of Christ. And they are his most obviously allegorical readings — those in which the relationship to the letter is tenuous, but the link to the story of Israel and church remains strong. Augustine seems to use no more technically specific language for them than he uses for any other acts of exegesis in the *Enarrationes*. Yet they may properly be called "allegorical," for here the text of the psalm is temporarily left behind to make a wider point meant for homiletical edification in preaching *about*

---

112. On Psalm 143 in *EP* VI, 360-63.

113. Daniélou was primarily concerned to designate allegory as a Jewish reading practice, one alien to the more specifically Christian one of typology. Hanson denigrates allegory as a Greek hermeneutic, divorced from Christianity's proper care of letter and history. See Daniélou's *From Shadows to Reality: Studies in the Biblical Typology of the Fathers*, trans. W. Hibberd (London: Burns & Oats, 1960), and R. P. C. Hanson, *Allegory and Event: A Study in the Sources and Significance of Origen's Interpretation of Scripture*, 2nd ed. (Louisville: Westminster/John Knox, 2002).

the psalm at hand. And here is the point they make, if I can summarize three major arguments of this book in a single paragraph: allegory is, properly speaking, the application of the biblical text to its hearers in a different way. A christological literalism applies the words directly, an allegorical departure driven by a narrative link applies them indirectly. That is the "sense" in which an allegorical reading is "other." Allegory names the way a preacher appeals to the broader narrative of scripture with which to draw hearers into scripture's story. It is a variant on the specifically *participatory* style of reading that we have examined in these pages. With allegory the words on the page are applied to hearers' lives through connection to the broader scriptural story. Allegory then is *evangelical*. It is about the entry of readers into the words, images, and story of scripture.[114] The primary sense of a passage from the psalms is always Christ, the whole Christ, head and members, as we have seen. The derivative sense that we are here calling "allegorical" is a text's indirect application to the lives of those listening to Augustine. We have here left behind Augustine's own vocabulary — as we have seen his own technical descriptions of his exegesis are less than helpful for categorizing what he does with the open page in front of him. We have however captured his spirit, over against modern categorizations of patristic exegesis and modern practices of biblical interpretation. The text literally refers to Christ, the *res* of all of scripture's *signa*. Derivatively, allegorically, it refers to us.

It is surely significant that Augustine tends to leave behind christological literalism for allegorical application of texts to hearers when prompted by narrative signals in the psalm. These allegorical moves signal for us anew the uniqueness of the Psalter for Augustine. The psalms are direct commerce between Israel and God. Christians naturally read their cries of jubilation and lament and everything in between through Christian lenses. Yet strict narrative portions of scripture may not lend themselves to christological literalism so readily as the psalms. To say that Gideon's fleece shows the change in relationship between Jew and gentile, or that the five smooth stones represent the gentiles' taking up of Torah in a different way, is to offer an interesting reading that can spark the imagination and desire of a sermon's hearers in ways

---

114. It is much like Hans Frei's description in *The Eclipse of Biblical Narrative* (New Haven: Yale University Press, 1974) of scripture absorbing the reader's world rather than the reader translating the scriptures' into some other idiom. Frei himself had no time for what he viewed as allegory, employing the common history-of-religions description of the Reformers' distinction between typology (as good) and allegory (as bad). Yet I think Frei's descriptions do well at describing Augustine's procedure here, in his most "allegorical" moments. Nor is it any accident that so many younger Yale School theologians are interested in figural exegesis: Dawson, Davis, Marshall, Reno, Radner, Rogers, and more.

we described in Chapter 3. But it is a strange reading. One can take it or leave it. It is held together more by the church's continuity in identity and history with Israel than by the words themselves. Here the *Enarratio* dealing with these narratives merely shows something about Christ. It does not engineer the christological exchange itself. As we have seen, through most of the *Enarrationes* Augustine reads the church's praying of the psalms and God's provision of scripture as themselves instantiating anew the divine exchange that is salvation. The reading of narrative portions of scripture participate in that exchange as well, to be sure, yet their relationship to it is somewhat less direct than with the psalms' own liturgical trajectory. One can adopt the five stones as a sign of gentile inclusion or not; one cannot but read lament as *kenosis,* and exultation as *theosis.*

The description of "allegory" here may seem a deviation from my description of "christological literalism" above, in which the words of the psalm refer directly to Christ's whole body, including his members in the church.[115] Yet this need not be so. To say that allegory is evangelical is to say that Augustine has great latitude for applying lines of psalms or whole psalms to the lives of his hearers as part of a general invitation to them to live as Christians. Allegory is homiletical exposition, done in detail. In the examples of the biblical stories above, Augustine rereads the beloved narratives for glimpses of Christ or the church, whether clearly or obscurely offered. We should see that as he does this he is not overly concerned with names for the particular type of reading being offered, nor even for the "way the words go" on the page. He is looking for something to convert his hearers, either for the first time, or more deeply innumerable times, into the mystery of Christ. Just so, the deepest purposes of scripture are fulfilled. Augustine offers his expositions in an effort to spark wonder at the beauty of Christ in a place unexpected in scripture, and so giving greater delight in following. "Our job," Augustine says in a moment of self-disclosure, "is to act on whatever is signified by these similes, not to spend too much time on debating whether they describe things that really happen."[116] Elsewhere, when the psalm itself announces God's admoni-

---

115. Worse, it suggests that words that apply to the *totus Christus* do not apply to "us," when of course for Augustine they do. What I am pushing toward experimentally here is a description such as this: christological literalism and allegory here name two different ways of applying the words to the body of Christ.

116. Psalm 66 in *EP* III, 322. This is not to say that Augustine does not assume that events happen as narrated in scripture — he does, far more regularly than we moderns (see Psalm 33 [1] in *EP* II, 13, where Augustine insists that the Psalm "derived from an event that really occurred"). It is simply to say that what *matters* is not so much the historicity of the occurrence but its reverberation in the lives of Augustine's hearers.

tion to "hearken to my law, O my people," Augustine insists, "This is the whole purpose of all that is narrated. These events took place as types and symbols, and whatever they signify can be realized spiritually in human beings."[117] The types and symbols of the Bible are to be immediately applied to Christ and the church, the cornerstone of Augustinian psalm exegesis. Then derivatively, but crucially, they are to apply to the lives of scripture's immediate readers and hearers. Exegesis is about closing the gap between what scripture says the church is and what the church currently is, on the way to its celestial destination. The delight that comes from allegory inches hearers forward just a bit toward that goal. Any form of biblical reading, whether for Augustine or any other patristic exegete, is not finally about meanings or texts or senses, if these words are meant in an abstract fashion. It is finally about the pursuit of a certain sort of life. If we miss this, we miss the entire heart of Augustine's exegetical endeavor.

This rigorously participatory exegesis is visible throughout the *Enarrationes*. In Psalm 25 Augustine defends a counter-conventional reading of the line, "I have not sat down in the assembly of fools," by arguing that "sitting" is genuinely taken to mean "compliance and collusion." At the Council of Carthage in 411 the Donatists took this verse as their rationale for not literally *sitting* in their chairs! Augustine replied that the psalm also says, "Neither will I go in with those who act unjustly," showing that the Donatists, who were presumably already in the doors (even if not seated), had acted out of concert with their own psalm exegesis. Notice that both Augustine and the Donatists take the psalm to apply directly to church life — whether to sit or go in with those deemed unjust. Neither makes our contemporary move of denigrating the particular words as "mere" imagery. The life of the church is directed in these pages; the only question is how precisely to interpret the details.[118]

---

117. Psalm 77 in *EP* IV, 103.

118. Psalm 25 (2) in *EP* I, 262-63. A parallel is the earlier debates during the Arian controversies over Proverbs 8:22, where Wisdom claims to have been brought forth as the first of God's works. Anti-Nicene readers see this as clear biblical evidence of the Logos' status as a creature, pro-Nicene ones must read it as a description of the *kenosis* of the Logos, but both agree it is indeed about Jesus. We would be hard-pressed to find a modern interpreter who would work with the same assumption. Just so, our christology is impoverished as well as our biblical exegesis.

In a volume edited by David Ford and Graham Stanton, a biblical and patristic scholar are paired together presumably to juxtapose modern and ancient ways of reading the "wisdom" described in Proverbs 8. Paul Joyce disparages any christological reading of the figure of wisdom, saying that such a reading makes it "hard to escape the sense that the biblical text is being distorted and even abused." Yet Joyce welcomes all manner of other fresh readings of the text in new historical contexts. The only sort of reading he rules out is a christological one. Frances Young is clearly meant to defend (or at least render intelligible) christological readings in re-

Augustine's exposition of Psalm 3 early in his career can give some insight into his procedure here. He reads the entire psalm with reference to Christ, as we might expect. Then he says, "This Psalm can also be understood with reference to Christ in another way, namely, that the whole Christ is speaking . . ." before ascribing it to the church. After these *two* christological readings, Augustine writes that "each one of us can also" apply this psalm individually to our own lives. In this instance the first two readings refer to Christ, and the third, based upon the two former, is an application to each reader.[119] Later in his career Augustine's *totus Christus* becomes more unified, and there is less of a transition from Christ to the church, yet the procedure of exegesis remains the same.[120] The way a psalm refers to Christ is unfolded, and then generally toward the end of an *Enarratio* the particular way this psalm refers to the lives of those listening is displayed. As Augustine writes at the end of a long exposition on Psalm 93, he wants his hearers not only to discuss and remember what they have heard, but also to "order your lives in conformity with it. A good life, conducted according to the commandments of God, is like a pen that writes on the heart what has been heard. . . . Write it on your hearts and in your conduct, and it will never be effaced."[121] Exegesis, *writing*, is finally done on the lives of hearers.

As Augustine applies texts to his readers, his allegorical readings have a remarkably consistent feature. They are *incarnationally* shaped. Augustine only rarely offers us allegories that are not christological. The few instances in which he does offer non-christological allegories include his reading of the whip of cords in John's Gospel. It reminds him of the way anger can twist a soul into an unbreakable knot of sin.[122] Judas reminds him of the Jews in Psalm 108. The ba-

---

sponse, yet she does not. For mostly textual reasons she disputes patristic claims that this text should be read christologically in the way Athanasius does. So, for Young, "the Lord created me at the beginning of his works" cannot apply to the human nature of Christ. For her, Eusebius is a hero for consulting the Hebrew text on the key word "created" and for interpreting neither along Arian nor Athanasian lines. Young seems here strangely modern in her praise of Eusebius for appealing to the "original" meaning of the Hebrew. Surely a patristic hermeneutic that would hold that the "wisdom of God," understood from such places as 1 Corinthians 1:25 to be Christ himself, might be helpful here. Yet, strangely, Young has little more place for such a reading than Joyce. See their essays in Ford and Stanton, eds., *Reading Texts, Seeking Wisdom*.

119. Psalm 3 in *EP* I, 83.

120. Michael Cameron makes this case in *Augustine's Construction of Figurative Exegesis Against the Donatists in the Enarrationes In Psalmos*. Based on Cameron's work we might say that Augustine grows *less* allegorical and indirect with his exegesis and more christologically literal as his career progresses.

121. *EP* IV, 408, in an echo of Jeremiah 31:33.

122. Psalm 139 in *EP* VI, 290.

bies whose heads are to be bashed refer to whining desires in the infamous Psalm 136. Occasionally, early in his career, Augustine suggests a psalm could be reread christologically at the end of his exposition, but then does not himself do so, in Psalm 7 and Psalm 17. Occasionally the words on the page inveigh against a christological reading. Psalm 87's description that "all day long I stretched out my hands to you" has deep exegetical roots in the tradition as a description of Christ on the cross. Yet Augustine is puzzled — Christ did not hang on the cross a full day, and the scriptures concentrate more on a three-day long *pasch*, which is not actually three calendar days. He decides instead it should refer with less specificity to Christ's unflagging doing of good all his life.[123] In Psalm 118's line, "Your word is a lamp for my feet," Augustine asks, "Does it mean the Word who was God-with-God in the beginning? . . . No, that cannot be right, for the Word is a light, not a lamp." The words rule out a christological interpretation, and so must be taken to refer to the scriptures — a light derivative of *the* Light.[124] The most unsatisfying portions of the *Enarrationes* are long portions that never mention christology, such as those referring to Psalms 26 and 48. These are taken to refer directly to the spiritual state of believers without much effort at christological mediation, and just so they fail to shed much light on the psalm. These exceptions can be attended to in a single paragraph here, since the vast majority of exegesis in the *Enarrationes* has a definitively incarnational character. It is this that keeps Augustinian allegory, even as we have narrowly defined it here, from "floating off" into absurdity or from being a wax nose in the hand of the exegete to move in whatever direction she fancies. The allegories Augustine offers are no more absurd, no more play-acting by the interpreter, than is the incarnation itself.

We can see this "incarnational shape" to allegory in the simplest of exegetical procedures: slogging through a grammatical problem, rooted in the difficulties of translation and manuscript transmission. Augustine stared down this unbelievable sentence in Psalm 67: "If you sleep in the middle of your allotted inheritances, the silvery wings of the dove, and between its shoulders in the fresh sheen of gold, will be made white by the snow on Zalmon." Obviously this is not a complete sentence. It could be translated somewhat differently to force it into comprehensibility, and each translation would create a different meaning. One translation would suggest the church's spoils tradition in which the "inheritances" taken from the Egyptians are pagan converts themselves, who beautify the house they go to join. In a second, it could be a reference to these people's actual conversions, when they are "made white" as

123. In *EP* IV, 265. Clearly there can be grounds for ruling out a christological reading.
124. Psalm 118 (23) in *EP* V, 450.

they come up from baptism. Third, the wings of the dove could refer to those borne up to higher things as part of church life. Fourth, the silver could refer to those purified through the refining fire of disciplinary instruction. Fifth, the word "middle" suggests to Augustine the need for the interpreter to show the balance, the concord, between the two testaments, in the "middle" of which he stands. Sixth, to sleep between the (two) allotted inheritances suggests the differing promises in the two covenants — one offering earthly happiness, the other eternal, with the latter promises obviously more important than the former. No wonder a grammatical and exegetical tangle like this could leave even Augustine wondering where he can find a good Hebraicist! Finally we see the seventh — that Zalmon means "Shadow." Here we see an explicitly christological shape in the reading Augustine takes to be the most satisfactory. Christians are not distinguished by any merit of their own, but rather by a sort of shadow "fame," through forgiveness of sins. A shadow is created by a combination of light and a body — just as the light of the world becomes incarnate in a body. In these interpretations, the sorts of "fanciful" attempts at coherence noted in options one through six find their resolution in the incarnational image of the seventh. This incarnational reading, in turn, makes the previous six possible for Augustine. They are not left behind but caught up in the incarnational *coup-de-grace*. That is to say that all the benefits of the spoils in the church, being borne up and purged, and mediating between the promises of the two testaments, all these things find their source and purpose in Christ, whose incarnation makes this sort of exegesis possible.[125]

When Augustine hears a significant biblical word or phrase or motif, his lexical imagination runs it through the entirety of the scriptural story, anchored as it is in Christ, until he thinks of a meaning supportable by the words on the page. When he hears "poor," he thinks of Paul's description of the incarnation in terms of wealth and poverty (2 Corinthians 8:9).[126] When he hears the "depths of the sea" he thinks of the depths to which Christ sunk in the crucifixion.[127] A "snake" naturally suggests evil and death, but also a strange sort of healing, by a glance at one in the wilderness (Numbers 21:9;

---

125. *EP* III, 338-43. We should note that this exposition seems to have been written for publication rather than transcribed by hearers, perhaps to complete the exposition of the entire Psalter, and so has a more academic and less homiletical style.

126. The destitution announced in Psalm 101:10, "the bread I ate was ashes, and my drink I would dilute with weeping" brings Augustine to think of 2 Corinthians 8:9, "though he was rich, for your sake he became poor, so that by his poverty you might be enriched." That is, an expression of utter desolation is a sign of the depth to which God the Son descends in his incarnation. Psalm 101 (1) in *EP* V, 45.

127. Psalm 68 in *EP* III, 371.

John 3:14), and so "being saved from death by believing in one who died."[128] The litany of allegories disciplined by the shape of the incarnation could include a reference to all the several hundred *Enarrationes*. The point is this: the incarnational shape of these allegories is their "control." It is the primary move one grows accustomed to in reading Augustine's exegesis, and it is the primary means by which we can judge whether an allegory is successful or not — if it conforms to the shape of the incarnation.

Many of these features we describe as "Augustinian allegory" were no less present in our description of his treatment of the *sensus literalis*. That is precisely the point. In Augustine's own practice, no less than in his description of his practice, the line between "allegory" and "letter" tends to blur. He himself signifies this blur with his effusion of terms for exegesis: "figure," "symbol," "mystery," and so forth. What we have tried to show here is the general shape of his exegesis. These words before the exegete refer first to the *totus Christus*, and last to the hearers of the sermon. Exegesis is not first and last about texts, though of course it is about them too. It is primarily about lives shaped in faithful ways. If Augustine shows less concern about accuracy in terminology than we would like, so much the worse for us. We can still imitate his procedure, and that is to read the text of the psalm with the presumption that the letters refer to Christ and the church, and just so, they refer to the people now reading, expositing, and listening. What Augustine's own exegetical practice shows is that modern discussions of what is "literal" or "allegorical" as though these were nothing more than a textual or hermeneutical matter are profoundly different exercises than actual patristic exegesis. The fathers read scripture to refer to the lives of those listening with reference to Christ. It is the rooting of biblical hermeneutics in the incarnation and in lives shaped after its pattern that finally keeps any charge of arbitrariness from sticking.

Perhaps the two claims we have made in this section — that allegory involves the application of texts to the lives of readers, and that it has a decidedly incarnational shape — can best be seen by looking at Augustine's allegorical readings of *New Testament* texts. It is not obvious that this is something Augustine ought to do. Allegory is supposed to be about particularly Christian readings of the Old Testament. Not a few contemporary apologists for allegory have argued that its application to the New Testament would be inappropriate.[129] Yet Augustine himself practices something that

---

128. On Psalm 73 in *EP* IV, 19.

129. Robert Wilken argues this in a passage that echoes de Lubac: "In its original sense, Christian allegory as an interpretive technique is a way of interpreting the Old Testament in light of the new things that have taken place with the coming of Christ. The New Testament

looks much like allegorical reading of the New Testament. On the other hand, some other recent apologists for allegory, resting their arguments on postmodern love of play of interpretation without constraints, have simply assumed the New Testament should be legible in this fashion, without serious theological argumentation for their position.[130] Augustine rests in the middle of these two. He seems not at all unwilling to read the New Testament allegorically in places, in ways that are incarnationally shaped, and aimed to apply texts to readers lives. For example, he reads Jesus' puzzling comment about the "woe" that is due "those who are pregnant in those days, or suckling their babies," to refer to those full of hope for some worldly thing, or those who have obtained it and are now nursing it, either of whom could be in danger at the judgment.[131] Both should shift their desire elsewhere. Jesus' pastorally troublesome comment that enough faith can make a mountain leap into the sea is read to refer to Christ, the Lord's mountain (Isaiah 2:2), leaping up and leaving the Jews to go to the nations, whose tumultuous nature is represented by the sea.[132] The Baptist's warning that Abraham's children could be raised from stones *has happened*, for the gentiles used to worship stones, and so can rightly be named by what they worshiped.[133] In a favorite exegetical move,

does not need an allegorical interpretation because it speaks directly about Christ. . . . The spiritual meaning of the New Testament events is the literal meaning" (Wilken, "In Defense of Allegory," *Modern Theology* 14, no. 2 [April 1998]: 201).

130. Graham Ward faults Henri de Lubac for limiting "allegory" to the interpretation of Old Testament events in light of the Christ event. Ward counters that God is not an event, as though finished and done with, but continual Act. He locates the need for Christian allegory in an understanding of God as continually revealing God's self and readers as journeying toward this God through "the mystical doctrine of the mysteries" (words he quotes from de Lubac against the overly static view of allegory in de Lubac's formal definition). "Revelation is progressive and temporal, for it develops in, through and as the vocation to personhood, to move towards becoming a person in Christ. . . . Analogy cannot present a frozen glimpse of the eternal truth. It is part of a larger and more dynamic symbolics" ("Allegoria: Reading as a Spiritual Exercise," 288). Earlier in the same essay he notes the double *entendre* present in both the Greek and English sense of "hand over" *(paradidomai)* as a suggestion that every interpretation, every "giving over" of Christ anew, is also a sort of betrayal. For Ward, scriptural exegesis is rooted in a postmodern philosophical understanding of meaning as pluriform and at least partially *misleading*, without intrinsic relationship to the work of God in giving the scriptures and fulfilling them in his incarnation. It is unclear then why we should not do allegory on New Testament texts at our own whim like the ancient Gnostics. Nor is there here sensitivity to the need for a christological plumb line against which to measure our exegesis' faithfulness.

131. Psalm 39 in *EP* II, 221, referring to Mark 13:17.

132. Psalm 45 in *EP* II, 314, Matthew 17:20 and parallels.

133. Psalm 46 in *EP* II, 332, Matthew 3:9. *HarperCollins Study Bible* notes here that "raising up *children to Abraham* from stones may allude to Gentiles (see Matthew 1:1)." Matthew notes by Dennis C. Duling (New York: HarperCollins, 1993), 1863.

the story of the healing pool in John 5:1-9 is read allegorically in every detail: the five porticoes represent the five books of Moses, which claim to heal, but can only heal one person at a time. That singleness is a glimpse at the unity of the church. The "disturbance" of the water is an image for what happens in Israel when Christ comes. Now anyone may be healed by coming "down" in their humility, into the water, to be made whole.[134] Elsewhere as Augustine reads one of the psalms' expressions of the momentary nature of trouble measured against the depth of joy, he reflects, "Look at the price we pay — a penny to gain everlasting treasures, a paltry mite of labor to win unbelievable rest," effectively placing a rhetorical "us" in the place of the widow in Jesus' storytelling.[135] In a comment on the psalm phrase "he repaid for me," Augustine seizes on the episode of Christ paying his and Peter's taxes from the mouth of a fish. He has Peter fish out a "stater," that is, two didrachmas, or the equivalent of four drachma coins. Now he has enough in place to offer a christologically shaped allegory: "Ours is indeed the first fish to be hooked, the first fish to be caught with a hook, the first to rise from the sea, the first-born from the dead." And enough, in the form of the number four, to say more: the four evangelists make it so we are no longer debtors as they render to us one who owed nothing, yet paid in our stead.[136] In an extraordinary mixing of New Testament metaphors, Augustine marvels in one place about Christ, "Did he not light the lamp of his flesh when he hung upon the cross, searching for his lost coin?"[137] This sort of exegesis may rightly be called "homiletical playfulness": Augustine seizes on an odd detail, normally at the end of an exposition, to read allegorically for the delight and edification of his hearers.[138] Yet that is precisely the nature of allegory, here performed on the New Testament, yet with no loss of christological shape.[139]

Perhaps even more daringly from our vantage, Augustine can even take great liberty by paraphrasing the actual wording of New Testament texts. In one place he wrestles with Christ's conclusion to his own parable that "many are called, but only few are chosen." Strangely, the story he has just told in Matthew 22:1-14 has only a single man being thrown from the wedding banquet for lacking the proper clothes. Augustine asks, "Would it not be more ac-

---

134. Psalm 70 (1) in *EP* IV, 433.

135. On Psalm 93 in *EP* IV, 403, Mark 12:41-44 and Luke 21:1-4.

136. On Psalm 137 in *EP* VI, 254-55, Matthew 17:23-26.

137. On Psalm 103 (4) in *EP* V, 169, Matthew 5:14 fused with Luke 15:8-10.

138. The phrase, "homiletical playfulness," is Robert Wilken's. As we saw in Chapter 3 on aesthetics, the delight of play is no insignificant matter for Augustine theologically!

139. Even if, perhaps, the execution of allegorical reading is here a bit more flat than when Augustine's hermeneutics become more incarnationally full-blown(see below).

curate to say, 'all were invited, many are chosen, but one is excluded?'"[140] Elsewhere, Augustine gives a long paraphrase of Christ's terrifying pronouncement, "I never knew you": this "implies, 'you do not fit into my body; you do not keep to my rules. You are like lapses of taste in a work of art, but I am art itself, free from all fault, and it is from me that anyone learns to avoid faults.'"[141] That's quite a paraphrase! Philosophically Augustine must explain how Christ can claim not to know someone when everything is created through him, and he lacks no knowledge. The statement has to be given christological import. For our purposes, the more striking thing to note is that Augustine feels such liberty paraphrasing Jesus' own words and scripture itself. The point of interpretation is not then to divine what might have been meant in Jesus' own context, nor in the evangelists', it is rather to say what Jesus is saying to the church now. To that end the preacher has a great deal of freedom with the actual words on the page. In a final striking example, Augustine wrestles with Jesus' claim that it is easier for a camel to pass through the eye of a needle than for a rich man to enter the kingdom. He notes that Abraham was a rich man, and that Paul condemns not so much riches as love of riches. In light of those two hagiographical examples he asks, "Will they get through the eye of the needle? Most certainly they will, for there was One who went through it first, One on whom no one could have laid the burden of his passion, as a camel is loaded, if he had not first lowered himself to the ground. He told us himself that 'what is impossible for human beings is easy for God.'"[142] Is this reading literal? It attends to the words on the page in great detail. Is it allegorical? One might not have guessed at the way Christ would be witnessed to with these particular words, yet he is, and the particular shape of this bit of exegesis is incarnational — focused on his *kenosis* and our *theosis*. In either case the words are taken to refer first to Christ, then to the readers and listeners, so that their lives may also be shaped incarnationally. Whether we call it "literal" or "allegorical," and either term may indeed apply, this is Augustine's own pattern in exegesis.

## Sacramental Exegesis

Christian worship that does not rotate, ellipse-like, around the two poles of preaching and sacrament, is an anomaly. Christians ought not to worship reg-

---

140. On Psalm 61 in *EP* III, 207.
141. On Psalm 34 (2) in *EP* II, 60, Matthew 25:12.
142. On Psalm 51 in *EP* II, 27, Matthew 19:24 and parallels.

ularly without both sacrament and preaching. Yet many do, especially in Protestant churches in our day, or in morning prayer in Augustine's, when he preached the *Enarrationes*. Yet the anomalous nature of such worship is shown in the fact that Augustine frequently uses sacramental language and imagery while preaching. As we have seen, Augustine often points to the liturgical invitation *sursum corda* as a rhetorical point in his preaching. Even when the eucharist is not to be celebrated in a given liturgical setting, it is still the heart of worship, frequently referred to and missed when absent, like a missing matriarch at a family table. For Augustine, Christian preaching, and just so Christian exegesis of the Bible, finds its home in sacramental practice. We might even be so bold as to say Christian exegesis is commentary on Christian liturgical practice. This last section of the chapter will show just how this is so.

Occasional comments shed light on Augustine's own posture toward scripture, especially in the Bible's role as the source for his preaching. He beseeches his listeners to approach scripture with him in an attitude of "reverent curiosity."[143] Readers must be curious enough to notice what puzzles, whether grammatical or narratival or theological. Then, their exegetical energy must be spent in the task of seeing how this surprising letter fits with the faith to which both reader and listener hold with such reverence: how these *signa* fit to the already known *res*. In many instances Augustine signals there could be abundant possibilities for multiple meanings. We have recently seen one where he describes as many as seven possibilities. Not infrequently Augustine warns his hearers that another reader could perhaps come up with more or better readings than he has or can.[144] Yet this polite demurring that others could do better and the suggestion that these texts must be approached with reverence hardly mean scripture's words should receive passive or meek acceptance from Christian readers. Augustine positively wrestles with scripture, like Jacob at the Jabbok. He bends it now this way, now that, in an effort to see it yield its meaning. He advises his hearers to be "assiduous creditors" in their approach to God through scripture. God has made extravagant promises to his people, though these have not yet seen their eschatological fulfillment. Christians should demand what they have coming to them: greater love and knowledge of God through liturgical practice, like the preaching they currently hear. "Even if you

143. On Psalm 34 (2) in *EP* II, 62.

144. "Some other person may produce a better interpretation, for the obscurity of the scriptures is such that a passage scarcely ever yields a single meaning only. But whatever interpretation emerges, it must conform to the rule of faith. Let us not be jealous of those with more powerful minds than our own, nor despair because we are so small. I am expounding to you, beloved ones, whatever seems right to us, but I do not want to close your ears against others, who may perhaps have better things to say." Psalm 74 in *EP* IV, 50.

are small or weak, exact the promised mercy. Haven't you noticed how the young lambs butt their mothers' udders with their heads to get the milk they need?"[145] As he advises his hearers to storm heaven in search of divine meaning, he invites no less zeal in the effort to *be* the subject of the psalms. With regard to the one who "longs for springs of water" in Psalm 41, Augustine asks, "Why bother to inquire any further who it is, when it is within your power to be yourself the answer to the question?"[146] As we have seen, many figural readings of scripture begin with reference to Christ and end with reference to us, as when he explores the word "foundation," notes its New Testament use as a christological term, and then turns to his hearers, to whom he defines it as a "squared stone, which a Christian ought to resemble. A Christian does not topple over, whenever temptation strikes."[147] This sort of interpretation is finally about the shaping of lives by scripture, not solely about texts in themselves. Elsewhere when Augustine admonishes his hearers to be like stones, he insists that psalms are not so much chanted vocally as vocationally: "let any such person sing the verses that follow, not so much with the tongue as by the honesty of a life. . . ."[148] When this prevalent exegetical motif comes up elsewhere, Augustine writes, "All the stones that make up the house need to understand what they have sung." Exegesis is *praise seeking understanding,* or in this case — stones learning how to become stones.[149] Exegesis occurs as Christians reflect on what is happening in the church's scripture-soaked liturgy.

The descriptions here are rooted in an account of theological language that occasionally shows on the surface of the *Enarrationes*. Its contours are familiar to anyone who has worked with Augustine's description of language in more famous works such as the *De doctrina christiana*. He occasionally offers up brief theologies of analogy, descriptions of the metaphorical nature of God-talk, as when he comments on the psalm verse, "with you is the fount of life, and in your light we see light." He reflects, "In our world a fountain is one thing, and light another; not so there. The reality that is a fountain is light also; you may call it what you will, *because it is not what you call it.*"[150] Whatever description one might use for God — here quite biblically central images such as light and fountain — God is *not* that, so one ought to feel a great deal of freedom to use a full range of biblical images. Apophatic theology opens up kataphatic theological speech here. If God were one thing, directly

145. On Psalm 39 in *EP* II, 197.
146. On Psalm 41 in *EP* II, 239.
147. On Psalm 86 in *EP* IV, 249.
148. On Psalm 111 in *EP* V, 292.
149. On Psalm 95 in *EP* IV, 423.
150. On Psalm 35 in *EP* II, 86; emphasis added.

namable by human speech, all terms but that one would be wrong.[151] Scripture's own God-talk shows this cannot be so. Less unequivocal theological speech would stumble over the New Testament's ascription to Christ of status as both the "foundation" (1 Corinthians 3:11) and the "cornerstone" (Ephesians 2:20) of the church: "in the buildings we know, the same stone cannot be at the base and the summit."[152] The trouble does not stop there, since Christ is also a shepherd and a door and any number of other objects throughout the New Testament. Augustine is unworried: "since the Godhead is immediately present everywhere, symbols of it may be drawn from everywhere, and it can be entirely present in the symbols because it is properly speaking none of these things."[153] Here we see a metaphysical premise undergirding a nascent theology of language. God is omnipresent, and any good thing God has created may bear witness to him, if it is kept clearly in mind that God is not directly to be identified with any one of them. Thus far this theology of language might fit comfortably into a typically modern scheme like Sallie McFague's, whereby all of our language is derivative, so no one may claim any exclusive or exhaustive revelation of the divine.[154] Yet this is not the last word for Augustine on language's reference to God. For the final piece of his theology of language is incarnational. Even if anything created may properly be used of God since it is all equally *not God,* we still need some more specific direction in what to say and what not to, in how to use material images for God to better or worse effect. We find precisely that in the incarnation. Augustine hints at this relationship between metaphysics and exegesis as he reads the troubling phrase that says God is "great and terrible to all who *surround* him." How precisely can an immaterial God be surrounded? "We must understand it in this way: he who is present everywhere willed to be born according to the flesh in a particular place, to pass his life in one nation, to be crucified in a unique place, to rise from one special location, to ascend to heaven from one particular place."[155] God is everywhere, yet not to be identified exclusively with any one thing — save the incarnation, and so the

---

151. As in the Eunomians' insistence on "unbegotten," as the proper name for God, thereby ruling the Son's divinity out of court.

152. On Psalm 86 in *EP* IV, 248.

153. *EP* IV, 248.

154. Sallie McFague, *Metaphorical Theology: Models of God in Religious Language* (Philadelphia: Fortress, 1982). I am indebted here to Verna Harrison's criticism of McFague in "The Relationship Between Apophatic and Kataphatic Theology," *Pro Ecclesia* 4 (1996): 318-32.

155. On Psalm 88 (1) in *EP* IV, 280. He explains the phrase by saying Christ did all these things in an Israel surrounded by gentiles, who would then be the object of the church's missionary outreach.

church. It is by matching the contour of an image to the *kenosis* of the Son of God that we learn whether speech has fittingly described God or not.

The fact that it can so describe God is nothing short of miraculous. Augustine the rhetor began his Christian career astounded that knowledge of God is ever communicated between two people. He imagined that it must be an unexplainable miracle when such a process takes place (not an uncommon observation for frustrated teachers on all levels!).[156] He grows in his reflection to see that human speaking of a word, the giving of physical life to an immaterial idea in the mind, is a little incarnation of sorts, patterned on Jesus' incarnation that gives all meaning. Likewise, the love that allows a disciple truly to know a subject is patterned on the pouring out of the love of the Spirit into the hearts of those in the church. Language is shaped after a divine pattern, which is no accident because it only exists among creatures out of the gratuitous goodness of God. As Augustine grows in his understanding of language he progresses from using older categories that specify three or four levels of meaning in a text (quoted ever after by medieval and other scholastic interpreters) to a more fully sacramental theology of scripture. The Bible is a material, created thing that through liturgical action comes to be a *locus* of God's saving power. The materiality of the sacrament, no less than the words on the page and the events they narrate, matter: "all these things quite clearly did happen. . . . No one will deny that . . . [yet] there is far more good in the reality symbolized than in the symbol itself."[157]

Scholars are quick and correct to point out that Augustine uses *sacramentum* frequently to describe a far wider range of ecclesial activities than the Roman Catholic Church's seven sacraments or Protestant churches' two. It can be used to describe "Easter, Easter's octave, Pentecost, the sign of the cross, spiritual songs, bowing of the head, contemplation, the great fasts, penitential garments, taking off of shoes, the rites of the catechumenate, entry into the period of being *competentes,* exorcisms, transmission of the *symbolum,* the font, salt, penance, laying on of hands, reconciliation, the eucharistic prayer, the Lord's prayer, and many other things."[158] Among these other things are the words of scripture. The name change in the inscription of Psalm 33 to which we have referred several times is a *sacramentum,* the reason for which should prompt careful investigation.[159] The ascription of several

---

156. For these claims see *De doctrina christiana,* trans. D. W. Robertson as *On Christian Doctrine* (Upper Saddle River, NJ: Prentice Hall, 1958), especially the preface and book I.

157. On Psalm 77 in *EP* IV, 93.

158. Emmanuel J. Cutrone, "Sacraments," in Fitzgerald, ed., *Augustine Through the Ages,* 741-47, 742.

159. *EP* II, 15.

psalms to "the sons of Korah" points to "a sweet mystery [*sacramentum*], hinting at a holy meaning hidden under a sign."[160] Elsewhere he exults, "These are great mysteries. Sacred signs [*sacramenta*] are here, wonderful, profound, fraught with mystery. How delightful it is to discover them."[161] Before he plunges into the etymological exploration of such names as Sehon, Og, Amorites, and Basan, he marvels that such names are "pregnant with sacramental meanings."[162] There will be no need for such sacramentals once the City of God is at rest, but for now they stoke our imagination and love. Augustine, reflecting on the promise that God "binds up your bruises," asks whether the Bible will need to be read, whether the bishop will need to lay hands on anyone, or any other such "sacramental" will be necessary eschatologically. "All these sermons we preach to you, the words that are heard and then fade away, all the temporal actions performed in the Church, are dressings applied to our bruises. . . . All these are splints for our fractures, and when our healing is perfect they will be removed."[163]

Scripture's sacramental role in the church of bringing about healing — or, better, of being a quite physical first dose of an anticipated eschatological healing — correlates strikingly to the human nature of Christ and its relationship to the divine. Augustine's view of scripture is that it is sacramental in the most profound sense. Scripture is analogous to the two natures of Christ.[164] Its letters are meant to lead to the divine promise sacramentally joined to them. If the scriptures are read aright in all their materiality, in conjunction with church doctrine and life toward the end of twin love of God and neighbor, they indeed bear witness to the incarnate God who gifts the church with them. If we do not read within those bounds, they do not so witness. Those who crucified the Lord of glory could not see him, in a favorite Augustinian text (1 Corinthians 2:8). There is a certain *commicatio idiomatum* between literal and allegorical readings of scripture, just as there is for any orthodox christology. The lines between literal and allegorical blur, and cannot be kept fixed in any clear way, for the "lines" are there only to be transcended in a larger soteriological purpose. Scripture is also sacramental in that its proper reading actually effects salvation for Augustine. Its form matches the form of God's own appearance to humanity in Christ: initial repulsion, eventual allure, slow recognition of fittingness, and finally worship. Figural reading cannot be seen without submission to the

---

160. On Psalm 46 in *EP* II, 324.

161. On Psalm 106 in *EP* V, 238.

162. On Psalm 134 in *EP* VI, 207.

163. On Psalm 146 in *EP* VI, 427.

164. Any analogy must equivocate, of course. See our discussion of Telford Work's use of this analogy in the conclusion below.

church, growth in humility and putting off of pride, an imagination increasingly stoked by the wide lexicon of scripture, and a heart expanding with love for the One from whom it comes and all his creatures.

Finally, this sort of reading is profoundly communal. Scripture is hard — no one who opens it and says otherwise can possibly be speaking the truth. This way of reading it is counterintuitive and cannot be created *ex nihilo* by even such an earnest and well-educated reader as the early Augustine. Yet through trustworthy teachers like the one Augustine found in Ambrose, and friends like Alypius, these sorts of habits of reading can be slowly learned, until the disciple can be as adept at such exegetical moves as the teacher, or more so in Augustine's case. This sort of slow and difficult process of teaching and learning is inextricable from the particularities of life in the church: difficult relationships, the opportunity and need for humility and forgiveness, the bumping up against quite material difficulties with other people and foreign words. In just such a matrix is scriptural exegesis born. The odd and often hilarious comments about the community to which Augustine preaches are crucial to his whole exegetical endeavor. Sometimes they applaud. Sometimes they sleep and are reprimanded. Sometimes they shout approval; sometimes they signal hostility or even boredom.[165] Sometimes they celebrate the martyrs' feast days with too much zeal; sometimes their pews are empty as they are present at some other spectacle across town. Sometimes they smell — leading Augustine to end his preaching early![166] Just such earthy, material examples of specific life in the church are what is necessary for learning to read scripture well. Other people praise, disappoint, approve or not; they smell. And it is precisely through such people that one learns to read like this, or in any other way. An Augustinian biblical hermeneutic is one that participates in God's drawing of ordinary persons toward himself in the church's liturgy, within and amidst all our smells, hostility, approval, and otherwise. For precisely such ordinary people are those being bound in the charity of the Spirit to Christ and one another.

165. At the end of a rather windy and not altogether interesting *enarratio* on Psalm 38, Augustine says, "Well, brothers and sisters, if I have burdened and wearied you, put up with it, for this sermon has been hard work for me too. But in fact you have only yourselves to blame if you feel overworked, because if I felt you were getting bored with what was being said, I would stop immediately." Then he stops! *EP* II, 193.

166. At the end of an *enarratio* on Psalm 72, "The Psalm is finished now, and from the stench in the building I surmise that I have given you rather a long sermon. But I can never keep up with your eager demands; you are extremely violent with me. I only wish you would be just as violent in seizing the kingdom of heaven." *EP* III, 492. Perhaps they were taking his advice seriously about demanding nourishment from God through the preacher like a lamb demands milk from its mother!

# Conclusion: Reading Like Augustine

*[Scripture] cannot be mapped, or its contents catalogued; but after all our diligence, to the end of our lives and to the end of the Church, it must be an unexplored and unsubdued land, with heights and valleys, forests and streams, on the right and left of our path and close about us, full of concealed wonders and choice treasures.*

John Henry Newman[1]

Newman's quote is not only significant as a representation of an important later-day Augustinian arguing for a return to allegorical exegesis. It is also important in its use of *topographical* imagery for scripture. After all our diligent work in exegesis, scripture remains wild, untamed, foreboding. It is precisely this perilous terrain through which we traverse on pilgrimage, with all the physical exertion, meticulous planning, and need for creativity *en route* the metaphor implies. To speak once more in dogmatic terms — scripture remains a place of mystery. For Newman it is only Christian doctrine that keeps scripture wild and unmapped, that points our way through it without allowing us to pretend to possess it.

A common complaint against allegory is that it domesticates scripture, flattens it into a monotonous sameness, and reduces its historical and linguistic particularity into mere dogmatic *apologia*. Perhaps allegory can and has done those and worse things. Yet notice that the Newman quote suggests an

---

1. *An Essay on the Development of Doctrine*, rev. ed. (London, 1891), 71. Quoted in Andrew Louth, *Discerning the Mystery: An Essay on the Nature of Theology* (Oxford: Clarendon, 1983), 109-10.

argument that runs in precisely the opposite direction. Allegory is necessary to remind us that scripture is untamed and untamable. It is not the science of historical criticism that keeps scripture *other* than a false projection of ourselves onto a blank screen; rather, it is allegory that keeps exegetes genuinely open to something new and unexpected on the page of holy writ. This is a theological argument in the proper sense — it rests upon the doctrine of God. When we speak of scripture, as when we speak of all else in theology, it is only Christ who can meet us in judgment and grace, correct our false motives and point us toward a truth other than that of our own making. Any other attempt at objectivity or self-guidance through the morass invites failure. It is a strong rhetorical argument for historical criticism to claim that it keeps Christians from assimilating scripture into something dogmatically palatable and easily useful, that it marks off history as other than an extension into past time of a flattened *now*.[2] It allows history to be genuinely other. This book has offered Augustine's exegesis as an argument in the opposite direction. It is a tempting mistake to place a modern set of scientific skills into that sort of salvific technique. But only Christ can liberate us from powers that enslave and give us the *sapientia* that renders us unable to do violence to scripture and other people. Further, it is the very simulacrum of a Christian argument that makes apologetics for historical criticism seem so powerful. But it is just that — a *simulacrum*.

The exegesis of scripture is, properly speaking, a liturgical practice. Liturgy, the "work of the people" in which God and humanity unite, is the locus for all Christian thought and action. Liturgy obviously takes on an extraordinarily wide variety of forms in the church — preaching, presiding, speaking the truth to power, caring for the needy — yet all these and more have their final coherence in the sanctifying meeting of God's people with God in prayer and praise. Liturgy is an activity as varied as Newman's description of a pilgrimage through terrain quoted above. Sometimes it involves climbing rocks, sometimes camping, sometimes gathering food or defense from enemies, but it has as its goal the arrival at a certain end. Exegesis is intertwined with liturgy, which has as its end the beatific vision.

There is no Christian liturgical act that does not involve biblical exegesis.[3]

---

2. For example, see the essays by Williams that we have cited several times: "Historical Criticism and Sacred Text," in *Reading Texts, Seeking Wisdom*, ed. David Ford and Graham Stanton (Grand Rapids: Eerdmans, 2003); and "The Discipline of Scripture," in *On Christian Theology* (Oxford: Blackwell, 2000). This strongly theological rationale for historical criticism leads Duke Old Testament scholar Stephen Chapman to describe the practice to students as a form of *lectio divina*, a spiritual exercise designed to establish scripture as something other than the reader.

3. Geoffrey Wainwright describes the intertwining of Christian theology of scripture with

Even when scripture is not opened or preached from on a particular occasion, as in a visit to an infirm parishioner or stranger, Christian scripture is enacted in tending to the least of Christ's body, or offering hospitality to a stranger. God's people meet over scripture taken up, prayed over, broken apart, and distributed, like the bread and wine of the eucharist. We celebrate scripture in song; we honor it in procession and standing or kneeling; we listen to it attentively in preaching, enact it in sacrament, and bear it into the world when we are sent forth. Scripture is at the heart of the Christian life.

Therefore any exegesis of scripture that is properly Christian must arise from and progress toward Christian liturgy. Any exegesis with some other origin or destination must be considered something else. This is not to say it cannot be useful for the Christian community or laudable for other reasons — many members of other religious communities have made fascinating use of scripture, opponents of the church may teach us more than our friends. The opposition I present here is not meant to suggest an impermeable boundary between church and world.[4] It is rather an argument over what Christians ought to recognize as specifically Christian exegesis and what as not — whether we judge what is not to be helpful as a secular parable, as plunder to be robbed from the Egyptians, or as a gift of the *logos spermatikos*.[5]

---

Christian liturgical practice in his *Doxology: The Praise of God in Worship, Doctrine, and Life* (Oxford: Oxford University Press, 1980).

4. Williams's essay "The Judgement of the World" (in *On Christian Theology*) expresses his concern with George Lindbeck's project of describing all of reality in a scriptural framework over against the project of "translating scripture into extrascriptural categories" (citing Lindbeck, *The Nature of Doctrine* [Philadelphia: Fortress, 1984]). Williams wishes the church's doctrine to be susceptible to the judgment of outsiders and for the church to benefit from doctrinal input from those not in its membership. In such "activity the Christian community is itself enlarged in understanding and even in some sense evangelized" (31). I share his sense that we should plan to be surprised about where the Spirit works and how we shall recognize Christ anew. Yet the examples Williams provides of outside input into the Christian community are all from writers who have some deep familiarity with biblical faith — Søren Kierkegaard, Erich Auerbach, and Wilfred Owen (we might especially note the oddity of pointing to Kierkegaard, a self-identified Christian thinker). These are not figures to whom the scriptural story was unfamiliar, even if it is not their own; rather, each had reflected upon scripture for so long that they could put it to surprising and powerful new use. The "boundary" between "church" and world may be blurrier here than Williams sees, even as he accuses Lindbeck of offering one too distinctly. Further, Lindbeck's primary point withstands Williams's criticism: that it is more salutary for Christian theology and conversation with religious others to speak in the language of their scriptures rather than to try and translate their scriptural thought into something else. Finally, as we argued in Chapter 3, the best way to "evangelize" the church anew is to offer readings that, surprisingly, conform to strange words and bring new delight to familiar teaching.

5. Karl Barth famously described an instance of the truth of God outside the covenant com-

For many years Christians have turned to historical-critical exegesis when we have engaged in biblical interpretation. This is as it should be. At first those interpretive approaches were new and innovative and required the marshaling of impressive arguments to overcome ecclesial opposition to their use. They also required rigorous academic acumen and the best technical skills of the church and the university. The widespread implementation of these tools has allowed exegesis that Augustine could only have envied and has empowered preaching ministries of extraordinary faithfulness. All the same, we as church have failed to digest the methods and results of historical criticism into something that can be fully nourishing to the whole of the church across time and space. And a church that fails to be nourished, like any living organism, runs a perilous risk.

The result of centuries of biblical scholarship and theological education is that pastors stepping into the pulpit or behind the altar table often approach the biblical text with no other skills than those of historical investigation. Whether the appointed text comes from the Pentateuch, the Gospels, the Epistles, the Psalter, the Wisdom literature, or apocalyptic material, we who are educated in the modern theological academy and certified by the church's licensing boards have a number of stock approaches. We are generally adept at framing the text's presumed historical context, speaking to the needs this piece of writing sought to address, debunking possible fundamentalist misinterpretations, and not much more. We have a general sense that the Pentateuch or the Gospels are made up of various and interweaving strands of authorship, some idea that the psalms likely evince multiple historical settings, some sense of the situation of powerlessness that produced Revelation, a vague concept that the historical writings are not very good "history." Yet we have been given too few skills in how to relate this otherwise disparate group of writings to the triune God of Christian confession, nor how to point out the intersections between these words, that confession, and the people seated before us. The very project Augustine and centuries of fathers before and af-

---

munity as a "secular parable," stemming from the one Word of God as all true words do, yet arising elsewhere as an instance of grace and judgment for those with eyes to see (*Church Dogmatics* IV/3.1 [Edinburgh: T&T Clark, 1961]). Patristic writers at least as ancient as Origen describe Christian borrowing from the wealth of pagan antiquity allegorically in terms of the Israelites' raiding of the treasure of their Egyptian former masters. As early as Justin Martyr Christians explained glimpses of wisdom outside the biblical witness and the church as instances of the one *Logos*, through participation in whom anyone says anything that is true, whom Christians know in incarnate (and conventional wisdom-defying) form in Jesus Christ (Justin, "First Apology," in *St. Justin Martyr*, vol. 56 in *Ancient Christian Writers*, trans. and ed. Leslie William Barnard [New York: Paulist, 1997], paragraph 46, p. 55).

ter him pursued relentlessly — relating every word of scripture to the whole scriptural confession of Christian faith — we simply have insufficient skills even to begin to carry out. The result is catastrophic for Christian preaching and liturgy more broadly. Huge swaths of the canon remain *de facto* closed for great numbers of Christians. If the psalms, with all their poetic and theological wealth, are neglected in preaching because of pastors' inability to analogize from the psalmist's cursing to this Sunday's gathering, how much more must Ecclesiastes, or Leviticus, or the travel notes in 2 Timothy, or Revelation go unattended? Without the sorts of skills Augustine brings to bear on scripture we necessarily have a fractured canon. Most of it remains present in the books in the pews, but it may as well be excised. Historical criticism can be a far more severe editor of the canon than Martin Luther was, with his, by comparison, charming suggestion that James and Jude be edited for failing to proclaim justification by grace alone.[6] Biblical closure must be the result if preachers are only given skills for saying whether Moses wrote the Pentateuch, David the Psalter, Mark the Gospel of Mark, or Paul the later Paulines, yet cannot show their church how to see Christ's lordship in the words of the Psalter.[7]

Now, this is not to say that we should jettison even the very historical critical points I raise here about authorship and integrity of biblical books as we have them. The historical-critical guild has outgrown a parochial fascination with authorship questions, and its members have often offered extraordinarily detailed, fruitful, and *faithful* readings of scripture.[8] Disabusing simplistic fundamentalist notions of textual inerrancy is a worthy goal. In fact, its very worthi-

6. See his "Preface to the Epistles of St. James and St. Jude," in John Dillenberger, *Martin Luther: Selections from His Writings* (New York: Anchor, 1962), 35-37.

7. Patrick Keifert and the late Donald Juel discuss the inutility of the modern paradigm for seminary studies in "A Rhetorical Approach to Theological Education: Assessing an Attempt at Re-Visioning a Curriculum," in *To Teach, to Delight, and to Move: Theological Education in a Post-Christian World*, ed. David Cunningham (Eugene, OR: Cascade, 2005), 281-96. Seminaries adopted this paradigm as a way to pry fundamentalist students away from naïve assumptions. Now, however, incoming students are so poorly catechized they have no naïveté from which to be disabused. They and other authors recommend "rhetoric" as a topic around which to reorient theological education.

8. Examples could stretch on *ad infinitem,* but I think of Francis Watson's rereading of the Jacob story in *Text, Church and World* (Grand Rapids: Eerdmans, 1994) and Elisabeth Schüssler Fiorenza, "Missionaries, Apostles, Coworkers: Rm 16 and the Reconstruction of Women's Early Christian History," *Word and World* 6 (1986): 420-33. That both Watson and Schüssler Fiorenza read over against prevailing interpretive tradition in favor of a feminist approach suggests a primary weakness of interpreters like Augustine, and a strength of our own age. Below I hope to show how my version of allegory can make space for ancient readers to be wrong and modern ones right, even as we favor the overall hermeneutical approach of the former.

ness is, I suspect, why schools and churches pursue historical-critical disciplines so rigorously. It still feels exciting, *evangelical,* to disabuse simplistic notions of faith. To do so is to bring up risky, contentious material, to overcome objections to it, and to see a student come around to a point of view on scripture that changes how they think about God, the church, and the world. Again, historical criticism can be its own form of evangelism.[9] Any preacher loves to see the unconverted come around to their point of view, especially on issues of such mighty importance as the nature of the Bible, the church, and God.

There are tasks at which historical criticism is quite adept that Augustine could have only envied. It has remarkable ability to reconstruct historical contexts previously lost to history. For example, the deeply political and Jewish nature of the Gospels was long obscured by ecclesial inattention, and arguably could only have been regained by secular disciplines such as these.[10] Its extraordinary facility with ancient languages and texts, born out of scores of careers marked by great patience and diligence, are gifts to the church and the world alike. Augustine himself was constantly frustrated with his own linguistic inability and with the difficulty of finding good translations and reliable texts, and he would have loved even a year at the most mediocre of modern academies to learn from this treasure trove of modern scholarship. Our wider knowledge of comparative religious literature has allowed enormous strides to be taken in interpreting texts that could only bewilder ancient readers like Augustine — such as in apocalyptic literature. It probably took modern scholarship to notice the important positions women held in early church leadership. The great similarity of biblical Wisdom literature with religious texts of surrounding cultures would have been a fertile source for Augustine's own musings on the nature of wisdom and where it can be discerned. Historical criticism continues to produce great scholars and great careers because it is so fascinating and also so productive toward the betterment of the church and the world.

Yet when Christians seek to carry out biblical interpretation *as Christians,* historical criticism alone cannot suffice. A sermon on an assigned text about the Exodus cannot finally be a discourse about the event's historicity. This

9. It is not merely an *ad hominem* smear to note how many deeply skeptical biblical scholars are recovering former fundamentalists (and readers of mystery novels — see Steinmetz's "Uncovering a Second Narrative: Detective Fiction and the Construction of Historical Method," in *The Art of Reading Scripture,* ed. Ellen F. Davis and Richard B. Hays [Grand Rapids: Eerdmans, 2003]). Bart Ehrman may have left behind the theology and hermeneutics he learned at Moody Bible Institute, but he is still evangelizing.

10. E. P. Sanders is the name most closely associated with this Copernican shift in biblical studies. See his *Paul and Palestinian Judaism: A Comparison of Patterns of Religion* (Philadelphia: Fortress, 1977) and *Jesus and Judaism* (Philadelphia: Fortress, 1985).

may indeed weigh into the homily, it may even affect it in crucial ways, but it is not enough. It can be digested into a call for humility in the face of questions about the historicity of Judaism's origins. It can suggest the text must be read allegorically to refer to flight from violence, or whatever, but the alleged "fact" about history must be transfigured into a sermonic claim about God and God's people. This is not to re-enshrine the fact/value distinction — those pursuing historicity questions often have heavily "value-laden" reasons for doing so — it is merely to point to the artificiality of trying to offer historical investigation, whether critical or conservative, where sermonic address is meant to be. And for that, the preacher must reflect upon the liturgical practices around meals in which the congregation participates regularly, as well as the way these words reverberate throughout the church's teaching since biblical times. To do any less would be to offer stone instead of bread, a scorpion in place of an egg (Matthew 7:9; Luke 11:11-13).

The problems are heightened all the more when a Christian turns to this text. For the New Testament's letter itself enshrines a reading of the Exodus as Christian baptism (e.g., 1 Corinthians 10:1-11). Just on an etymological level it is not non-literal to read the Exodus liturgically, for a literal reading of Paul demands as much. Yet even to read the Exodus baptismally is not sufficient for a specifically Christian literal reading of the text. For no reading is without audience, no biblical exegesis without a congregation. That reading must be made to intersect with the body of readers on whose behalf the exegete reads if the reading aspires to be Christian. A "literal" reading of the Exodus then must be shown to intersect with the particular pastoral needs of the community gathered around the text at hand. To do so is not non-literal. It is simply a recognition of how scripture invites the baptized to read.

A crucial first lesson in any modern biblical course is the insistence that these texts must be read in their own context. No good reading of Genesis can take place without some sense of the events surrounding the writer as he or she wrote. Yet texts have multiple "contexts." After Gadamer we are more sensitive to the "context" of the interpreter, without attention to which we run the risk of bad readings. Biblical texts often have dogmatic contexts that include exegetical histories of readings of the text as part of dogmatic disputes, such as those over Proverbs 8:22.[11] The psalms bring into particular focus the liturgical context of many biblical texts, both in their writing, their transmission, and their reading today. It may be instructive to speak for a moment of these multiple "contexts" of the biblical text rather than multiple "senses" as

11. See the applicable discussion in *Reading Texts, Seeking Wisdom* and my note 118 on p. 226.

the medievals did. It is to be hoped that discussion of the former will clarify what our forebears meant by the latter.

## The Fourfold Sense after Augustine:
## Reading in Light of the Trinity

The first and most obvious context of a biblical text is merely the act of reading the words. Now, this "literal" context cannot possibly be thought of as pre-reflective. We are always already analyzing arguments, sifting information through our interpretive categories, making a sort of "sense" of words according to prior categories. Every translator knows they are also something of an interpreter. As I argued in Chapter 5, Augustine is an exemplar of "christological literalism." He makes "sense" of the "letters" on the page of the Psalter through the christological lenses given him by the church and exercised in pursuit of sermon preparation and delivery for God's people. As not a few theorists theologically inclined and otherwise in recent decades have pointed out, the physical object of the book before us is never neutral. Christians bind holy books in ways that invite prayer — with leather, soft pages, colored markers. Alternately the physical object can be worn down, dog-eared through years of devotion, or left unused and dusty. Any exterior says certain things about the text before the book is even opened. It makes an enormous degree of difference whether one uses a bare devotional Bible in church or a lectionary book, with lessons assigned according to the time of the church year and framed with prayer and song. The former suggests a more Protestant confidence in *sola scriptura* and avoidance of intrusion from any marginal gloss, the latter a more Catholic trust in the preeminence of the tradition that has organized scripture in wise ways for subsequent generations' edification. Once opened, books always present the biblical material in certain ways. Ancient gloss-based Bibles had running commentary from the fathers and medieval church doctors. Modern study Bibles carry glosses from preeminent biblical scholars. Fundamentalists are drawn to texts that can be coherently included in Cyrus I. Schofield's map for the end-times. My own use of the Psalter is sifted through the *Liturgy of the Hours'* framing of it into sections for morning prayer.[12] Such prayers open with a trinitarian invoca-

---

12. Unfortunately the Catholic breviary does not include the Psalms' superscriptions, as important as these are to Augustine. See *The Liturgy of the Hours According to the Roman Rite*, 4 vols., English trans. by the International Commission on English in the Liturgy (New York: Catholic, 1975).

tion, follow with an antiphon that frames the central prayer motif of the psalm, then lead into the psalm itself with an ancient authority pointing to its christological significance. Before I begin to make literal sense of the words of the Psalter I have already been led in a certain interpretive direction by the physical object of the book (leather, gold pages, worn, but not as worn as it ought to be) and by the organization of the text into components of a wider life of prayer along christological lines. Note again — there is nothing non-literal about any of this. In fact, these activities rest on at least some coordination between the literal sense of the psalm and the ancient prayers, invocations, and biblical allusions that fill the breviary.

I suggest we should situate historical criticism within this literal context of the biblical text. We should see it as part of a larger project of determining the *construction of the letter*. Under this rubric we can turn the best of our critical historical skills to questions of communities behind texts and layers of interpretive tradition before the present state of the words as we have them. We can also apply the best linguistic and manuscript reconstruction skills available. Linguists and poets can tune us into the skilled employment of rhetoric. The full critical glance of a hermeneutics of suspicion can be employed. Yet the use of the word "construction" can remind us that all our best historical investigation always remains inconclusive, admitting the potential fallibility such inquiry (like any other) is always inclined to forget. The word also makes plain the fact that grappling toward a text's letter is always a communal process. The letter never sits still. This scholar thinks it is this, that one that. In that ongoing process the "sense" Christians will make of the letter's construction will perhaps differ from others. There is no moment when psalm texts of revenge, exultation, and forgiveness can ever be read without awareness of the church's christological categories.[13] These, along with our best critical skills, should be brought to bear as we argue about the construction of the text's letter.

Allegory is often mistakenly seen as an opponent of literal interpretation, especially when the word "literal" is conflated with historical criticism. On

---

13. It is time for the church to recognize that literal readings cannot be thought of as non-christological and non-liturgical, as we have now for so long. In fact, the medieval habit of speaking of four senses of biblical texts, derived from hints in patristic literature, may have unwittingly led to a sense in which the "letter" can be discerned apart from attention to the other more obviously dogmatic "senses" of a scriptural text. Historical critics with sensitivity to classical, ecclesial forms of reading will often claim to be offering precisely the "literal" sense described by Augustine or Aquinas. Yet for the ancients the "letter" was only discernible in concert with the "Spirit"; the "literal" was a designation in partnership with the "allegorical." In short, the letter of scripture is not dogmatically neutral territory.

the contrary, it is only allegory that can properly take account of competing claims to literal (and other) interpretation. For example, Augustine can read a psalm text christologically without denying he is interpreting literally. He can also read it as a description of the historical episode there narrated, without necessarily glossing that story in christological terms. He can explore the linguistic or historical or manuscript problems behind the letter in front of him. Or he can read a text with an eye to the sacramental celebration into which his community is about to enter. In a more meditative gaze he can see it as a road to prayer, whether personal or communal. In a doctrinal one he can explore it as a locus for trinitarian exploration (though rarely this). "Allegory" claims that history, theology, prayer, all of these can legitimately be claimed as part of Christian practices of reading without any having to "win" and the others to "lose." Historical criticism has often claimed to be offering the literal sense of a text, perhaps for the first time. It subtly suggests that it has privileged access to a text against which all other readings must be measured. Allegory is not bound to such exclusivity.

Allegory might best be described as a habit of remaining open to God while reading scripture. Contrary to whatever sort of reading that becomes rote, with pat answers to standardized questions, allegory is a fundamental openness to making sense of these words with reference to the God worshipped in the church. This stance of openness to God is the stance of one in prayer — eager to receive a word from the God who has spoken in scripture, whose speaking in scripture has been reflected upon by those open to allegory in the history of the church, and who will speak anew to us now. Its physical illustration is the believer in the stance of the *orans*, the "praying one" from ancient church art, standing upright, hands outstretched, offering words to God and quite physically awaiting a response. Now, it is important to say that *any* form of reading, including allegory, can become a static "technique" for policing anything but pat answers. This is no more a problem for historical criticism than for allegory. Yet allegory at its best functions as it does in Augustine's hands. He pays exacting attention to the detail of the words on the page, constructing the letter, as I have called it. He reads in light of the God known in the church, making christological sense of the letters before him. He reads in light of the great sweep of church history, cognizant of readers who have read before him, approving and slightly amending and occasionally forthrightly disagreeing with them. Perhaps most importantly he reads in the midst of the great dynamism of God's work on this particular people to whom he is appointed in service. Openness to God, who speaks his Word in scripture, is concurrently an openness to the God whose Spirit is actively building love in the church. Such openness requires detailed attention to the particular persons in one's pastoral charge, as Augustine himself shows in de-riding the astrologer who wanders before him while preaching (alas, perhaps without much tact).[14] Notice here that exegesis is as specifically a trinitarian affair as any other liturgical activity. The Word and the Spirit cannot be di-vided from one another, since each trinitarian *persona* is fully God. To read a text without reading the church invites a specifically trinitarian heresy: an at-tempt to separate the work of the *logos* from that of the *pneuma*. Further, to attempt to read the Word without reading what the Word has said in the past to saints attentive to the Spirit's community-creating work also risks a trini-tarian heresy, in this case a new form of Pneumatomachianism. Whatever we make of Augustine's success in exegesis, and I have given him high (if mixed) marks here, we must attend to it. At least we must do so if God is indeed the triune God of Christian confession, whose work in history is not incidental to his nature.

If the construction of the letter is a particular attention by practitioners of many disciplines to the words of scripture in light of Christ, all other non-literal forms of reading that we call "allegory" should be thought of as a par-ticular openness to the Spirit's work in God's people as we read. Traditionally "allegory" has been distinguished in an extraordinary variety of ways — de Lubac's work catalogues these and runs to thousands of pages. One common medieval distinction was made among an "allegorical" sense properly speak-ing, in which texts are brought to bear on dogmatic matters; a "tropological" sense in which they are read to inform moral issues; and an "anagogical" sense in which they inform matters of eschatological import.[15] The danger of distinguishing multiple senses in this way is they seem to refer to "properties" in texts, or worse, "kinds" of texts: here is a "dogmatic" psalm, there an "es-chatological" text. Yet Christians know that no interpretive issue even of mere literary import can be discussed apart from our christological, moral, and es-chatological convictions. For example, Christ has already shown us that curs-ing psalms are prayers for enemies to be changed into friends — prayers that may only be answered in the eschaton. Augustine himself slips among these "senses" in a way that belies even his rather loose distinction of senses in *De*

---

14. Comment on Psalm 61 in *Expositions of the Psalms*, trans. Maria Boulding, OSB, *Works of Saint Augustine: A Translation for the 21st Century* III/18 (Hyde Park, NY: New City Press, 2002), III, 227-28 (referred to hereafter as *EP*). We offered our reading of this psalm at the end of Chap-ter 3.

15. Steinmetz in "The Superiority of Pre-Critical Exegesis" (in *The Theological Interpreta-tion of Scripture: Classic and Contemporary Readings*, ed. Stephen Fowl [Oxford: Blackwell, 1997]) describes each of these briefly. Henri de Lubac in his *Medieval Exegesis* does so at much greater length.

*doctrina christiana.* All matters christological necessarily transcend whatever artificial borders assigned to them, just as specifically Christian doctrine cannot be spoken of without impinging on matters of morality and hope.[16]

Perhaps then in addition to speaking of a text's multiple "contexts" to show the goals and achievements of multi-sense exegesis we may also need to speak of the variety of "skills" brought to bear on any given text. It takes time and talent to read the words of the psalm christologically. It takes pastoral savvy and an ability to read the Spirit's work in community to learn to offer "persistent patterns of signification" from morally or theologically challenging texts for the sake of listeners' sanctification.[17] It requires a particular openness in prayer to learn to see God's extravagant hope refracted through whatever words the lectionary presents. The "senses" of scripture seek merely to name the skills being brought to bear in exegesis. These can change as quickly and fluidly as steps in a dance. They can also fail to be integrated into an aesthetic whole as easily as missteps in a dance. Or, like dance, they can edify and produce beauty.

To shift metaphors again: the skills that multi-sense exegesis involves are not unlike the skills involved in a pilgrimage, as Newman envisions. Those on pilgrimage deploy skills not only for survival and the completion of their journey. They also employ skills required to seek the Lord's presence along the way. Natural topological signs become markers of the kingdom — as conch shells did on the *Via de Santiago* in northern Spain during the Middle Ages. Difficulties along the journey become metaphorical markers for the things against which Christians marshal their energies — such as sin and death. Beauty on the journey is a sign of One coaxing the pilgrims along into the joy of life in the divine presence. Pilgrims live in a universe full of signs, each of which refers either to other signs or to the God who created them as markers of divine creation and intention to save. We might say then that a properly Christian doctrine of allegory is inextricably intertwined with a properly Christian ac-

---

16. I suspect that we moderns err when we overread patristic and medieval writings that look like modern "hermeneutics" and underread their actual exegesis. The ancients did not know they were doing something other than "theology" when they outlined how they were to read before offering actual readings. Those disciplinary boundaries only affect us, and must be unlearned before we can read them aright. In other words, what Augustine says in *De doctrina* cannot be read without attention to exegetical work like the *Enarrationes*, "moral" works like his many writings on marriage, and "political" works like the *City of God*. This is all the more the case with Michael Cameron's argument that *De doctrina* is not as christologically fleshed out as most of the later *Enarrationes* ("Transfiguration: Christology and the Roots of Figurative Exegesis in St. Augustine," *Studia Patristica* 33 [1997]: 40-47).

17. The language is Ayres', borrowing from von Balthasar, as we saw in Chapter 1.

count of creation.[18] The world indeed shows forth the glory of God, to paraphrase the psalmist. Those who live in this world journeying to its source are
given eyes to see marks of its createdness in all things, not least in the scriptures that bear witness to the story that marks their lives. It is hardly surprising
that Christians of a certain ilk become adept at spotting christoform patterns
throughout Christian scripture, when they are indeed busy looking for such
patterns throughout creation as they journey salvifically through it.[19]

It is important for allegory to be used with care, however. One rationale
for using "allegory" bends it so far out of shape as to make it unrecognizable.
This is the popular description in which a biblical text that makes claims that
appear unreasonable to the "modern mind" are taken to be "allegorical." This
is especially often employed in the case of miracle stories. For example, Jesus'
walking on water cannot be taken "literally," to be about him walking physically upon water, for we know this to be impossible. Rather, it must be taken
"allegorically," spiritually, with the husk of the fable left behind and the kernel
of the spiritual teaching embraced. In effect, these descriptions seem simply
to mean that one should not take such passages very seriously. This rehashing
of Enlightenment and modernist skepticism toward the miraculous seems especially beloved of church leaders (like Bishops John Spong and Joseph
Sprague) and disaffected (and formerly more religiously conservative) scholars (Dominic Crossan, Marcus Borg) of a certain generation who are now
bent on making nineteenth-century German historical scholarship available
at Barnes and Noble.

The greatest danger in this way of speaking in the church is not merely
that there is no end to it — Jesus' resurrection itself likely falls to the test of
what modern people can be expected to believe. It is not only that ancient

18. Carol Harrison and Michael McCarthy offer significant descriptions of Augustine's
treatment of creation in the *Enarrationes*. See Harrison, *Beauty and Revelation in the Thought of
Saint Augustine* (Oxford: Clarendon, 1992), 97-139, and McCarthy, *The Revelatory Psalm* (Ann
Arbor: University Microfilm, 2003), 74-151. For McCarthy the psalmist's praise of nature must
also be a description of human reformation in Christ, for no account of creation can be complete without an account of re-creation. McCarthy offers the especially important argument
that Augustine is no less interested in "history" than any historical critic; he merely has a different, and particularly theological, understanding of what "history" is. Namely it is "creation,"
called forth from nothing in Christ to participate in the fullness of God, on its way to that goodness through its restoration in Christ.

19. Ephraim Radner has even suggested that Christians ought again to look for specifically
Christian symbols in creation as the fathers are often lampooned for doing — as when Justin
Martyr sees in a ship's mast the sign of the cross (this is a famous stock example, not one Radner
uses). See his "Sublimity and Providence," in *Hope Among the Fragments: The Broken Church
and Its Engagement of Scripture* (Grand Rapids: Brazos, 2004), 91-108.

writers and readers were untroubled by the miraculous in itself — the question is only what a miracle "means." It is more the gnosticism inherent in the suggestion that the story that offends be left behind and the spiritual teaching accepted. This fits well with a consumer society with no desire to be burdened by such cultural baggage as that provided by gullible religious forebears. And it is finally too easy to leave behind what is inconvenient and accept what pleases us.[20]

My criticisms here of historical criticism might be seen in a similar light to Augustine's criticisms of attention to the world without reference to its origin. When someone, for example, the early Augustine in *Confessions,* is overly taken with ephemeral love, beauty, or peace, Augustine (now the later one) turns his full rhetorical powers against them. These poignant moments in his *oeuvre* are why Augustine is still often derided as an unrepentant Platonist, for his inability to see the goodness in materiality, human relationship, society, and so on. Yet these accusations represent a mistake. Augustine's criticism of materiality *in se* is but the flipside of his love for creation as the expositor of God's saving work, for materiality as that to which God-enfleshed is joined to bring about its holiness. Historical criticism by itself has no more value than any other human enterprise. Worse, it can lead practitioners and readers to think no more can be said about the Bible than what can be ascertained through scientific inquiry. But viewed aright, placed within God's saving economy as part of Christians' liturgical practice of reading scripture while *en route* to the City of God, it has an esteemed place. Like all of materiality it can be mistakenly viewed as an end of itself; and like all of creation it can be seen in light of God's saving purposes.

Finally, let me offer a Jewish image for my vision of biblical exegesis. Christian exegesis should have a *midrashic* shape. Jews have famously harsh things to say about those who would attempt to read Torah without *halakhic* interpreters and their correlative forms of life. Likewise, as we approach a verse or text in question, we should first see what our earliest interpreters said about it, both Jewish and Christian. Then what the fathers said, then the medievals, then the Reformers, and then Enlightenment-era critics, finally modern saints and exegetes. This must be a conversation mindful of each expositer's place in the history of the church. Historical critics have their place at the end of that conversation, where they fall in the history of exegesis (just prior to more radical postmodern interpretations). They can indeed trump exegesis that has come before if they offer the best reading, just as a

---

20. This is the prime instance of the "cut and paste" approach to allegory so often derided by its critics. If, as I have argued, the shoe does not fit with Augustine, it does here.

medieval interpreter can improve upon an ancient Jewish one (or vice-versa), or a twentieth-century saint upon Augustine. Yet what we cannot do is position historical criticism as though it offers us the first and most reliable historical assessment of a text against which others must be compared. Historical criticism is no less rooted than Augustine was in its own historical situation amidst the lives that produce it, with its own strengths and weaknesses, productive of certain virtues and vices. It can win out, but only if it offers the best reading. Exegesis is a conversation with the saints about scripture for the sake of contemporary faithfulness. All ages of the church, and other interested parties, have their place in that endeavor.

## Dogmatic Rationale for Exegesis

It is not uncommon for Christian theologians to offer dogmatic reasoning for why the church should embrace historical criticism, as we have seen. Ernst Käsemann offered an early and influential version of the argument.[21] If the word of God that is scripture indeed bears a relationship with the Word of God incarnate, then the flesh, the words, the particularity of the human medium in which God is present, all matter. Therefore Christians must pay rigorous attention to the historical particularity of the text as discoverable only through historical criticism. To fail to do so is to fall prey to the Docetic heresy, in which Christ only seems to be human but is in truth an untouchable phantom, floating above history. A more explicitly trinitarian defense of historical criticism is offered by the Pentecostal theologian Telford Work.[22] Work establishes a "divine ontology" of scripture in a trinitarian shape: just as the Father speaks a Word who is anointed by the Spirit, so the divine word that is scripture descends among us and works in the church in the power of the Spirit. This is a strong claim for an analogy almost without equivocation between Christ and scripture, one that mandates Christian use of historical criticism for its study. Just as the flesh of Christ is no threat to his saving work but rather its precondition, so the particular history of scripture is not to be shunned by Christian exegetes without dire consequences.

These suggestions of the great similarity between the Word incarnate and the word of scripture are to be welcomed for their use of dogmatic categories

---

21. In "Vom theologischen Recht historisch-kritischer Exegese," *Zeitschrift für Theologie und Kirche* 64, no. 3 (1967): 281. See A. K. M. Adam, "Docetism, Käsemann, and Christology," *Scottish Journal of Theology* 49, no. 4 (1996): 391-410.

22. *Living and Active: Scripture in the Economy of Salvation* (Grand Rapids: Eerdmans, 2002).

to speak of the Bible. Yet they also offer something of a bait-and-switch. Granted that the flesh of Christ is prerequisite to any properly Christian view of salvation, how precisely does it follow that Christians' use of historical criticism in their practice of reading scripture is mandated? Dozens of generations of Christians had no access to the modern tools of historical criticism, and yet neither Käsemann nor Work would wish to argue their salvation was thereby endangered, as a "heresy" must do by definition. Further, the very Christians who forged the arguments that led to Chalcedon were not arguing about the ontological status of scripture. On that most Christians were agreed on what would look to modern eyes like a "fundamentalist" doctrine of revelation and of the Bible: God speaks here; we must listen accordingly and read allegorically at times. Most importantly, the sorts of biblical arguments that led to and arose from Chalcedon were often deeply intertwined with allegorical practices of reading — against which modern techniques have often been deployed. Further, all the historical investigation in the world is not going to settle the questions of Chalcedon: did Jesus have one divine nature, or two natures, one divine and one human? Was his flesh life-giving flesh? Those are properly dogmatic questions. To suggest historical inquiry can grant an answer to them is simply a category mistake. We may have strong reasons for insisting Christians should use all available means, ancient and modern, to read scripture. Yet we cannot take an ancient dogmatic category — arrived at and then defended allegorically — to argue that historical critical (and *not* allegorical) exegesis is mandatory for those who hold that ancient dogma.[23]

Two other distinguished theologians have offered variants of these dogmatic arguments for historical criticism: Kevin Vanhoozer and Francis Watson. Vanhoozer is, like Work, an evangelical committed to ongoing discourse with modern despisers of Christian faith as well as its adherents.[24] Vanhoozer's own area of critical discourse is that of literary theory, where the works of Jacques Derrida and others offer a fundamental threat to what Vanhoozer sees as the central Christian category of "meaning." If there is indeed no "meaning" in texts, if radical inquiry can do away with the very idea of an author's communicative speech-act, then the Christian notions of a *deus loquens*, of an incarnate *Word*, of scriptures that reveal, are lost. He of-

---

23. Adam's important and unjustly underread article offers these and further responses to Käsemann. See note 21 above.

24. Vanhoozer, *Is There a Meaning in This Text? The Bible, the Reader, and the Morality of Literary Knowledge* (Grand Rapids: Zondervan, 1998); *First Theology: God, Scripture, and Hermeneutics* (Downers Grove, IL: InterVarsity, 2002); and, most recently, *The Drama of Doctrine: A Canonical-Linguistic Approach to Christian Theology* (Louisville: Westminster, 2005).

fers, in contrast, a trinitarian hermeneutical vision, in which the Father speaks a Word to which Christians have some textual access in the Spirit. Christian doctrines of the incarnation, of revelation, and of scripture indicate that there indeed must be an intelligible concept of "meaning," however we identify that with what was intended by a text's author. Watson also worries over Christians' willingness to dispense with concepts such as authorial intent and textual meaning.[25] He castigates Christian theologians in the post-liberal school, such as Lindbeck and Frei, who are willing to sell the store to post-moderns in their giving up of authorial intent. There must indeed be something like authorial intent if a Christian vision of God's communicating himself inner-trinitarianly and to us in scripture is to be tenable. Vanhoozer's and Watson's work both offer the virtues of a Reformed insistence on the primacy of the Word, attention to divine address as of the first import in exegesis, and a willingness to argue with the leading intellectual lights of the day.

Yet their worry about the loss of "meaning" as a central category in theology is misplaced. Both Vanhoozer and Watson give the impression that Trinitarian doctrine should commit Christians to specifically modern forms of biblical interpretation. In their eagerness to save Christian faith from the death of meaning, both use the Trinity to buttress the crumbling concept, lest the house be ruined. Yet this is a misuse of trinitarian dogma. As we argued above about Chalcedon, ancient Christians argued toward and from Nicea without the benefit of modern scriptural exegesis or concepts of "meaning." Post-liberal theologians' willingness to dispense with modern notions of "meaning" is simply an admission that interpretation cannot be discerned abstractly, without reference to a community's specific location, its virtues, and its ends. Further, Christians have no stock in defending "meaning" without reference to Christ. A pyrrhic victory in the former argument would advance us no further in the effort to proclaim Christ as Lord. A way forward in these extraordinarily complicated arguments over hermeneutics and texts is for Christians to display to the world the kind of meaning-making shown in the *Enarrationes:* here is how our confession of Christ's lordship drives us to read the psalms.

Another significant dogmatic argument for historical criticism in the last century has been Brevard Childs's brilliant work, now widely known as "canonical criticism."[26] Childs takes the reality of the church's two-part canon as a fun-

25. Watson, *Text, Church and World* (Grand Rapids: Eerdmans, 1994), and *Text and Truth* (Grand Rapids: Eerdmans, 1997). See Stephen Fowl's critique of Watson in *Engaging Scripture,* 21-24.

26. I work here especially from Childs's *Biblical Theology of the Old and New Testaments: Theological Reflection on the Christian Bible* (Minneapolis: Fortress, 1993). See also "Does the Old Testament Witness to Jesus Christ?" in *Evangelium, Schriftauslegung, Kirche* (Göttingen:

damental starting point in his program for exegesis. The two testaments of the Christian Bible fold over a binding that is christological. Both the Old and the New Testaments witness to Jesus Christ. Yet they do so in different ways. The Old Testament witnesses to Christ (perhaps counterintuitively) by not mentioning him. That is, its many documents can be seen in retrospect to point toward him, but proper exegesis of the Old Testament now must not force it into christological categories. Let Isaiah and the Psalter and Deuteronomy witness to Christ in their own ways as they would have been audible to the Jews who wrote, canonized, and kept those documents — without the full display of christological contours there hinted. To use Childs's language, the Old Testament must be allowed to speak in its "own discrete voice," so that its particular witness to Christ can be heard. On the other hand, Childs insists upon a robust willingness to interpret the New Testament christologically, since that Testament witnesses to Christ quite openly. Hence it would be a christological and finally trinitarian mistake to interpret the Old Testament in terms of the New, or vice versa. God has revealed himself in history in a particular order, and particularly Christian exegesis of the two-testament Bible must reflect that reality. Further, while Childs is well aware that Paul practices allegorical exegesis, we must realize that we are not Paul. "We are not apostles and prophets," Childs argues repeatedly. Our major difference from the apostles is that we now have the two-testament canon, and so we need not perform the kind of allegorical readings Paul does — which is a good thing, because we cannot.

Childs includes some cryptic comments about the possibility of multi-sense exegesis at the end of his *Biblical Theology,* and many friends and students have testified that Childs was more sympathetic with patristic exegetes at the end of his life. Early in his career he even said, "At the head of any list [of works of exegesis for the church] stands the *Enarrationes* of Augustine, . . . the prism through which the Psalter was refracted during the larger part of Christian history. The exposition is not easy reading and runs counter to everything that the historical critical method assumes as obvious. Augustine does not interpret the text to discover what the biblical author originally meant, but he replays the chords of the text as one plays an organ in order to orchestrate one's praise to the God and Father of Jesus Christ."[27]

---

Vandenhoeck & Ruprecht, 1997); "Toward Recovering Theological Exegesis," *Pro Ecclesia* 6, no. 1 (1997): 16-22; and his groundbreaking *Introduction to the Old Testament as Scripture* (Philadelphia: Fortress, 1979). I am also indebted to Childs's student Stephen Chapman for helpful conversation about his work.

27. Childs, *Old Testament Books for Pastor and Teacher* (Philadelphia: Westminster, 1977), 62ff., cited in Michael Cameron, *Augustine's Construction of Figurative Exegesis Against the Donatists in the Enarrationes In Psalmos* (Ph.D. dissertation, University of Chicago, 1996), 12.

More recently Childs produced an important work on the history of exegesis with material researched for his Isaiah commentary, *The Struggle to Understand Isaiah as Christian Scripture*.[28] In it he shows that he is up-to-date in recent developments in history of exegesis, especially on new readings of Origen that make it impossible to call allegory "arbitrary." While he can appreciate allegory on its merits, he still worries that it occludes our ability to hear the Old Testament witness to Christ "in its own discrete voice." Childs would rather not have explicit christological exegesis done on the Old Testament, but that he is enough of a churchman not to rule it out in principle and broad-minded enough intellectually to appreciate it to some degree. His commentary on Isaiah has occasional christological interludes when he cannot do otherwise — but only a handful in more than 550 pages. He writes in one place in the commentary, "It is quite impossible to conclude an exposition of Isaiah 6 without some brief attention to the reverberations from the Old Testament text within the New Testament."[29] In this book I have argued that it should be similarly "impossible" to attend to Old Testament passages that reverberate throughout the Christian tradition, from the New Testament to Augustine and beyond. How else can we discern the form of Christ without attention to patient, extended christological readings of the whole of Isaiah? Childs's work is ably defended and furthered by his student Christopher Seitz. Especially in his *Word without End*, Seitz makes room for a specifically Christian reading of Isaiah along Childsean lines.[30] He draws a key distinction between a reading of the Old Testament *per se* and one done by the church *in novo receptum*. The former attends to the "plain sense" of Isaiah as heard in the covenant community before or without reference to Christ. The latter refers to Christians' hearing of the text in light of Christ's messiahship and drawing of the gentiles. These two must remain distinct for Seitz lest Christians "obliterate" or simply move beyond the particularity of the Old Testament in Marcionite fashion. Yet they must also be held in tandem for exegesis to be specifically Christian.

Seitz's work may be the best interlocutor for the kind of renewal of Augustinian exegesis for which I call in this book. He is more polemical than Childs against the historical-critical guild, and far more so than this work. His individual observations occasionally dazzle — as when he writes, "The

28. Childs, *The Struggle to Understand Isaiah as Christian Scripture* (Grand Rapids: Eerdmans, 2004).

29. Childs, *Isaiah*, The Old Testament Library (Louisville: Westminster/John Knox, 2001), 59.

30. Seitz, *Word without End: The Old Testament as Abiding Theological Witness* (Grand Rapids: Eerdmans, 1998).

Old Testament is not authoritative only where it is *referred* to in the New, but also when it is *deferred* to," a comment with which Augustine could not have agreed more.[31] He rightly argues that seminaries should teach courses in "Christian scripture" lest they be tempted to think that courses in ancient Semitic history can suffice for those preparing for careers of preaching from the Old Testament.

Yet any genuine dialogue must include disagreement. Seitz continues to hold a fairly strict distinction between "allegory" and "typology," especially in his more recent book *Figured Out: Typology and Providence in Christian Scripture.* He also continues to trade in such stock dismissals as the claim that christological reading ought "not entail tracking down types of Christ inside every burning bush or rock in the wilderness."[32] Not only must Augustine disagree — why else do rocks exist, and why else does God intervene savingly in response to Israel's distress, other than to bring glory to the triune God? — but Paul does as well (Romans 10:4). Further, the *per se* and *in novo receptum* distinction may function like the ones Nicholas Lash criticizes, as we saw in Chapter 1. That is, it may suggest, in a positivist fashion, that attention to a *per se* reading is not itself an act of interpretation. We have argued that if Christians are always already interpreting in light of their community's specific claims and ends, then they cannot be required to ignore Christ in order to produce non-christological readings of, say, Isaiah. As we saw in Chapter 5, Augustine can produce christological readings that are not at all "allegorical" for him, but are simply an exercise in making christological sense of the letters on the page — a sort of christological literalism. Such readings, far from being absurd, can be beautiful in their fittingness to the words on the page. Just so, for Augustine, they make a claim to truth.

It may be that the best arbitration between an approach like Seitz's version of Childs' hermeneutic and ours is to compare their readings of actual passages both in their aesthetic richness and as to what sort of Christian people they produce. That is, that we cannot finally know who is to be preferred before years of exegesis, preaching, and attempts at faithful living. Or, it may be that allegory can incorporate both Seitz's best observations and Augustine's, whereas Seitz seems to remain *a priori* committed to excluding much of Augustine's approach to the Old Testament.

It is impossible to do justice to the depth and breadth of Childs's learning or the greatness of his theological legacy here. Yet we can say that his argu-

---

31. Seitz, *Word without End*, 222.

32. Seitz, *Figured Out: Typology and Providence in Christian Scripture* (Louisville: Westminster/John Knox, 2001), 8.

ment is similar to those of Käsemann, Work, Vanhoozer, and Watson. Here again a specifically Christian dogmatic category — canon — is mobilized to insist that Christians *not* interpret the Old Testament christologically. To do so for Childs would be to violate the particular nature of the Old Testament canon as that testament witnesses to Christ obliquely. The result, in Childs's hands, is a particularly sensitive employment of historical critical exegesis by someone who is himself a master interpreter and churchman. But it is not, on Augustine's grounds, fully *Christian* interpretation of the Old Testament, for Christ himself is not present in the interpretation.

Augustine is also sensitive to the change of conditions that marks the New dispensation from the Old: "At that time, the New Testament was hidden within the Old, as fruit is in the root. If you look for the fruit in the root, you will not find it; yet you will not find any fruit on the branches either, unless it has sprung from the root."[33] Nor, we might add, can we fail to be attentive to the signs of the fruit in the root now that it is present and full-blown. Childs's insistence that we are not apostles and prophets is justly attentive to the difference between the first century and our own. Yet the humility in the statement veils a crucial gap between how the fathers interpreted this difference and how Childs does. For Augustine, our not being able to imitate Paul's situation fully is a blessing, for we now have Paul's exegetical example to follow and generations full of further exegetical exemplars between Paul and us. Paul himself repeatedly tells his readers to imitate him, as he in turn imitates Christ (e.g., 1 Corinthians 4:16; 11:1; Philippians 3:17; 4:9). We can presume he includes in this command the injunction to follow in one of the most important activities of faithful Jews: the interpretation of Israel's scripture.[34] Augustine certainly holds this to be so: "By the explanation of one [figure] he made sense of the rest."[35] Paul's exegesis is not merely true in its results, like some *brutum factum*. Its procedure is exemplary. Most importantly, the church's decision to close the canon during its fight against the gnostics was never interpreted as an argument against allegorical exegesis, as Childs treats it. In fact, both sides in that great debate argued allegorically. Yet Irenaeus sought to anchor his allegory more properly in the *kerygma*, and hence defeated his gnostic opponents who would allegorize without reserve. Later Origen would complete Irenaeus's arguments about the nature of the Chris-

---

33. On Psalm 72 in *EP* III, 470.

34. Richard Hays's powerful argument for Christians to imitate Paul precisely in his biblical interpretation was an instigator of this book. See his *Echoes of Scripture in the Letters of Paul* (New Haven: Yale University Press, 1989).

35. Cited in Cameron, *Augustine's Construction of Figurative Exegesis*, 210.

tian Bible with a display of allegorical exegesis that the church has only recently begun to question.[36]

I write with great appreciation for these scholars, each with a commitment to the Reformed tradition's rigorous attention to scripture. Each is
working creatively to reappropriate ancient Christian dogma for modern
times. Yet each misuses an ancient dogmatic benchmark to shoehorn Christians into doing historical criticism. Surprisingly, each could be put to particularly unwelcome use by fundamentalists. If the Bible is to be so closely
equated with the incarnation, with the Trinity, why should Christians not
worship it? Not take every word as straight from the divine, in a more Islamic
vision of revelation? In contrast, an Augustinian vision of creation in which
the created order participates in the divine and so shows forth God's glory
would allow for the Bible to be revelatory, to be full of signs, and yet not itself
to be divine.

A more fitting Christian dogmatic analogy to scripture than Trinity,
christology, or canon would be the sacraments.[37] Augustine's exegesis of the
psalms can be described as an avid search for *sacramenta* — saving mysteries
of Christ and the church, figured in the words of the psalmist. His list of sacraments is often extraordinarily long, despite other places in his work[38] that
would suggest a limitation to a few liturgical signs in the new covenant over
against the many in the dispensation before Christ.[39] One historian surmises

36. Joseph Leinhard has argued that Origen properly filled out Irenaeus's argument for the
Old Testament against the gnostics by showing how Christians could read allegorically those
parts of the Old Testament that were literally confusing or problematic. Without Origen, we
would be left with an Irenaean approach to scripture that merely "hits the highlights" and leaves
huge portions of scripture unread. See Leinhard, "Origen and the Crisis of the Old Testament in
the Early Church," *Pro Ecclesia* 9, no. 3 (2000): 355-66.

37. See the previous discussion in Chapter 5, pp. 233-39.

38. Such as *De doctrina christiana* III.9.13: "In these times, since there has been revealed to
us a clear sign of our liberty in the Resurrection of the Lord, we are not heavily burdened with
the use of certain signs whose meaning we understand; rather we have a few in place of many,
which the teaching of the Lord and the Apostles has transmitted to us, and these are very easy to
perform, very sublime in implication, and most upright in observance. Such are the sacrament
of Baptism and the celebration of the Body and Blood of the Lord" (trans. D. W. Robertson
[Upper Saddle River, NJ: Prentice Hall, 1958], 87).

39. Emmanuel Cutrone lists the following sacraments of the old covenant in his article
"Sacraments" in *Augustine Through the Ages: An Encyclopedia*, ed. Allan Fitzgerald OSA (Grand
Rapids: Eerdmans, 1999), 741-47: the Sabbath, circumcision, the temple, sacrifice, sacrificial vic-
tims, altars, priesthood, Passover, and unleavened bread, "to name just a few" (742). Those Augustine lists as falling under the new covenant include not only the obvious baptism and eucharist, not only those that would become the medieval church's seven, but also Easter, the octave
of Easter, Pentecost, the sign of the cross, spiritual songs, bowing of the head, contemplation,

that the word normally connotes for Augustine "something of spiritual importance, externally visible, and most frequently but not always connected with the rituals of the church."[40] Cameron describes the christological turn in Augustine's biblical hermeneutic as a move toward a sacramental vision of biblical language. That is, though in *De doctrina* Augustine could write as though *signum* and *res* could be spoken of separately, and performed figural exegesis in which the sign and thing were somewhat extrinsically related, years of pastoral pondering of scripture and the incarnation pushed him toward a conjunctive sense of the unity of *signum* and *res*,[41] first in Christ and then in the scriptures. Cameron calls this the "completion of a sacramental understanding of language," in which the "conjunctive sign or sacrament paradoxically mediates a knowledge of the unknowable."[42] Augustine asks rhetorically in his first major work after this shift, "What else are the corporeal sacraments but as it were certain visible words which have been sanctified?"[43] To speak of scripture in sacramental terms is to recognize its home in the liturgy of the church, and its part in God's saving work among his people. Cameron gets at this vision of scripture as full of *sacramenta* by contrasting it with an understanding in which scripture merely gives historical or religious knowledge. He writes, "The Paschal celebration communicates not only the dying and rising of the Lord," as in a limited epistemological view of scripture, but "also that of the Church and the believer."[44] It is not just Christ's dying and rising about which we read, and into which we live. It is also our own, mediated to us sacramentally in text and liturgy.

---

the great fasts, penitential garments, taking off of shoes, the rites of the catechumenate, entry into being *competentes*, exorcisms, transmission of the *symbolum*, the font, salt, penance, laying on of hands, reconciliation, the Eucharistic prayer, the Lord's prayer, "and many other things" (742).

40. Cutrone, "Sacraments," 742.

41. One wonders how intelligible it was ever to speak as though "signs" and "things" can be spoken of as separate — what thing can be spoken of without speech? Not God, without whose Word we cannot speak of him. Rowan Williams notes this difficulty in "Language, Reality, and Desire in Augustine's *De Doctrina*," *Journal of Literature and Theology* 3, no. 2 (July 1989): 138-50. Oliver O'Donovan argues that *De doctrina* was something of a false start in Augustine's exploration of the relationship between love of God and neighbor (to love the former only with delight and the latter only with use). Perhaps also *De doctrina*, coming before the christological turn that Cameron narrates, is a false start in his understanding of language. All the more reason that we should not read that document as though it were his final word on the matter. See Oliver O'Donovan, *The Problem of Self-Love in St. Augustine* (New Haven: Yale University Press, 1980).

42. Cameron, *Augustine's Construction of Figurative Exegesis*, 180.

43. Cameron, *Augustine's Construction of Figurative Exegesis*, 180, citing the *Contra Faustum*, 19.16; Cameron's translation.

44. Cameron, *Augustine's Construction of Figurative Exegesis*, 178.

It is important to speak of how this should look in current church life as well as in Augustine's work. In the eucharist, for example, God's people bring all their gifts forward as an offering of all God has given to us: "of thine we have given thee," to cite the *Book of Common Prayer*. My own Methodist congregations have often baked homemade bread that fills the sanctuary with a smell almost as delicious as its taste, literally (well, almost) the bread of angels. Churches without teetotaling traditions often smell similarly luxuriant with wine, poured out up front and breathed out by those who have returned from the altar. It has been traditionally important that the eucharistic elements are made by human hands, and not just picked randomly from a store shelf or manufactured by strangers. We offer a sign, a first-fruit of the labor through which we transform what God has given us in creation into something we can offer at the altar, for the whole community to eat and drink. So too with the monetary fruit of our labor — a first portion of it is gathered up and offered back to God. Now, this is a fitting place to think of the various labors, or skills, that go into biblical interpretation. Linguistic skill, manuscript skill, skills of historical reconstruction, and a faithful hermeneutic of suspicion can here be gathered up and made into offering. Just as in church life we would refuse certain offerings — bread that is inedible or wine that is not potable or money from illegitimate sources — so there could be skills the offering of which the church should refuse. A church on the ground would have to decide what to embrace and what to exclude on a case-by-case basis. One possible example would be the second-rate historical scholarship *cum* media savvy offered by the Jesus Seminar. Just as the presider at table acting for the community would be wise to reject moldy bread for the eucharist, so she should reject such an offering.

Now, with the presentation and offering of the church's gifts the minister stands for the Great Thanksgiving. The magisterial Protestant and Roman Catholic communities have made such enormous strides toward commonality with each other via return to ancient Christian forms of liturgy that we can speak with a broad degree of generalization. The triune God is invoked throughout the eucharistic liturgy, beginning with an address appropriate to the Father's work in creation, including the gifts at table, concluding with the *sanctus*. The Son through whom all things were made is praised for being joined with that creation in his ministry and now again in the eucharist. That entire story is remembered and retold in the proclamation of the mystery of faith, "Christ has died, Christ is risen, Christ will come again." Most dramatically the Spirit is invoked with arms raised, in a supplication to make these elements be the body and blood of Christ. And the people file forward, "the body of Christ, broken for you, the blood of Christ, shed for you." My own

Wesleyan tradition has shied away from strict dogmatic descriptions of when and how the elements become the body and blood, but our best formulations of their transfiguration are in our hymns.[45] Charles Wesley asks his hearers in "Come, Sinners to the Gospel Feast" to "behold the bleeding sacrifice," invoking a eucharistic realism no less substantial than many Roman Catholic celebrations.[46] We Methodists have tended to insist that the elements are indeed the body and blood of Christ and to leave off any technical description of how this takes place. We choose instead to name it a "mystery." "Who shall say how bread and wine God into us conveys?" Wesley asked.[47]

Now, just as communion elements and offerings made from any number of professions are brought forward just before the communion liturgy, so too any number of disciplines can contribute directly or indirectly to biblical scholarship. And just so, these are only as good as they are helpful to the people of God being made holy in the liturgy. They must finally be something over which a minister can raise her hands, pray the liturgy, and offer to God's people for their sanctification. That liturgy is at once biblical and traditional in the best sense. Its primary story and its very language are all drawn from scripture, yet it has also been passed on through the ages — amended, improved upon, changed. Even churches like mine that are quite reticent to speak of a role for the fathers in exegesis already unwittingly give them one in our eucharistic liturgy. The church, here as anywhere, is theoretically open to new "fathers" and "mothers" reshaping the liturgy for changed circumstances, though here as ever the burden of proof must be on those who would change rather than accept what is old, tested, and reliable.[48] So too with biblical interpretation. The church has a long heritage of exegesis that served it for many generations. This heritage has been significantly questioned of late, to the point where the tradition I have described using Augustine in this book is now all but unrecognizable to us. Yet it sufficed to make people holy for a millennium or more, as it narrated God's works to a new day's assembly of God's people.

---

45. Geoffrey Wainwright has shown that the Methodists' most important contribution to the greater church theologically is in its hymnody. See his introduction to the Wesleys' *Hymns on the Lord's Supper* (Madison, NJ: The Charles Wesley Society, 1995), v-xiv.

46. "Come Sinners to the Gospel Feast" is in the *United Methodist Hymnal* (Nashville: United Methodist Publishing House, 1989), no. 616.

47. In "O the Depth of Love Divine" in the *United Methodist Hymnal* (Nashville: United Methodist Publishing House, 1989), no. 627.

48. Even the Orthodox tradition, with its great antipathy to change of any kind, adds new saints as the church's work continues, such as St. Isaac of the Americas and St. Herman of Alaska in this country.

Above all, in the eucharist, God saves us. In it God again deigns to be *kenotically* present in bread and wine, in dramatic continuity with his presence in Israel and Jesus, now re-enfleshed in the church. The church is sent out from this meal refreshed to be the body of Christ for the sake of the conversion of the world. This too should be the goal of biblical interpretation. It works for the refreshment of a people for mission. Because this people will change in any one gathering of the local church, we cannot be overly meticulous in stipulating in advance how exegesis will look. Yet it must be recognizable no less than the eucharist is: offering, trinitarian prayer, fraction, *agnus dei,* and so forth. Even with local variety and attention to particular needs in various settings the eucharist is still recognizable to God's people as eucharist, no less than an ordinary meal is recognizable as a meal by someone who is hungry. So too it should be with biblical interpretation. That which does not work for the saving and growth in grace of a people is simply something other than biblical interpretation. God's people go hungry; their sanctification is neglected. But something that can be so offered, even if it expands or challenges our notions about what "counts" as exegesis, should be included.

This dogmatic analogy for exegesis improves on those offered by Käsemann, Work, Vanhoozer, and Childs in several ways. One, it avoids the trap into which Work's model often falls of implying Christian worship, or almost *latreia,* of the letter. An analogy that fails to equivocate in its identity between the Word in flesh and the word that is scripture threatens to be more Islamic than Christian. The Bible has and continues to be used in horrible ways. It is, unlike Christ in flesh, unable to speak for itself. It can be easily manipulated and used for abuse in ways to which many of us can attest. Scripture is rather like bread and wine. It can be misused, either causing obesity or famine, wars can be fought to secure it or take it. Or, it can be offered to God's glory in the liturgy, and shared to ease hunger and create community. This model leaves space to name scripture's potential for abuse as well as for sanctification. Unlike Vanhoozer, Watson, and Childs, this model opens space not just for formal arguments drawing on dogma for some already desired end (the Trinity says we should do historical criticism, the canon rules out allegory, etc.). It rather points to the central truth that allegorical exegesis defends and demonstrates — that at the center of scripture is the story of Christ's saving work, attention to which is the purpose of the church's gathering and reading any portion of that scripture. Those who participate in the eucharist are being trained to see divine *kenosis* everywhere, to participate in it themselves, and so will not be surprised to find this fundamental *kenotic* and *theotic* movement throughout scripture, their own lives, and even elsewhere in creation. Finally the eucharistic analogy keeps us from offering a stiffly formal doctrine of scripture that fails to attend to the particulars of lives of those gathered in the sanctuary. The sermon is nothing more than a commentary on the liturgy, a drawing of attention to points in the eucharist to which *these people* should be attentive at this time. No reading of scripture can be legitimate, however "orthodox" or historically correct, that fails to attend to the sins and graces, desires and fears, of the people for whom the reading is offered.[49] Allegory offers a vision for faithful congregational practice. Because it intends to be beautiful — to delight — it has to know what its hearers will think is beautiful, and respond accordingly. No doubt this will be contested ground. Sinners that we are, we are drawn to things that are actually ugly, and our spiritual senses have to be renewed constantly. That is, indeed, one of the key jobs of the church's preaching — to "convert" our senses into the proper beauty that is God, that is finally good for us.

Another way to put my argument for christological allegory, then, is that it should be seen as a fundamentally *evangelical* practice. The process of allegorical reading matches the contours of Christ's confrontation with his hearers, both those depicted narratively in the Gospels and those that take place whenever the church preaches or presides. Initial hostility or puzzlement yields either rejection or enticement. If the latter, questions follow: if this is as true as it is aesthetically compelling, what of this objection, or this? Finally conversion results — given that Christ is Lord, how must life now look? This sort of conversion in response to a strange, appealing, and finally liberating word preached is matched in the process of allegorical reading. Moral or theological puzzlement gives way to allegorical possibility, and finally further light cast on the nature of God and so of his people. Allegory and evangelical call to conversion are hardly alien to one another. That they are now so seen is merely an accident of our historical situation — centuries old as it is — of a perceived "Catholic" reading practice set off against a perceived Protestant one. But they are natural allies, even twins.

A final dogmatic reason for allegory over against these alternatives is this: allegorical exegesis makes for good literal reading of scripture. One cannot claim to attend to scripture's letter without seeing allegory there inscribed. An extraordinary generation of biblical scholars is demonstrating in its work that allegory is not an extra-scriptural import, it is rather a deeply biblical practice. Richard Hays's work on Paul's reading of the Old Testament has demonstrated that he was not thoughtlessly offering "proof-texts" for positions already ar-

---

49. Liberation theologians, both for their liberationist commitments and for many their Catholic ones, might heartily agree here. See for example Gustavo Gutiérrez's *On Job: God-Talk and the Suffering of the Innocent,* trans. Matthew O'Connell (Maryknoll, NY: Orbis, 1989).

rived at. He was rather offering an ecclesiocentric reading of scripture. Israel's messiah has come, gentiles are streaming to Zion as scripture foretold as they are drawn to the church, so scripture must be read with new eyes. Further, Hays argued, Paul is well aware of the biblical context of the passages from which he quotes. For example, when he cites the psalmist in Romans 8 with his lament that "we are being led as sheep to the slaughter," he knows and expects his readers to know that Psalm 44 ends in exultation, as must any Christian suffering with the sort of deprivations described in Romans 8. The scriptural key of the notes Paul sounds reverberate throughout his many quotations, even as he offers "another sense" to these through his use of them on behalf of an eschatological gathering of gentiles and Jews around Israel's messiah. Paul is a model for allegory of a specifically biblical sort.[50]

Ellen Davis has offered to fellow Old Testament scholars abundant evidence that Old Testament texts were written to be read figuratively.[51] For example, she writes over against a near-consensus among scholars that would have the Song of Songs be read merely as a piece of ancient love poetry celebrating human sensuality, canonized and treasured by rabbis and church fathers who remained ignorant of its true nature. Davis points to good scriptural reasons to the contrary. She shows intertextual connections between the Canticle and the Garden of Eden, and descriptions of the building of Israel's temple to show the Song was written to be read on multiple levels. Further, the rabbis of Israel and fathers of the church have been appropriately sensitive to the ways scripture can resonate in new settings, and so have offered profound spiritual readings of the Canticle in new settings.

50. Hays, *Echoes of Scripture in the Letters of Paul*, 57-61. The import of Hays's book is that it argues that Paul had a consistent biblical hermeneutic, but that unlike other readers of scripture in the early church his was not primarily christological but ecclesiological. This is a fine example of a modern reader of Paul seeing something that ancient ones would not have. Hays is also a master at suggesting the rationale behind allegorical exegesis that looks bizarre to modern readers, and then at recommending that the church "go and do likewise." While his account of Paul rests on eccesiological rather than christological grounds, he does not argue those are the only acceptable Christian reasons for reading allegorically. Augustine's christological grounds for allegory on the psalms may be a step beyond Paul, but one I hope is in keeping with the best biblical tradition that Hays helps us properly to identify. Further, if as Hays shows Paul is an ecclesiocentric reader, and as Augustine shows on Pauline grounds that the church is never separable from Christ her head, then these two views are profoundly consonant with one another.

51. See her "Romance of the Land in the Song of Songs," *Anglican Theological Review* 80, no. 4 (1998): 542; *Getting Involved with God: Rediscovering the Old Testament* (Boston: Cowley, 2001); and *Proverbs, Ecclesiastes, and the Song of Songs*, Westminster Bible Companion (Louisville: Westminster/John Knox, 2000). Davis's recommendations are also not primarily for christologically shaped allegory, while like Hays she is also not opposed to such readings. Unlike him she makes use of christological readings of the Song from patristic and medieval readers.

Another Old Testament scholar, Gary Anderson, has written a compelling account of the interpretation of Genesis 1–3 in the ancient church and synagogue, offering Augustine, Gregory of Nyssa, and Ephrem as model interpreters no less than Michelangelo of Sistine Chapel fame.[52] Jon Levenson, a Jewish scholar of Hebrew Scripture, has written about the effort of modern biblical interpretation to remove all parochial investment that could occlude objective historical inquiry — including such parochialisms as Jewishness.[53] In contrast, his own Jewish sources and life enable him to offer brilliant readings of scripture, such as a prophetic objection to the common celebration in scholarship of the Exodus as a paradigm for liberation. In contrast to its frequent use by modern liberationist exegetes, Levenson sees the Exodus as liberation only in order to be rightly bound — to YHWH.[54] Each of these brings out aspects of Genesis that other modern readers using historical skills often miss, but yet, once pointed out, these throw extraordinary light on the text.[55]

These scholars are at the top of their field, doing work that represents the best of modern biblical studies. In each of these cases their critical eyes have seen warrant in the letter and history of scripture to read against the letter in some fashion. We could have included not a few more biblical scholars, such as Luke Johnson and Stephen Fowl, who have argued for a greater place for church tradition in the exegete's vocation. Yet Hays, Davis, Anderson, and Levenson do enough to show us that the text itself applies "pressure" on the exegete to read in ways that resemble ancient Christian and Jewish forms of reading.[56] Christians have always cared about the letter of scripture, about "the way the words go." We have rightly insisted that no dogmatic formulation can rest solely on allegorical support, but must also have a deep literal foundation in the Bible. Just so, here allegory has deep literal roots in scripture. It is no wonder that faith communities that not only wish to glean information from the Bible but wish also to read biblically find themselves continually returning to allegory.

---

52. *The Genesis of Perfection* (Louisville: Westminster/John Knox, 2001). Anderson's strength in showing the way Jews and Christians read in light of their respective ends is to show brilliant readings from ages past that we often ignore.

53. Levenson, *The Hebrew Bible, the Old Testament, and Historical Criticism: Jews and Christians in Biblical Studies* (Louisville: Westminster/John Knox, 1993). The title essay makes this argument most forcefully.

54. "Exodus and Liberation," in Levenson, *Hebrew Bible*, 127-60.

55. We draw attention here to Levenson not because he is a practitioner of specifically Christian allegory, of course, but rather because his work indicates the inseparability of a form of life with a biblical hermeneutic. He may have more in common with ancient Christian allegorical readers however than either he or they would recognize.

56. The language of the biblical text applying theological "pressure" is Childs's.

## What Now?

Where can one learn to read this way? There are now very few living masters who can teach such skills. These have been diverted to careers in biblical studies, or if they found such study spiritually unedifying, into preaching careers. One can, of course, study with one of the professors whose work I have drawn upon here. Yet their own appropriation of allegory remains hedging for the most part, provisional rather than abundantly practiced. It is time for *sacra doctrina* to be knit back together in a new era of biblical interpretation in which theology reigns anew among Christians as queen of the theological sciences.[57] Masters must be adept at the literal skills we have rightly long prized in modernity — language, history, antiquity. They have also to be doctrinally adept enough to know that no literal exploration is complete without seeing a text's letter after the pattern of Christ. Masters must also be pastorally skilled in order to teach exegesis. Ability to read the Spirit's work in the church is crucial for good reading of the Word's words on the page, and vice versa. The homiletical skill of offering models for imitation from the raggedy band of characters in scripture is not only an act of allegorical acumen in its own right, it is a key *a priori* skill for reading well. Finally a trust in the Lord of history is indispensable. If the claims Christians make to the eschatological inbreaking of the kingdom are false, readers of scripture should give up their task. Yet if God's kingdom is among us, announced in Christ, embodied in church and hoped for (even if inchoately at times) by all people, we can continue with the difficult tasks of reading scripture and living as Christians. This is an extraordinarily demanding set of tasks. And just so, we need masters willing to teach them anew to students. In short, nothing may be more crucial to a transfiguration of our practices of reading scripture than a radical reworking of seminary education. Our professors should be working pastors or active lay people, preaching and presiding and serving with great care, with students looking over their shoulder, then making first attempts to pastor for themselves, under faithful supervision. Seminary teachers should primarily be evaluated on the basis of the faithfulness of the pastoral careers of seminarians they train, rather than on books published, contributions to journals, or offers of employment from rival institutions. Such a restructuring would require no diminution in intellectual skills. For there is no more demanding task, linguistically, theologically, or morally, than training pastors to conduct faithful ministry in the church.

---

57. I am making no claim here for non-theological fields such as biology, though perhaps such a case could be made. Rather, I am claiming that *sacra doctrina*, holy reading, should unite all we do in the theological academy.

A working model for this reconfiguration of seminary education would be the ancient and continuing monastic tradition — with its rigorous attention to prayerful and liturgical reading of texts amidst the negotiation of difficult relationships and a community's effort to feed itself and others. Yet it would depart from the monastic tradition's cloisters, and be present in all the parts of the world to which ministers are called to go. It would then more resemble the mendicant and preaching orders of the Middle Ages, or the Jesuits, or the early Methodists, with their uniting of prayer and study with active work for the kingdom in the world. Seminaries should be communities that instill Augustinian habits in students in preparation for these to read scripture for the sake of the community to which they are called in ministry. Only a reintegration of the seminary's disciplines can move us toward this vision.[58]

There are hopeful signs of progress back toward these ways of reading. Impressive publishing ventures are in progress with InterVarsity and Eerdmans that attempt to make the fathers easily accessible to pastors who prepare sermons. The former series tends to rely on shorter snippets, often previously translated, organized around the text at hand. The latter series has longer pericopes that are previously untranslated. The former's strengths are those of the medieval *glossa ordinaria:* it is easily accessible and legible without reference to the larger context of the interpreter's work. The latter shows more of the strengths of modern patristic scholarship, with precision in translating, manuscript work, and identifying the literary context of the patristic or medieval figure. There are older publishing ventures that count as resources, including the Catholic missal, with its daily readings from the fathers on the scriptures at hand, and the still-useful *Ante-Nicene* and *Post-Nicene* fathers translations. A more intentionally avant-garde approach is shaping up at Brazos Press, with its major new initiative to publish specifically theological commentary on books of scripture. So rather than snippets of the fathers we will have commentary on Genesis from Rusty Reno, Leviticus from Ephraim Radner, the Psalter from Ellen Charry, Ezekiel from Robert Jenson, and so on.[59] While these figures will be familiar with and possibly draw on modern

58. Such a dramatic reorganization of theological education seems unlikely. Yet it is not impossible. The Roman Catholic Church could reorganize its seminaries posthaste if its bishops wished. Evangelical schools could not rule out a conversion of sorts from board members. As far-reaching as my claims are here, they have some similarities to the already cited book of essays, *To Teach, to Delight, and to Move,* whose Protestant authors have prestigious positions in several prominent American institutions.

59. The first several volumes are now available: Jaroslav Pelikan's *Acts,* Brazos Theological Commentary of the Bible (Grand Rapids: Brazos, 2006); Peter Leithart, *1–2 Kings* (2006); and Stanley Hauerwas, *Matthew* (2007).

exegesis, their own expertise in the modern academy is elsewhere. Their work promises to look more like the fathers' in both form and content. A further series now coming out with Blackwell that seeks to integrate the observations of contemporary exegetes with those working in history of interpretation is also welcome, for similar reasons.[60]

In addition to publishing endeavors, another encouraging sign is renewed interest in radical forms of discipleship among Christians.[61] These sorts of reading practices take the kind of time that only a monastic setting can give — that is, a place organized to feed and further its material life only so as to enable long stretches of time for *lectio divina,* prayer, and growth in grace. Seminaries will do well to appropriate both the gifts of recent publishing efforts and to incorporate monastic and other radical forms of life if they wish to further such practices of reading.

A difficulty with my set of proposals here, besides that of our current state of seminary education, is that of the divided church. Augustine can accuse the Donatists of removing themselves from the one body of Christ, severing themselves as members from the head, because such a charge had purchase. The Donatists cannot respond to it with indifference, but most somehow return the same charge back to Augustine. Membership in the one body united to the one head was a prerequisite for Augustine's christological readings of the psalm, and that membership in turn formed Augustine's readings. That is to say the resonance of the word "member" was as in the phrase "member of a body" rather than our "member of an organization." It may sound odd to say, but ecclesial division does render allegory problematic. It does not necessarily follow that denominational reunification must precede christological reading of the Old Testament. Life is rarely that neat. Yet we must, like Augustine, see the unity of the church and the coherence of allegory as interdependent. In fact, it may be that attention to the sorts of christological and ecclesiological readings that Augustine offers in the *Enarrationes* encourages us to "discern the body" among Christians with whom we are not now in communion. If Augustine's problem was that one part of the body had knowingly severed itself from the head, ours may be that several hundred parts of the body are severed from one another and so also from the head, and must work to rejoin one another, in whatever piecemeal fashion we can, if a specifically biblical vision of allegory is to become tenable again.

---

60. See Judith Kovacs, *Revelation Through the Centuries,* Blackwell Bible Commentaries (Oxford: Blackwell, 2004), and subsequent volumes.

61. For example, see *School(s) for Conversion: 12 Marks of a New Monasticism,* edited by the Rutba House (Eugene, OR: Cascade, 2005).

A final test for allegory, as for any Christian theological claim, is the kind of people it produces. I have no full-blown sense of how precisely to instantiate the kinds of scriptural reading practices I recommend here.[62] But I have claimed here that the Christian life itself is "allegorical," continually producing new "readings" of texts that beautify the words while living them out in ever different forms of life. How exactly we can read like Augustine and can produce preachers who preach like Augustine is no more clear to me than before undertaking this writing. And this is as it should be. My proposal is for an experiment. It must be submitted for testing to the community of the church. If the church were to take up my suggestions of reading scripture like Augustine, and to find that she was producing greater faithfulness than she was before, then this book will have been proved right at least to that degree. If no church finds that greater faithfulness is produced, or none even experiments toward answering the question, so much the worse for this work. In our age what is called for is a third naiveté.[63] Post-liberals have rightly spoken of their work in Ricoeur's terms as a "second naiveté" — a willingness, after learning all critical scholarship has to offer about texts and communities, to read the Bible as the word of God again. That move is quite right and justified. It has produced an extraordinary generation of scholars whose work can allow for me to claim as I do here that christological allegory is the best hermeneutical approach to the Old Testament. Now what is called for is a third naiveté — not just reading scripture as though it were true, and as though Christian doctrine mattered, but *structuring Christian community* as though scripture were true and as though the God of scripture rules, reading scripture as though references to the people of God and even to Christ always already include "us." Augustine assumed as much, and preached accordingly. The monastic tradition assumed that it had to produce Christians who read scripture like Augustine, and it structured its community accordingly. Post-liberals have scratched out a way for us to read scripture with confidence and say after having done so that God has spoken. Now we must, no less naively, structure our common life as though this is the right way to read scripture. Only then could we tell whether we ought read scripture like Augustine, as I here propose we do.

---

62. Chapter 4's suggestion that it should make the church more philo-semitic is the strongest specific recommendation I have to offer.

63. See here Mark I. Wallace, *The Second Naiveté: Barth, Ricoeur, and the New Yale Theology* (Macon, GA: Mercur, 1990).

# Bibliography

## Augustine

*The City of God Against the Pagans.* Ed. and trans. R. W. Dyson. Cambridge: Cambridge University Press, 1998.

*Confessions.* Trans. Maria Boulding, OSB. New York: Vintage, 1998.

———. Trans. Henry Chadwick. Oxford: Oxford University Press, 1991.

"The Excellence of Marriage." In *Marriage and Virginity,* trans. Ray Kearney. Vol. I/9 of *The Works of Saint Augustine.* Hyde Park, NY: New City, 1999.

*Expositions of the Psalms 1–32.* Trans. Maria Boulding, OSB. Vol III/15 of *The Works of Saint Augustine: A Translation for the 21st Century,* ed. John Rotelle, OSA. Hyde Park, NY: New City, 2000.

*Expositions of the Psalms 33–50.* Vol. III/16 of *Works of Saint Augustine.* 2000.

*Expositions of the Psalms 51–72.* Vol. III/17 of *Works of Saint Augustine.* 2001.

*Expositions of the Psalms 73–98.* Vol. III/18 of *Works of Saint Augustine.* 2002.

*Expositions of the Psalms, 99–120.* Vol. III/19 of *Works of Saint Augustine.* 2003.

*Expositions of the Psalms, 121–150.* Vol. III/20 of *Works of Saint Augustine.* 2004.

*Homilies on the First Epistle of St. John.* In *Augustine: Later Works.* Ed. and trans. John Burnaby. Philadelphia: Westminster, 1955.

*On Christian Doctrine.* Trans. D. W. Robertson. Library of Liberal Arts. Upper Saddle River, NJ: Prentice-Hall, 1958.

*On Genesis: Two Books on Genesis Against the Manichees and on the Literal Interpretation of Genesis, An Unfinished Book.* Washington: Catholic University, 1991.

*The Political Writings of St. Augustine.* Ed. Henry Paolucci. Chicago: Gateway, 1962.

*St. Augustine: Letters.* Trans. Sr. W. Patterson. New York: Fathers of the Church, 1953.

*Tractates on the Gospel of John.* 5 vols. Washington: Catholic University, 1988-1994.

*The Trinity.* Trans. Edmund Hill, OP. Vol. V of the *Works of Saint Augustine,* 1991.

## Secondary Literature on Augustine

Arnold, Duane, and Pamela Bright, eds. *De Doctrina Christiana: A Classic of Western Culture.* Notre Dame, IN: University of Notre Dame, 1995.

Ayres, Lewis. "The Christological Context of Augustine's *De Trinitate* XIII: Toward Relocating Books VIII-XV." *Augustinian Studies* 29 (1998): 111-39.

———. "The Discipline of Self-Knowledge in Augustine's *De Trinitate* Book X." In *The Passionate Intellect: Essays on the Transformation of Classical Traditions Presented to Professor Ian Kidd,* ed. L. Ayres, 261-96. Brunswick, NJ: Transaction, 1995.

———. "'Remember That You Are Catholic' (serm. 52.2): Augustine on the Unity of the Triune God." *Journal of Early Christian Studies* 8 (2000): 39-82.

Babcock, William. *The Christ of the Exchange: A Study in the Christology of Augustine's Enarrationes In Psalmos.* Ph.D. dissertation, Yale University, 1971.

Barnes, Michel. "The Arians of Book V, and the Genre of De Trinitate." *Journal of Theological Studies* 44 (1993): 185-95.

———. "Exegesis and Polemic in *De Trinitate* I." *Augustinian Studies* 30 (1999): 43-59.

———. "Rereading Augustine's Theology of the Trinity." In *The Trinity: An Interdisciplinary Symposium on the Trinity,* ed. Stephen T. Davis et al. Oxford: Oxford University Press, 1994.

———. "The Visible Christ and the Invisible Trinity: Mt. 5:8 in Augustine's Trinitarian Theology." *Modern Theology* 19, no. 3 (2003): 329-55.

Bernard, Robert W. *In Figura: Terminology Pertaining to Figurative Exegesis in the Works of Augustine of Hippo.* Ph.D. dissertation, Princeton University, 1984.

Bonner, Gerald. "Augustine as Biblical Scholar." In *The Cambridge History of the Bible.* Vol. 1, *From the Beginnings to Jerome.* Ed. P. R. Ackroyd and C. F. Evans. Cambridge: Cambridge University Press, 1970.

Bowlin, John. "Augustine on Justifying Coercion." *The Annual of the Society of Christian Ethics* 17 (1997): 49-70.

Bright, Pamela, ed. *Augustine and the Bible.* Eng. trans. of *Bible De Tous Les Temps,* vol. 3, *Saint Augustin et la Bible,* ed. Anne-Marie La Bonnardière. Notre Dame: University of Notre Dame Press, 1986.

Brown, Peter. *Augustine of Hippo: A Biography.* Berkeley: University of California Press, 1967; 2nd ed., 2000.

———. *The Body and Society: Men, Women, and Sexual Renunciation in Early Christianity.* New York: Columbia University Press, 1988.

Burnaby, John. *Amor Dei: A Study in the Religion of St. Augustine.* London: Hodder & Stoughton, 1938.

Cameron, Michael. *Augustine's Construction of Figurative Exegesis Against the Donatists in the Enarrationes In Psalmos.* Ph.D. dissertation, University of Chicago, 1996. Ann Arbor: University Microfilms, 1997.

———. "Transfiguration: Christology and the Roots of Figurative Exegesis in St. Augustine." *Studia Patristica* 33 (1997): 40-47.

Cavanaugh, William T. "Coercion in Augustine and Disney." *New Blackfriars* 80 (1999): 283-90.

Dagens, Claude. "L'Intériorité de l'homme selon saint Augustin: Philosophie, Théologie, et vie spirituelle." *Bulletin de littérature écclesiastique* 88 (1987): 249-72.

Daley, Brian. "A Humble Mediator: The Distinctive Elements in Saint Augustine's Christology." *Word and Spirit* 9 (1987): 100-117.

Dodaro, Robert, and George Lawless, eds. *Augustine and His Critics*. New York: Routledge, 2000.

Drobner, Hubertus. "Grammatical Exegesis and Christology in St. Augustine." *Studia Patristica* 18 (1990): 49-63.

Evans, C. F. "Augustine as Biblical Scholar." In *The Cambridge History of the Bible*. Vol. 1, *From the Beginnings to Jerome*. Ed. P. R. Ayckroyd et al. Cambridge: Cambridge University Press, 1970.

Evans, G. R. *Augustine on Evil*. Cambridge: Cambridge University Press, 1982.

Fiedrowicz, Michael. *Psalmus Vox Totius Christi: Studien zu Augustins "Enarrationes In Psalmos."* Freiburg: Herder, 1997.

Finn, Thomas. "It Happened One Saturday Night: Ritual and Conversion in Augustine's North Africa." *Journal of the American Academy of Religion* 58 (1990): 589-611.

Fitzgerald, Allan D., OSA. *Augustine Through the Ages: An Encyclopedia*. Grand Rapids: Eerdmans, 1999.

Frederiksen, Paula. "*Excaecati Occulta Justitia Dei:* Augustine on the Jews and Judaism." *Journal of Early Christian Studies* 3, no. 3 (1995): 299-324.

Hanby, Michael. "Augustine and Modernity." In *Radical Orthodoxy*. London: Routledge, 2003.

Harmless, William. *Augustine and the Catechumenate*. Collegeville, MN: Liturgical, 1995.

Harrison, Carol. *Beauty and Revelation in the Thought of Saint Augustine*. Oxford: Clarendon, 1992.

Lienhard, Joseph T., SJ, et al. *Augustine: Presbyter Factus Sum*. From Collectanea Augustiniana. New York: Peter Lang, 1993.

———. "Reading the Bible and Learning to Read: The Influence of Education on St. Augustine's Exegesis." *Augustinian Studies* 27, no. 1 (1996): 7-25.

Louth, Andrew. "Augustine on Language." *Journal of Literature and Theology* 3 (1989): 151-58.

McCarthy, Michael. *The Revelatory Psalm: A Fundamental Theology of Augustine's Enarrationes in psalmos*. Ph.D. dissertation, University of Notre Dame; Ann Arbor: University Microfilms, 2003.

McWilliam, Joanne. "The Study of Augustine's Christology in the 20th Century." In *Augustine: From Rhetor to Theologian*. Waterloo, ON: Wilfrid Laurier University Press, 1992.

Madec, Goulven. "*Christus, Scientia et Sapientia nostra.*" *Recherches Augustiniennes* (1975): 77-85.

O'Connell, Robert J., SJ. *Art and the Christian Intelligence in St. Augustine*. Cambridge: Harvard University Press, 1978.

O'Donnell, James J. *Confessions/Commentary*. 3 vols. Oxford: Clarendon, 1992.

O'Donovan, Oliver. *The Problem of Self-Love in St. Augustine*. New Haven: Yale University Press, 1980.

Oden, Amy. *Dominant Images for the Church in Augustine's 'Enarrationes in Psalmos': A*

*Study of Augustine's Ecclesiology.* Ph.D. dissertation, Southern Methodist University; Ann Arbor: University Microfilms, 1990.

Rondeau, M. J. *Les commentaries patristiques du Psautier (IIIe-Ve siècles).* Vol. 2, Orientalia Christiana Analecta 220. Rome, 1985.

Schlabach, Gerald. *For the Joy Set Before Us: Augustine and Self-Denying Love.* Notre Dame: University of Notre Dame Press, 2000.

———. "'Love Is the Hand of the Soul': The Grammar of Continence in Augustine's Doctrine of Christian Love." *Journal of Early Christian Studies* 6, no. 1 (1998): 59-92.

Studer, Basil, OSB. *The Grace of Christ and the Grace of God in Augustine of Hippo: Christocentrism or Theocentrism?* Trans. Matthew J. O'Connell. Collegeville, MN: Liturgical, 1997.

———. *Trinity and Incarnation.* Edinburgh: T&T Clark, 1993.

Taylor, Charles. *Sources of the Self: The Making of Modern Identity.* Cambridge, MA: Harvard University Press, 1989.

Turner, Denys. *The Darkness of God: Negativity in Christian Mysticism.* Cambridge: Cambridge University Press, 1995.

Van Bavel, Tarsicius J., OESA. *Recherches Sur La Christologie De Saint Augustin: L'Humain Et Le Divin Dans Le Christ D'Après Saint Augustin.* Fribourg: Éditions Universitaires, 1954.

Van Fleteren, Frederick, and Joseph C. Schnaubelt, OSA. *Augustine: Biblical Exegete.* Collectanea Augustiniana. New York: Peter Lang, 2001.

———. *Augustine: Mystic and Mystagogue.* Collectanea Augustiniana. New York: Peter Lang, 1994.

Williams, Rowan. *"De Trinitate."* In *Augustine Through the Ages,* ed. Allan D. Fitzgerald. Grand Rapids: Eerdmans, 1999.

———. "Language, Reality, and Desire in Augustine's *De Doctrina.*" *Journal of Literature and Theology* 3 (1989): 138-50.

———. "*Sapientia* and the Trinity: Reflections on the *De Trinitate.*" In *Collectanea Augustiniana,* ed. B. Bruning et al. Leuven: Leuven University Press, 1990.

Young, Frances. *Biblical Exegesis and the Formation of Christian Culture.* Cambridge: Cambridge University Press, 1997.

## Other Literature

Abraham, William J. *Canon and Criterion on Christian Theology: From the Fathers to Feminism.* Oxford: Oxford University Press, 1998.

Adam, A. K. M. "Docetism, Käsemann, and Christology: Why Historical Criticism Can't Protect Christological Orthodoxy." *Scottish Journal of Theology* 49, no. 4 (1996): 391-410.

Anderson, Gary. *The Genesis of Perfection: Adam and Eve in Jewish and Christian Imagination.* Louisville: Westminster/John Knox, 2001.

Athanasius of Alexandria. *The Life of Antony and the Letter to Marcellinus.* Trans. Robert C. Gregg. New York: Paulist, 1980.

————. *On the Incarnation.* Trans. by a religious of the CSMV. Crestwood, NY: St. Vladimir's, 1998.

Ayres, Lewis, and Gareth Jones, eds. *Christian Origins: Theology, Rhetoric, and Community.* London: Routledge, 1998.

————, and Stephen Fowl. "(Mis)Reading the Face of God: *The Interpretation of the Bible in the Church.*" *Theological Studies* 60 (1999): 513-28.

————. *Nicaea and Its Legacy: An Approach to Fourth-Century Trinitarian Theology.* Oxford: Oxford University Press, 2005.

————. "On the Practice and Teaching of Christian Doctrine." *Gregorianum* 80 (1999): 33-94.

Balthasar, Hans Urs von. *Mysterium Paschale.* Trans. Aidan Nichols, OP. Grand Rapids: Eerdmans, 1990.

Barth, Karl. *Anselm: Fides Quaerens Intellectum. Anselm's Proof of the Existence of God in the Context of his Theological Scheme.* Trans. Ian Robertson. London: SCM, 1960.

————. *Church Dogmatics.* Trans. G. W. Bromiley et al. Edinburgh: T&T Clark, 1975- .

————. *The Word of God and the Word of Man.* Trans. Douglas Horton. New York: Harper & Row, 1957.

Barton, Stephen C. "New Testament Interpretation As Performance." *Scottish Journal of Theology* 52 (1999): 179-208.

Basil of Caesaria. *On the Holy Spirit.* Trans. David Anderson. Crestwood, NY: St. Vladimir's, 1997.

————, and St. Gregory Nazianzus. *The Philocalia of Origen.* Trans. George Lewis. Edinburgh: T&T Clark, 1911.

Beasley-Murray, George. *John.* Word Biblical Commentary. Waco, TX: Word, 1987.

Behr, John. "The Word of God in the Second Century." *Pro Ecclesia* 9 (2001): 85-107.

Blowers, Paul, et al., eds. *In Dominico Eloquio: In Lordly Eloquence.* Festschrift for R. L. Wilken. Grand Rapids: Eerdmans, 2002.

————. "The *Regula Fidei* and the Narrative Character of Early Christian Faith." *Pro Ecclesia* 6, no. 2 (1998): 199-228.

Bonhoeffer, Dietrich. *Christ the Center.* Trans. Edwin Robertson. San Francisco: HarperCollins, 1960.

————. *Creation and Fall: A Theological Exposition of Genesis 1–3.* Trans. Douglas Stephen Bax. Vol. 3, Dietrich Bonhoeffer Works. Minneapolis: Fortress, 1997.

————. *Letters and Papers from Prison.* Ed. Eberhard Bethge. New York: Macmillan, 1972.

————. *Life Together and Prayerbook of the Bible.* Trans. Daniel W. Bloesch and James H. Burtness. Vol. 5, Dietrich Bonhoeffer Works. Minneapolis: Fortress, 1996.

————. *A Testament to Freedom: The Essential Writings of Dietrich Bonhoeffer.* Ed. Geffrey B. Kelly and F. Burton Nelson. San Francisco: HarperCollins, 1995.

Bossy, John. *Christianity in the West, 1400-1700.* New York: Oxford University Press, 1987.

Braaten, Carl, and Robert Jenson. *Jews and Christians: People of God.* Grand Rapids: Eerdmans, 2003.

Calvin, John. *The Institutes of the Christian Religion.* Trans. Ford Lewis Battles. Vols. 19 and 20, Library of Christian Classics. Philadelphia: Westminster, 1960.

Candler, Peter. *The Grammar of Participation: Theological Reading as Manuduction*. Ph.D. dissertation, Cambridge University, 2002.

Cartwright, Michael. "Ideology and the Interpretation of the Bible in the African-American Christian Tradition." *Modern Theology* 9 (1993): 141-58.

Casey, Michael. *Sacred Reading: The Ancient Art of Lectio Divina*. Liguori, MO: Triumph, 1995.

————. *Toward God: The Ancient Wisdom of Western Prayer*. Liguori, MO: Triumph, 1989.

Charry, Ellen. *By the Renewing of Your Minds: The Pastoral Function of Christian Doctrine*. Oxford: Oxford University Press, 1997.

————. "Is Christianity Good for Us?" In *Reclaiming Faith: Essays on Orthodoxy in the Episcopal Church and the Baltimore Declaration*, ed. Ephraim Radner and George R. Sumner. Grand Rapids: Eerdmans, 1993.

Childs, Brevard. *Biblical Theology in Crisis*. Philadelphia: Westminster, 1970.

————. *Biblical Theology of the Old and New Testaments: Theological Reflection on the Christian Bible*. Minneapolis: Fortress, 1992.

————. "Does the Old Testament Witness to Jesus Christ?" In *Evangelium, Schriftauslegung, Kirche: Festschrift für Peter Stuhlmacher zum 65. Geburtstag*, ed. Jostein Adna et al. Göttingen: Vandenhoeck & Ruprecht, 1997.

————. *Isaiah*. Old Testament Library. Louisville: Westminster/John Knox, 2001.

————. "The *Sensus Literalis* of Scripture: An Ancient and Modern Problem." In *Beiträge zur alttestamentlichen Theologie*, ed. Herbert Dranner et al. Göttingen: Vandenhoeck & Ruprecht, 1977.

————. *The Struggle to Understand Isaiah as Christian Scripture*. Grand Rapids: Eerdmans, 2004.

Clark, Elizabeth. *Reading Renunciation: Asceticism and Scripture in Early Christianity*. Princeton: Princeton University Press, 1999.

Coakley, Sarah. "Can God Be Experienced as Trinity?" *Modern Churchman* 28 (1986): 11-23.

————. *Powers and Submissions: Spirituality, Philosophy and Gender*. Oxford: Blackwell, 2001.

————, ed. *Re-Thinking Gregory of Nyssa*. Oxford: Blackwell, 2003.

————. "Why Three? Some Further Reflections on the Origins of the Doctrine of the Trinity." In *The Making and Remaking of Christian Doctrine*, ed. Sarah Coakley and David A. Pailin. Oxford: Clarendon, 1993.

Countryman, William. "Tertullian and the Regula Fidei." *Second Century* 2 (1982): 208-27.

Cyril of Alexandria. *On the Unity of Christ*. Trans. John A. McGuckin. Crestwood, NY: St. Vladimir's, 1995.

Daley, Brian E., SJ. "Is Patristic Exegesis Still Usable? Reflections on Early Christian Interpretation of the Psalms." *Communio* 29 (Spring 2002): 185-216.

Daniélou, Jean. *From Shadows to Reality: Studies in the Biblical Typology of the Fathers*. Trans. W. Hibberd. London: Burns and Oates, 1960.

Davis, Ellen. "Critical Traditioning: Seeking an Inner Biblical Hermeneutic." *Anglican Theological Review* 82, no. 4 (2000): 733-51.

————. *Getting Involved With God: Rediscovering the Old Testament*. Cambridge, MA: Cowley, 2001.

————. "Losing a Friend: The Loss of the Old Testament to the Church." *Pro Ecclesia* 9 (2001): 73-84.

————. *Proverbs, Ecclesiastes, and the Song of Songs.* Westminster Bible Companion. Louisville: Westminster/John Knox, 2000.

————. "Reading the Bible Confessionally in the Church." *Anglican Theological Review* 84, no. 1 (2002): 25-35.

————. "Romance of the Land in the Song of Songs." *Anglican Theological Review* 80, no. 4 (1998): 533-46.

————, ed. *Imagination Shaped: Old Testament Preaching in the Anglican Tradition.* Valley Forge, PA: Trinity, 1995.

Davis, Ellen F., and Richard B. Hays, eds. *The Art of Reading Scripture.* Grand Rapids: Eerdmans, 2003.

Dawson, John David. *Allegorical Readers and Cultural Revision in Ancient Alexandria.* Berkeley: University of California Press, 1992.

————. *Christian Figural Reading and the Fashioning of Identity.* Berkeley: University of California Press, 2002.

————. *Literary Theory.* Guides to Theological Inquiry. Minneapolis: Fortress, 1995.

Donoghue, Denis. *Speaking of Beauty.* New Haven: Yale University Press, 2003.

Drury, John. *Critics of the Bible 1724-1873.* Cambridge: Cambridge University Press, 1989.

Ehrman, Bart. *The Orthodox Corruption of Scripture: The Effect of the Early Christological Controversies on the Text of the New Testament.* Oxford: Oxford University Press, 1993.

Ephrem the Syrian. *Selected Prose Works,* ed. Kathleen McVey. Vol. 91 of *The Fathers of the Church.* Washington: Catholic University Press, 1994.

Finan, Thomas, and Vincent Twomey. *Scriptural Interpretation in the Fathers: Letter and Spirit.* Cambridge: Cambridge University Press, 1995.

Ford, David, and Graham Stanton. *Reading Texts, Seeking Wisdom: Scripture and Theology.* Grand Rapids: Eerdmans, 2003.

Fowl, Stephen. *Engaging Scripture.* Oxford: Blackwell, 1997.

————. *Rethinking Metaphysics.* Oxford: Blackwell, 1995.

————. "The Role of Authorial Intention in the Theological Interpretation of Scripture." In *Between Two Horizons: New Testament Studies and Systematic Theology.* Grand Rapids: Eerdmans, 2000.

————, and L. G. Jones. "Living and Dying in the Word: Dietrich Bonhoeffer as Performer of Scripture." In *Reading in Communion.* Grand Rapids: Eerdmans, 1991.

Frei, Hans. *The Eclipse of Biblical Narrative: A Study in Eighteenth and Nineteenth Century Hermeneutics.* New Haven: Yale University Press, 1974.

————. "The 'Literal Reading' of Biblical Narrative in the Christian Tradition: Does It Stretch or Will It Break?" In *Theology and Narrative,* ed. George Hunsinger and William Placher. Oxford: Oxford University Press, 1993.

Frymer-Kensky, Tikva, et al. *Christianity in Jewish Terms.* Boulder: Westview, 2000.

Gadamer, Hans-Georg. *Truth and Method.* Trans. Joel Weinsheimer and Donald G. Marshall. New York: Continuum, 1999.

Green, Garrett. *Imagining God: Theology and the Religious Imagination.* Grand Rapids: Eerdmans, 1989.

——. *Theology, Hermeneutics, and Imagintion: The Crisis of Interpretation at the End of Modernity.* Cambridge: Cambridge University Press, 2000.

Green, Joel B. "Reading the Bible as Wesleyans." *Wesley Theological Journal* 2 (1998): 116-29.

Greer, Rowan. *Broken Lights, Mended Lives: Theology and Common Life in the Early Church.* University Park, PA: Penn State University Press, 1986.

——. *Christian Life and Christian Hope: Raids on the Inarticulate.* New York: Crossroad, 2002.

Gregory of Nyssa. *Commentary on the Inscriptions of the Psalms.* Trans. Casimir McCambley, OCSO. Brookline, MA: Hellenic, n.d.

——. *The Life of Moses.* Trans. Abraham Malherbe and Everett Ferguson. New York: Paulist, 1978.

——. *The Lord's Prayer and Beatitudes.* Trans. Hilda C. Graef. New York: Paulist, 1954.

——. *On Virginity.* Trans. H. A. Wilson. Vol. 5, *The Nicene and Post-Nicene Fathers,* ed. Philip Schaff and Henry Wace. Reprinted in Edinburgh: T&T Clark, 1994.

Grieb, A. Katherine. "Feminist or Faithful? How Scripture Teaches a Hermeneutic of Suspicion." *Sewanee Theological Review* 41 (1998): 261-76.

Gutiérrez, Gustavo. *On Job: God-Talk and the Suffering of the Innocent.* Trans. Matthew O'Connell. Maryknoll, NY: Orbis, 1989.

Hadot, Pierre. *Philosophy as a Way of Life.* Trans. Michael Chase. Oxford: Blackwell, 1995.

——. *What Is Ancient Philosophy?* Trans. Michael Chase. Cambridge, MA: Belknap, 2002.

Hanson, R. P. C. *Allegory and Event: A Study of the Sources and Significance of Origen's Doctrine of Scripture.* Louisville: Westminster/John Knox, 2002.

——. *The Search for the Christian Doctrine of God: The Arian Controversies, 318-381.* Edinburgh: T&T Clark, 1998.

*HarperCollins Study Bible.* Gen. ed. Wayne A. Meeks. New York: HarperCollins, 1993.

Harrison, Verna. "Allegory and Asceticism in Gregory of Nyssa." *Semeia* 57 (1992): 113-30.

——. "The Fatherhood of God in Orthodox Theology." *St. Vladimir's Theological Quarterly* 37 (1993): 183-212.

——. "The Relationship Between Apophatic and Kataphatic Theology." *Pro Ecclesia* 4, no. 3 (1996): 318-32.

——. "Word as Icon in Greek Patristic Theology." *Sobornost* 10 (1988): 38-49.

Hart, David Bentley. *The Beauty of the Infinite: The Aesthetics of Christian Truth.* Grand Rapids: Eerdmans, 2003.

——. "A Gift Exceeding Every Debt: An Eastern Orthodox Appreciation of Anselm's *Cur Deus Homo.*" *Pro Ecclesia* 7 (1998): 333-49.

——. "No Shadow of Turning: On Divine Impassibility." *Pro Ecclesia* 11 (2002): 184-206.

Harvey, Barry. *Another City: An Ecclesiological Primer for a Post-Christian World.* Harrisburg, PA: Trinity, 1999.

Hauerwas, Stanley. *Unleashing the Scriptures: Freeing the Bible from Captivity to America.* Nashville: Abingdon, 1993.

Hays, Richard. "Can the Gospels Teach Us How to Read the Old Testament?" *Pro Ecclesia* 11 (2003): 402-18.

——. *Echoes of Scripture in the Letters of Paul.* New Haven: Yale University Press, 1989.

————. *The Moral Vision of the New Testament: A Contemporary Introduction for New Testament Ethics.* San Francisco: HarperCollins, 1996.

Howell, James C. "Christ Was Like St. Francis." In *The Art of Reading Scripture,* ed. Ellen F. Davis and Richard B. Hays. Grand Rapids: Eerdmans, 2003.

Hughes, Kevin. "The 'Fourfold Sense': De Lubac, Blondel and Contemporary Theology." *Heythorp Journal* 42 (2001): 451-62.

Hütter, Reinhard. *Suffering Divine Things: Theology as Church Practice.* Trans. Doug Stott. Grand Rapids: Eerdmans, 1997.

*Irenaeus of Lyons.* Trans. Robert M. Grant. In *The Early Church Fathers,* ed. Carol Harrison. London: Routledge, 1997.

Jennings, Willie James. "Wrestling with a Wounding Word: Reading the Disjointed Lines of African American Spirituality." *Modern Theology* 13 (1997): 139-70.

Jenson, Robert. "A Second Thought about Inspiration." *Pro Ecclesia* 13, no. 4 (2004): 393-98.

————. *Systematic Theology.* 2 vols. Oxford: Oxford University Press, 1997 and 1999.

————. "Toward a Christian Doctrine of Israel." *CTI Reflections* 3 (2000): 2-21.

————. "What If It Were True?" *CTI Reflections* 4 (2003): 1-20.

John, Jeffrey. *The Meaning in the Miracles.* Grand Rapids: Eerdmans, 2004.

Johnson, Luke Timothy. "Imagining the World Scripture Imagines." In *Theology and Scriptural Imagination,* ed. L. G. Jones and J. J. Buckley. Oxford: Blackwell, 1998.

————. *The Real Jesus: The Misguided Quest for the Historical Jesus and the Truth of the Traditional Gospels.* San Francisco: HarperCollins, 1997.

————. "So What's Catholic about It? The State of Catholic Biblical Scholarship." *Commonweal* 12 (1998): 12-29.

————. *The Writings of the New Testament: An Interpretation.* Philadelphia: Fortress, 1986.

Juel, Donald. *Messianic Exegesis: Christological Interpretation of the Old Testament in Early Christianity.* Philadelphia: Fortress, 1988.

————, and Patrick Keifert. "A Rhetorical Approach to Theological Education: Assessing an Attempt at Re-Visioning a Curriculum." In *To Teach, to Delight, and to Move: Theological Education in a Post-Christian World,* ed. David Cunningham, 281-96. Eugene, OR: Cascade, 2005.

Justin Martyr. *The First and Second Apologies.* Vol. 56, *Ancient Christian Writers,* trans. and ed. Leslie William Barnard. New York: Paulist, 1997.

Käsemann, Ernst. "Vom theologischen Recht historisch-kritischer Exegese." *Zeitschrift für Theologie und Kirche* 64, no. 3 (1967): 281.

Kelsey, David H. *Proving Doctrine: The Uses of Scripture in Modern Theology.* Harrisburg, PA: Trinity, 1999.

Kermode, Frank. *The Genesis of Secrecy: On the Interpretation of Narrative.* Cambridge: Harvard University Press, 1979.

Koester, Craig R. *Symbolism in the Fourth Gospel: Meaning, Mystery, Community.* Minneapolis: Fortress, 2003.

Ladner, Gerhart. *The Idea of Reform: Its Impact on Christian Thought and Action in the Age of the Fathers.* Cambridge: Harvard University Press, 1959.

Lampe, G. W. H., and K. J. Woollcombe. *Essays on Typology.* Naperville, IL: Allenson, 1956.

Lash, Nicholas. *The Beginning and the End of 'Religion.'* Cambridge: Cambridge University Press, 1996.

———. *Believing Three Ways in One God.* Notre Dame: University of Notre Dame Press, 1993.

———. *Holiness, Speech, and Silence: Reflections on the Question of God.* Burlington, VT: Ashgate, 2004.

———. "The Ministry of the Word." *New Blackfriars* 6 (1987): 472-83.

———. *Theology on the Way to Emmaeus.* London: SCM, 1986.

Levenson, Jon. *The Hebrew Bible, the Old Testament, and Historical Criticism: Jews and Christians in Biblical Studies.* Louisville: Westminster/John Knox, 1993.

———. *Sinai and Zion: An Entry into the Jewish Bible.* San Francisco: HarperCollins, 1987.

———. "The Universal Horizon of Biblical Particularism." In *Ethnicity and the Bible,* ed. Mark G. Brett. Vol. 19, Biblical Interpretation Series, ed. R. Alan Culpepper and Ellen van Wolde. Leiden: E. J. Brill, 1996.

Lewis, C. S. *Reflections on the Psalms.* New York: Harvest, 1959.

———. *The Weight of Glory.* New York: Macmillan, 1949.

Lienhard, Joseph T., SJ. *The Bible, the Church, and Authority: The Canon of the Christian Bible in History and Theology.* Collegeville, MN: Liturgical, 1995.

———. "Origen and the Crisis of the Old Testament in the Early Church." *Pro Ecclesia* 9 (2001): 355-66.

Lindbeck, George. *The Church in a Postliberal Age.* Ed. James Buckley. Grand Rapids: Eerdmans, 2002.

———. *The Nature of Doctrine.* Philadelphia: Fortress, 1984.

———. "Postcritical Canonical Interpretation: Three Modes of Retrieval." In *Theological Exegesis,* ed. Chris Seitz and Kathryn Greene-McCreight. Grand Rapids: Eerdmans, 1999.

———. "Scripture, Consensus, and Community." In *Biblical Interpretation In Crisis,* ed. R. J. Neuhaus. Grand Rapids: Eerdmans, 1989.

———. "The Story-Shaped Church: Critical Exegesis and Theological Interpretation." In *The Theological Interpretation of Scripture,* ed. Stephen Fowl. Oxford: Blackwell, 1997.

Lischer, Richard. "In the Mirror of the Bible." In *The Preacher King.* Oxford: Oxford University Press, 1995.

*The Liturgy of the Hours According to the Roman Rite.* 4 vols. English trans. by the International Commission on English in the Liturgy. New York: Catholic, 1975.

Long, D. Stephen. *The Goodness of God.* Grand Rapids: Brazos, 2001.

Louth, Andrew. *Discerning the Mystery: An Essay on the Nature of Theology.* Oxford: Clarendon, 1983.

de Lubac, Henri. *Origen, Histoire et Esprit, l'intelligence de l'Écriture d'après Origène.* Paris, 1950.

———. *Medieval Exegesis: The Four Senses of Scripture.* Vol. 1, trans. Mark Sebanc. Vol. 2, trans. E. M. Macierowski. Grand Rapids: Eerdmans, 1998, 2000.

Lull, Timothy F. *Martin Luther's Basic Theological Writings.* Minneapolis: Fortress, 1989.

Luther, Martin. *Lectures on Genesis Chapters 1–5.* Trans. George Schick. In *Luther's Works,* ed. Jaroslav Pelikan. St. Louis: Concordia, 1958.

MacIntyre, Alasdair. *After Virtue*. Notre Dame: University of Notre Dame, 1981.

Marshall, Bruce. "Absorbing the World: Christianity and the Universe of Truths." In *Theology and Dialogue: Essays in Conversation with George Lindbeck*, ed. Bruce D. Marshall. Notre Dame: University of Notre Dame Press, 1990.

―――. "Aquinas as Post-Liberal Theologian." *The Thomist* 53, no. 3 (1989): 353-406.

―――. "Do Christians Worship the God of Israel?" In *Knowing the Triune God: The Work of the Spirit in the Practices of the Church*, ed. James Buckley and David Yeago, 231-64. Grand Rapids: Eerdmans, 2001.

*Maximus the Confessor*. Trans. Andrew Louth. In *The Early Church Fathers*, ed. Carol Harrison. London: Routledge, 1996.

Mays, James L. *Psalms*. Interpretation: A Bible Commentary for Teaching and Preaching. Louisville: Westminster/John Knox, 1994.

McCabe, Herbert. *God Matters*. London: Chapman, 1987.

―――. *God Still Matters*. Ed. Brian Davies. New York: Continuum, 2002.

McFague, Sallie. *Metaphorical Theology: Models of God in Religious Language*. Philadelphia: Fortress, 1982.

Meeks, Wayne. "A Hermeneutics of Social Embodiment." *Harvard Theological Review* 79 (1986): 176-86.

Milbank, John. *Being Reconciled*. London: Routledge, 2003.

―――. "'Postmodern Critical Augustinianism': A Short *Summa* in Forty-Two Responses to Unasked Questions." *Modern Theology* 7 (1991): 225-37.

―――. *Theology and Social Theory: Beyond Secular Reason*. Oxford: Blackwell, 1990.

―――. *The Word Made Strange: Theology, Language, Culture*. Oxford: Blackwell, 1997.

Miller, Patrick. *Interpreting the Psalms*. Philadelphia: Fortress, 1986.

Moltmann, Jürgen. *The Trinity and the Kingdom: The Doctrine of God*. Trans. Margaret Kohl. Minneapolis: Fortress, 1993.

Mühlenberg, Ekkehard. *Die Unendlichkeit Gottes bei Gregor von Nyssa: Gregors Kritik am Gottesbegriff der Klassischen Metaphysik*. Göttingen: Vandenhoeck & Ruprecht, 1966.

Murphy, Roland. "What Is Catholic about Catholic Biblical Scholarship? — Revisited." *Biblical Theology Bulletin* 28 (1998): 112-19.

Newman, John Henry. *An Essay on the Development of Christian Doctrine*. Notre Dame: University of Notre Dame Press, 1989.

Norris, Frederick. "Black Marks on the Communities' Manuscripts." *Journal of Early Christian Studies* 2 (1994): 443-66.

―――. *Faith Gives Fullness to Reasoning: The Five Theological Orations of Gregory Nazianzen*. Ed. and introduced by Frederick Norris. Trans. Lionel Wickham and Frederick Williams. New York : E. J. Brill, 1991.

O'Donovan, Oliver. *The Problem of Self-Love in St. Augustine*. New Haven: Yale University Press, 1980.

O'Keefe, John J. "Christianizing Malachi: Fifth-Century Insights from Cyril of Alexandria." *Vigiliae Christianae* 50 (1996): 136-58.

―――. "Impassible Suffering? Divine Passion and Fifth-Century Christology." *Theological Studies* 58 (1997): 39-60.

―――. "'A Letter That Killeth': Toward a Reassessment of Antiochene Exegesis, or

Diodore, Theodore, and Theodoret on the Psalms." *Journal of Early Christian Studies* 8, no. 1 (2000): 83-104.

————, and R. R. Reno. *Sanctified Vision: An Introduction to Early Christian Interpretation of the Bible*. Baltimore: Johns Hopkins University Press, 2005.

Ollenburger, Ben C. "What Krister Stendahl 'Meant' — A Normative Critique of 'Descriptive Biblical Theology." *Horizons in Biblical Theology* 8 (1986): 61-98.

Origen. Trans. Joseph W. Trigg. In *The Early Church Fathers*, ed. Carol Harrison. London: Routledge, 1998.

————. *On First Principles*. Trans. G. W. Butterworth. Gloucester, MA: Peter Smith, 1973.

————. *The Song of Songs: Commentary and Homilies*. Trans. R. P. Lawson. New York: Newman, 1956.

Ouspensky, Leonid, and Vladimir Lossky. *The Meaning of Icons*. Trans. G. E. H. Palmer and E. Kadloubovsky. Crestwood, NY: St. Vladimir's, 1983.

Phillips, Edward. *The Ritual Kiss in Early Christian Worship*. Cambridge, MA: Grove, 1996.

Pontifical Biblical Commission. "The Interpretation of the Bible in the Church." *Origins* 23, no. 29 (1994): 497-524.

————. "The Jewish People and Their Sacred Scriptures in the Christian Bible" (2004), at www.vatican.va.

Presbyterian Church (USA). "A Theological Understanding of the Relationship Between Christians and Jews: A Paper Commended to the Church for Study and Reflection by the 199th General Assembly" (1987), at www.pcusa.org.

Quenot, Michel. *The Icon: Window on the Kingdom*. Crestwood, NY: St. Vladimir's, 1996.

Radner, Ephraim. *The End of the Church: A Pneumatology of Division in the Christian West*. Grand Rapids: Eerdmans, 1998.

————. *Hope among the Fragments: The Broken Church and Its Engagement of Scripture*. Grand Rapids: Brazos, 2004.

Reno, Russell. *In the Ruins of the Church: Sustaining Faith in an Age of Diminished Christianity*. Grand Rapids: Brazos, 2002.

Rogers, Eugene. "How the Virtues of an Interpreter Presuppose and Perfect Hermeneutics: The Case of Thomas Aquinas." *Journal of Religion* 76 (1996): 64-81.

————. *Sexuality and the Christian Body: Their Way into the Triune God*. Oxford: Blackwell, 1999.

Rossé, Gérard. *The Cry of Jesus on the Cross: A Biblical and Theological Study*. Trans. Stephen Wentworth. New York: Paulist, 1987.

Rowe, Kavin. "Biblical Pressure and Trinitarian Hermeneutics." *Pro Ecclesia* 11 (2002): 295-312.

Ruether, Rosemary Radford. *Faith and Fratricide: The Theological Roots of Anti-Semitism*. New York: Seabury, 1974.

Rutba House. *School(s) for Conversion: 12 Marks of a New Monasticism*. Eugene, OR: Cascade, 2005.

Sanders, E. P. *Jesus and Judaism*. Philadelphia: Fortress, 1985.

————. *Paul and Palestinian Judaism: A Comparison of Patterns of Religion*. Philadelphia: Fortress, 1977.

*Sayings of the Desert Fathers*. Trans. Benedicta Ward, SLG. Kalamazoo, MI: Cistercian, 1975.

Scalise, Charles. "Allegorical Flights of Fancy: The Problem of Origen's Exegesis." *Greek Orthodox Theological Review* 32, no. 1 (1987): 69-88.

Scarry, Elaine. *On Beauty and Being Just.* Princeton: Princeton University Press, 1999.

Schüssler Fiorenza, Elisabeth. "Missionaries, Apostles, Coworkers: Rm 16 and the Reconstruction of Women's Early Christian History." *Word and World* 6 (1986): 420-33.

Seitz, Christopher R. *Figured Out: Typology and Providence in Christian Scripture.* Louisville: Westminster/John Knox, 2001.

———. *Word without End: The Old Testament as Abiding Theological Witness.* Grand Rapids: Eerdmans, 1998.

Smalley, Beryl. *The Study of the Bible in the Middle Ages.* Oxford: Blackwell, 1952.

Soulen, R. Kendall. *The God of Israel and Christian Theology.* Minneapolis: Fortress, 1996.

Steinmetz, David. "Calvin and the Irrepressible Spirit." *Ex Auditu* 12 (1996): 94-107.

———. *Calvin in Context.* Oxford: Oxford University Press, 1995.

———. *Luther in Context.* Grand Rapids: Baker, 1995.

———. "The Superiority of Pre-Critical Exegesis." In *The Theological Interpretation of Scripture: Classic and Contemporary Readings,* ed. Stephen Fowl. Oxford: Blackwell, 1997.

———. "Uncovering a Second Narrative: Detective Fiction and the Construction of Historical Method." In *The Art of Reading Scripture,* ed. Ellen F. Davis and Richard B. Hays. Grand Rapids: Eerdmans, 2003.

Stendahl, Krister. "Biblical Theology, Contemporary." In *The Interpreter's Dictionary of the Bible,* ed. G. A. Buttrick. 4 vols. Nashville: Abingdon, 1962.

Surin, Kenneth. " 'The Weight of Weakness': Intratextuality and Discipleship." In *Turnings of Darkness and Light: Essays in Philosophy and Systematic Theology.* Cambridge: Cambridge University Press, 1989.

Tanner, Kathryn. *God, Humanity and the Trinity: A Brief Systematic Theology.* Minneapolis: Fortress, 2001.

———. "Theology and the Plain Sense." In *Scriptural Authority and Narrative Interpretation,* ed. Garrett Green. Philadelphia: Fortress, 1987.

Torjeson, Karen Jo. *Hermeneutical Procedure and Theological Method in Origen's Exegesis.* Berlin: de Gruyter, 1986.

*United Methodist Hymnal.* Nashville: United Methodist Publishing House, 1989.

Vanhoozer, Kevin. *First Theology: God, Christ, and Hermeneutics.* Downers Grove, IL: InterVarsity, 2002.

———. *Is There a Meaning in this Text? The Bible, the Reader, and the Morality of Literary Knowledge.* Grand Rapids: Zondervan, 1998.

Van Rompay, Lucas. "The Christian Syriac Tradition of Interpretation." In *Hebrew Bible/ Old Testament: The History of Its Interpretation.* Vol. 1, *From the Beginnings to the Middle Ages,* ed. Magne Saebo, 612-41. Göttingen: Vandenhoeck & Ruprecht, 1996.

Volf, Miroslav. *Exclusion and Embrace: A Theological Exploration of Identity, Otherness, and Reconciliation.* Nashville: Abingdon, 1996.

———. *Free of Charge: Giving and Forgiving in a Culture Stripped of Grace.* Grand Rapids: Zondervan, 2006.

———. "'The Trinity Is Our Social Program': The Doctrine of the Trinity and the Shape of Social Engagement." *Modern Theology* 14, no. 3 (1998): 403-23.

Wainwright, Geoffrey. *Doxology.* Oxford: Oxford University Press, 1980.

———. "Towards an Ecumenical Hermeneutic: How Can All Christians Read the Scriptures Together." *Gregorianum* 76 (1995): 639-62.

Wallace, Mark I. *The Second Naiveté: Barth, Ricoeur, and the New Yale Theology.* Macon, GA: Mercur, 1990.

Ward, Graham. "Allegoria: Reading as a Spiritual Exercise." *Modern Theology* 15 (1999): 271-95.

Watson, Francis. "A Response to Professor Rowland." *Scottish Journal of Theology* 45 (1995).

———. *Text and Truth: Redefining Biblical Theology.* Grand Rapids: Eerdmans, 1997.

———. *Text, Church and World: Biblical Interpretation in Theological Perspective.* Grand Rapids: Eerdmans, 1994.

Wells, Samuel. *Improvisation: The Drama of Christian Ethics.* Grand Rapids: Brazos, 2004.

White, Victor, OP. *Holy Teaching: The Idea of Theology according to St. Thomas Aquinas.* London: Aquin, 1958.

Wilken, Robert. "Gregory the Great as Biblical Interpreter: The Moralia." *Pro Ecclesia* 10 (2001): 213-26.

———. "In Defense of Allegory." *Modern Theology* 14 (1998): 197-212.

———. "*In Dominico Eloquio:* Learning the Lord's Style of Language." *Communio* 24 (1997): 846-66.

———. "In *Novissimis Diebus:* Biblical Promises, Jewish Hopes and Early Christian Exegesis." *Journal of Early Christian Studies* 1 (1993): 1-19.

———. *John Chrysostom and the Jews: Rhetoric and Reality in the Late Fourth Century.* Berkeley: University of California Press, 1983.

———. *Remembering the Christian Past.* Grand Rapids: Eerdmans, 1995.

———. *The Spirit of Early Christian Thought: Seeking the Face of God.* New Haven: Yale University Press, 2003.

Williams, Rowan. *Christ on Trial: How the Gospel Unsettles Our Judgement.* London: HarperCollins, 2000.

———. "Does It Make Sense to Speak of Pre-Nicene Orthodoxy?" In *The Making of Orthodoxy: Essays in Honor of Henry Chadwick,* ed. Rowan Williams. Cambridge: Cambridge University Press, 1989.

———. *The Dwelling of the Light: Praying with Icons of Christ.* Grand Rapids: Eerdmans, 2004.

———. *On Christian Theology.* Oxford: Blackwell, 2000.

———. *Ponder These Things: Praying with Icons of the Virgin.* Franklin, WI: Sheed and Ward, 2002.

———. *Ray of Darkness: Sermons and Reflections.* Boston: Cowley, 1995.

———. *Resurrection: Interpreting the Gospel.* Harrisburg, PA: Morehouse, 1982.

———. *The Wound of Knowledge: A Theological History from the New Testament to Luther and St. John of the Cross.* Eugene, OR: Wipf & Stock, 1998.

Willimon, William H. *Calling and Character: Virtues of the Ordained Life.* Nashville: Abingdon, 2000.

Wolterstorff, Nicholas. *Divine Discourse: Philosophical Reflections on the Claim That God Speaks.* Cambridge: Cambridge University Press, 1995.

Work, Telford. *Living and Active: Scripture in the Economy of Salvation.* Grand Rapids: Eerdmans, 2002.

Wright, N. T. *Jesus and the Victory of God.* Vol. 2, *Christian Origins and the Question of God.* Minneapolis: Fortress, 1997.

———. *The New Testament and the People of God.* Vol. 1, *Christian Origins and the Question of God.* Minneapolis: Fortress, 1992.

Wyschogrod, Michael. *Abraham's Promise: Judaism and Jewish-Christian Relations.* Ed. Kendall Soulen. Grand Rapids: Eerdmans, 2004.

———. "Incarnation." *Pro Ecclesia* 2 (1993): 208-15.

Yeago, David. "The New Testament and Nicene Dogma: A Contribution to the Recovery of Theological Exegesis." In *The Theological Interpretation of Scripture,* ed. Stephen Fowl. Oxford: Blackwell, 1997.

Yoder, John H. "The Hermeneutics of Peoplehood: A Protestant Perspective." In *Priestly Kingdom.* Notre Dame: University of Notre Dame Press, 1984.

———. *The Jewish-Christian Schism Revisited.* Ed. Michael Cartwright and Peter Ochs. Grand Rapids: Eerdmans, 2003.

———. *The Politics of Jesus.* Grand Rapids: Eerdmans, 1972.

Young, Frances. *The Art of Performance: Towards a Theology of Holy Scripture.* London: Darton Longman and Todd, 1990.

# Index of Names and Subjects

# Index of References to the Psalms